RICHARD RHODES
THE TWILIGHT
OF THE BOMBS

Richard Rhodes is the author or editor of twenty-three books, including *The Making of the Atomic Bomb*, which won a Pulitzer Prize in Nonfiction, a National Book Award, and a National Book Critics Circle Award, and *Dark Sun: The Making of the Hydrogen Bomb*, which was a finalist for a Pulitzer Prize in History. He is the recipient of fellowships from the Ford, Guggenheim, MacArthur, and Alfred P. Sloan foundations, among others. He has been a visiting scholar at Harvard, MIT, and Stanford, and a host and correspondent for the public television series *Frontline* and *American Experience*. He lectures frequently in the United States and abroad. He lives near Half Moon Bay, California.

www.richardrhodes.com

ALSO BY RICHARD RHODES

THE TWILIGHT

OF THE BOMBS

RECENT CHALLENGES, NEW DANGERS,
AND THE PROSPECTS FOR A WORLD
WITHOUT NUCLEAR WEAPONS

RICHARD RHODES

Vintage Books
A Division of Random House, Inc.
New York

FIRST VINTAGE BOOKS EDITION, SEPTEMBER 2011

The Library of Congress has cataloged the Knopf edition as follows:
Rhodes, Richard.
The twilight of the bombs : recent challenges, new dangers, and the prospects for a world without nuclear weapons / Richard Rhodes.
p. cm.
Includes bibliographical references and index.
1. Nuclear arms. 2. Arms race. 3. Nuclear nonproliferation.
4. Nuclear disarmament. I. Title.
US64.R49 2010
327.1'747—dc22
2010003901

Vintage ISBN: 978-0-307-38741-7

Author photograph © Nancy Warner
Book design by M. Kristen Bearse

www.vintagebooks.com

146028962

FOR THOMAS GRAHAM, JR.

A grant from the John D. and Catherine T. MacArthur Foundation supported the research and writing of this book.

The problem of nuclear weapons is nuclear weapons.

RICHARD BUTLER

CONTENTS

PART FOUR AN INTOLERABLE THREAT TO
ALL HUMANITY

THE TWILIGHT
OF THE BOMBS

PROLOGUE

A DIFFERENT COUNTRY

It did not take atomic weapons to make war terrible. . . . It did not take atomic weapons to make man want peace, a peace that would last. But the atomic bomb was the turn of the screw. It has made the prospect of future war unendurable. It has led us up those last few steps to the mountain pass; and beyond there is a different country.   ROBERT OPPENHEIMER, 1946

WHEN THE ICE BROKE on the river of history in the final years of the Cold War, the world had lived with nuclear weapons for almost half a century. Forty nations had attained the capability to build them, but only nine had yet done so: the United States, the Soviet Union, Britain, France, China, Israel, India, Pakistan, and South Africa. Together, these nine nations had accumulated about sixty thousand nuclear weapons—about three thousand pounds of explosive force for every man, woman, and child on earth, more than enough to destroy the human world. Their reasons for going nuclear varied from the United States's conviction that only nuclear weapons could protect the West from a Communist empire it believed to be bent on world domination, to the Soviet Union's belief that it stood surrounded by enemies and alone in a hostile world, to France's and Britain's doubts that the United States would make itself a nuclear target to come to their aid, to South Africa's curious notion that brandishing a small nuclear arsenal should it be attacked by other African states would compel the major nuclear powers to intervene on its behalf.

Yet in all the years since the first two atomic bombs destroyed the Japanese cities of Hiroshima and Nagasaki at the end of the Second World War, no more nuclear weapons had been exploded in anger. Those who believed in deterrence, in the power of the bombs to prevent their use, naturally believed that half a century free from major war meant that deterrence had worked—and, by extension, should continue to work in perpetuity. Those who doubted the efficacy of deterrence noted that both the United States and the Soviet Union had accepted stalemate, as in Korea, or even defeat, as in Vietnam and Afghanistan, rather than risk nuclear escalation. Nuclear arsenals might promote caution in relations among hostile states, the doubters therefore argued, but they clearly did not compel, while a world awash with tens of thousands of nuclear weapons gravely risked accidental or inadvertent nuclear holocaust.

During the Cold War most of the nations of the world had aligned themselves with one or the other superpower, freezing into place the contending hegemonies that had followed from the victories and defeats of the Second World War. With the warming of relations between the United States and the Soviet Union initiated by the Soviet reformer Mikhail Gorbachev in the 1980s, that seizure of international relations began to release.

At a summit meeting between Gorbachev and the U.S. president Ronald Reagan in Reykjavik, Iceland, in 1986, the two leaders had come close to agreeing to lead the world to the complete elimination of nuclear weapons. To that purpose Gorbachev had championed common security, a principle formulated out of Europe's Cold War experience of zero-sum division between East and West. As a United Nations commission chaired by the Swedish prime minister Olof Palme had defined it in a 1982 report, "The principle of common security asserts that countries can only find security in cooperation with their competitors, not against them." In a speech to the 27th Soviet Communist Party Conference early in 1986, Gorbachev had applied the principle to the ongoing nuclear arms race between the Cold War antagonists. "The task of insuring security," he told the delegates, "is more and more taking the form of a political task and can be resolved only by political means. . . . In our time, genuine equal security is guaranteed not by the highest possible but by the lowest possible level of strategic balance, from which it is essential to exclude entirely nuclear and other types of weapons of mass destruction." Reagan, however, believed that only physical security in the form of space-based antimissile defenses could guarantee nuclear disarmament. The Soviet government was not prepared to undertake such an expensive and ultimately chimerical technological competition, and the agreement on nuclear elimination failed. Reykjavik was not fruitless, however; it put both sides' commitment to nuclear-arms reductions, rather than merely arms control, firmly on the table, and led directly to the 1987 Intermediate Nuclear Forces Treaty, which eliminated an entire class of particularly destabilizing nuclear weapons carried on 2,692 U.S. and Soviet medium-range missiles.

Despite their seemingly implacable differences, the two superpowers had worked both separately and jointly during the Cold War to limit nuclear proliferation, implicitly cooperating for common security. Their most significant cooperation drove the negotiation of the Nuclear Nonproliferation Treaty (NPT), opened for signature in 1968, which offered extensive security guarantees and the advantages of commercial nuclear power to countries willing to forgo acquiring nuclear arsenals; by 1990, 140 states had signed on. More than any other factor, the NPT had limited the proliferation of nuclear weapons across the world.

Actions had also been directed against specific states. In 1975 a threat by the United States to withdraw its military forces from the Korean Peninsula had compelled South Korea to abandon its program of nuclear-weapons development. In 1976 and again in 1987, partly under pressure from the People's Republic of China, the United States had forced Taiwan to abandon clandestine nuclear weapons programs. Satellite images indicating an impending South African nuclear test that the Soviet Union passed to the United States for timely action in 1977 led to intense U.S. diplomatic pressure that delayed the South African nuclear weapons program by several years.

But the very predominance in nuclear weapons that the two superpowers had achieved had worked against their security. Neither side had been sufficiently confident of the authority of its nuclear arsenal to limit itself to minimum deterrence, as China had done, and both the Soviet and American military-industrial complexes had taken advantage of that uncertainty to repeatedly expand and modernize their nations' nuclear arsenals. Actions that were justified domestically as defensive were perceived by the other side to be hostile. In 1983, shaken by the Reagan administration's belligerent military buildup, and misjudging the intent of a major NATO field exercise in West Germany called Able Archer, which included a practice run-up to nuclear war, the Soviet leadership under Yuri Andropov had very nearly launched a preemptive nuclear strike against the United States. Though it all but escaped public notice, the Able Archer incident was the Cuban Missile Crisis of its day. By the time Gorbachev came to power in 1985, both sides threatened each other with total and mutual annihilation. "If one country keeps building weapons while the other one doesn't do a thing," Gorbachev told Richard Nixon in the summer of 1986, "the one that arms will not gain anything from it. The weaker party could just explode its nuclear stockpile, even on its own territory, which would mean suicide for it and a slow death for the opponent."

The progress at Reykjavik, and the arms proposals that Gorbachev offered in its aftermath, foundered on American suspicions of Soviet intentions, but gradually, during the presidency of George H. W. Bush, through the good offices of Secretary of State James A. Baker III and the Soviet foreign minister Eduard Shevardnadze, relations began to warm. That improvement prepared the way for cooperation between the two former enemies to beat back the aggression of Iraqi president Saddam Hussein, who misread the Reagan and Bush administrations' tilt toward his country and against its enemy Iran as license to plunder Kuwait and threaten Saudi Arabia, a prime U.S. client. By the time the Persian Gulf War ended, in February 1991, however, the struggle for power in the Soviet Union was straining Gorbachev's control and the Soviet economy was collapsing. After a coup attempt against the beleaguered Soviet leader the following August, U.S. policy shifted from support to salvage. When the Soviet Union fractured into fifteen independent nations on 25 December 1991, one nuclear power suddenly metastasized into four—Russia, Belarus, Ukraine, and Kazakhstan—each with substantial nuclear arsenals. Thereafter the United States scrambled to support the consolidation of the former superpower's nuclear weapons on Russian soil, to subsidize the scientists and engineers of the former Soviet nuclear weapons complex, and to secure nuclear materials dispersed in manufactories and institutes across eleven time zones.

The example of the superpowers' nuclear arms race had not been lost on smaller nations. The overwhelming majority had the good sense to recognize that mutual security under the NPT would spare them a financial burden and keep them safe. A few, stigmatized by the international community for their repressive policies or locked into long-standing conflicts, concluded that nuclear weapons could protect them from conventional as well as nuclear attack and even secure them a place at the banquet table of the superpowers. India, pursuing a nuclear option after losing a border war with China in 1962, tested a first-generation nuclear weapon underground in 1974 (calling it a "peacful nuclear explosive") but then confined itself to research and plutonium stockpiling until the 1990s. Pakistan, after losing a devastating war with India in 1971, began developing a uranium-enrichment program for nuclear weapons with Chinese technical support. In the early 1980s, China supplied Pakistan with a simple and sturdy bomb design, and allowed its ally to test its first nuclear weapon at a Chinese test site, Lop Nur, in May 1990. Pakistan too would extend development of its nuclear arsenal in the 1990s.

Iraq, in contrast, pursued nuclear weapons initially as a shield against Iran, with which it fought a devastating war between 1980 and 1988, and subsequently against Israel and the United States.

North Korea first sought nuclear-power reactors from the Soviet Union to replace the hydroelectric capacity it had lost almost totally to American strategic bombing during the U.S.-Korean War of 1950 to 1953. Repeatedly rebuffed by its Cold War patron, its leader, Kim Il Sung, authorized an indigenous nuclear power and weapons program in 1979; the weapons program was intended to produce a deterrent to the arsenal of U.S. tactical nuclear weapons positioned in South Korea and to compel the United States to negotiate. A five-megawatt gas-graphite-type nuclear reactor went critical at the North's research center at Yongbyon in 1986 and began breeding plutonium in the course of its operation. By 1990, U.S. satellite surveillance had revealed that North Korea was building a plutonium-separation facility at Yongbyon as well.

The 1968 Nuclear Non-Proliferation Treaty had been an exception to the rule that treaties are usually ratified indefinitely—that is, permanently, without a termination date. The nonnuclear signatories had been concerned that the five nuclear powers grandfathered into the treaty would fail to reduce their arsenals or work actively for nuclear disarmament, and that the treaty's safeguards requirements would put countries without nuclear power at a commercial disadvantage. These concerns had led them to insist that the NPT should be reviewed after twenty-five years and then either indefinitely extended or extended only for a limited term or terms. Since the treaty had entered into force in 1970, two years after it had been opened for signature, this review and extension conference was scheduled for 1995.

Yet only five years prior to that deadline, as protective Cold War alliances fell away, a new wave of nuclear proliferation appeared to be surging through the second and third tier of nations. At the same time, the unfettering and simultaneous impoverishing of the Soviet Union had opened the world's largest nuclear arsenal—previously secure within borders guarded by barbed wire and minefields—to theft or criminal diversion. In *Nuclear Ambitions,* a study published in 1990 subtitled *The Spread of Nuclear Weapons 1989–1990,* the nonproliferation expert Leonard Spector worried about the proliferation tendencies he saw evolving:

> Despite certain promising developments during 1989 and 1990 in the field of nuclear non-proliferation, a number of disturbing trends in this area point to the need for continued vigilance and intensified international efforts to curb the spread of nuclear weapons. Even as the risk of nuclear confrontation between the superpowers has diminished, for example, concerns have increased that conflict may erupt between the two *de facto* nuclear powers in South Asia [i.e., India and Pakistan], a conflict in which nuclear weapons would inevitably play a role. Similarly, as hopes have been raised that South Africa may join the NPT and thereby reduce the number of states outside the international non-proliferation regime, anxieties have increased over the nuclear intentions of North Korea and Iraq and over the commitments of these two NPT parties to the treaty. . . . Argentina and Brazil have undertaken important confidence-building measures through their exchanges of visits to nuclear facilities, but fears of unconventional warfare continue to mount in the Middle East, as evidenced by Iraqi President Saddam Hussein's threats to destroy half of Israel with chemical weapons, if attacked, and by Israel's threats to respond to such an act a hundred times over.

These trends implied that for all the elation and fresh energy that followed the release of Eastern Europe and the Soviet people themselves from Communist authoritarianism, the post–Cold War era might be more hazardous than the Cold War years had been. While the threat of global nuclear war between two hostile superpowers had faded, the risk of regional nuclear war among nations with seemingly modest nuclear arsenals had intensified.

A regional nuclear war between India and Pakistan, for example, would be unlikely to involve more than about one hundred Hiroshima-scale fifteen-kiloton weapons, merely 1.5 megatons of total explosive force, less than the yield of many individual Soviet and U.S. hydrogen bombs. The primary destructive effect of nuclear weapons is mass fire, however, and with highly combustible South Asian megacities as the likeliest targets, such a nuclear exchange would kill between three million and sixteen million people. Smoke from mass fires would loft into the stratosphere, drift around the world, and darken and chill the earth for a decade, reducing global average temperatures below those of the European Little Ice Age of the sixteenth to mid-nineteenth centuries, when crops failed and millions starved. Even a "small" regional nuclear war, that is, would be an unmitigated disaster for the entire world.

Yet Spector's catalog of dangerous trends incorporated only a limited view of post–Cold War challenges and opportunities. Another perspective revealed realistic opportunity in the last decade of the twentieth century and the first decade of the twenty-first to move toward drastic reductions in the number of nuclear weapons in the world, down to minimum deterrence or even to zero. Both the United States and the former Soviet Union, for example, undertook a radical withdrawal and reduction of their nuclear arsenals. Both sides endorsed and supported the indefinite extension of the Nuclear Nonproliferation Treaty. Both sides supported and signed the Comprehensive Nuclear Test-Ban Treaty, although conservative Republicans in the U.S. Senate bent on discrediting President Bill Clinton prevented its American ratification in 1999.

Before governments could act responsibly to eliminate nuclear arsenals, a debate among government and public organizations throughout the world was necessary to test the logic and work out the process of doing so. That debate opened in the 1990s in the context of securing the nuclear remnants of the former Soviet Union, aiding states with nuclear ambitions in abandoning those ambitions, and coercively dismantling the nuclear infrastructure of Iraq. Those in the U.S., France, Britain, and Russia who believed nuclear weapons armored their national sovereignty vociferously defended nuclear possession for deterrence even as proponents of nuclear elimination, including many military leaders, identified the weapons themselves as the fundamental danger. "As long as any state has nuclear weapons," Australia's 1996 Canberra Commission on the Elimination of Nuclear Weapons postulated, "others will seek to acquire them."

Although the world continues at risk, by the second decade of the twenty-first century the end of the Cold War and its transformative aftermath have opened the clear prospect of moving to a world free of nuclear weapons, Oppenheimer's "different country," where common security rather than the threat of nuclear retaliation will guard the peace. How the dangerous post–Cold War transition was managed, who its heroes were, what we learned from it, and where it carried us are questions that have not yet been fully explored. Doing so is the purpose of this narrative.

PART ONE

FOLLOWING THE CALUTRON TRAIL

ONE "PRESIDENT BUSH'S FRANKENSTEIN"

F OR GEORGE H. W. BUSH'S secretary of state James A. Baker III, the Cold War ended on 3 August 1990. That day at Moscow's Vnukovo International Airport Baker and the Soviet foreign minister, Eduard Shevardnadze, stood side by side and jointly condemned Saddam Hussein's massive and ongoing invasion of Kuwait, a small, wealthy, but largely undefended country southeast of Iraq on the Persian Gulf that produced about 10 percent of Middle Eastern oil. Iraq, the Soviet Union's most important client in the region, was heavily armed with Soviet tanks, missiles, and artillery; Shevardnadze's willingness to condemn Iraqi aggression signaled to Baker the beginning of a real partnership between the United States and the U.S.S.R.

During the long Iran-Iraq War that had ended in 1988, two years before Iraq invaded Kuwait, Saddam Hussein had been the enemy of America's enemy Iran, and thus, if not a friend, at least something of a surrogate. The United States had remained neutral during the first two years of the war, but when an Iranian offensive in spring 1982 succeeded in breaking through the Iraqi line and forcing the Iraqis to retreat, the Reagan administration had begun to favor Iraq. An affidavit sworn by a National Security Council (NSC) staff member, Howard Teicher, who helped develop the new policies, describes the result:

In June 1982 . . . President Reagan decided that the United States would do whatever was necessary and legal to prevent Iraq from losing the war with Iran. President Reagan formalized this policy by issuing a National Security Decision Directive (NSDD) to this effect in June 1982. . . . CIA Director [William] Casey personally spearheaded this effort to ensure that Iraq had sufficient military weapons, ammunition and vehicles to avoid losing the Iran-Iraq war. Pursuant to the secret NSDD, the United States actively supported the Iraqi war effort by supplying the Iraqis with billions of dollars of credits, by providing U.S. military intelligence and advice to the Iraqis, and by closely monitoring third country arms sales to Iraq. . . . The CIA, including both CIA Director Casey and Deputy Director [Robert] Gates, knew of, approved of, and assisted in the sale of non-U.S. origin military weapons, ammunition and vehicles to Iraq.

In the same spirit, the State Department removed Iraq that year from its list of states that sponsored terrorism. Two years later, in 1984, Donald Rumsfeld, a corporate executive at that time who was serving as a Reagan special envoy to the Middle East, met with Saddam Hussein in Baghdad to discuss areas of cooperation, including restoring diplomatic relations after a seventeen-year hiatus. That meeting, on 20 December, produced the video, later to become notorious, of Rumsfeld shaking Saddam's hand. Saddam "was pleased that [the] US wished to see further development in its relations with Iraq, including exchange of ambassadors," a secret State Department summary noted. "Iraq valued this positive appreciation by the US of the need for a high level of relations."

Israel, which had been selling arms to the Iranians, also offered at that time to assist Iraq. ("I do not remember even one discussion about the ethics of the matter," an Israeli defense ministry official told the Israeli journalist Ronen Bergman about the sales to Iran. "All that interested us was to sell, sell, sell more and more Israeli weapons, and let them kill each other with them.")

Teicher, the NSC staff person, testified that he attended the meeting in Jerusalem at which the Israeli foreign minister, Yitzhak Shamir, briefed Rumsfeld on the offer, as well as the meeting in Baghdad when Rumsfeld passed the offer along to the Iraqi foreign minister, Tariq Aziz. Aziz was horrified, Teicher recalled: "Aziz refused even to accept the Israelis' letter to Hussein offering assistance, because Aziz told us that he would be executed on the spot by Hussein if he did so."

Despite the warming of U.S.-Iraq relations, both the United States and Israel were aware that Iraq was pursuing a program of nuclear development; Israel at least was following the Iraqi program with concern. Iraq had signed the Nuclear Nonproliferation Treaty as a nonnuclear state, thus committing itself not to develop nuclear weapons, but the U.S. and Israel suspected that it was cheating on its commitment. Iraq allowed the International Atomic Energy Agency (IAEA) to inspect its nuclear facilities, as its NPT commitment required. At that time, however, the treaty terms restricted IAEA inspections to facilities that the parties to the treaty had officially declared; nor was the IAEA authorized to conduct surprise inspections or to probe beyond official declarations. The United States might collect intelligence and bide its time; Israel was not prepared to depend on Iraq's honesty and goodwill. In 1981, striking from the air with sixteen 2,000-pound slick bombs selected and spin-balanced for accuracy, the Israeli Air Force destroyed a French-built 40-megawatt light-water reactor at Al Tuwaitha, a large nuclear-research complex eleven miles southeast of Baghdad on the Tigris River. The reactor had not yet been loaded with fuel. France had delivered the first of six fuel loads, however—twenty-six pounds (11.8 kilograms) of uranium enriched to 93 percent U235 (highly-enriched uranium, or HEU), about two-thirds of the amount needed to charge one first-generation atomic bomb—and that uranium survived the raid undamaged in a bunker.

Iraq, which also operated a five-megawatt Soviet research reactor at the Al Tuwaitha complex fueled with twenty-two pounds (ten kilograms) of 80-percent enriched uranium, made no effort to rebuild the larger French reactor, but in consequence of the Israeli raid it reorganized its entire nuclear program away from plutonium production by reactor to the clandestine production of HEU by uranium enrichment.* David Kay, the American expert who would play a major role in investigating the Iraqi bomb program after the 1991 Gulf War, writes that "the deciding factor in this decision was the desire of the military and security services not to attract any undue attention to Iraq's developing nuclear program. . . . The argument ran: 'Let Israel believe it destroyed our nuclear capacity, accept the sympathy being offered for this aggression, and proceed in secret with the program.' "

In the 1980s, even while fighting its costly war with Iran, Iraq rebuilt and extended Tuwaitha. Building after building was added to the complex, which was divided into four subsections by earthen berms a hundred feet high that kept IAEA inspectors unaware of the expansion (and protected the complex from another Israeli bombing attack). It was perfectly possible for IAEA inspectors to tour one section of the complex while clandestine activity continued beyond its walls, screened as well by

---

*An atomic bomb can be made with either HEU or plutonium. Uranium, refined from common minerals, is enriched through a large-scale, laborious industrial process; plutonium, a man-made element, is bred from uranium by neutron bombardment in a nuclear reactor and then chemically separated. Natural uranium consists primarily of two variant physical forms called isotopes and designated by the total number of protons and neutrons in their nuclei: $U238$ (99 percent of natural uranium) and $U235$ (0.7 percent). Only $U235$ both fissions and chain-reacts. A reactor with the right moderator—material such as graphite or deuterium oxide ("heavy water") that slows down neutrons produced in fission without absorbing too many to allow the chain reaction to continue—can be fueled with natural uranium. Reactors moderated with ordinary water ("light water"), however, require uranium enriched to more than 2 percent $U235$ to function. (The higher the enrichment, the smaller the volume of fuel a reactor requires.) Nuclear weapons, which produce an uncontrolled fast-neutron chain reaction, use either uranium enriched to at least 90 percent $U235$—HEU—or plutonium. Enrichment (for uranium) or breeding in a nuclear reactor (for plutonium) thus represent alternative paths to a bomb.

trees and the careful placement of interior roads. If Iraq chose not to declare some of the nuclear facilities at Tuwaitha or elsewhere in the country, there was no IAEA mechanism for discovering that fact. The building additions were visible to U.S. and Soviet intelligence satellites, but the clandestine activities that went on inside them were shielded from overhead surveillance.

Nor were IAEA inspectors necessarily alert to diversions, David Kay comments:

> Al Tuwaitha was visited every six months by IAEA safeguard inspectors who announced, at the conclusions of such visits, that there was no sign of diversions of nuclear material. The inspectors gave a general clean bill of health to the facility; two deputy director generals of the IAEA and many staff members visited Al Tuwaitha, all of whom indicated that they saw no suspicious activity. . . . The IAEA inspectors were only allowed to visit portions of three of the almost one hundred buildings at Al Tuwaitha. . . . While the restrictions on the movements of these visitors could have been viewed as a warning sign, they were not recognized as such by most of the visitors at the time. The safeguard inspectors were routinely subjected to such restrictions in almost every country they visited.

Saddam Hussein himself had been the president of the Iraqi Atomic Energy Commission beginning in 1973, when he was the vice president of Iraq. He gave up the position when he became the Iraqi president in 1979 but he accelerated the commission's work. Iraq began buying uranium abroad that year, purchasing more than 11 tons of unenriched uranium dioxide from Italy under IAEA safeguards. Uranium dioxide is a form of uranium that can be converted directly into reactor fuel, though not fuel useable in the type of reactor Iraq was then building. In 1980 Iraq bought 138 tons of yellowcake—partly refined uranium ore— from Portugal, notifying the IAEA that it had done so. Niger supplied another batch of yellowcake, something more than 200 tons, in February 1981, four months before the Israeli strike on Tuwaitha, and once again Iraq notified the IAEA. After the air strike, however, Iraq no longer reported its purchases: 148 tons of yellowcake from Portugal in 1982 and a total of 32 tons of uranium dioxide from Brazil in 1981 and 1982, without notifying the IAEA. Iraq also hired a Belgian company to design and build a plant for producing yellowcake from indigenous phosphate ore (phosphate rock contains an average of 50 to 200 parts per million of natural uranium). Construction began in 1982 and was completed in 1984; the plant delivered its first batch of Iraqi yellowcake in December 1985, producing a total of 168 tons by 1991.

Why Iraq might be buying large quantities of uranium ore which it had no known facilities for using—no natural-uranium-fueled reactor and no machinery for enrichment—is not a question that anyone has publicly acknowledged asking during this period. Just as, after the Second World War, the United States had doubted if the Soviet Union possessed the industrial capabilities to develop a nuclear-materials complex, so also did U.S. and international experts in the 1980s underestimate Iraq.

In another historical parallel with the early American atomic-bomb program, Iraq in 1987 designed and tested a radiological weapon—a "dirty" bomb. In 1943, shortly after the secret Manhattan Project bomb-design laboratory at Los Alamos, in northern New Mexico, opened its doors, concerned that Nazi Germany might be ahead in the race to build the atomic bomb, the Italian physicist and Nobel laureate Enrico Fermi had proposed to Los Alamos's director, Robert Oppenheimer, that the pioneering nuclear reactor Fermi had recently started up at the University of Chicago might be used to make radioactive material to poison the German food supply. Responding to Fermi's proposal, Oppenheimer had commented, "In this connection I think that we should not attempt a plan unless we can poison food sufficient to kill a half a million men, since there is no doubt that the actual number affected will, because of non-uniform distribution, be much smaller than this." As bomb development advanced, Fermi's project lapsed, although U.S. experiments with radiological weapons continued after the war.

Iraq developed its dirty bomb to use against Iranian troop concentrations and human wave attacks and to contaminate contested building complexes and territory. "The fact is that during the Iran/Iraq war, it was masses of people attacking Iraq," an Iraqi senior government official testified later. "I have to say that these masses, if they do not die, they would be unhappy. Because they know that by dying, they go to heaven. So it was masses of people attacking Iraq. Any idea that was presented to us to find a solution to this problem on the border of 1,200 kilometers was welcomed." Zirconium, the metal selected for irradiation, with a half-life* in its irradiated form of only 75.5 days, would lose most of its radioactivity in a matter of weeks, allowing Iraqi forces to secure contaminated areas after radiation levels declined.

But the 1987 Iraqi tests proved to be both incompetent and ineffective. The bombs tested, twelve feet long and weighing more than two thousand pounds, were built around three-foot-long, lead-lined capsules containing the radioactive zirconium powder, to be dispersed at the appropriate time by high explosives. They "produced only minimal levels of radiation," writes the proliferation expert Gary Milhollin, who reviewed the 1987 Iraqi test report when Iraq finally disgorged it a decade later. For the third and most successful test, the Iraqi Air Force dropped two bombs from a plane. They generated large radioactive clouds, but most of the radiation dispersed with the clouds. "The maximum level of radiation was only 3 millirem per hour at a distance of 10 meters from the point of impact," Milhollin notes. "According to the report, this is only equal to the dose allowed to be received internationally by radiation workers. . . . Such a dose, by definition, would have little or no health effect over the lifetime of

---

*The "half-life" of a radioactive element is the time required for half a given quantity of the material to undergo radioactive decay, a natural process; the shorter the half-life, the more intense the radiation.

the person receiving it." The bombs would have to be recharged in a nuclear reactor every week to be even minimally effective, another fatal defect. Iraq abandoned its radioactive-bomb program after the 1987 field tests and continued to work toward a real nuclear weapon. In 1988 it decided formally to develop a nuclear arsenal, with the expectation that a first bomb would be ready by summer 1991.

The next clear sign that Iraq was advancing toward developing nuclear weapons appeared in 1988, when an Iraqi representative contacted two U.S. companies seeking to obtain a quantity of a special type of vacuum tube known as a krytron. In previous years both Israeli and Pakistani agents had been caught shipping krytrons to their respective countries; now it was Iraq's turn. Krytrons are extremely fast electronic switches; triggered by an electric current, they can open in as short a time as five nanoseconds to pass that current through. In 1988 they were used in high-speed flash photography and in copying machines, but the rugged krytron the Iraqis were seeking was designed specifically to trigger the detonators of a nuclear weapon. Its export required a U.S. government permit, and the Iraqi request for such a permit was denied.

The Iraqi procuring agents regrouped. If they couldn't buy krytrons directly, perhaps they could buy another necessary and more generic element of a nuclear-weapon firing set, a device known as a capacitor. Capacitors accumulate and store electric charge. Attached to a battery, they can accumulate charge from the battery current up to whatever capacity they've been designed to hold; when they discharge, they discharge the entire stored charge at once. An electric fence uses a capacitor to accumulate charge between discharges, typically five thousand volts or more, which is why a mere nine-volt electric-fence battery can deliver such a painful shock. A firing set for a nuclear weapon might thus consist of one or more batteries, which are connected to an array of capacitors, which are connected to krytrons, which are connected to exploding-wire detonators, which are inserted into

high-explosive blocks arranged in the form of a sphere of con-
centric shells of explosives and other components, at the center
of which is a sphere of HEU or plutonium. This method of detonating a subcritical mass of fissile material—by squeezing it to a
denser supercritical state with an inwardly moving shock wave
generated by shaped charges of explosives ("explosive lenses")—
is called implosion.

Ali Daghir, an Iraqi agent with dual British and Iraqi citizen-
ship, operated a front company in London known as Euromac.
Its official business was buying heating and ventilation equipment for export to Iraq; its unofficial and partly illegal business
was buying every kind of material for weapons of mass destruction, including anthrax and gangrene cultures and mustard gas
and sarin nerve gas precursors, as well as computers and computerized machine tools for weapons manufacture. According
to a British Customs report, "In September 1988 an American
company specializing in the design and manufacture of capacitors . . . received an enquiry from its UK representative. . . . From
the specifications quoted . . . [the American company] suspected
that the capacitors were for use in a nuclear device. . . . [It was
established] that the initial enquiry had come from Euromac
(London) Ltd., who were attempting to source the capacitors,
and some high-speed switches"—i.e., krytrons—"for end-use in
Iraq." The company Daghir contacted was CSI Technologies, a
small electronics manufacturer located in San Marcos, California, near San Diego. The company's president, Jerry Kowalsky,
thought the order suspicious. "I came immediately to the conclusion," he later testified, "that this was the specification for a
capacitor designed as the triggering device for a nuclear weapon."
He contacted both U.S. Customs and the CIA, and Customs set
up a sting. Before that could proceed, however, a story about
renewed Iraqi efforts to develop nuclear weapons appeared in
The Washington Post and Daghir backed off.

The Iraqi agent inquired again of CSI Technologies nine
months later, in June 1989. After communicating back and forth

across the summer with Euromac, Kowalsky and a U.S. Customs undercover agent, Daniel Supnick, traveled to London in September to pursue the sting. They met in a hotel café with Daghir; his export manager, Jeanine Speckman; and two Iraqis whom Daghir introduced as engineers representing the Iraqi Ministry of Industry and Military Industrialization's rocket research branch, Al Qaqaa. Kowalsky introduced Supnick in turn as Daniel Saunders, his finance and export manager. Supnick then led the Iraqis through an incriminating Socratic dialogue: What use? Laser research. Fine, we'll make some that only work in lasers. Side talk in Arabic. No, aerospace research. Fine, what altitude? Sea level. Fine, but they'll only work at sea level. Side talk in Arabic. And so it went, until everyone understood what the capacitors were for. "A purchase order for $10,500 was signed at that time," *The New York Times* would report. "The next day, Miss Speckman telephoned the Americans suggesting that they misdescribe the items as components of computer-room air-conditioning units." Supnick and Kowalsky returned to the United States. When the payment was wire-transferred to CSI, the payer was listed as the Iraqi Embassy in London.

Daghir dithered for months about how CSI should ship the capacitors. Supnick, in turn, tried to lure Daghir to San Diego to pick them up in person. It was March 1990 before the two sides agreed that the devices would be shipped to Euromac in London for transshipment to the Middle East. Daghir sent an end-user certificate issued in the name of the Baghdad University of Technology and declaring that the capacitors were destined for use as part of a carbon-dioxide laser system.

Supnick alerted British Customs to the impending shipment of forty capacitors, which arrived at Heathrow on 20 March 1990. According to a subsequent parliamentary inquiry, "On arrival at Heathrow the crate was secured by officers in Customs ID and substituted by a similarly packaged crate containing inert and inoperable capacitors." Seven days later, the inoperable capacitors were delivered to Euromac, where Daghir and his staff repack-

aged them in two boxes. The next day, 28 March, Daghir, Speckman, and an assistant drove the two boxes to Heathrow to deliver
them to an Iraqi Airways flight. "At this stage," the parliamentary
inquiry concludes, "the boxes were intercepted and detained by
Customs ID officers. Various individuals were arrested, including Mr. Daghir, Mrs. Speckman, and Mr. Amyuni. The business
premises of Euromac (London) Ltd. were searched." The three
were jointly charged with attempting to export illegal goods.

Just as the U.S. government had been puzzled about why Iraq
would be buying large quantities of uranium ore when it supposedly lacked facilities for enrichment, so also was it puzzled, after
the Euromac arrests, about why Iraq would be buying firing-set
components for nuclear weapons when it was believed to be years
away from actually building such weapons. The defense correspondent of the London *Guardian* speculated in a story published the day after the Euromac arrests that "Iraq may be close
to testing a weapon, perhaps using the enriched uranium it had
prepared for its Osirak reactor"—at Tuwaitha—"until the Israeli
air force bombed it in 1981." It was a good guess, better certainly
than U.S. estimates, which put an Iraqi atomic bomb five years
or more away.

One explanation for the differing estimates is simply differing
interpretations of what a bomb program might be. One bomb
doesn't make a program, nor would any rational leader destroy
his only cache of fissile material in a test. On the other hand,
efforts to buy krytrons and capacitors should have signaled the
possibility that Iraq was advancing in the development of a working bomb design, which could be tested and perfected with an
inert core to be made ready when sufficient fissile material came
to hand. That was, in fact, the case; in that strategy also, the Iraqi
bomb project of the 1980s was modeled on the American Manhattan Project of the 1940s, proceeding along multiple parallel
lines of development with the expectation that some would fall
by the wayside while others progressed. In Iraq's case, some had
already fallen by the wayside by 1988—in particular, uranium

enrichment by gaseous diffusion, for which the Iraqis had been unable to develop an effective diffusion material, called "barrier." (Gaseous diffusion involves forcing a gaseous compound of natural uranium at high pressure through a material with microscopic pores; the lighter U235 component diffuses at a slightly faster rate than the heavier U238 component, and by piping off the enriched gas and diffusing it repeatedly, hundreds or thousands of times, any degree of enrichment can be attained.) A 1987 test with uranium hexafluoride gas had failed when the barrier clogged. Laboratory-scale gaseous-diffusion research continued in Iraq using anodized aluminum as a barrier material, but the larger program turned to other approaches.

Little or none of this was known to the administration of George H. W. Bush, who took office as president in January 1989 promising vigilance against nuclear proliferation. During the Reagan years, when he was vice president, Bush had championed the tilt toward Iraq, and he continued to seek rapprochement with Saddam Hussein in the first years of his presidency. National security was certainly one reason he did so. The prospect of Iran under the Ayatollah Khomeini turning off the spigot of Middle Eastern oil argued for supporting Iraq as a counterweight. And anti-Communist fervor still fogged the mirrors in the State Department: "The Soviets have strong cards to play" in the Middle East, a deputy secretary of state wrote in a secret memo to senior government officials in 1988; in the official's view, the United States for that reason alone should pursue closer ties with Iraq.

More generally, Bush and his new secretary of state, James Baker, saw an opportunity to increase American influence in the Middle East, commercial as well as strategic, by rewarding improved Iraqi behavior. According to the investigative journalist Alan Friedman, a transition-team policy review at the outset of Bush's presidency "had advised the president-elect that it was time to set a new direction for U.S. policy toward Iraq." The new administration now had the choice, the review proposed, "to decide whether to treat Iraq as a distasteful dictatorship to be shunned where possible, or to recognize Iraq's present and potential power in the region and accord it relatively high priority. We strongly urge the latter view." The lessons of war, the review continued, "may have changed Iraq from a radical state challenging the system to a more responsible, status-quo state working within the system and promoting stability in the region." The review offered no evidence for this hypothetical Iraqi transformation; in fact, it judged that "few expect a humane regime will come to Iraq any time soon." It nevertheless endorsed "military exchanges" and "higher level dialogue." Trade was the key, Friedman says in summarizing the review's culminating argument, despite "the risk of 'diversion' of U.S. exports to Iraq's war machine."

Indeed, the policy review articulated a prime U.S. business interest that influenced Bush and Baker in their thinking: Iraq's "vast oil reserves," which promised "a lucrative market for U.S. goods." The review noted that U.S. oil imports from Iraq had skyrocketed after Iraq began offering American oil companies "large price incentives."

The idea, as one of the officials involved in preparing these recommendations at Baker's State Department summarized it, was "to embrace Saddam in a cocoon of moderation."

Bush agreed. On 2 October 1989 he signed National Security Directive 26. Its gist: "Normal relations between the United States and Iraq would serve our longer-term interests and promote stability in both the Gulf and the Middle East. The United States Government should propose economic and political incentives for Iraq to moderate its behavior and to increase our influence with Iraq." Before the end of the month, Baker endorsed extending Iraq up to a billion dollars in Commodity Credit Corporation (CCC) agricultural-product loan guarantees even though it faced "severe financial difficulties" that might prevent repayment; doing so, the action memorandum noted, was "in line with NSD-26."

At least one tough-minded, skeptical senior congressman—Henry Gonzalez, the Democratic chairman of the House banking committee—thought the explanation for Bush's Iraq initiatives was straightforward: oil. Tall, elegant, eloquent, and a relentless crusader, Gonzalez had begun dogging the Bush administration about Iraq after the FBI raided the Atlanta offices of the Banca Nazionale del Lavoro—BNL—in August 1989. BNL, Gonzalez would tell the House in 1992 in one of his biting hour-long speeches, was "one of the largest banks in Italy, with assets of over $100 billion." It was "98 percent owned by the Italian Government" and had operations around the world. As the FBI raid had established, former employees of the Atlanta branch had "conspired to provide the Government of Iraq with over $4 billion in unreported loans between 1985 and 1990. . . . The $4-billion-plus in BNL loans to Iraq . . . were crucial to Iraqi efforts to feed its people and to build weapons of mass destruction. In addition, the BNL loans were crucial to Reagan and Bush administration efforts to assist Saddam Hussein." An intense Bush administration effort at stonewalling and cover-up, led by Brent Scowcroft at the National Security Council and Lawrence Eagleburger at the State Department, followed the BNL revelations. Bush himself participated in stonewalling Congress.

In one of his most devastating House speeches, Gonzalez took note of the correlation between U.S. oil imports from Iraq and U.S. sales to Iraq of military and dual-use equipment. "That raid by the FBI on August 4, 1989," he told the House, "led to the unraveling not only of one of the biggest banking scandals of all time, it also laid bare that the United States was carrying on a strange, secretive, clandestine relationship with Iraq, which was at that time and still is today one of the most notorious governments in the world. It was Iraq, after all, that had used chemical weapons not just against its Iranian enemies but against its own Kurdish minority." Gonzalez continued:

Despite all this, the United States allowed Iraq to become the biggest customer of the Commodity Credit Corporation, a guaranteed program. Guaranteed by whom? The taxpayers, of course. That was financed largely through loans made by the BNL Atlanta office. Not only that, Iraq operated an extensive secret military procurement network in this country and in Europe which was also financed through BNL Atlanta, not through CCC guarantees but through commercial loans.... The U.S. Government knew about the secret procurement network, and it made a decision, and that decision was to tolerate it, even after the BNL office was raided in 1989.

Consider this: the BNL Atlanta office was raided on August 4, 1989. The raid revealed that BNL was funding Matrix Churchill Ltd. and Matrix Churchill Corp., known Iraqi procurement fronts. The raid also revealed that Iraq was funding several other firms, including TDG, TEG and Euromac, that the CIA linked to Iraq's clandestine military procurement network. Our intelligence knew all of this.... The Secretary of State was advised, the President was advised.... Yet just a few months later, after warning its allies in Europe to be alert to Iraqi efforts to buy glass fiber technology,* the U.S. Government—that is, this administration and the immediate past one—approved a Matrix Churchill export license for the sale of the complex fiber factory to Iraq's largest armaments producer.

In fact, the Bush administration continued to approve the sale of military-useful technology to Iraq even when that technology was known to be destined for Iraqi arms factories. This policy was in place right up until Iraq invaded Kuwait.

Then Gonzalez drew the link with oil sales, citing a "recently-declassified State Department memorandum to Secretary Baker dated March 23, 1989."

---

*Glass-fiber technology adapted to use carbon fiber would allow Iraq to manufacture advanced centrifuges for uranium enrichment.

The memo states:

"Iraq would also like freer export licensing procedures for high tech."

The memorandum also states:

"As part of its approach to the United States, Iraq has in the last year given favorable deals to U.S. oil companies; oil exports to the U.S. have soared to around 500,000 barrels per day."

Giving favorable oil deals to U.S. firms furthered Iraq's ultimate strategy of increasing its importance to the United States. The success of this plan, as measured by oil sales, is illustrated in a recently declassified CIA report dated April 1990 which states:

"The U.S. purchase of Iraqi oil has jumped from about 80,000 barrels per day in 1985–1987 to 675,000 b/d so far in 1990— about 24 percent of Baghdad's total oil exports and eight percent of new U.S. oil imports."

By the time Iraq invaded Kuwait, United States purchase of Iraqi oil had grown to over 1.1 million barrels per day. The largest single purchaser was Exxon, but there were many others.

Within days of Iraq's invasion of Kuwait, Bush signed a conflict-of-interest waiver to protect high-level officials of his government from prosecution for conflicts of interest—oil holdings in particular—related to what the waiver called "the current Middle East crisis." The waiver included James Baker, Brent Scowcroft, and nine other cabinet members and security advisers.

Gonzalez concluded his House presentation with a devastating summary of the Bush administration's collusions with Saddam Hussein:

In short, these are the facts: First, the administration wanted to help Iraq; second, Iraq had cheap oil to offer and the United States was eager to buy—as shown by the amazing 50 percent growth in Iraqi oil sales to the United States in the two years before the Gulf war; third, the Bush administration was so eager to please Saddam Hussein that it deliberately tolerated Iraq's military procurement activities in the United States; fourth, companies like Matrix Churchill were used by Iraq to provide everything from steel mills to nuclear-weapons-useful technology—right up to the day the Gulf war started; and fifth, even after the BNL raid made it impossible to hide Iraq's procurement activities in this country, the Bush administration did nothing to stop Iraq. They even showed support by having the Department of Energy purchase Iraqi oil just a few months before our Government went to war against Iraq. Favorable oil deals made it all possible.

WHEN NEW YORK CONGRESSMAN Charles Schumer surveyed the wreckage of Bush policy later, he called it "President Bush's Frankenstein." Saddam Hussein, Schumer charged, had been created "in the White House laboratory with a collection of government programs, banks and private companies."

If greed played a part in the Bush administration's collusion with Iraq, an alliance with the secular Middle Eastern state against a revolutionary Muslim state that had shown itself to be passionately hostile to the United States—Iran—was clearly Bush and Baker's larger motive, as it had been the Reagan administration's before. The strategy backfired in 1990 as Saddam Hussein, after repeated delays and defaults, found his sources of income increasingly reduced or cut off and began looking upon his neighbor, Kuwait, as an ill-guarded bank to rob. Demanding forgiveness of his debts and support for reconstruction, he told the Arab Cooperation Council at a February 1990 summit in Jordan, "Let the Gulf regimes know that if they do not give this money to me, I will know how to get it." Whether convinced himself or simply bluffing, he portrayed the United States as a paper tiger, fearful of conflict after its loss in Vietnam: "Brothers," he told the council, "the weakness of a big body lies in its bulkiness. . . . We saw that the United States as a superpower departed Lebanon immediately when some marines were killed, the very men who are considered to be the most prominent symbol of its arrogance. . . . The United States has been defeated in some combat arenas for all the forces it possesses, and it has displayed signs of fatigue, frustration, and hesitation." In a television speech on 2 April, to warn off Israel, he threatened it with chemical weapons and perhaps alluded to a nuclear capability (which he did not yet have): "By Allah, we will make the fire eat up half of Israel if it tries to do anything against Iraq."

Crucially, he took the American government's years of support as a sign that the United States would tolerate an Iraqi invasion of Kuwait. His notorious 25 July 1990 meeting with the U.S. ambassador to Iraq, April Glaspie, added to that conviction. He used the occasion to rehearse his grievances:

> Iraq came out of the war burdened with $40 billion debts, excluding the aid given by Arab states, some of whom consider that too to be a debt although they knew—and you knew too—that without Iraq they would not have had these sums and the future of the region would have been entirely different. We began to face the policy of the drop in the price of oil. . . . When planned and deliberate policy forces the price of oil down without good commercial reasons, then that means another war against Iraq. Because military war kills people by bleeding them, and economic war kills their humanity by depriving them of their chance to have a good standard of living. As you know, we gave rivers of blood in a war that lasted eight years, but we did not lose our humanity. Iraqis have a right to live proudly. We do not accept that anyone could injure Iraqi pride or the Iraqi right to have high standards of living. Kuwait and the U.A.E. [United Arab Emirates] were at the front of this policy aimed at lowering Iraq's position and depriving its people of higher economic standards.

Grievances against his brother Arab states led Saddam next to make veiled threats against the United States in response to threats he felt the U.S. had recently made against Iraq:

So what can it mean when America says it will now protect its friends? It can only mean prejudice against Iraq. This stance plus maneuvers and statements which have been made have encouraged the U.A.E. and Kuwait to disregard Iraqi rights. . . . The United States must have a better understanding of the situation and declare who it wants to have relations with and who its enemies are. . . . It is not reasonable to ask people to bleed rivers of blood for eight years then to tell them, "Now you have to accept aggression from Kuwait, the U.A.E., or from the U.S. or from Israel."

Glaspie responded, when the Iraqi dictator finally gave her a chance, by emphasizing that she had "a direct instruction from the President to seek better relations with Iraq." Saddam asked, "But how? We too have this desire. But matters are running contrary to this desire." Glaspie emphasized the importance of continuing to talk, criticized the "American media" for portraying Saddam in a bad light—"These are the methods the Western media employs," she said disdainfully—and then segued to a discussion of the importance of keeping the price of oil low. Abruptly, in almost a non sequitur, she added: "But we have no opinion on the Arab-Arab conflicts, like your border disagreement with Kuwait. I was in the American Embassy in Kuwait during the late sixties. The instruction we had during this period was that we should express no opinion on this issue and that the issue is not associated with America. James Baker has directed our official spokesmen to emphasize this instruction. We hope you can solve this problem using any suitable methods via [Chedli] Klibi [the secretary-general of the Arab League] or via [Egyptian] President [Hosni] Mubarak."

Apparently Glaspie was indicating that her government hoped for a peaceful negotiation, perhaps through the intervention of the Arab League or of Egypt. Saddam's response was to rehearse his grievances once again, lugubriously, this time emphasizing Kuwait:

We want to find a just solution which will give us our rights but not deprive others of their rights. But at the same time, we want others to know that our patience is running out regarding their action, which is harming even the milk our children drink, and the pensions of the widow who lost her husband during the war, and the pensions of the orphans who lost their parents. . . .

Brother President Mubarak told me [that the Kuwaitis] were scared. They said [Iraqi] troops were only 20 kilometers north of the Arab League line. I said to him that regardless of what is there, whether they are police, border guards or army, and regardless of how many are there, and what they are doing, assure the Kuwaitis and give them our word that we are not going to do anything until we meet with them. When we meet and when we see that there is hope, then nothing will happen. But if we are unable to find a solution, then it will be natural that Iraq will not accept death, even though wisdom is above everything else. There you have good news.

Glaspie told Saddam she would carry the good news to America.

Before she left Iraq, Glaspie cabled a report to the State Department on her meeting with Saddam. George Bush responded with a message mollifying the Iraqi leader that Glaspie delivered on 28 July. Coming from the president, it carried far more weight with Saddam Hussein than the representations of a mere ambassador:

The United States and Iraq both have a strong interest in preserving the peace and stability of the Middle East. For this reason, we believe that differences are best resolved by peaceful means and not by threats involving military force or conflict. I also welcome your statement that Iraq desires friendship, rather than confrontation, with the United States. Let me reassure you . . . that my administration continues to desire better relations with Iraq. . . . We still have fundamental concerns about certain Iraqi policies and activities. And we will continue to

raise these concerns with you, in a spirit of friendship and candor, as we have in the past, both to gain a better understanding
of your interests and intentions and to ensure you understand
our concerns.

What Saddam Hussein made of Bush's message is evident
from what followed. Iraq had begun massing forces on the
Kuwaiti border in July. While a travesty of negotiations played
out between Iraq and Kuwait, all international flights from
Kuwait City sold out, and so many Kuwaitis moved funds out
of the country that the government blocked all further overseas
electronic funds transfers. Kuwait's small army, on the other
hand, having finished its midsummer maneuvers, stood down,
and most of its officers left on vacation.

At eleven p.m. on 1 August 1990, American technicians from
Westinghouse who were manning a tethered radar-observation
balloon near the Kuwait border with Iraq called the commander
of the U.S. Army unit that advised the Kuwaiti Army. "Their
reports were very pointed," writes one of the U.S. officers posted
to Kuwait at the time. "They described the radar paint as a mass
armor formation resembling an iron pipe several kilometers
long and rolling downhill. They were advised to cut the tether
and move out smartly. By 0100, 2 August 1990, the Iraqi formation was rapidly moving south along the Abdaly highway totally
unopposed."

TWO **CUTTING SADDAM'S SINEWS**

G EORGE H. W. BUSH had been shocked by Saddam Hussein's perfidy in the run-up to Iraq's invasion of Kuwait at the beginning of August 1990. The invasion itself stunned and then outraged him. The United States had bent over backward to mollify the Iraqi dictator; bitterly, his response was betrayal. On 2 August the United Nations Security Council condemned the invasion and demanded that Iraq withdraw. Iraqi tanks continued to roll into Kuwait through the weekend, and when Bush helicoptered back from Camp David on Sunday, 5 August, he announced emotionally from the White House lawn, "This will not stand, this aggression against Kuwait." James Baker says he reminded the president later that month, when the two old friends were alone in the Oval Office, "I know you're aware of the fact that this has all the ingredients that brought down three of the last five Presidents: a hostage crisis, body bags and a full-fledged economic recession caused by forty-dollar oil." According to Baker, Bush responded, "I know that, Jimmy, I know that. But we're doing what's right; we're doing what is clearly in the national interest of the United States. Whatever else happens, so be it."

Several thousand Americans had been trapped in Kuwait and Iraq by the invasion. In the weeks and months to come, the primary responsibility for protecting them and securing their release fell to a forty-year-old U.S. foreign service professional named Joseph Wilson. Joe Wilson's conflict a decade later with the administration of Bush's son George W. Bush about whether or not Iraq had recently attempted to buy yellowcake from Niger would make his name and that of his second wife, Valerie Plame Wilson, well known. For now, his challenge was representing the hundred Americans who had taken shelter in the American embassy in Kuwait City and the several thousand more who were lying low throughout the city. At the same time, he would work to gather up a large contingent in Baghdad, mostly employees of Bechtel, the American engineering company, and to free the hundred-plus hostages whom the Iraqis had seized.

Wilson met with Saddam himself on 6 August. "Convey to President Bush that he should regard the Kuwaiti emir and crown prince as history," the Iraqi dictator vaunted. He used the occasion to offer America a supply of cheap oil in exchange for its tolerance of his taking over what he liked to call Iraq's "nineteenth province." (He announced the annexation of Kuwait two days later.) He also fished for clues about the United States's intentions. Wilson didn't know those intentions, he writes, but after their discussion the dictator was visibly relieved. "Saddam was worried about the possible American response, and may have concluded that the confusing statements coming from different parts of the U.S. government meant there would be no consensus to respond militarily to his invasion of Kuwait."

While Wilson was meeting with Saddam in Baghdad, secretary of defense Richard Cheney was meeting with King Fahd of Saudi Arabia in Jedda. Among others accompanying him on his mission to convince the Saudi king to allow the United States to use his country as a base of operations were Norman Schwarzkopf, the American Army general in charge of the U.S. Central Command; Deputy National Security Adviser Robert Gates; and Cheney's senior aide Paul Wolfowitz. Schwarzkopf delivered the main briefing, using satellite photos of the Iraqi buildup along Kuwait's border with Saudi Arabia to support his argument.

Cheney closed the sale. The king recognized the looming threat to his country and was easily persuaded despite the skepticism of Crown Prince Abdullah and other advisers on hand. "After the danger is over," Cheney concluded, "our forces will go home." In Arabic, Abdullah quipped acidly, "I should hope so." At 3:30 p.m. that day, the chairman of the Joint Chiefs of Staff, Colin Powell, recalled, "Dick Cheney called me from Jedda. He had just left King Fahd, he said. 'We've got his approval. I've informed the President. Start issuing orders to move the force.' " The first U.S. muscle—a squadron of F-15 Eagles—arrived in Saudi Arabia the next day. By mid-August, Powell had airlifted almost thirty thousand combat troops into the country. "Within a couple of weeks we'll have completed the deterrent buildup," he told Bush. "We should have enough power to discourage Saddam from attacking, if that's what he has in mind."

ON 2 AUGUST, the second day of the Iraqi invasion, Norman Schwarzkopf had mused aloud that his science adviser should investigate the feasibility of exploding a nuclear weapon in a high-altitude airburst over Iraq at the outset of a war to generate an electromagnetic pulse to short out Iraqi communications and missile launch controls. The Joint Chiefs would soon decide not to move nuclear weapons into the Persian Gulf, writes the intelligence analyst William Arkin—in any case, there were nuclear bombs stored at an American air base in southern Turkey, well within range of Baghdad—"but a variety of military organizations quietly began to examine nuclear options. Led by the 'special weapons branch' in the Operations Directorate and the office of the Scientific Advisor at Schwarzkopf's headquarters, the Army staff, Defense Nuclear Agency (DNA), Strategic Air Command (SAC) and the Department of Energy's national laboratories all contributed ideas and proposals."

Unknown to anyone outside the Iraqi government, Saddam was also examining what he imagined to be his nuclear options. In the days after the invasion, through his cousin and son-in-law Hussein Kamel, he ordered his scientists to initiate an eight-month crash program to build an atomic bomb. They could divert the 93-percent-enriched uranium left unloaded when Israel bombed the French-built reactor at Tuwaitha and the 80-percent-enriched fuel in the Soviet reactor as well. Allowing for processing losses, that would not be enough for one bomb, so they would somehow have to enrich a few more kilograms from their reactor supplies. The goal of the crash program was to produce a total of twenty kilograms of weapons-grade uranium metal to serve as the pit of an implosion warhead that could be mounted on a missile capable of reaching Tel Aviv—a mission of national suicide considering Israel's certain nuclear response.

The previous May, Kamel's scientists had completed a series of twenty high-explosive tests evaluating five different designs for an implosion lens system. The high-explosive components of the Nagasaki implosion bomb, Fat Man, had been made from an explosive called RDX; that bomb had weighed five tons. The Iraqi design used HMX—"high-melting explosive," a more powerful RDX derivative—and was much lighter. "These tests were credited with reducing the bomb weight to about half a ton," a U.S. Defense Special Weapons Agency report concludes. At a thousand pounds, the weapon could be delivered by either one of Iraq's larger, longer-range missiles (the Aabed or the Tamuz), although it would require advanced engineering to stabilize it against the large g-forces of missile acceleration and reentry. A less sophisticated assembly could be delivered by bomber. With some eighteen kilograms of HEU packed into its core, the bomb would be notably unstable, barely subcritical, and ready to go off. "It was a stupid idea," writes a knowledgeable former U.S. official, "because they would have to master several chemistry steps never before tried in Iraq to get the [uranium oxide] reactor fuel turned into metal, and they would have to suddenly succeed at centrifuge enrichment when they were already having lots of problems. The only advantage would have been that the amount needed, with the already enriched reactor fuel on hand, would have been much smaller [than a gun bomb would require]. Otherwise, it was a knee-jerk project, the dictates of a mad dictator."

At the end of August Saddam announced that the women and children among the U.S. refugees would be allowed to leave Kuwait. With all Western airlines banned, Wilson and his staff had to ticket the exodus on Iraq Air. September saw two or three flights a week out of Kuwait via Baghdad. Hostages had increased by then to about 125, Wilson recalls:

> We had learned that they were routinely being moved from one strategic site to another inside Iraq. As some were released they brought purloined letters from others to us, so that after a while we were able to identify some fifty-five sites that were being used around the country. We sent this information to Pentagon planners for their use.
>
> As it turned out, Saddam had unwittingly shown us, by where he put the hostages, which locations were most important to him. I was gratified when several months later, on the first night of Desert Storm, long after the hostages had been released, many of those sites were ones hit by American bombs.

Bush initially condemned the Iraqi invasion with inflated analogies to Hitler and the Second World War. "A half-century ago our nation and the world paid dearly for appeasing an aggressor who should and could have been stopped," the president told a crowd in mid-August. "We're not about to make that same mistake twice. Today Saddam Hussein's Iraq has been cut off by the Arab and Islamic nations that surround it. The Arab League itself has condemned Iraq's aggression. We stand with them, and we are not alone."

Whether the U.S. should stand with other countries through the United Nations or challenge Iraq alone was becoming a matter of debate within the administration at that time. The political analyst Christian Alfonsi has identified "sharp divisions within

George Bush's war cabinet over what the U.N.'s role in the Gulf crisis should be. It had become apparent to [U.N. Ambassador Thomas] Pickering that Dick Cheney and the Pentagon 'really didn't want to stay with the UN activity. They basically wanted to free themselves from the need to consult with anyone.' . . . [But] Bush intuitively sensed the widespread suspicion of American motives in the Islamic world and wanted to build a broad international coalition against Iraq that included significant participation by other Arab and Islamic states. For this, the legitimacy conferred by the UN was essential."

A second strategic debate went on within the Bush administration over whether and how long to allow sanctions and diplomacy to continue before going to war. Baker supported diplomacy because it strengthened the burgeoning new partnership between the Soviet Union and the United States. Scowcroft, on the other hand, writes Alfonsi, "was convinced that military action in the Gulf would become inevitable, and not just because he doubted that sanctions and diplomacy alone would be enough to drive Saddam out of Kuwait. The United States needed to demonstrate a willingness to use force against Iraq, so that future challengers to American global leadership would think twice before acting." Scowcroft, that is, wanted to make an example of Iraq to scare away potential competitors in the new world that was opening to American hegemony with the withdrawal and weakening of the Soviet Union.

Bush's longer-term problem was what to do about Iraq after his coalition drove the invaders out of Kuwait. The Middle Eastern dictatorship would still be a formidable military power, the fourth largest in the world. The solution, devised by Thomas Pickering, was to leave Saddam in authority but to shrink Iraq's military, destroy most of its arms, wall off sections of the country with exclusionary zones, and eliminate its weapons of mass destruction. Cutting Saddam's sinews to that extent went beyond what was required for liberating its tiny neighbor, however, and required a larger rationale. "The Bush administration," Alfonsi writes, "which had rarely mentioned Iraq's weapons of mass destruction in its public (or private) comments during the first month of the Gulf crisis, would now increasingly use Saddam Hussein's attempts to acquire these weapons as justification for taking decisive action against Iraq." At that time, however, according to the International Atomic Energy Agency's David Kay, "the consensus opinion of the intelligence agencies and all was there was nothing there."

So one consequence of these internal Bush administration policy debates was to endorse fear-mongering as an acceptable stratagem to sell the American people on war in the Gulf, as it had been an acceptable stratagem for building and sustaining an economically burdensome U.S. military-industrial complex during the long Cold War with the Soviet Union. Bush believed, correctly, that the Gulf conflict was the first post–Cold War challenge to world order, historically significant and precedent-setting. Tragically, choosing to lie about the known extent of Iraq's nuclear capabilities set a dangerous precedent; what Bush did with the best of intentions in 1990 would be available to be repeated with less justified intentions a decade later by his son.

AT THE BEGINNING OF October 1990, a representative of the Pakistani metallurgist A. Q. Khan turned up in Baghdad with a sensational offer: Khan, the so-called father of the Pakistani bomb, was prepared to sell the Iraqis a tested bomb design and support for centrifuge enrichment of uranium. The unspecified bomb design was the Pakistani derivative of the Chinese design designated CHIC-4, which was passed to Pakistan in the 1980s, when China under Deng Xiaoping was intentionally proliferating nuclear-weapons technology to the developing world; Pakistan had tested its version of CHIC-4 in China at the Lop Nur test site the previous May. Khan wanted a preliminary technical meeting with Iraqi experts to review the documents he was prepared to sell. He wanted $5 million up front and a 10 percent commission on any machines or materials the Iraqis bought. His motive, an Iraqi intelligence report judged bluntly, was "gaining profits for him and the intermediary."

Hussein Kamel's people were wary of the offer. They suspected that it might be an American sting. They asked Iraqi intelligence—the Mukhabarat—to acquire samples of the materials Khan was offering to sell. The Mukhabarat passed the request along to the intermediary, but it was never fulfilled. The public records of the Khan approach are too scanty to determine why. Khan did sell the Iraqis a chain-reaction-initiation system more sophisticated than the World War II–era polonium-beryllium initiator developed at Los Alamos that the indigenous Iraqi design used. Had the Iraqis bought the Pakistani design, it's barely conceivable that they might have been able to piece together enough enriched uranium to make one bomb. Their suspicions got in the way, and soon enough American conventional bombs obliterated their nuclear installations.

THERE WAS STRONG RESISTANCE in the U.S. Congress to liberating Kuwait by force. Georgia's Democratic senator Sam Nunn, the chairman of the Senate Armed Services Committee, favored sanctions and diplomacy and found many retired government and military leaders to support him in televised Senate hearings in late November 1990. He was concerned that the continuing U.S. buildup in Saudi Arabia would make war inevitable; Colin Powell had almost doubled his troop requirements, from 250,000 to 400,000, earlier that month. Bush sketched the resistance in his diary:

> November 28 [1990]
>
> The debate is raging now and Sam Nunn, I think running for president, is trying to decide how hard to push. [Congressman Richard] Gephardt "breaks" with the President, saying "no use of force, sanctions must work." None of them seem concerned

about the hostages, none of them share my anxiety about the Embassy.... It's ironic, the isolationistic right lined with the [Yale president and anti-Vietnam War activist] Kingman Brewster left [voicing the] Vietnam syndrome. Bob Kerrey, a true war hero in Vietnam and John Glenn, also a hero, "no force, no force."

Projections of American casualties for a ground war with Saddam Hussein, whose forces in Kuwait were approaching the half-million mark—he had even called up seventeen-year-olds—ranged from military estimates of below two thousand U.S. combatants to civilian projections of twenty thousand or more. The former secretary of defense Robert McNamara put the number at thirty thousand, former senator and Democratic presidential candidate George McGovern at fifty thousand. Beyond the conflicting casualty estimates, however, the war decision had become a debate over presidential versus congressional authority in this first major U.S. confrontation since Vietnam. Congress wanted the president to seek its approval to wage war with Iraq, as the U.S. Constitution required. Bush was willing to do so, but he worried that Congress might vote war down.

Secretary of Defense Dick Cheney had been a congressman at the time of the Reagan administration's Iran-Contra scandal, which revealed, in Reagan's words, that "what began as a strategic opening to Iran deteriorated, in its implementation, into trading arms for hostages." Cheney had always been a denizen of the far right—"somewhat to the right of . . . Genghis Khan," a waggish colleague had observed of him as far back as his early days in the Gerald Ford White House—and he emerged from his party's Iran-Contra disaster vehemently opposed to seeking congressional approval of presidential decisions in foreign affairs. Discussing the lessons of Iran-Contra on a 1987 television news program, he had argued:

I think you have to preserve the prerogative of the President in extraordinary circumstances not to notify the Congress at all [of covert actions]. Or to exercise discretion to wait for days or weeks, or even months [before doing so]. I think that's within his constitutional prerogative. . . . I don't think that you can pass a law that will guarantee no future president will make mistakes, and I think we have to guard against passing laws now that will restrict some future president in a future crisis that we can only guess at at present.

Armed with this extreme view of presidential prerogative, Cheney pointedly disagreed with Senator Edward Kennedy in a December 1990 Armed Services Committee hearing about needing congressional approval to go to war against Iraq:

SENATOR KENNEDY: Secretary Cheney, you're a former member of the House of Representatives, and you're fully aware of what the Constitution says with regards to the war-making power. . . . But the President still refuses to ask the one body that the Constitution requires him to ask, which is the United States Congress, about the declaration of war. . . .

Yesterday, Secretary Baker suggested more ominously that if President Bush does go to war, he expects that Congress will rally around the President after he has committed the troops to combat. And one would gather that the President effectively is thumbing his nose at Congress. He's really daring us to act if we disagree with him. He's telling us that the decision whether to go to war is his, and effectively his alone, to make. And he apparently is not going to let Congress interfere with him.

Now, barring an act of provocation, do you agree that the President must obtain the approval of Congress in advance before the United States attacks Iraq?

SECRETARY CHENEY: Senator, I do not believe the President requires any additional authorization from the Congress before committing US forces to achieve our objectives in the Gulf.

"It's such a vital problem," Cheney argued with Bush, "that we have no choice but to move in and liberate Kuwait. Even if the Congress votes no, we'd still have to do it. Asking for their approval and being turned down would create a major confrontation with the Congress of having asked for their authority and having it denied. We would then have to say, 'Well, we don't need them anyway, we've got the authority to proceed.' "

Rejecting Cheney's arguments, Bush chose to seek a congressional resolution supporting a war. He lobbied Congress intensely through December and early January against a U.N. deadline for Iraqi compliance set for 15 January 1991. James Baker met one final time with Iraq's foreign minister, Tariq Aziz, in Geneva on 9 January and told him bluntly what would happen to his country if it failed to comply with the U.N. deadline. "I also warned him of severe reprisals for using chemical or biological weapons," Baker writes. " 'This is not a threat,' I said, 'it's a promise.' " Baker was hinting at a nuclear response, although Bush had ruled out the use of nuclear weapons in the impending war. Aziz responded by refusing to deliver a letter summarizing Baker's warnings from Baker to Saddam, calling it an insult.

Both houses of Congress approved war resolutions on 12 January, three days before the U.N. deadline, but the margins were narrow: 250–183 in the House, 52–47 in the Senate. Despite Cheney's objections, Bush had taken the risk and won the support he needed. Congress, and by extension the American people, would share responsibility for the war.

IN BAGHDAD, Joe Wilson had been working behind the scenes to persuade Saddam Hussein to release the hostages he was holding. Wilson met with the Arab press and dogged the Iraqi foreign ministry, arguing that "holding on to the hostages was not in Saddam's interest, unless he wanted to go to war over that issue rather than over his continued occupation of Kuwait." Through an influential Arab journalist with whom he had lunch, Wilson believes, his message reached King Hussein of Jordan. The king and Yasir Arafat met with Saddam in Baghdad in early December; Wilson says they laid out the same case he had made against continuing to hold the hostages:

> That meeting with the king and Arafat was the real clincher. Saddam, who had just invited the wives of the hostages to return to Baghdad to see their husbands, announced on December 6 that Iraq's defenses were now strong enough to withstand an American offensive, so the hostages could now go home. We were elated and went back into the charter aircraft business.

When the hostages got home to the United States, they found themselves invited to turn in the clothes they had worn during their captivity. From the clothing of hostages who had been held at Tuwaitha, who had been transported to the gymnasium there for exercise on buses that were also used by Tuwaitha workers, U.S. scientists extracted microscopic particles of uranium. "They ran the analysis," David Kay told me, "and to their surprise the uranium was depleted"—i.e., it was anomalously low in U235— "at a level that would only be possible if you were sitting on top of a calutron, essentially." A calutron is a machine that accelerates uranium atoms through a magnetic field to separate U235 from U238, a process known as electromagnetic isotope separation, or EMIS; it was invented at the University of California early in the Second World War and first used to enrich uranium for the Hiroshima atomic bomb. Jere Nichols, a chemical engineer at the Oak Ridge National Laboratory who was involved in the investigation, said later that the uranium isotopics "showed that there was uranium-238 in the sample—and essentially none of the other uranium isotopes. These isotopics could only have been obtained as the tailings from an electromagnetic isotope separation system."

Kay called this information "the initial clue" to the fact that Iraq was using EMIS technology to enrich uranium. It was not a clue that the U.S. intelligence community judged to be credible, however. "Some of us believed that EMIS was the primary method of uranium separation in Iraq," Nichols recalled, "but the deciding votes, back in those days, were cast by people who believed that a proliferator would not use that old-fashioned, power-intensive technology. They had concluded that Iraq must be using centrifuge technology for uranium enrichment." Since knowing what you're looking for is the key to successful investigation, looking for centrifuges when they should have been looking for Baghdadtrons, as the Iraqis called their version of the calutron, would be at least a misdirection of time and resources.

The other problem with assessing the Tuwaitha collections was that the process used to analyze the Tuwaitha uranium dust, called neutron-activation analysis, involved irradiating the particles in a nuclear reactor. "The reactor that did it was out in California," David Kay says, "and it was not big and it was almost a handicraft process to do it. It took almost six weeks, so the results weren't available until after the war was over."

IN NOVEMBER, visiting U.S. marines in the Saudi desert on a Thanksgiving tour, George Bush emphasized the urgency of Iraq's race toward nuclear weapons. "Those who would measure the timetable for Saddam Hussein's atomic weapons program in years," he claimed, "may be underestimating the reality of the situation and the gravity of that threat. No one knows precisely when this dictator may acquire atomic weapons or who they may be aimed at down the road. But we do know this for sure: He has never possessed a weapon that he hasn't used."

By emphasizing weapons of mass destruction (WMD), Bush was pursuing his political agenda of enlarging the purpose of a war beyond the liberation of Kuwait. He also, writes William Arkin, had received an early November analysis from the Joint Atomic Intelligence Committee, an interagency group, "which concluded . . . that with a 'crash program' Iraq could produce one or two 'crude nuclear explosive devices' in as little as six months to a year." As the possibility of going to war hardened toward certainty, the problem also emerged of keeping Israel pacified, to avoid shattering the largely Arab coalition Bush was assembling should the Jewish state opt in. Israel made its price clear in a message to James Baker on 4 December: for Israel to stay out of the war, the U.S. would have to eliminate Iraq's WMD. An analyst at the U.S. Embassy in Tel Aviv explained Israel's reasoning three days later in an assessment: "In the [government of Israel's] view, even a complete [Iraqi] withdrawal would be problematic if it left Iraq's conventional and especially nuclear arsenal [sic] intact."

Bush intended to destroy the Iraqi nuclear-weapons program anyway as part of reducing Saddam's war-making capabilities. But what if Saddam pulled his forces out of Kuwait as soon as the war began and stood down? An order went out to the air-war planners in Riyadh that the Iraqi "capability to produce and use weapons of mass destruction" should be destroyed as early as possible in the war. "Thus," Arkin writes, "two weeks before the air war would begin, a new plan emerged. It would compress six days of attacks into three, nearly doubling the number of sorties flown during the first 72 hours and emphasizing Washington's requirement that all nuclear, biological and chemical (NBC) targets be visited by the end of Day Two." The price of compressing the attacks into a shorter period of time was that the targets would be hit with fewer bombs. Instead of eight F-117As dropping eight bombs on each target, the targets would be "functionally impaired" with one or two bombs each. As it turned out, the high-precision attacks were effective despite their limited scale; but only about half of the eighteen nuclear-production sites in Iraq were known to the coalition at the outset of the war. The other half were left unscathed.

THE UNITED NATIONS coalition attack on Iraq began at seven p.m. Eastern Standard Time on Wednesday, 16 January 1991—three a.m. on 17 January in Baghdad. I was traveling with my wife-to-be at the time on a careening speed-freak-driven bus across Thailand from Bangkok to Chiang Mai, and caught CNN's green night-vision coverage of the initial air assault on a television set in the bar of a rest stop, a bowling alley surrounded by paddy fields in the middle of the country; the Thais gathered around the TV, who still remembered their flush days as purveyors of R & R to U.S. soldiers fighting next door in Vietnam, were cheering as the bombs exploded and the streaking antiaircraft fire swayed across the green sky. The green night-vision images, surging white as the explosions overloaded the amplifier, hinted at the high technologies the U.S. would first introduce in that brief, overwhelming war.

The primary targets of the air assault that first night were Iraq's air defenses and electric grid. Decapitating the Iraqi leadership—preferably by killing Saddam—received equal weight, Arkin writes:

> This was indeed a new era of warfare. Despite all the attention heaped on Stealth [technology], in the first wave more [U.S. Navy Tomahawk] cruise missiles were directed at Baghdad targets than were [F-117A] Stealth fighters.
>
> Though the Tomahawks' reliability and accuracy were questioned, even by many in the Navy, their use did not put pilots' lives at risk. Eight missiles were targeted on Saddam's New Presidential Palace along the Tigris River, six on Ba'ath Party headquarters to its south.
>
> Electrical power plants were attacked with special variants of the Tomahawk that dispensed a spider-like web of filaments to cause them to short-circuit. . . . The special warheads would disable electrical distribution without destroying generating capacity, minimizing the long-term effect on the civilian population.

Tuwaitha was hit on 18 January, the second night of the air war. Sea-launched Tomahawks and F-111F fighter-bombers carrying laser-guided bombs totally destroyed the reactors and other installations there. Targeters could not target what was unknown to them, but one installation that proved to be an important nuclear site was fortuitously hit later. As David Kay tells the story:

> During the second week of the air campaign there was a pilot rolling out of Baghdad who still had armament left. The rule of thumb is, one does not land aircraft with armament still aboard, especially on carrier decks. So pilots, if they have an approved secondary target, will dump, and if they don't have an approved secondary target, they'll still dump. So he looked down, he had a secondary target and the AWACS plane told him there wasn't much anti-aircraft in that direction. So he rolled on the secondary target, he found the biggest building he could find and he just dumped the bombs on it and went home.
>
> Because it had been a secondary target, the battle damage assessment took about two days—two days before anyone flew a photo mission. Well, the photo mission saw these big circular objects and something like six big cranes and over a hundred people around this building pulling things out. Now a good rule of military intelligence is, if something happens in combat that you don't understand, blow the shit out of it and worry later about figuring out what it was. So they directed a B-52 raid across this site. It was like clearing a swath for a freeway; they just started at one end and dumped it.

The mystery site, located about eighteen miles northwest of Baghdad on the Tigris River, was called Tarmiya, but what the "big circular objects" were, no one yet knew.

Smoke from burning Kuwaiti oil wells first showed up on satellite images on 8 February 1991. By 15 February, at least 50 wells were billowing fire and dense black smoke. These first fires were probably ignited accidentally by coalition aircraft bombing Iraqi forces holding defensive positions in the oil fields. On television shortly after the beginning of the war, Saddam had threatened to "use oil for self-defense," and beginning on 16 February, as his forces moved to retreat from Kuwait, they began systematically blowing the caps off Kuwaiti oil wells with plastic explosives and deliberately igniting the gush. By 24 February, 792 wells had been set ablaze; the oil burned so hot that air temperatures in the immediate vicinity of the fires were raised to nearly 1,000° F. Every day, six million barrels of oil—more than 10 percent of the world's daily production—went up in flames. It took eight months to blow out the fires and cap the wells; in the end, Kuwait lost 85 percent of its oil-production capacity.

The air war gave way to the ground war. Hostilities continued until 27 February 1991. "The Gulf War was the war against the Russians we didn't have," Colin Powell would say. "There were no trees and no hills, but that's what we were trained to fight. The Iraqis sat there and we kicked the shit out of them." In some 110,000 combat air sorties flown, the coalition lost only thirty-eight aircraft. Only 148 Americans died in battle; only 467 were wounded. Iraqi losses were substantial: up to 65,000 combat casualties. Where Iraqi troops defended from a line of World War I–style trenches, U.S. engineers in armored bulldozers simply dozed them under. By the end of the war, 86,000 Iraqi soldiers had surrendered, most of them young and frightened conscripts.

DESERT STORM WAS a limited war, and deliberately so. Although Colin Powell would have been happy, as he said, to have killed Saddam Hussein, George Bush had no desire to push on to Baghdad and take over the country once Kuwait was liberated and Iraq's military potential reduced. Responding to critics at a postwar press conference who said he should have gone into Baghdad, Bush answered impatiently, "Yes, and do what?" Cheney also defended the administration's limited goals at a Washington symposium in late April 1991:

I think that the proposition of going to Baghdad is . . . fallacious. I think if we're going to remove Saddam Hussein we would have had to go all the way to Baghdad. We would have to commit a lot of force, because I don't believe he would wait in the Presidential Palace for us to arrive. I think we'd have had to hunt him down. And once we'd done that and we'd gotten rid of Saddam Hussein and his government, then we'd have had to put another government in its place. What kind of government? Should it be a Sunni government or Shia government or a Kurdish government or Baathist regime? Or maybe we want to bring in some of the Islamic fundamentalists? How long would we have had to stay in Baghdad to keep that government in place? What would happen to the government once U.S. forces withdrew? How many casualties should the United States accept in that effort to try to create clarity and stability in a situation that is inherently unstable? . . . It's my view that the President got it right . . . that it would have been a mistake for us to get bogged down in the quagmire inside Iraq.

The United States introduced a revolutionary new class of military systems into Desert Storm. They had been conceived and developed in the 1970s under the direction of William J. Perry, a tall, soft-spoken mathematician who had served as undersecretary of defense for research and engineering in the Carter administration. The best known of Perry's innovations was the Lockheed F-117A Nighthawk, the sixty-five-foot-long, black, batlike attack bomber configured with radar-dispersing facetings and coatings so effective that its radar reflection was comparable to a small bird's. Although Nighthawks flew thirteen hundred sorties during Desert Storm and delivered twenty-one hundred bombs, of which 81 percent struck within ten feet of their aim points, not one of the futuristic new planes was even damaged by antiaircraft fire, much less shot down.

Other innovations that Perry tallied in a postwar report included space satellite systems "used to generate data for maps, locate military units, identify military systems and pinpoint the location of the air defense and command-and-control installations of the Iraqi forces"; tactical reconnaissance supplied for the first time by AWACS (airborne warning and control system) aircraft using radar for all-weather air surveillance and air-traffic control and JSTARS (joint surveillance and target attack radar system) aircraft for detecting and locating ground vehicles such as tanks; night-vision systems; global-positioning systems (GPS); high-volume satellite communications systems; digital radios; and laser-guided missiles and bombs. "Operating together," Perry wrote, "these systems made a vital contribution to shortening the war, to dramatically reducing coalition casualties and to reducing Iraqi civilian casualties." Compared to Iraqi losses ("tanks destroyed, prisoners captured and, not least, casualties incurred") coalition losses "were so lopsided—roughly a thousand to one—that there is virtually no historical precedent."

Perry saw these transformations as a promising new kind of nonnuclear deterrence. "While it is certainly not as powerful as nuclear weapons," he argued, "it is a more credible deterrent, particularly in regional conflicts vital to U.S. national interests"— the only kind of conflict that the United States was likely to encounter in the post–Cold War world. "It can play a potentially significant role in deterring those regional conflicts that would involve the confrontation of armed forces (as opposed to guerrilla wars). . . . It should strengthen the already high level of deterrence of a major war in Europe or Korea." Former national security adviser McGeorge Bundy concurred with Perry's assessment in a lecture, commenting, "Our wisest defense experts have understood for a long time that the threat of initiating nuclear warfare has been declining in military value. . . . In the final analysis of strategy, politics and morals we are better off keeping [nuclear weapons] unused except in deterrence."

The nuclear threat was declining in value in part because injuring and killing large numbers of civilians, in an era of live television reportage from war zones, was fast becoming politically embarrassing to the leaders of democracies; the mass killing that nuclear weapons produced would generate horror on a world scale. Even as precision weapons shortened conventional wars and reduced civilian casualties, they raised expectations of limiting conflict to combatants and infrastructure. Limited war, by definition, was not nuclear war; it was war fought for limited objectives.

George H. W. Bush was proud that the U.S. had shown restraint, but as a World War II veteran he also missed the satisfaction of a clear victory. Limited war, he wrote in his diary on 28 February, means "no feeling of euphoria. I think I know why that is. After my speech last night [announcing the Iraqi surrender], Baghdad radio started broadcasting that we've been forced to capitulate. I see on the television that public opinion in Jordan and in the streets of Baghdad is that they have won. It is such a canard, so little, but it's what concerns me. It hasn't been a clean end—there is no battleship *Missouri* surrender. This is what's missing to make this akin to WWII, to separate Kuwait from Korea and Vietnam." Well, Bush consoled himself, "when the [Iraqi] troops straggle home with no armor, beaten up, 50,000 and maybe more dead, the people of Iraq will know. Their brothers and their sons will be missing, never to return. . . . Bob Gates told me this morning, one thing historic is, we stopped. We crushed their 43 divisions, but we stopped—we didn't just want to kill, and history will look on that kindly."

THREE TRUE COURAGE

IRAQ'S DEFEAT IN late February 1991 offered the world a unique opportunity to track down and eliminate the troublesome country's weapons of mass destruction. By its aggression against Kuwait, Thomas Pickering would say, Iraq "had forfeited any capacity on its part to resist or to non-comply with a very expansive program to root out and destroy . . . to provide permanent assurance to the international community that this particular proliferator . . . would no longer be a danger or threat to peace and security."

The obvious organization to carry out this program of inspection and destruction, at least as far as Iraq's nuclear infrastructure was concerned, was the International Atomic Energy Agency, an independent body responsible to the United Nations that had long experience with conducting nuclear inspections. The U.S. government, however, was sharply divided in its opinion of the IAEA's competency for such an assignment. One faction favored the IAEA to carry out inspections in Iraq; another favored appointing a special U.N. commission instead. "There were those who looked at the creation of a special commission as a threat to the IAEA," recalled Robert Gallucci, a State Department Middle East specialist who became involved in the dispute. "Those of this view had, I would say, a principal objective of preserving the role of the IAEA in the international community. In other words, the proliferation problem and the IAEA's role in it were bigger than the Iraqi problem, and we shouldn't go fix the Iraqi problem and destroy the Agency in the course of doing that." With the NPT extension conference coming up in less than five years, the IAEA needed a victory, the agency's Dimitri Perricos explains. "For the international community to just disregard the IAEA as an effective organization capable of doing the inspections in Iraq could have a serious effect on the way that the NPT and its indefinite extension might be considered over the next five-year period." Another faction, Gallucci noted, argued to the contrary "that the [IAEA] had failed in Iraq, and that it was structurally incapable of dealing with Iraq. I think that some of these critics also held a belief that the agency really wasn't up to doing what it was supposed to do more generally . . . and this led to some bloodletting within the U.S. government."

The solution Pickering and others found was to create a special commission directly responsible to the U.N. Security Council (rather than through the U.N. secretary-general and his sluggish bureaucracy), to assign responsibility for IAEA participation to the IAEA director general personally rather than to the agency as a whole, and, most significant in Gallucci's view, to give the executive chairman of the U.N. special commission "the responsibility to designate sites not declared for inspection by the Iraqis. This led to inevitable, intermittent tensions [with the IAEA]—that's possibly an understatement." Resolution 687 was hammered into shape during discussions with the British, the French, the Chinese, and the Russians. It authorized the creation of a United Nations special commission, UNSCOM, which would oversee the destruction of Iraq's chemical, biological, and nuclear weapons production complexes. At the insistence of Britain and France, the IAEA was assigned responsibility for "nuclear weapons or nuclear-weapons-usable material or any subsystems or components or any research, development, support or manufacturing facilities related to the above," with "the assistance and cooperation of the Special Commission." That formulation embedded the conflicts over the IAEA's mission and competence within the structure of the inspection process itself, whence they would emerge in the early weeks of inspections to complicate the organizations' work.

Gallucci had been called back to the State Department in March 1991 from teaching at the National War College to work on drafting Section C of Resolution 687, the section concerned with "the destruction, removal or rendering harmless" of Iraq's chemical, biological, and nuclear weapons (if any) and weapons-related facilities. At the War College, he told an audience later, he had been busy "twisting middle-aged minds . . . when Iraq invaded Kuwait and the coalition put together Desert Shield. I got to watch that from the War College. I even got to watch Desert Storm from the War College, which was a really good place to watch it from."

A trim, witty, combative forty-five-year-old in 1991, Gallucci had a long-standing interest in preventing nuclear proliferation. Brooklyn-born, Staten Island–raised, Hollywood-handsome, he had cut his teeth at State in the 1970s working on preventing Pakistan from acquiring a nuclear arsenal. It was one of many Sisyphean assignments he undertook in his years of government service, after which, as he liked to joke, he always got promoted. Working for the United Nations was hardly a promotion—"New York is such a little sideshow for Washington," the Swedish diplomat Hans Blix once told me—but Gallucci had nevertheless been brevetted to the U.S. mission immediately after the Iraq cease-fire to draft the necessary Security Council document.

Gallucci's father had immigrated to the United States from Italy. His mother's heritage was Italian as well, making him, he said, "sort of first or one-and-a-half-generation" American. As a high school student he had been strongly affected by the 1962 Cuban Missile Crisis. In his senior year of high school he read the U.S. diplomat Robert D. Murphy's lively 1964 memoir of Second World War experiences, *Diplomat Among Warriors*, "and I was," he recalled, "ever since then, fascinated by war . . . [by] a diplomat's view of war and a diplomat's role in war. I was very impressed with that, and I think that had a lot to do with the direction I ultimately headed in my life." Nuclear war—"the magnitude of the destruction and the need to do something about it"—was a focus of his concern during college, when he studied international relations, but he turned his attention in graduate school at the end of the 1960s to the Vietnam conflict, writing a Ph.D. dissertation about its bureaucratic politics.

Along the way, he lost faith in the abstractions of political science. He wanted to do policy, the real thing, and in 1974 he left teaching for the U.S. Arms Control and Disarmament Agency. In 1978 he moved over to the State Department, served in the field as deputy director general of the Sinai peacekeeping force from 1984 to 1988, then returned to Washington to his National War College post.

The Security Council approved Resolution 687 on 3 April 1991; Iraq acceded to it officially three days later. His duty done, Gallucci returned to Washington, assuming he could resume teaching, "but I was told I was mistaken. I was told that I was the perfect person to help make sure that the right people ended up in the right places, and that this special commission got off to a good start. So I was given three quick objectives. The first was to go up and establish [UNSCOM]." The second was to promote the appointment of a Swedish diplomat named Rolf Ekéus as executive chairman. "The third: I was to be the deputy executive chairman."

To find out what a special commission might do, Gallucci checked in with the State Department's international organization bureau, where he learned that "there are lots of commissions doing lots of different things, but there had never been a commission established that was supposed to go over to another country—a country that the United States had just defeated in a war, and where there might be some hostile feelings—and destroy their weapons of mass destruction."

Back in New York, Gallucci took a call from David Kay in

Vienna. A Ph.D. in international affairs from the University of Texas with years of experience in managing nuclear development, Kay was then Blix's bulldog at the IAEA for UNSCOM. "I had never met David before," Gallucci said later. "To my recollection, he was very agitated on the phone, and he wanted to get the inspections going right away. He argued that the IAEA was ready to begin inspections; it was in a big hurry to get out there. I told him that UNSCOM was not ready; we didn't have anything in place yet, in terms of capability or support. He did not want to hear any of that. The IAEA wanted to get going, because its reputation was on the line."

Kay's concern, he told me, was that "the U.S. military was anxious to get out of Iraq, there were these hanging accusations about WMD, and I thought if we didn't start inspections soon and we left Saddam in control we weren't going to find anything. You just have to start inspections while there's heat and support behind them. So when I called up Bob, I told him, 'We don't have a lot of time.' The U.N. system in particular is constitutionally very difficult to move fast." After they talked by phone, Kay flew to New York to meet Gallucci. "Bob told me, 'Well, what we've got to do is watch out for the U.N. process. It's the mushroom theory—keep them in the dark and feed them shit.' So we immediately formed a bond. We decided we were going to do this job the right way and get really intrusive inspections going—intrusive compared to the usual IAEA inspection regime, which was based on permission."

The IAEA, which grew out of U.S. President Dwight Eisenhower's "Atoms for Peace" speech at the U.N. in 1953, both supports the development of nuclear power and attempts to prevent nuclear proliferation. It had long conducted "safeguard" inspections to verify that nuclear materials such as enriched uranium were not being diverted from civilian applications to nuclear weapons. Safeguard inspections were required of signatories to the Nuclear Non-Proliferation Treaty. But since safeguard inspections involved only sites that a state formally declared, and inspectors gave advance notice of their intention to inspect, they depended for their credibility on the state's willingness to cooperate—like paying your taxes, Blix liked to say. That limitation was adequate when the materials and equipment involved had been provided under IAEA auspices, since the inventory was known at the outset and the only question was diversion. With a clandestine proliferator like Iraq, the system broke down. As Jay Davis, a physicist at the Lawrence Livermore National Laboratory who served as a technical adviser to UNSCOM, testified at a Congressional hearing in 1993:

> Many of the IAEA staff, and some of its leadership, were burdened by the perceived need to protect the Agency's role, to defend its past performance in Iraq, and to protect themselves from criticism (and possible career damage) within the Agency. Institutionalizing leadership for the [Iraq] nuclear inspections in the Agency made it difficult to remove timid leaders and resulted in an opening between UNSCOM and the IAEA that made possible both information loss and Iraqi political intrigue. The IAEA has been accused of being both politicized and of suffering from clientitis. From my perspective, both these accusations are justified. The IAEA shows little appetite for intrusive inspection or aggressive behavior, both of which are essential to this inspection regime.

The inspections that Kay and Gallucci wanted to demand of Iraq fell well outside IAEA custom, though they were well within UNSCOM's mandate. "We had a different view," Gallucci explains. "We were dentists here, and we were about to go pull some teeth."

There could be no inspections of any kind until UNSCOM was up and running. "The first thing we needed was inspectors," Gallucci said. "For inspectors, I need experts. So I called the State Department and they told me that I had better plug into the Defense Department. So they gave me the numbers in DoD.

I was in the politico-military bureau [of the State Department], so of course I was very comfortable talking to the Department of Defense. I had a very comfortable conversation in which my interlocutor told me, in sum: 'We've had a discussion about supporting the Special Commission. It is the DoD's view that we, on behalf of the United States, led the coalition in the war. You, on behalf of the State Department and the UN, can lead on behalf of the peace. Have a nice day.' "

Gallucci had a similar experience when he approached the U.S. intelligence community. "Not only did they not show up," he says, "but they were aggressive about not showing up." Cooperation came later when UNSCOM began producing results; at the outset, "a lot of people walked into the room intent on telling me how much they were not going to tell me. I still had my clearances, but as soon as you start working on assignment to the U.N. you are persona non grata. You are not going to get anything. It was a very cold reception." Resourcefully, Gallucci turned to other governments—"permanent members of the Security Council principally, and then others"—to loan him experts in each of the weapons areas that UNSCOM needed to inspect: chemical, biological, missile, and nuclear. Nuclear inspection was the expertise which the United States contributed most extensively, "because we had our national laboratories to support us." No one wanted to do explosive-ordnance disposal (EOD), a vital but dangerous task in a recent war zone. Gallucci resorted to searching out EOD contractors in the *Yellow Pages*. "There were two groups along the Beltway. I hired them, and then I had to buy them insurance."

David Kay thought the U.S. bureaucracy's initial resistance to supporting UNSCOM was defensive. "We had no secure telephones, for example, none of any type in Vienna or New York. We had no safes that met government standards for security. We had to go out and buy all these things commercially. The government could have bought them. It was really a standoff. The U.S. military wanted to declare victory and get out of Dodge. They remembered Vietnam and they didn't want to hang around to see what happened afterward—they were smarter this time." The State Department was similarly conflicted, Kay said. Ambassador-at-large Richard T. Kennedy, a nonproliferation specialist and the U.S. representative to the IAEA, "was very, very ambivalent about the inspection process. He took me aside and said, 'Look, this is a poisoned chalice. You're not going to get the support you think you're going to get. It's going to be harder and they're going to blame the IAEA'—'they' being the U.S. government. Why? Because the Iraqi program originated in part in deals with the French involving commercial nuclear power. Kennedy was closer to the truth than a lot of people have recognized. This was going to be a difficult experience for the IAEA, who would have to explain, if anything was found, how it got there, and for the government, because the government would have to cover its ass."

Blix recalls "no frictions with the U.S., nor with the CIA," but the CIA refused at first to share any information with UNSCOM. "Some other intelligence services did, but the U.S. would not, and I respected that. They probably said to themselves, 'Why should we? Intelligence is always sensitive; why should we give them anything at all unless we see that they really do some work?' " (Later, Blix told me, after the inspections began to show results, "then they came and they wanted to tell us how we should do our work. Mohamed ElBaradei"—the IAEA's legal adviser at the time; later Blix's successor—"said that they shouldn't try to teach us how to suck eggs.")

Some recruiting difficulties were personal, Jere Nichols, the Oak Ridge chemical engineer, recalled. "We were all scared. I was, for example, the fourth choice to be the EMIS person, and I didn't know a whole lot about EMIS [electromagnetic isotope separation]. Two of the three people who did know were older guys. The third said he was basically a coward and didn't want to do it. Some of the rigors we were told about, which frightened some of us, were: temperatures of 50 degrees Celsius [122° F.] or more; the humidity; the possibility of poison gas remnants from the war; the possibility of unexploded bombs; snakes and scorpions; bacteria in the food and water; spies who searched and placed electronic bugs in our hotel rooms."

"I had to go out and lease a plane to get to Baghdad," said David Kay. "Romanian Airlines. They had a Romanian knockoff of the British Aircraft Corporation 111. I'd actually flown a lot on the BAC-111 and I hated it. You never knew if the thing was going to get off the ground. When we took the aircraft, the first thing the Romanian pilot showed us—proudly—was a plaque that said it was the first BAC-111 produced in Romania. It was slow, one of the restrooms was taped shut—it was awful." The equipment the inspectors pulled together commercially, Kay said, came from "the West Coast version of Crazy Eddie. Two inspectors from Lawrence Livermore National Laboratory in California cleaned out the place so we'd have cameras and communications gear. I took the first digital camera into Iraq. It was a Kodak camera and it cost eleven thousand dollars. Two megapixels or some such. So much of what we did had never been done before. We made up the rules as we went along."

"The first few trips required true courage," Gallucci remembered. "For mobility, once we got there, the Iraqis provided these unair-conditioned buses and I rented us a couple of cars from Avis. For medical support—this was a dangerous mission—we had first-aid kits. For secure communications, we used a book cipher—two copies of the same book, with the code designating the location of the word. It takes about three days to decode 'Hi, Mom,' but you can do it. It was very crude." On the first mission Kay led into Baghdad, he said, "the city was still struggling with the aftermath of the war. There was one functioning traffic light in the entire city. We had no U.S. military support, and, in fact, the U.S. government had refused to give us almost anything. The vehicles we initially used were diesel-fueled British Land Rovers, and we had a real problem getting fuel."

Once they began work, conditions improved. They staged out of an American air base in the micro-kingdom of Bahrain, a small island in the Persian Gulf connected by a causeway to Saudi Arabia. "The inspectors came from all over the world," Gallucci recalled. "Our lift was eventually provided by German C-160s [turboprop military transport aircraft] and our mobility by CH-53s [U.S. marine medium-lift twin-engine helicopters] and Norwegian-supplied SUVs. We had good medical support from New Zealand. The intelligence picture really picked up quickly. The U.S. intelligence community cottoned on to the fact that we were actually walking around Iraq. Someone, someplace in the CIA, figured this out, and all of a sudden we were nearly besieged with intelligence. We built up our staff at headquarters. Within a month or so, headquarters was doing what it was supposed to do. We recruited the specialized teams, did mission planning, conducted briefings, evaluated mission results, created an archive—the offices in Bahrain and Baghdad functioned pretty well."

If logistic conditions improved, there was still serious conflict between the IAEA leadership and UNSCOM. Blix felt that UNSCOM meant to treat the agency "as a dog on a leash"—letting it sniff out the contraband but allowing it no further authority. "An even more serious matter," he wrote later, "was the difference in inspection style between the organizations: to UNSCOM the IAEA inspectors seemed too much like proper civil servants; to the IAEA, some of the UNSCOM inspectors seemed to act Rambo-style." Blix claimed that the friction made the work unpleasant without reducing its effectiveness. Kay and Gallucci disagree; they think their effectiveness was compromised as well until Blix saw the light.

By accepting Security Council Resolution 687, Iraq had agreed to disclose fully its WMD programs and stockpiles within fifteen days—that is, by mid-April 1991. In secret high-level meetings in Iraq following its capitulation, senior managers of the Iraqi programs for missile, chemical, biological, and nuclear weapons had assembled complete inventories of their programs and materials along with options for how to respond. The documents went to Hussein Kamel, who decided in consultations with Saddam

Hussein to declare part of Iraq's chemical-weapons and missile programs but to conceal its biological- and nuclear-weapons programs. Foreign Minister Tariq Aziz, among others, speculated later that the biological and nuclear programs were concealed in the hope that Iraq could develop a deterrent against the United States, Iran, and Israel, its three most dangerous enemies.

"This first declaration was rejected by the IAEA because it didn't contain anything," Blix's deputy Dimitri Perricos said. "There was a full denial that anything existed, in terms of any important nuclear material, in Iraq." Iraq submitted a second declaration on 27 April that "had a little bit more content, which at least gave the agency a starting point. Iraq admitted that it did have highly-enriched uranium, which everyone already knew about because it was part of the HEU fuel used in the Tammuz reactor"—a small Russian-supplied reactor. "Iraq also admitted that it had buildings and facilities at Tuwaitha other than those that had been visited by safeguards inspectors."

Perricos, a Greek chemist, was the chief inspector for the initial inspection, which went from 15 through 21 May 1991. "The first inspection had a very defined objective," he said later: "to get custody of all the nuclear material in Iraq—find out where the material was located and take control of it so that there would be no danger that the material would disappear." David Kay handled logistics and delivered the initial briefing but did not accompany the crowd of thirty-four inspectors of twenty different nationalities when it left Bahrain for Baghdad.

Southeast of Baghdad at Tuwaitha the team was startled by the complex's scale, Perricos recalled. "To our surprise, Tuwaitha was a very, very large center. It was not just the three or four buildings that safeguards inspectors had visited before the war—the two reactors, a small storage facility, and a small laboratory-scale fabrication plant. We found that there was a whole new area of Tuwaitha where safeguards inspectors had never been before. This area was only known to those people who had access to aerial surveillance. It was in this area, called the new R & D area, where Iraq did most of its clandestine development work." The extensive complex was now largely ruined, Perricos saw:

> Tuwaitha was very badly damaged by the Gulf War bombardment. The bombing had done its work, but it also caused some difficulties for us, because it gave the Iraqis an excuse to hide a lot of things and tell us that they had been lost during the bombing, hidden by the rubble, or burned. . . . Some chores were more difficult then others. You had to go through the rubble to try to find out what was there. Inspectors spent a lot of time digging, really digging, into rubble in order to be able to find material or equipment that we were told had been lost in the bombing.

Searching could be dangerous. "Inspectors had to walk carefully among the ruins, because there were still unexploded ordnance. We had explosive ordnance disposal experts who were going ahead, and you had to follow in their steps to avoid getting into danger."

The two Tuwaitha reactors—the French reactor the Israelis had bombed in 1981 and the smaller Russian one—were heavily damaged, the team reported, to such an extent that "they would be difficult to restore"; in any case, Perricos said, their significant component was their HEU fuel:

> The surprise that we had was that the nuclear material was not where it was supposed to be. We spent some time in the beginning—the first days—persuading the Iraqis to tell us where the fresh HEU was located. We found out that the HEU had been removed for storage in the physical protection control bunker at the entrance of Tuwaitha. . . . Then we looked for the spent [reactor] fuel. We were not able to find any spent fuel, except for that spent fuel that was buried in the rubble at the site. We finally were told by the Iraqis that they had taken all the spent fuel—one [fuel assembly] by one, over a long operation, they said, during the bombardment period—and put all of it in an

agricultural farm somewhere closer to Baghdad. In a deserted area, they had dug some holes and they put the fuel assemblies in barrels with water and kept them in there.

The team confiscated any nuclear materials it located. "We had not only to measure the fuel," Perricos recalled, "we also had to take it under control and eventually, during subsequent inspections, we had to be able to take it and store it in areas where it could later be shipped out of the country." Besides the reactor fuel, they found large quantities of uranium ore stored near Tuwaitha. "There were hundreds of barrels of yellowcake. Some of this was material that had been imported before the Gulf War. At this particular location . . . we started to collect all the natural uranium and low-enriched uranium from other locations in Iraq." A later report gives the volume of nuclear materials confiscated in the Tuwaitha area during the first inspection:* 31 kilograms of fresh 72-percent-enriched uranium; 17 kilograms of irradiated 52-percent-enriched uranium; kilogram quantities of uranium enriched to less than 30 percent; an estimated 327 kilograms of natural or depleted uranium buried under the rubble by the bombings; and 204 tons of yellowcake.

Most of the damage at Tuwaitha had obviously been caused by bombing, the inspectors reported, "but in some significant cases by extensive clearing operations carried out by Iraqi authorities during and after the conflict. In almost all cases documentation and records had disappeared and were not available. . . . It is clear that much of the equipment which once existed at Al-Tuwaitha has been removed to other locations, most of which were not disclosed" to the IAEA inspectors. Despite this plain indication of deceit, the report nevertheless concluded, "The overall

*Uranium enriched to above 80 percent U235 is considered bomb-grade; uranium enriched to above 90 percent U235 is considered highly enriched (HEU). All of the Tuwaitha materials would therefore require further enrichment to be used in nuclear weapons.

impression is of a site where most significant buildings have been thoroughly destroyed or cleared and, with only a few exceptions noted below, provide only limited concern for future verification unless substantial rebuilding takes place."

When the action team returned to Bahrain, Kay told me, disagreement flared between Blix, Dimitri Perricos, and some of the team members. "Dimitri talked to the director general"—i.e., Blix—"and the director general was prepared to have a report that said, 'There's nothing there. We've looked, there's nothing there.' Because that was the belief. I mean, Blix, during the run-up to the war, had told me that there was nothing there and he was confident that the inspection process had worked." Two American inspectors on the team disagreed. "They said that if the report took that position, they would have to issue a dissenting report, and that would have been a serious embarrassment. So the report just said, 'We have looked at what the Iraqis gave us and here is what we found.' "

Fortunately for the investigation, the U.S. intelligence community was watching Iraq from space and the air. While Perricos and his team were digging for contraband at Tuwaitha, Kay recalls, "a photo analyst noticed that the Iraqis were clearing stuff out and burying it across the road. He thought they were clearing up the site, so he didn't tell the team or his superiors. Then, the day the action team left, there happened to be a [high-altitude photo-reconnaissance] U-2 pass over the site and the same photo analyst got the pictures, which is remarkable. He noticed they were unburying things and putting them on trucks and moving them."

The analyst had seen similar objects before; again by happenstance, he had reviewed the first poststrike photos from Tarmiya, the mystery site northwest of Baghdad, after it had been bombed during the war, and remembered the "big circular objects" the photos had revealed. Since the end of the war, the intelligence community had observed the objects—massive, discus-shaped metal plates, about fifteen feet in diameter—being moved and buried. They had nicknamed them Frisbees after the plastic disks used in throwing games. "At that point he called someone," Kay says, "and told them, 'That's the same shape I saw at Tarmiya.' This was the initial lightbulb going off. Some people said, 'Might be related to uranium enrichment,' and others said, 'No, the only things that fit that shape are the electromagnets for a calutron process.' Unfortunately, there were damn few people left around who even thought about calutrons."

The calutron ("California University cyclotron"), so named by its developers at the University of California at Berkeley, is a machine for separating isotopes. It was invented at Berkeley early in the Second World War to separate isotopes of uranium for the Manhattan Project. It does so by generating and injecting a beam of electrically charged uranium tetrachloride gas into a vacuum tank that is set between the poles of a powerful electromagnet. Lighter atoms of U235 are displaced more than heavier atoms of U238 and follow a tighter curve around the magnetic field, so that when they arrive at the bucket-like collectors at the other end of the tank, more U235 atoms will be captured in one collector than in the other. By repeating the process with the enriched portion of the product, any level of enrichment is possible up to pure U235. In the Manhattan Project operation, two stages of calutrons produced almost all the highly enriched uranium used in Little Boy, the 13.5-kiloton uranium gun bomb that was detonated over Hiroshima, Japan, on 6 August 1945.

One American inspector at Tuwaitha was an expert on uranium-enrichment technology. When he and the action team moved on from Tuwaitha north past Baghdad to the even larger site at Tarmiya, they expected to discover a full-scale centrifuge plant for enriching uranium. "The team found that, on the whole, the area was in ruins," Perricos recalled. "In the beginning, they couldn't make anything out of it; they could not really understand what was happening. They were told that the facility was not important . . . but the inspectors were extremely skeptical. There was all sorts of new construction and there were walls in the large hall that did not make sense. But one thing was very clear: the facility did not have the profile of a centrifuge enrichment facility."

The American expert "didn't find what he was looking for," Jere Nichols added, "but he did take some very good notes. He sketched the buildings, many of which had been significantly destroyed by bombing and Iraqi demolition, and made notes about the electricity requirements at each." The team's formal report described the Tarmiya buildings as "unusual . . . with unusually large installed electrical power co-allocated with buildings with large chemical processing capabilities. . . . Building 33 was stated by the Iraqis to be used for transformer fabrication. . . . This is simply not credible. . . . The building had two ten-ton bridge cranes and two twenty-five-ton bridge cranes, an enormous installed electrical supply (over 100 megawatts) and a supply of purified and chilled water." Once again, however, the expert was puzzled by the team's findings.

Perricos said his inspectors "took hundreds of pictures of Tarmiya, and they were collected in Vienna and shown to experts." One of those experts was a sixty-nine-year-old veteran of the Manhattan Project, John Googin, a down-easter who had taken a chemistry degree at Bates College in his hometown of Lewiston, Maine, in 1944, and plunged immediately into working on electromagnetic isotope separation at the U.S. Army Corps of Engineers' Y-12 EMIS plant in Oak Ridge, Tennessee. "John's first assignment," wrote his eulogist, "was the daunting task of recovering and recycling the large fraction of precious uranium-235 that was deposited everywhere except in the product stream"—EMIS is a notoriously wasteful technology, which is why in 1991 it had long been obsolete and nearly forgotten. After the war, when the United States shut down its EMIS plants and moved on to more efficient gaseous diffusion and centrifuge enrichment technologies, Googin earned a Ph.D. in physical chemistry while continuing to work at Oak Ridge in the production of nuclear materials. He knew enrichment technologies from the ground up. "I can still see him in Vienna sorting out the pictures," Perricos said. When Googin finished his analysis, he announced that the process the Iraqis were developing at Tarmiya was electromagnetic isotope separation.

But even Googin's expert conclusion was not yet enough to overcome the UNSCOM leadership's incredulity that any nation would appropriate a fifty-year-old technology when far more efficient methods of uranium enrichment were available— missing the point that EMIS was a better fit to a marginal industrial structure than more sophisticated (and correspondingly more difficult to construct and operate) technologies might be, and that buying its more commonplace components abroad was less likely to trigger export controls.

David Kay remembered the day he realized that most of the IAEA inspectors had never heard of a calutron. Kay said that one of the IAEA team leaders, Mauricio Zifferero, an Italian, "may have had a dim memory of it, but no one else at the IAEA knew what calutrons were." Kay had carried a copy of my 1987 book *The Making of the Atomic Bomb* with him into Bahrain. It discusses EMIS technology at length and includes a schematic drawing of a calutron. He showed it to Zifferero and his IAEA colleagues. "I said, 'Well, look, I'll explain—here it is, it's in the book.' Because they were extraordinarily skeptical," Kay said. That was my small contribution to Iraq's disarming.

By the beginning of June 1991 the inspectors had returned to the United States, where one of them learned that an Iraqi defector had identified EMIS as the technology Iraq was developing to enrich uranium. "We analyzed all the available information for about two weeks," Jere Nichols recalled, "and prepared a document concluding that Tarmiya, and Ash Sharqat"—another site far up in Iraq's northern desert—"by extension, were large-scale EMIS production plants."

Nichols and his colleagues presented their EMIS findings to Ekéus, Gallucci, and other UNSCOM leaders on 12 June. "One of the intelligence people was a lawyer," Nichols remembered;

"he presented all of the information in the form of a case that he concluded would convict Iraq in an international court. The other two intelligence people presented incriminating overhead photography and a summary of information derived from the defector. I presented information derived from building layouts and electric power [supplies] and estimates of the uranium-235 production capacity of the plants at Tarmiya and Ash Sharqat." Googin made a similar presentation to the IAEA in Vienna on the same day.

Three days later, Bob Gallucci and Mauricio Zifferero led a team of UNSCOM and IAEA inspectors back into Iraq to begin a second round of inspections, armed this time with strong evidence that Saddam Hussein's government was covertly enriching uranium in violation of its commitments under the Nuclear Non-Proliferation Treaty. Still unanswered was a graver question: Were the Iraqis also working on an atomic bomb?

FOUR FOLLOWING
THE CALUTRON TRAIL

THE OVERHEAD IMAGERY that the Gallucci-Zifferero team had seen had placed the EMIS Frisbees—the massive magnet iron calutron disks, fifteen feet in diameter and each weighing some sixty tons—at a large military base twenty miles west of Baghdad, out past war-damaged Saddam International Airport at Abu Ghraib. "We got on our bus and rode out there on June 23," Jere Nichols said, "but the Iraqis had blocked the road in that particular area and they just wouldn't let us in. They said that they didn't have permission to do that." The inspectors were reduced to photographing boxed material through a fence. They spent the next day "running around Tuwaitha," Nichols said, "trying to get permission to go back."

The time at Tuwaitha wasn't wasted. American intelligence had passed along a tip, Bob Gallucci recalled, "that it might be a good idea to go to a particular site, the 'grove site,'" not far from there:

> We had, as it turned out, nothing much to do at Tuwaitha. We knew the facility; the IAEA people knew Tuwaitha particularly well. So I said I wanted to go to this nearby site, and so we went. I was looking for a particular building, and I had made a sketch of where I thought the building was. And they told me, very hesitantly, that I did not want to go there, because that building

was an automobile maintenance facility, and it is now an empty automobile maintenance facility. So I said: "That sounds really interesting, and I would love to see what that looks like, because I've not seen one of those in Iraq."

So we went down there, and it was, indeed, a big, empty, open garage-like area. But there were very large overhead cranes at the facility, and that was strange. They were large enough, as one of my colleagues said, to take a two-and-a-half-ton dump truck and turn it upside down to drain the oil out. So it didn't look like an automobile maintenance facility. On one side of the crane, I saw some Arabic writing, and I was going to get one of our interpreters. But I walked around to the other side and I didn't need the interpreter, because stenciled there in English was "Atomic Energy Commission of Iraq." . . . This turned out to be a magnet test-stand facility for the EMIS program.

What the action team had found was equipment for winding and testing large electromagnets, for which the soft iron Frisbee disks would serve as cores. "I had brought a magnetometer," Nichols recalled, "and used it to measure magnetic fields in the building. The magnetometer went off scale, indicating a very high magnetic field in many places including the bridge crane above the suspected winding machine. My watch stopped in this building and didn't run again until we returned home and I sent it to the manufacturer."

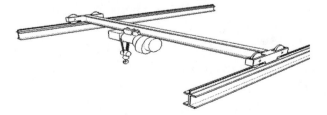

BRIDGE CRANE

An electric current generates a magnetic field around the wire that carries it. If the wire is wrapped around a core of magnetizable metal such as iron, cobalt, or nickel, it induces a magnetic field in turn in the core. Soft iron—pure iron without alloy—doesn't retain its magnetism when the electric current is shut off, but many metals do. The intense magnetic field generated in testing the calutron electromagnets had induced permanent magnetism in the steel crane; the magnetized crane, in turn, had magnetized Nichols's stainless-steel watch. But where were the Frisbees?

David Kay had joined the team by then. When the Iraqis had denied entry to Abu Ghraib, Maurizio Zifferero had gone to New York to inform the U.N. Security Council; Kay had replaced him as acting chief inspector. Kay's action team finally received permission to visit the storage area on Wednesday, 26 June 1991. It was predictably empty, Nichols recalled, "just a dusty area with a few pieces of loading machinery around, and poor, tired Iraqi soldiers sleeping out on cots in the heat. Over those two days, those poor men had moved all of that metal somewhere else."

Accumulating satellite images and U-2 photographs, the intelligence agencies supporting UNSCOM decided that they had a hard fix on where the Frisbees might be—at a place called Fallujah, out beyond Abu Ghraib. The problem for Kay was how to get there when Blix expected them to give the Iraqis advance notice and the Iraqis were blocking them from sensitive sites. A meeting was scheduled with an Iraqi minister for Thursday night to give notice of where the team next intended to inspect. "We quite literally wrote the script for Fallujah while walking through Baghdad back alleys after midnight," Jay Davis would tell a Congressional committee. "Decidedly not the IAEA style." Kay told me he "took a walk beforehand with a couple of the inspectors and hashed it out. I said, 'Look, in my experience working abroad, the hardest thing to acquire in another language is prepositions. So what I'm going to tell the Iraqis tonight is that we're going *to* Abu Ghraib. Odds are, they'll assume we want to see Abu Ghraib, and since we've inspected it before, they'll be happy to let us go there.' So sure enough, I met with the Iraqi minister that night and said, 'Tomorrow morning we will be conducting an inspection *to* Abu Ghraib.' Fine, no problem."

In the heat of Friday morning the eighteen-member action team and its minders set out together for the base, the Iraqis leading the way, Kay behind them in a Land Rover "with the steering wheel on the wrong side and a crapped-out fuel gauge," his inspectors following in a bus. "My communications officer and driver was a Kiwi—a New Zealander—absolutely first-rate guy. I told him, we'll follow them to the checkpoint, but as soon as we get through the checkpoint I want you to cut in front of the Iraqis and floorboard it. We've only got about five miles from there to get to where we're really going." At the checkpoint, as ordered, the driver raced ahead. "The Iraqis were a little bit slow to react. They started honking horns and giving chase and we just kept going. We followed directions and got to the place, but the photo interpreters had identified it as being on the right side of the road. Funny business, how they do things. They'd studied the photos upside down and they'd forgotten to make the translation when they wrote their directions. Stuff started appearing on the wrong side of the road. We went about a quarter mile too far before I figured out the problem. It was a divided highway, so I said, 'Do a wheelie across.' " The driver bounced across the median, skidded around, and headed back for the gate. The Iraqis and the bus had to go on to the next interchange to reverse direction because they couldn't navigate the median.

Kay and his driver beat the crowd by ten minutes. They were about to attempt the first zero-notice inspection in IAEA history. "As soon as we hopped out," he told me, "I walked up to the Iraqi guard—this was a little dinky base for training truck drivers—and demanded access. The base commander turned up then, a colonel, and I got on my best high horse: 'On behalf of the United Nations Security Council,' the pope, and anyone else I could think of, 'I have a resolution, we demand access.' It was standard procedure as soon as we got anyplace for my driver to set up the telephone satellite dish even if we didn't need it. It was a big antenna back then, a big fanned-open suitcase. Imposing. You could act as if you had capability even if you didn't. I told the Iraqi colonel I was going to call New York, call the Security Council. He said, 'I can't give you access to this base without permission from Baghdad. There's nothing on this base.' I said, 'That's for me to determine.' Then he made a fatal mistake— literally, because subsequently Saddam had him executed for it. He said, 'I can't give you access to this base, but you can put people up there'—he pointed to a water tower inside the fence line— 'and you can inspect from there until we sort this business out.' " By then the bus had arrived with its crowd of inspectors; Kay realized he'd be able to search and film from the water tower and jumped at the chance. "I said immediately, 'That's what we need. Let's get on top of that and look.' So three guys went up there with cameras."

What they photographed was astonishing. "It literally looked like dinosaurs in heat," Kay said, laughing. Sixty-foot tank transporters—big forward-cab military trucks with flatbed trailers for hauling tanks—fifty or more in a long line, were starting up and roaring out the base's back exit loaded with big iron Frisbees and tarp-covered crates. "I immediately had a couple of guys take a Land Rover and go around the base and try to get more film. They chased the trucks down the road, snapping away." The truck guards started firing into the air to scare them off. When they turned back and rejoined the others at the base, they had hundreds of frames of evidence that the Iraqis had been building calutrons to enrich uranium. Kay reported immediately to the U.N., and in New York that evening the president of the Security Council deplored Iraq's denial of access to the site and requested that the secretary-general send a high-level mission to Baghdad. "The David Kay cowboys really cut loose," Gallucci said later. "They were following the calutron trail. That put the inspection team on the map. . . . It caught the Iraqis in a huge lie, which was very useful for public support, and which made it clear to everybody that this was a game of hiding and finding."

The delegation the U.N. sent out consisted of Hans Blix, Rolf Ekéus, Mohamed ElBaradei, and the U.N. under secretary-general for disarmament affairs, Yasushi Akashi, with Ekéus in charge. (To finesse any conflicts with Blix, Ekéus asked for and got written confirmation of his authority from U.N. secretary-general Javier Pérez de Cuéllar—the two Swedes, from different Swedish political parties, often disagreed.) They departed New York immediately and arrived in Baghdad around noon on 30 June. During the next three days they met with Iraqi officials up to and including Hussein Kamel and Tariq Aziz, debates that generated more heat than light. Blix eventually conducted a long inspection at Fallujah, but the site had been scrubbed. Worse, wrote an Ekéus senior adviser, "Rolf Ekéus felt that both Hans Blix and Mohamed ElBaradei had been too quick and too willing to accept Iraqi protestations that there had never been a nuclear weapons program and that the inspectors under David Kay must have been mistaken if they thought they had seen calutron components on the trucks leaving Fallujah."

The special delegation left Iraq on 3 July 1991—David Kay and his inspectors left then as well—and reported to the Security Council the next day. In the meantime, in the wake of the warning shots at Fallujah, George H. W. Bush had implicitly threatened military action against Iraq if it continued to resist cooperating with the inspections. "We can't allow this brutal bully to go back on this solemn agreement and to threaten people that are there under U.N. jurisdiction," Bush told the media. He put eighteen ships of the U.S. Central Command on alert in the Persian Gulf. Its two carriers supported 155 aircraft; seven other ships in the fleet loaded Tomahawk cruise missiles.

The message got through. Abruptly, just as the third IAEA inspection group under Dimitri Perricos was heading to Baghdad on 6 July 1991, Saddam Hussein authorized full disclosure of the Iraqi uranium-enrichment program. In early May the Iraqi dictator had formed a Concealment Operations Committee headed by his son Qusay. It was Qusay's Special Republican Guard which had been playing hide-and-seek with the U.N. teams, moving equipment around, burying it in the desert, scrubbing former production sites. Recognizing now that U.S. satellite collections made further concealment impossible, wrote the senior inspector Scott Ritter, Saddam directed "all concealment task forces . . . to initiate emergency procedures for the identification of critical components and material that would continue to be hidden. . . . The unilateral destruction of the remaining material was also decided." As a result of this decision, Iraq would destroy most of its WMD program materials and production equipment across the summer of 1991, without recording what it destroyed. The absence of such evidence, which made it impossible to prove that the destruction had taken place, would fatally compromise Iraq's future security.

"The inspectors arrived in Baghdad," Perricos recalled, "and on the next morning"—7 July 1991—"they were delivered a big list of items that Iraq now wanted to declare. There was a long list of facilities, but—more important than anything else—there were the names of the places where the inspectors could find all these calutrons from the EMIS program. We went to one of these locations, and the first thing that we requested was 'roll the trucks in.' And the trucks arrived, and the inspectors were happy."

Perricos's action team spent the next week and a half working to verify the Iraqi government's declarations. The EMIS program was the furthest along of Iraq's nuclear research-and-development efforts, but as with the U.S. Manhattan Project, it had not been the only line of attack. "At one time or another," the IAEA team reported to the Security Council, "gaseous diffusion, electromagnetic isotope separation (EMIS), gas centrifuge and chemical exchange technologies were examined by Iraq. The commitment to EMIS for production-scale development and deployment followed early successes with the method and, most importantly, the demonstration that the separator units and magnets could be made in Iraq."

Another reason the Iraqis chose EMIS as their primary technology for enriching uranium was revealed to Perricos's team at a seminar with the Iraqi technical staff, Perricos said, "where the inspectors asked questions about the enrichment program. [At one point] the Iraqis in the front of the room could not provide any answers. Finally, from the back of the room, a voice says, 'Well, I will explain that.' That was the first time we saw Dr. Jaffar." Jaffar Dhia Jaffar, handsome even behind his de rigueur Saddam mustache, was a British-educated high-energy physicist who turned out to be the head of the Iraqi program. His grandfather had been a comrade-in-arms of T. E. Lawrence, his father an adviser to King Faisal II until the king's assassination in 1958, but the Jaffars were Shiite, and rather than remain in Iraq under its radical new Sunni leadership, Jaffar's father had chosen comfortable exile with his family in England. Jaffar graduated from the University of Birmingham in 1968 and then trained at Manchester. He worked for a time at Harwell, the British Los Alamos, though not on nuclear weapons. In 1975, when he was thirty-three, he was passed over for a professorship at Imperial College, London, where he had taught since 1969, and decided to return to Iraq. There, then–vice president Saddam Hussein recruited him for the Iraqi nuclear program. By 1979 he was vice chairman of the Iraq Atomic Energy Commission.

Jaffar has maintained, and most official accounts report, that the Iraqi atomic-bomb program only turned to an enriched-uranium approach to bomb development after the Israelis destroyed the Osirak reactor in 1981. There is evidence, however, that Jaffar was researching electromagnetic-isotope separation before he returned to Iraq, and even stronger evidence that he was doing so on his country's behalf by 1979.

For a brief time in the late 1960s, Jaffar worked at the Iraqi Nuclear Research Center in Baghdad. He published twelve scientific papers between 1967 and 1976, a productive period in his life. Some of the papers were researched at Birmingham, others at CERN, the European Organization for Nuclear Research, located on the Franco-Swiss border near Geneva, where he worked in the early 1970s. When Jaffar returned to Iraq in 1975, one of his colleagues reported, he took with him the entire CERN library of computerized magnet-design programs. Several were standard American programs that CERN had used to design its own magnets.

In 1979 Jaffar sent one of his engineers to CERN to learn about a large magnet that was nearing completion for use in a high-resolution spectrometer the organization was building. The CERN magnet, like the disk-shaped magnets built later for the Iraqi calutron program, had hexagonal symmetry, although it differed from the Iraqi magnets in being toroidal—doughnut-shaped, with a large hole in the middle to allow a particle beam to pass through. A Swiss physicist, André Gsponer, who was working on the CERN experiment at the time, learned from a colleague about the Iraqi engineer's visit and realized later, when the Iraqi calutrons were discovered by the IAEA inspection teams, that Jaffar had drawn on the CERN technology in designing his calutron magnets. The Iraqi physicist ultimately settled for an alternative design with a solid iron core, but it retained some of the superior features of the CERN design. The Stanford University theoretical physicist Sidney Drell was one of the several dozen scientists who participated in the development of the big mass spectrometer at CERN. "If that was the model for the Iraqi calutron magnets," he told me, "that was way beyond the Manhattan Project calutrons." Based on the technical questions the Iraqi engineer asked, Gsponer concluded that "it was quite possible that Iraq, at the time, was already comparing the engineering problems of various options for the construction of an industrial-scale EMIS plant."

Jaffar later revealed the strategic thinking behind Saddam Hussein's summer 1991 decision to destroy most of his WMD infrastructure. "There was no sense in developing a nuclear-weapons program against the United States," the Iraqi scientist told the BBC in 2004. "That was why the program was stopped in July

1991, hoping that the sanctions would be lifted soon. Because it was far more important to lift sanctions than to continue with these programs. The strategic aim of these programs became more or less useless when the United States and Great Britain became involved." Saddam had pursued nuclear and other terror weapons since the early 1970s for a deterrent against Iran and Israel and to further his goal of becoming the unchallenged leader of the Arab Middle East. Giving up his nuclear and other WMD programs acknowledged the reality of U.S. and British military and nuclear dominance.

What Saddam was not prepared to admit even then, Perricos noted later, was the nuclear program's real purpose: to make nuclear weapons:

> Jaffar tried to explain—in his own way—what the EMIS program was all about. As he said, the program, of course, was a peaceful program; it had nothing to do with any intention to weaponize. Iraq had to supply the fuel for its own power reactor and research reactor projects. But in a subsequent visit to Tarmiya, they gave us a video that for the first time enabled us to assess the magnitude of the project that was being built in the large halls at Tarmiya.
>
> The video showed the big magnets as they had been set up in place. You could see the various pumps and vacuum systems. There were supposed to be a large number of them; they followed exactly the classical recipe learned from the Manhattan Project. They used a large number of calutrons in the beginning of the process to enrich the feed material to a low level with high efficiency. Then they had set up the second part in another building where there were a smaller number of calutrons to enrich this low-enriched material to 93 percent uranium 235.

"Near the end of our stay in Iraq on that inspection," Jere Nichols said, "our minders took us in a bus to a desert site called Resala. Here for our benefit the Iraqis dug up four EMIS magnet pieces—a coil and three pole pieces—that had outside diameters of about four meters. These, most likely, were among those spirited away from Fallujah by truck on June 28." It was brutally hot at the desert site, Perricos remembered. "The place that they took us had a lot of buried equipment that was related to the EMIS project. We found calutrons and parts of the large vacuum chambers, destroyed vacuum pumps, and parts of coils that had been used to magnetize the huge iron cores. People could fry their eggs or heat their MREs on the jeep windows."

The unearthing of the calutrons prompted a visit from Hans Blix, who flew in from New York to inspect. "When Blix suddenly realized that the Iraqis had lied to him," one of the inspectors recalled, "he looked thunderstruck. It was absolutely a new concept to him that a nation-state would lie to a U.N. official. He had a religious experience." Blix, nobody's fool, was probably responding to the sheer magnitude of the deception, not merely the fact of it, but it's certainly true that his experiences with Iraq affected his view of the kind of inspections the IAEA would need to conduct thereafter. "The revelation that Iraq had secretly enriched uranium without being detected shook the world," Blix wrote. "In the board of the IAEA there was agreement with my conclusion that a sharpening of the safeguards system was necessary. It also now became politically possible, which it had hardly been earlier." At the U.N. Security Council in mid-July, Blix added, "the Soviet ambassador, Yuli Vorontsov, asked me whether it was certain that the Iraqi enrichment program was not peaceful. I replied that it was not plausible that a developing country would devote a billion dollars to enriching uranium for power reactors when there was an ample supply of cheap enriched uranium in the world markets and when, in any case, it had constructed no such reactors."

Through the summer of 1991 the Iraqis cooperated, at least so far as their EMIS and centrifuge programs were concerned. They gave the inspectors seminars and guided them to the desert sites where equipment was buried. "We traveled all around Iraq going to disposal sites," Frank Pabian, a senior analyst at Los Alamos, recalled. "These had been intended for concealment and deception, to hide the extent of their program. They took any materials related to enrichment out into the desert and buried them. There were a number of sites near Lake Tharthar"—seventy-five miles north of Baghdad—"and there were other sites around the country. We basically dug up tons of stainless-steel valves, some new and still in plastic, in crates buried underground. The Iraqis would take us out into the desert and they'd say, 'Well, it's out here somewhere,' and we'd say, 'Well, where?' They'd say, 'Kind of in that area.' They could drive you to the general area and then they'd work off of fence posts—'I think it's the third fence post.'" John Phillips, another Los Alamos recruit to the inspector ranks, told a laboratory newsletter of finding "a sand-covered Los Alamos report on nuclear technology that the wind had scattered from a concealment site." The work could be dangerous. "Much of the equipment had been buried or blown up," the newsletter paraphrased Phillips, "and the disposal sites were littered with Soviet TNT, primers and detonators." When the Iraqis started digging, Phillips recalled, "we would back up a respectful distance."

The primary site where the Iraqis had been pursuing electromagnetic-isotope separation proved to be one that had been unknown to the IAEA prior to the war: Tarmiya, the site that the pilot returning from Baghdad with his bomb load during the war had inadvertently struck and that B-52s had then all but excavated. Of the truckloads of Frisbees and calutron parts that David Kay's inspectors had chased down the road and photographed at Fallujah, Kay and Jay Davis wrote, "most of the material . . . was from Tarmiya, where 8 first-stage [calutron] separators were in operation at the time of the bombing and 17 in assembly. . . . The process bay in building 33 at Tarmiya was designed to hold seventy [primary-stage] separators. Initial installation had begun in January 1990, at the rate of approximately one separator per month, and the 8 in operation when the war began were at various points of development." With a full complement of ninety primary and secondary calutrons, Tarmiya could have produced enough HEU for one or two bombs per year.

But that was not all. Iraq had hired a Yugoslavian construction company to build the vast Tarmiya complex. In the mid-1980s Iraq had then taken the construction plans and used them to secretly *duplicate* Tarmiya at Ash Sharqat, a remote desert site 160 miles northeast of Baghdad. The Ash Sharqat EMIS installation, had it been completed, would have doubled Iraq's capacity to produce HEU, to as much as one hundred kilograms per year—five to eight bombs' worth, depending on design. It would also have served as a backup facility in case Israel or some other belligerent bombed Tarmiya. When Tarmiya was spotted and bombed during the Persian Gulf War, however, its duplicate at Ash Sharqat was also recognized because of its identical buildings (despite their different layout) and bombed to destruction by B-52s.

Blix reported the EMIS discoveries to the IAEA Board of Governors on 17 July. "The facility at Tarmiya," he told the board, "which was first described to our inspectors as a factory for the production of transformers, was, as the inspectors had concluded, a facility for the production of enriched uranium through the EMI separation method. It has been learnt that this huge facility was designed to house 90 electromagnetic isotope separators and that eight such separators were actually placed in operation in September 1990, resulting in the production of around half a kilogram of 4% enriched uranium." Blix used the occasion to lobby the board diplomatically to stiffen its spine:

> It is now being asked, and we must ask ourselves, whether major changes are needed to strengthen the safeguards system. The case of Iraq demonstrates the inspection challenges that may need to be met and the ability of the Agency to meet them. This ability was appreciated by members of the Security Council at the meeting on 15 July. May I conclude that the lesson to

be learnt from the present case is that a high degree of assurance can be obtained that the Agency can uncover clandestine nuclear activities if three major conditions are fulfilled.

First, that access is provided to information obtained *inter alia* through national technical means regarding sites that may require inspection;

Second, that access to any such sites, even at short notice, is an unequivocal right of the Agency;

Third, that access to the Security Council is available for backing and support that may be necessary to perform the inspection.

Iraq was the first nation caught attempting to develop nuclear weapons under cover of its commitment to the Nuclear Non-Proliferation Treaty; changing the rules to interdict further such breakouts was clearly a necessity.

A third inspection team arrived in Baghdad on 18 July to replace the breakthrough group, a fourth on 27 July that continued documenting, destroying, or applying seals to indicate if equipment was being used. But something was missing, Gallucci knew. "What we didn't have was a clear statement from the Iraqis that they did, in fact, have a nuclear-weapons program. We all thought that this was pretty obvious. They had all these programs to enrich uranium; they had been working on plutonium chemistry. Come on! 'Well, no, that is not the case,' said the Iraqis. The Iraqis, as they described it, were just really interested in the advanced nuclear fuel cycle, and they still maintained that there was no interest in nuclear weapons. So we still had not nailed it down. We had tried everything. We had a lot of folks come and present our views at the United Nations, but the case, we were told, was not proved when we went into August of 1991."

"SOMETIME DURING THAT AUGUST," Gallucci then recalled, "I was approached by someone in our intelligence community, who told me that they had extraordinary information on the location of documents that were quite relevant and directly related to the nuclear-weapons program of Iraq. We could finally make the case if we could get in, do the inspections, get the documents, and get out—or, as he put it, at least get the documents out. That was a degree of precision I didn't really appreciate until somewhat later."

Gallucci encountered resistance from Blix about conducting a document inspection. He talked to Ekéus and then tracked down David Kay at a conference at Los Alamos where the results of the first inspections were being reviewed. "Bob said, 'Let's walk the fence,' " Kay recalled. "We went outside and walked and he said, 'We've got confirmation of the location of the documents and we're going to carry out an inspection of it.' I'd come back from Iraq frustrated about the disagreements between Blix and Ekéus. I told Zifferero that unless we sorted it out I wasn't going to do any more inspections. So I said to Bob, 'What does "we" mean?' He said, 'Well, UNSCOM's going to do it.' I said, 'Bob, that's a mistake. If they're nuke documents, then it ought to be the IAEA.' 'Well, Ekéus talked to Blix and Blix won't let you lead it. Blix doesn't want to conduct the inspection at all.' I said, 'No, that's wrong. It's got to be an IAEA-led inspection.' And Bob said, 'Well, Ekéus said the only way he'll let the IAEA do it is if you lead it.' I told him, 'Wait until I get back to Vienna.' "

Kay returned to Geneva and confronted Blix, who said he was uncomfortable about raiding government documents. "It just went against his Swedish sensitivity," Kay said he thought. "He didn't like to accuse government people of cheating or lying. He didn't like the idea of purloining documents and all that. This went on for about two days, with discussions between him and Ekéus and him and me. I said, 'Look, it's a nuke inspection. If you don't lead it, UNSCOM will do it and UNSCOM will get more credit for it, not less credit.' Finally he agreed."

Ironically, Kay then advised Gallucci that he needed a different team from the IAEA experts who handled technology inspections. "Inevitably, the different team was drawn heavily from the intelligence agencies," Kay told me. "It was way too senior. Everyone in the CIA wanted to get in on it. Some of them had last done things like this in Vietnam, and they were out of shape. I brought two inspectors from the IAEA, only two, because Blix really didn't want the IAEA mixed up in raiding documents. And that was all right, because we weren't going to do a lot of technical analysis. We were breaking into buildings and photographing documents."

Gallucci rounded up thirty-nine team members from what he calls "elsewhere," a group that included American and British nuclear-weapon designers as well as private security specialists who were former military:

> The team was very, very special. I remember sitting in the back of an SUV with an Iraqi minder in the front. He looked at the fellow who was driving the vehicle, who was one of our "special people" and he said to me: "He does not look like a physicist." And I said: "It's just because he has a really thick neck. Is that what you're thinking?" And he said: "Yes, that . . . and the crew cut. Where did you get him?" I answered: "Well, there was an ad in the *New York Times*."
>
> We had a lot of team members with special skills, especially people who knew how to search buildings. Nothing in my training as a civil servant had taught me how to search a building properly, but we learned. We had a lot of special stuff, which was very useful for us, as it turned out.

The team first assembled at the British Cabinet Office in London, of all places, for a briefing and a first lecture on how to search for documents. From there the group flew to Bahrain and practiced searching the airport buildings from which the British had staged during the war. "We took people through and taught them how you systematically search a room for documents," Kay said. "You don't go straight for the desk; you start at the perimeter and work inward. And sure enough, we found a top-secret British document, which the Brits did not appreciate."

Kay, Gallucci, and their team flew from Bahrain into Baghdad on Sunday morning, 22 September 1991. They had intelligence on two sites they meant to inspect: the Design Center, an international conference area with multiple buildings located diagonally across from the Al-Rashid Hotel, just outside what would become the Green Zone; and an administrative facility, Petrochemical-3 Center, in a building across from the Palestine Hotel in the city center. They planned to inspect the Design Center first. "We had a description of the insides of the building," Kay told me, "and the location of all of the documents. Useful information like don't get on the elevator, not even the Iraqis use the elevator."

Concerned about leaks, Kay posted a team outside the Design Center at two a.m. on the morning of 23 September, the day of the inspections, to prevent the Iraqis from carting away any evidence. "The Iraqis, of course, rolled up and found them and were very upset." The full squad of inspectors arrived just before six a.m. and poured into the designated building without Iraqi resistance. "We had good luck and we had bad luck," Kay recalled. "The facility clearly had been sanitized partially before. Documents were in huge disarray—someone had gone through them." That was the bad luck. The inspectors worked for the next four hours searching through the building. Then, just after ten, they struck gold. "The good luck was, the basement of the building was L-shaped, with a very small room at the foot of the L. The people who had cleared documents must not have been the people who had put the documents there, because the people who had stored the documents had put the most valuable ones in this little back part of the L, a little room with a door. We opened the door and it was untouched. Everything was there."

Four boxes of documents awaited inspection. Kay had only a few Arabic linguists. "You usually have to triage. If you're looking at scientific documents, they usually include schematics, so you don't have to read everything. You do a quick triage. You try to seize or photograph as many as you can, but you really do have to reduce the volume. But when we hit this room, almost the first document we found when we opened the first case was a six-month interim report on the progress of the nuclear-weapons program." The report was in Arabic, but it included calculations and drawings of the levitated-core implosion-bomb design that the Iraqis had been developing. It was titled "Al-Atheer Plant Progress Report for the Period 1 January 1990 to 31 May 1990." The next several lines their translator read out made their hearts pound:

The goal of the Al-Atheer plant program is the design and manufacture of the mechanism which is composed of the following principal parts:
    Nuclear initiator (polonium-210 metal/beryllium)
    Core (enriched uranium metal)
    Reflector (natural uranium metal)
    Tamper (hardened iron)
    Explosive lenses (prepared by the Al-Qa' Qa' [Al Qaqaa] General Establishment)
    Electronic systems (triggering, control, and guidance)

This list of parts described the spherical implosion bomb starting from the center of the device—the walnut-sized initiator of gold-plated polonium-210 and beryllium that, when crushed by an inward-moving detonation wave from the high explosives surrounding the core, would release a burst of neutrons to start the fission chain reaction at the moment when the core was fully compressed and supercritical—and moving outward through the highly enriched uranium core that surrounded the initiator: the natural uranium reflector shell, which would reflect neutrons back into the core; the hardened iron tamper, which would hold the explosion together through a few more exponential neutron generations (which would account for most of the bomb's yield); the explosive lenses, which would compress the assembly; and the electronic systems connected to exploding-wire electric detonators that would ignite the thirty-two lenses with a simultaneity, as the document reported, "within time variations not exceeding 10 nanoseconds." And if there was any question about the reality of the Iraqi effort, they could read that as of the date of the report, 11 November 1990, "20 detonation tests have been carried out by using explosive lenses which have been prepared at Al-Qa' Qa' general facility."

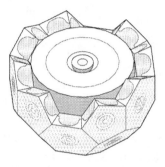

CUTAWAY OF IMPLOSION BOMB

According to a reactor physicist, Imad Khadduri, who worked in the Iraqi bomb program, the incriminating documents had originally been removed from their files and loaded into a welded train car that avoided U.N. inspection by traveling up and down Iraq when the inspectors were in the country. As the IAEA team asked more and more questions, however, Khadduri writes, "our scientists requested to refer to the scientific and technical reports amassed during the ten years of activity. A fatal error was committed and the order was issued to return the project's documents . . . to be deposited back again in their original location. That is where David Kay pounced on them in the early morning hours of [23] September 1991."

"You didn't have to read Arabic to figure out you had gotten a hot document," Kay told me.

Gallucci was working elsewhere in the building when the documents were discovered, but he and Kay had radios. "We had two sets of radios," Gallucci said, "one set that we were pretty sure the Iraqis were monitoring and another set which we were very confident that they couldn't monitor. And at that point, the message came over the secure radio: 'We found it.' This was one of the best moments of my nonproliferation life."

Gallucci rushed downstairs and joined Kay. "We looked at the document. We went out into the parking lot with one of our more nuclear-weapons-knowledgeable people, but it didn't take an expert to know what you were looking at. The schematics were just what you would want them to be, and so was everything else. These were nuclear-weapons designs and the status of the nuclear-weapons program. It was really terrific stuff." Even with the Iraqis watching, Gallucci started to get excited. "Wow! Right? I had a big sign on my back that said, 'Not Field-Capable.' The guy we were with said, 'Nothing here' and threw it back in the box."

Kay took up the story. "So then the issue we faced was, how in the hell do we get it out? Because in those days you didn't have the capability in the field of quickly scanning documents and getting them up on satellite, and the physical document we had was so important." His solution was low-tech and effective:

> I had one inspector, a U.S. military officer, who had one of the worst cases of diarrhea I'd ever seen. I'd decided I had to send him out to be rehydrated—we couldn't do that in the field. I was going to send him back to the Canal Hotel, which was our base in Baghdad. We had a Kiwi medical officer and a medical team with one of our four-by-fours rigged up as a medical vehicle. I told them we had a few documents that really had to get out. The great thing about the Kiwi medical staff is that they were all military. We probably violated the Geneva Conventions by using medical cover, but I literally had no other way to get the job done, and it was important to do. So they carried them back to the Canal Hotel along with the dehydrated inspector, and from the

Canal Hotel they went out the same day to the Habanya airport. We had NATO pilots flying, Germans, a regular supply mission that went out at two p.m. It was good cover. And here's the final piece of luck. As our guys were taking off, the Iraqis drove a fuel truck across the runway in a harassment move and—pilots are very cool—they barely cleared the truck.

Back inside the Design Center, Kay, Gallucci, and the others continued searching and cataloging throughout the day. As they finished an inventory, they carried the boxes of documents out to their vehicles and bungee-corded them onto the roof racks. Fully loaded at 3:45, they attempted to leave, but the Iraqis barred their way. "The Iraqi security personnel," Kay told me, "who in previous inspections had been around in the background, all overweight, always with a gun showing, stuffed into their waistbands—maybe there was a shortage of holsters?—were really starting to take control." Around 4:30 the Iraqis began reviewing the documents that the team had removed. An hour later, Jaffar arrived. "It was the first time he'd ever shown up at a site while we were there. He said to me, 'You've got to leave. We're closing down the inspection.' I protested. And then he said, 'And we've got to have the documents back.' " Jaffar didn't know that many of the documents had been filmed and many others marked as key documents and at least roughly inventoried, but that hardly protected the inspectors. "That was a very, very tense period," Kay said. "There were a lot of Iraqi security and military personnel around him and we were unarmed. We informed New York via satellite radio and all that, but I finally said, 'Look, we're not going to die over this.' They came in and very roughly cut the bungee cords and took the documents off the top and emptied the SUVs. It was pretty nasty."

After that tense day's work, the inspectors drove back to the Al-Rashid, except for Kay, who had reports to file at the other hotel, the Canal, where UNSCOM had its offices and communications. "I didn't get back to the Al-Rashid until around midnight," Kay told me. "I had just gotten to sleep when someone pounded on the door. I looked at my watch and it was two a.m. The Iraqis were downstairs and wanted to see me. I got dressed and went downstairs and there was Sami Al-Araji, the deputy minister of industry. 'We will give you your documents back now,' he told me. So I had to roust a group of inspectors who were going to get rousted at five a.m. anyway to go with me to retrieve the documents. After we had them it took ten minutes to discover we didn't get all of them back. I filed a protest, of course."

Short on sleep, Kay and his team hit the Petrochemical-3 Center at 6:20 a.m. on 24 September. "It was a sensitive facility," Kay recalled, "because it had the personnel records for the bomb program. Personnel records allow you to identify who's working where and what they might have been doing, so you can subject them to interviews. The Iraqis were tremendous bureaucrats, the best of British and Arabic training. So if they denied they had a program on, say, chemical enrichment, and you found guys whose personnel records said they worked in chemical enrichment, then . . ." The inspectors searched and photographed until just before eleven in the morning, when Araji arrived with a security squad and told them they had to give up the documents as well as their film and leave the building.

"He said to me," Kay said, "'I have no control over this. You've got to get out of the building and no documents. We take all documents.' So that was a tougher one." Jaffar arrived at 12:30 to press the issue. "That's when we dug in our heels. I said, 'Well, you can force us out of the building, but we're not giving you the documents.' I wish I'd been privy to the full Iraqi internal discussion at that point. Because there we were. They'd seized the documents from us the previous day. This time we were in the center of Baghdad. There was a hell of a protest going on back in New York about their behavior the day before. We had satellite communications. And they blew it. They delayed. They just told us, 'You can go back to your hotel but you can't take any documents.' I said, 'We're not going back to the hotel, we're staying here with the documents.' They allowed the pressure to build and didn't do anything."

Gallucci recalled how they protected the documents. "I don't remember whose idea this was," he said. "It might well have been David Kay's. We told everybody to put the documents on their body someplace, so that it would be harder for the Iraqi authorities to take the documents without essentially stripping us. We thought they might not want to strip-search a U.N. team. We weren't sure they wouldn't do it, but we thought it would be less likely. As it turned out, we were correct. They asked for documents, but we wouldn't give them up. So they told us that we would not be allowed to leave." Forty-three men and one woman, their shirts and pants stuffed with documents, loaded into their bus and SUVs in a parking lot in downtown Baghdad that was soon ringed with Iraqi security forces, and settled down to wait. "And this began the parking lot tour," Gallucci summarized, "which went on for four days. We slept, ate and sang songs and had a wonderful time. We celebrated at least one birthday in the parking lot. David Kay became a media star, and I was nothing but jealous."

They had the documents. They had their vehicles. They had water and MREs. And they had a satellite telephone that linked them to the outside world. "Ekéus called me on the satellite phone," Kay told me. "He said, 'CNN would like to talk to you. How do you feel about that?' He made the right call; he left the decision where it belonged, with the people in the field, and I'll always respect him for that. And I decided, yes, I'd talk to the media, because I was interested in keeping as much pressure as possible on the Iraqis—because I thought that was the only hope we had of getting out of there. I didn't know whether it was very much of a hope, but it was all we had."

Kay did that first CNN interview and the world turned its attention to a parking lot in Baghdad, the coverage spreading from one time zone to the next. "Suddenly you could track the traffic as various newspapers and networks got the phone number. It was just continuous after that. We were continuously on, the dominant news story of the week. The phone became our lifeline. The Iraqis could have taken us down. We ran the phone on a Honda generator. Boy, Honda deserves credit, that generator ran continuously and never burped once. But the Iraqis could have gone in and smashed the satellite phone. I think they couldn't figure out the consequences of us suddenly going off the air. A totalitarian regime doesn't know how to deal with a free press. Suddenly the world is watching."

Not only the world. The U.S. Navy was watching from the aircraft carrier U.S.S. *Abraham Lincoln,* on station in the Persian Gulf. "Apparently they'd prepared a strike package," Kay recalled. "Thank God they never executed it, because we were smack in the middle of it. These were the days of less-than-precision-guided weapons. As a rescue operation, it would have been a bloody disaster."

The team members operating the office at the Canal Hotel sent over food. The Iraqis tried to inspect it, but they let it pass through. "The biggest problem in the parking lot was sanitation. There was one one-holer. That was the first inspection when I'd taken in a woman inspector, the first woman inspector in Iraq. She was actually CIA; her specialty was computer hacking. After a day the sanitation got to be pretty god-awful. The Iraqis came up and said, 'We don't like treating a woman like this. We'd be happy to let her go back to the hotel.' I told them, 'Don't ask me. Ask her.' They did, and she let out a string of profanity that really shocked them. She said, 'I'm part of this goddamned team, I'm not leaving until Kay says we're leaving.' "

A CNN telephone interview with Kay found him emphasizing team spirit:

We are currently in nighttime in Baghdad, coming up slightly after eight o'clock, and we're pulling our inspection vehicles together in a circle so that we'll have light during the night and preparing to settle down for the evening. . . . We've had no official contact with the Iraqis now for over four hours. Other U.N. colleagues in the city managed to bring in a supply of water, MREs and watermelon, fortunately, which greatly improves MREs. So we're in adequate shape with regard to food and items, and in quite good spirits. This I should emphasize again is a very, very, good scene, very professional, very disciplined, and in quite high spirits at this time.

Kay was determined to keep pressure on the Iraqis. He also had to keep his team occupied. "In a hostage situation you don't want the pressure to be on the team—that's a losing proposition. But you had to keep everyone busy because just sitting around waiting for something to happen that you have no control over is terribly demoralizing. So we continued to inventory documents and wrote up as much as we could about it. Bob Gallucci organized a football game using a water bottle stuffed with a paper bag. It was one of the weirdest passing contests Baghdad had ever seen. We also had to establish procedures where some of the team would be awake all the time. Both Bob and I were concerned that the Iraqis would move in when it was dark. Some guys were on knife's edge, the Special Forces guys particularly. If someone had started shaking them in the middle of the night, there might be violence."

Gallucci would hint, in a talk he gave later, that the U.S. military was prepared to resume full-scale war in any case on the slightest provocation. The Bush administration had already concluded that the only long-term solution to the Iraq problem was to depose Saddam Hussein. All the arguments against regime change that Bush's son and his son's vice president would later ignore were brought to bear—by Secretary of Defense Dick Cheney in particular, of all people—against George H. W. Bush's visceral urge to take Saddam down. "Even in the parking lot," Gallucci said, "I had a sense that the threat of resuming [coalition] military operations was right there. I'm making up what was in the Iraqi minds, but I think it should have been there. It certainly was in my mind." Kay said the number of Iraqi military personnel surrounding the parking lot increased on the second night to several hundred. If no assault followed, Iraqi concern for a large-scale American military reprisal may well have been the reason.

On the second day of the standoff, Kay recalled, "a Winnebago camper pulled up right outside the parking-lot fence. This was an area where you couldn't get through unless the Iraqi security personnel let you through. The windows were shielded so you couldn't see inside. It sat there for about four hours. There was great speculation as to who was there. There were reports during the war that Saddam and his body doubles all traveled around in Winnebagos that way. He had six, ten, I forget what the number was of Winnebagos. There was a contest during the war to see how many Winnebagos the Air Force could bomb. I heard later that some people in the intelligence community thought they had signal intelligence from the parking lot indicating it was one of Saddam's sons. We never knew. But the incident is indicative of what must have been a serious, high-level discussion about how to deal with us. They were doing all sorts of things. They had a protest outside the fence with people gesturing and shouting at us. It was a game. They were clearly trying to figure out what the rules were. They didn't know them any more than we knew them."

Halfway through the four-day ordeal, at a moment when the satellite phone was briefly unoccupied, it rang. "The communications officer passed it to me," Kay told me, "and it was this flat sort of Midlands English voice saying he was the satellite systems operator. He said, 'We've noticed you've been on your telephone for something like twenty-three of the last twenty-four hours. We need a new credit-card number.' He literally had no idea who we were or where we were. I said, 'Well, two things. First, you're not getting my credit-card number. But let me tell you where we are and what's going on.' Which I did. He was extraordinary. He said, 'Eh, is there anything we can do to help you?' I said, 'Well, as a matter of fact . . .' We were on the edge of the satellite's cover-age. So they *moved the satellite*. We had great coverage after that."

The satellite phone was in almost constant use partly because the team had organized a phone-home lottery. "The lottery determined the order you could use the phone to call anyone you wanted to call. And since the guys' families lived in various time zones, they spent the rest of the day trading numbers so their call would match their home zones. Well, that kept them busy. Plus, calling home established that they were all right. If you know your family knows you're okay, it's a lot easier to endure. It's lack of contact that makes it severe. The telephone was as valuable to us in that way as it was for media contact."

Finally, at five-thirty on the morning of 28 September, the Iraqis gave in. "The deal was, we would go through the documents with them. They were arguing that some of the documents had nothing to do with the nuke program and were too sensi-tive. We'd take the documents to the hotel and they could go through them with us. They could protest if they wanted to, and if I accepted their protest they could have the document back. If I didn't, we kept it. Some of us had a chance to shower and shave before the document review started at eight a.m.; some of us didn't. It went on for hours and hours, until seven o'clock that night, until they got tired of the game. There were a few docu-ments that had no relevance that I agreed to give up." And then it was over. Amazingly, the team ran another round of inspections the next day—searching a warehouse and several other govern-ment buildings—before departing Iraq for Bahrain on 30 Sep-tember 1991.

"I think," Kay told me, "quite frankly, that it was the interna-tional pressure that carried the day. I've always credited what-ever success we had on this mission to the satellite telephone. It's an early example of international communications being used in a political situation, before any of us really understood the ground rules." Gallucci didn't disagree, but he emphasized what was behind the communications: "There was always the plausible prospect of the resumption of hostilities, and I don't mean tit-for-tat bombing. That's my conclusion about how we got out of that parking lot."

BOB GALLUCCI WOULD say later that the September 1991 inspections "did a lot to energize and legitimize an aggressive inspection process, which then continued for some period of time." A seventh inspection in October finally exposed Iraq's primary nuclear weapons research site at Al Atheer, east of the Euphrates River forty-two miles southwest of Baghdad near Al Musayyib. A CIA summary describes this site as "Project 6000, also known as Al Atheer: This factory was designed to fabricate the uranium shells [i.e., pits] for atomic bombs. The two most important buildings at the site . . . are the materials halls in building 6210 and building 6220. Building 100 at the factory is involved with explosive tests." Building 100 was a bunker where implosion systems could be detonated indoors, out of sight of satellite imaging. Besides uranium metallurgy, Al Atheer served for hydrodynamic experiments, explosive-lens development, and core assembly. Once the site was exposed, Iraq finally acknowledged that it was working on nuclear weapons.

In the months to come, U.N. inspectors filled the Al Atheer bunker with tons of concrete to render it useless. Swedish and Swiss engineers called in by the U.N. rigged the buildings at Al Atheer, Tarmiya, and Ash Sharqat with explosives and demolished them. All weapons-usable nuclear material and plutonium-laden spent fuel was flown out of the country. "The proud calutrons," Dimitri Perricos said later, "were also completely destroyed."

Iraq learned from its experiences of exposure, however. "Finding this smoking gun," Perricos concluded, referring to the documents uncovered in September, "told the Iraqis that they must protect their sources as much as possible." Three years would pass before the inspectors found any more important documentation.

In the meantime, another parking-lot standoff in July 1992 lasted three weeks, was accompanied by an intensive Iraqi challenge to the United Nations, and had destructive long-term consequences for both Iraq and the United States. As the political scientist Christian Alfonsi would recognize, "Saddam had witnessed firsthand in 1992 that the White House—any White House—was at its most vulnerable in the months preceding an election. His first 'across the board' challenge to the will of the international community in July of that year had been timed to capitalize on a Bush White House distracted by a reelection campaign in free-fall and by the crisis in Bosnia." George Bush's son George Walker Bush, the governor of Texas, who was serving as one of his father's campaign advisers, took note of the threat. So did Dick Cheney.

PART TWO

BREAKDOWN AND REFORMATION

FIVE **THE LITTLE SUITCASE**

I N EARLY AUGUST 1991, when David Kay, Bob Gallucci, and their fellow UNSCOM/IAEA inspectors were closing in on the documents that would expose the Iraqi atomic-bomb program, Mikhail Gorbachev, the first and last president of the Soviet Union, was preparing to leave Moscow with his family for a two-week vacation. Gorbachev had struggled for six years to reform his battered, tragic country, and he was exhausted. "I'm tired as hell," he told his aide Anatoly Chernyaev, who was flying to the Crimea with the Gorbachevs on the presidential plane. "Everything has become so petty, vulgar, provincial. You look at it and think, to hell with it all! But who would I leave it to? I'm so tired."

It was a bad time for the president to leave Moscow. His country was in crisis, suspended between retreat and transformation. Everyone else knew, or claims to have known, that a coup attempt was gathering among the venal men Gorbachev had appointed to high positions when he veered to the right the previous winter. Eduard Shevardnadze, his foreign minister since 1985, had resigned in December in protest against Gorbachev's appointments and the dictatorship he believed they presaged. "For those in the know," wrote the journalist and editor David Remnick, an eyewitness that summer, "the clues were unending."

Gorbachev had heard the rumors, but he didn't believe

them. Always optimistic, he believed he had at least temporarily restrained the centrifugal forces that were pulling his country apart. He thought his policies had broad support. Just before he left on vacation, Gorbachev had met with Boris Yeltsin, the recently elected president of the Russian Federation, and Nursultan Nazarbayev, the president of Kazakhstan, and finished negotiating a treaty transforming the Soviet republics into sovereign states within a federalized union. The three leaders had discussed throwing the hard-liners out of Gorbachev's government once the Union treaty was signed. Gorbachev was due to return from the Crimea on 19 August, and they had scheduled the treaty signing for the next day.

Unknown to its principals, however, the meeting had been bugged. Through that mechanism Vladimir Kryuchkov, the chairman of the KGB and one of the hard-liners they had talked about dismissing, had learned of their discussions.

A heavy brown briefcase accompanied Gorbachev on his flight to the Crimea. Code-named *Cheget* after a mountain in the North Caucasus, it contained the communications terminal that the Soviet president needed to convey to the military his authority to retaliate against a nuclear attack—or to start a nuclear war. Gorbachev called this doomsday machine by its insouciant Russian nickname *chemodanchik,* "little suitcase." (The United States's counterpart is nicknamed the football.) *Cheget* technology for nuclear command and control had been developed during the administration of Gorbachev's predecessor Yuri Andropov; Gorbachev was the first Soviet leader to have access to such a device. To service it around the clock in the Crimea, three teams of military officers traveled with it that August, each team consisting of a communications specialist and two members of the Soviet general staff. The general staff, according to a CIA expert, was "responsible for directing the activities of the Soviet strategic and general purpose forces throughout the world, and for maintaining reliable, secure links with them. . . . [It had] physical custody of the unlock codes for many nuclear delivery systems."

The presidential plane landed at Belbek military air base, near Sebastopol on the southwestern Crimean coast. After conferring for an hour with Ukrainian officials, Gorbachev traveled with his wife, Raisa, their daughter, Irina, her husband, Anatoly, and their two granddaughters, Ksenia and Anastasia, south by limousine another thirty kilometers to a lavish presidential dacha near the resort village of Foros. The dacha, called Zarya—"dawn"—had cost the Soviet government twenty million dollars to build; it was sited on a pine-covered bluff overlooking the Black Sea. Outside, barrel-vaulted arches supported its white decks under a peaked pink roof; inside, facings of marble and light wood framed its showy spaces, including a wide front hall, lounges, a billiard room, a theater, an office, and a cantilevered central staircase that wound up through the four interior floors. From the dacha grounds the Gorbachevs could descend on a covered escalator to an Olympic-sized swimming pool at beach level, or walk from there oceanward onto a kilometer-long private beach where the rocky debris that littered this sweep of the Crimean coast had been cleared and replaced with sand.

It was hot in Foros that August, ninety degrees and hotter in the afternoon. Gorbachev exchanged his suits for shorts and casual shirts, conferred with Moscow by phone, worked with Chernyaev on speeches and a long essay about the future of his country and of perestroika, but made time to sleep in, to enjoy his grandchildren, to walk on the beach in the evening with his wife. An old back injury was bothering him; the two physicians who traveled with him supervised heat treatments and massages. A well-armed thirty-two-man KGB personal bodyguard—a counterpart to the U.S. Secret Service—protected him and his family from intrusion.

In a guesthouse on the grounds some distance from the main house, the *Cheget* teams had plugged Gorbachev's *chemodan-chik* into a special national leadership network called Kavkaz, which supported crisis communications among senior government officials. The Kavkaz network, in turn, was plugged into a military network, Kazbek, which allowed the general staff to authenticate senior leadership decisions before passing them through to the strategic nuclear forces. In the United States, where the president has sole authority to launch a retaliatory nuclear strike, only the president has access to the football. The Soviet system, in contrast, divided that authority among three senior government leaders—the president, the minister of defense, and the chief of the general staff—who were required to respond together to authorize action. To make such a coordinated response possible, not only the president but also the other two senior leaders were issued *chemodanchiki*. During the period of Gorbachev's 1991 vacation, those two other senior leaders were Defense Minister Dmitri Yazov and Chief of the General Staff Mikhail Moiseyev. Each *Cheget* team on duty at Zarya performed regular checks on the ready status of the *chemodanchik* terminal and on the telephone link that connected their station with Gorbachev's office in the main house.

The essay that Gorbachev was writing with Chernyaev described a Soviet Union in crisis. It was an economic crisis first of all, with food shortages as well as increasing joblessness, but it was also a sharpening political crisis. The hard-liners were urging Gorbachev to proclaim a state of emergency, but such a radical retreat would suspend democratic processes and could potentially return the Soviet Union to Communist Party control. The appeals for a state of emergency that Gorbachev recalls most vividly in his memoirs had been shouted during a Central Committee plenum in April; "Let him either introduce a 'state of emergency,' " Gorbachev paraphrases his critics, "or quit." He called their bluff and resigned; by the next day they had turned tail and voted not even to discuss his resignation.

But when the KGB chairman, Vladimir Kryuchkov—"a quiet old man with a steely gaze," as Boris Yeltsin described him—called together his fellow conspirators on 17 August at a KGB Moscow safe house, the governing collective he proposed to form named itself the State Committee for the State of Emergency.

Kryuchkov had begun plotting the coup as far back as November 1990. He was moving quickly now to beat the 20 August deadline of the Union treaty signing, and by the time his fellow conspirators arrived, late in the afternoon, he had already sent a deputy to Foros to cut Gorbachev's communications and seal him off from the world. "The situation is catastrophic," Remnick quoted one of the conspirators, Prime Minister Valentin Pavlov, telling his confederates to justify their treason. "The country is facing famine. It is in total chaos. Nobody wants to carry out orders. The harvest is disorganized. Machines are idle because they have no spare parts, no fuel. The only hope is a state of emergency." Closer to the truth was the testimony of Dmitri Yazov, the minister of defense, that they all were unhappy with the Union treaty and were sure that "the state would fall apart" if it was implemented—their state, at least, and with it their privileges.

Others who participated in the coup planning that day included Boris Pugo, the minister of internal affairs, who had sneaked off from the very resort in Foros where Chernyaev was staying; Gorbachev's trusted aide Valery Boldin, the head of his personal staff; the deputy chief of the Defense Council, Oleg Baklanov, who represented the Soviet military-industrial complex; the Central Committee secretary Oleg Shenin, representing the Politburo; Vladimir Ivashko, deputy chairman of the Communist Party of the Soviet Union; Anatoly Lukyanov, the chairman of the Supreme Soviet and a friend of Gorbachev since their student days; and the Soviet vice president, Gennady Yanayev. They were all Gorbachev's men, nearly the entire Soviet leadership. They were nervous, if not afraid. "Yanayev," testified Yazov, "was already rather drunk," and with bottles of whiskey and vodka set out on the table, Pavlov soon would be. Kryuchkov designated Boldin, Baklanov, Shenin, and the army general in charge of Soviet ground forces, Valentin Varennikov, to fly to the Crimea the next day to present Gorbachev with a fait accompli.

Before Gorbachev, his family, or Chernyaev in his separate office knew that the delegation had arrived on the afternoon of

18 August, the *Cheget* team knew; at 4:32 p.m. their *Cheget* terminal signaled that it had been disconnected from its network. They tried to call Moscow headquarters on the military radio but got no further than the regional exchange, which simply confirmed a breakdown. A few minutes later the *Cheget* watch commander found himself called out to report to Varennikov. "[He] asked me about the condition of our communications center," the officer testified later. "I answered that communications had been cut off. He responded that that's the way it should be and that our communications center should be switched off." The watch commander asked Varennikov how long the situation would continue. " 'Twenty-four hours,' " the general said. "He added that the president [i.e., Gorbachev] was aware of it all." Varennikov went off to join the plotters approaching the main house—"Many cars were piling up at the entrance of our official workplace," Chernyaev said, "all of them with antennas and some with flashing lights . . . a crowd of chauffeurs and guards"—while the *Cheget* team, responsible to its own chain of command, went back to trying to reconnect with its headquarters, unsuccessfully.

Gorbachev was suspicious when a bodyguard told him a delegation had arrived unscheduled; when he discovered that the phones didn't work he recognized mortal danger. He put off the delegation long enough to call his family together. "Evidently they are going to try and blackmail me into something," he told Raisa, Irina, and Anatoly, "or they will try to arrest me, or kidnap me or something else." He would stand his ground to the end, he forewarned them. Then so would they: "The whole family said that the decision was up to me: they were ready to share with me whatever might happen."

Elsewhere in the dacha the impatient conspirators had already presumed to occupy Gorbachev's office. He went there and confronted them, heard their demands that he declare a state of emergency or resign the presidency, tried and failed to win them over—"It was a conversation with deaf-mutes"—insulted Varennikov, told the others they were fools to think their plot could succeed, railed at them, called them criminals, and swore at their backs as they hastily departed.

The *Cheget* watch commander saw them leave. By then it was half past five. He had tried to reach Gorbachev on the presidential phone and found the line dead. He sought out the KGB major general in charge of the coup lockdown to ask if he could contact his senior officer at the military vacation facility in Foros where the *Cheget* teams were bunked. Impossible, the KGB officer snapped.

In Moscow, at about the same time, the commander of the general staff division that maintained presidential communications with Soviet strategic nuclear forces was informed that the *Cheget* team was out of contact. "I was told that the cause of the breakdown was not known," he testified, "and was being looked into." He learned nothing more until the following morning. Soviet strategic nuclear forces were headless that night but not disarmed, since the general staff in an emergency could launch a retaliatory attack on its own. In the nuclear era a nation's sovereignty has come to be invested in its nuclear arsenal, its ultimate defense; with the president of the Soviet Union cut off from nuclear command and control, that sovereignty was temporarily adrift. Who might claim it depended on how the Soviet military—at that point, not itself a unified organization—assessed the authority of the Emergency Committee.

THE WORLD SHARED the public events of the next two days. The Emergency Committee took over central television and radio on Monday morning, 19 August, and began hourly announcements of its decrees and resolutions, including the mendacious claim that Gorbachev was "no longer capable of performing his duties due to the state of his health." Boris Yeltsin, wearing a bulletproof vest under his shirt and suit jacket, left his dacha outside Moscow by car early in the morning and arrived undetected at the vast, marble-faced Russian parliament building called the White House, on a bend of the Moscow River a little less than two miles southwest of the Kremlin. At nine a.m. Yeltsin and other Russian government leaders issued a declaration from the White House that the Emergency Committee was illegal and unconstitutional and called for a general strike. Red Army tanks, trucks, and armored personnel carriers began rolling into Moscow on Emergency Committee orders at nine-thirty. By noon, tanks had taken up positions outside the White House, where demonstrators were crowding the streets to protest the coup, but the tank commanders allowed the demonstrators onto the tanks, and within the hour Yeltsin himself emerged.

The defenders erected barricades of concrete blocks and Dumpsters around the White House even as assault troops and snipers took up positions across the city and the Central Telegraph in Moscow cut off both intercity and international communications. Decrees and counter-decrees flew back and forth between the Kremlin and the White House throughout the gloomy, rain-soaked afternoon. At the end of the day, five of the conspirators, led by a drunken and trembling Vice President Yanayev, now claiming to be the acting president, held a burlesque press conference at the foreign ministry press center that was televised around the world.

After a tense night when the Russian military backed away from supporting the coup attempt, the plot fell apart. In what came to be called "the race to Foros," Kryuchkov, Yazov, and two other members of the Emergency Committee lit out for Vnukovo Airport the next afternoon with Russian police forces giving chase. The plotters commandeered the presidential plane and skirred off to the Crimea, desperate to persuade Gorbachev to take their side. Yeltsin's people located another government plane. It departed Vnukovo for Belbek at five that afternoon carrying ten Russian parliamentarians; the Russian vice president, Aleksandr Rutskoi; the Soviet Security Council member Yevgeny Primakov; and thirty-six militia officers armed with submachine guns. The presidential plane had reached Belbek by then and limos had rushed the coup leaders to Zarya, but Gorbachev had his bodyguards arrest them. Later that night the presidential plane carried the Gorbachevs out of their exile, landing in Moscow at about two in the morning. The extremity of the experience was evident on their faces.

SUCH WERE THE PUBLIC EVENTS of the August coup. The Gorbachevs in the isolation of their house arrest lived through another, private reality at Zarya. Their seventy-two hours of uncertainty ramped up at times to intense anxiety and even terror, especially for Raisa, as they waited out an implicit threat of death that might consume not only their lives but also the lives of their daughter and son-in-law and their grandchildren.

Gorbachev's bodyguards remained loyal throughout the three-day ordeal. At his request that Monday, one of them passed a series of demands to the KGB officer in charge, a general named Generalov: restore the president's telephones and television, deliver the mail and newspapers, and send a plane to return him to Moscow. Gorbachev got no response. Late in the afternoon he learned that the *Cheget* team had been removed. The order had come from Moscow, from the chief of the division of the general staff that controlled strategic communications. The team had left with its equipment for Belbek at two; at about eight that evening, a security expert writes, the three *Cheget* teams "left for Moscow in the president's plane, taking with them his terminal, rendered useless by erasing its magnetic memory." Without the unique code that only Gorbachev possessed, the presidential *Cheget* was inoperative; the teams erased its memory to protect its secrets.

Midafternoon on Wednesday, 21 August, the day the coup collapsed, a BBC transmission that the Gorbachevs picked up on their Sony pocket radio, their only uncensored contact with the outside world, reported that Kryuchkov had sent a delegation to Foros to see for itself that Gorbachev was incapacitated. This was, in fact, the gang of panicked plotters the Russian police had chased to Vnukovo Airport, but the family had no way of assessing the ominous report. "We consider this a sign that the worst is to come," Raisa wrote. "Within the next few hours actions may be carried out to translate the infamous lie into reality." Gorbachev ordered his guards to block all the drives leading up to the dacha and to use force if necessary to prevent any unauthorized entry. Guards with Kalashnikovs stationed themselves at the entrance to the dacha and along the central staircase inside. The Gorbachev grandchildren were locked into their bedroom and the housekeeper assigned to take care of them. Raisa's distress was extreme, so much so that she suffered a transient stroke, with numbness in her arms and garbled speech. There were doctors at hand to care for her; she was treated and put to bed.

The desperate men of the coup arrived. Gorbachev's bodyguards arrested them and herded them into the dacha to wait until the president chose to receive them. Gorbachev demanded that they restore his telephones before he would speak with them; when they did so, he kept them waiting while he reconnected himself to the world. "I talked on the telephone with Yeltsin, Nazarbayev, [Nikolai] Dementi [of Belarus] and leaders of the other republics. I said to them: 'I'm holding the fort here with my garrison.' I also got in touch with President Bush. I began issuing orders. Yazov was dismissed and his duties as Minister of Defense were entrusted to [Mikhail] Moiseyev, who was to ensure that the flight carrying Rutskoi and his comrades could land at Belbek. The chief of government communications was instructed to disconnect the telephone lines of all the plotters. The Kremlin commandant was to secure the buildings and to isolate all the conspirators who had stayed behind there." By the time he was finished, says Chernyaev, "judging by their reaction . . . they were standing at attention."

For Gorbachev, when the Russian delegation arrived, "It was then that I really felt that I was free." He and his family still had to negotiate the uncertain situation at Belbek, pretending to board the presidential plane that the plotters had commandeered, then ducking back into the limo and racing across the airfield to the secure plane that had brought the Russian leadership to the Crimea. They landed at Vnukovo at two a.m. on the morning of 22 August, Raisa stricken, Gorbachev looking haunted. As soon as their daughter found the privacy of the waiting limo, "she threw herself on the seat and broke down in wracking sobs," Chernyaev reports. "We lived through those three August days," Gorbachev said afterward, "on the brink of human endurance." Walking to the Kremlin the next morning, Gorbachev assessed the change to his nation and himself. "I have come back from Foros to another country," he told reporters, "and I myself am a different man now."

SAM NUNN, IN 1991 the fifty-three-year-old United States Democratic senator from Georgia and chairman of the Senate Armed Services Committee, happened to be attending an Aspen Institute conference in Budapest when the August coup occurred. The conference was about America's relationship with the Soviet Union, Nunn recalls, and among those attending was his Soviet friend Andrei Kokoshin, a political scientist and America specialist whom Nunn had known for more than a decade. "The conference was probably a third of the way through," Nunn told me, "when the Soviet delegation got the call about Gorbachev and the coup taking place. Andrei immediately went back, and then when Gorbachev was released, he called me and said, 'Sam, there are big things happening in Russia.' He said 'Russia' about five times. I'd never heard him say 'Russia' before. He said, 'You've got to come over here; big things are happening. You've got to meet some of these new people.' "

Nunn didn't have a Soviet visa, and he assumed that this would be a fatal impediment, since visas usually took weeks to work their way through the Soviet bureaucracy. Kokoshin said he'd have the resident Soviet ambassador there in an hour. Nunn didn't believe him, but an hour later the ambassador showed up with a visa. Nunn alerted the U.S. Embassy in Moscow, which cautioned him to stay away—"Don't come," he was told. "This place is total confusion; we don't even know who the players are." Undeterred, he flew to Moscow the next morning, confident his Russian friends would take care of him. He visited the Russian White House on the afternoon of his arrival, in time to find "thousands of people still milling around" and to meet "all the new key players, the ones who were going to be in charge of Russia."

For the next two days Nunn attended the historic sessions of the Supreme Soviet convened in the wake of the coup attempt. Another Russian friend, Sergei Rogov, the deputy director of the Institute for U.S. and Canadian Studies of the Soviet Academy of Sciences, translated for him. "The leaders of the Soviet Union were sitting up there, including Gorbachev, and the leaders of the republics, and they were debating, with a lot of floor activity, the breakup of the Soviet Union. Rogov always spoke his mind. He'd say, 'So-and-so said this and So-and-so said that,' and then he'd mutter under his breath, 'Lying son of a bitch.' It was fascinating."

At the end of the second day's session, Nunn walked out with the delegate Roald Sagdeev, a wry Tatar astrophysicist and Gorbachev adviser whose 1990 marriage to Susan Eisenhower, the former president's granddaughter, had symbolized on a personal level the changed relationship between the U.S. and the Soviet Union. Sagdeev, like Nunn, was deeply worried about the security of the Soviet nuclear arsenal during the coup. "You have to assume that the leaders of the coup had effective control over the nuclear weapons," Sagdeev said publicly on the day after the coup collapsed. "This is what makes such a type of coup very dangerous. I think what happened—when they arrested Gorbachev, from that very moment, they switched all the electronic keys from him to somebody else, to someone who was declared commander-in-chief. From what we heard, they probably had a special technique to do it without Gorbachev's consent. . . . The worst-case scenario, in deterrence planning, is the leaders could have committed suicide this way." Nunn remembers noticing Sagdeev surreptitiously removing his delegate's badge as they pushed through the noisy mob of demonstrators outside the building. "I thought the crowd was friendly," he says. "I never felt threatened." After they were clear he asked Sagdeev why he'd taken off his badge and what the crowd was chanting. "He said, 'They were chanting "Down with the Soviet Union, down with the people's delegates." ' "

Nunn carried his concern with the Soviet nuclear arsenal into a meeting with Gorbachev himself:

> I went to see Gorbachev and I thought I'd just go in and say hello, but I ended up spending about forty-five minutes with him. He'd been out of captivity for about three days by then, something like that. We had a good, friendly conversation. He was bewildered—I mean, you could just tell. He was trying to be candid, but he still was clinging to empire and clinging to the Soviet Union staying together and saying he was going to do everything he could to do that. But he did tell me he wasn't going to shed blood. He made it clear that whatever they did they were going to do peacefully. That's when I asked him about the security of the weapons. Because I'd heard from people during that trip—my friends as well as the military people I talked to—that one of their biggest concerns was how they were going to control the nuclear, chemical and biological stuff when the whole country was splitting up and this stuff was everywhere.
>
> I asked Gorbachev. I said, "Did you have control of the nuclear chain of command during your captivity, or who did?" He just turned—he didn't answer the question. He said, "Goodbye, Senator Nunn."

It was not only his conversation with Gorbachev that late-August day in Moscow that made Nunn determined to find a way to help the fracturing Soviet Union secure its weapons of mass destruction. "That was one part of it," he told me, "but the whole thing was so apparent to me: that we had to act and act quickly to help them, certainly, but also to *focus* them, to move the problem way up on their list of priorities."

AS LATER TESTIMONY REVEALED, the Soviet nuclear arsenal was never at risk during the coup, thanks partly to what the American command-and-control expert Bruce Blair called its "ingenious" design. Blair, a solid, handsome man who apprenticed in his field as a U.S. missile-control officer, told a Senate subcommittee a month after the coup that the Soviet system's safeguards "are more stringent than those of any other nuclear power, including the United States. The overall design of Soviet nuclear command and control is ingenious and its designers were deservedly awarded Lenin prizes for their efforts." Blair and his Soviet counterpart, command-and-control expert Gennadi Pavlov, explained to the subcommittee in some detail how the Soviet system worked.

"We do not invest any authority to use nuclear weapons in a single individual," Pavlov began, "in contrast with the United States." In the American system, the president acting by himself can key the order to alert and launch nuclear weapons. The Soviet system was multileveled, with built-in checks and balances. At the leadership level it was a four-key system; the president, the minister of defense, and the chief of the general staff accounted for three *Chegets,* and any one of three commanders in chief of Soviet strategic forces (the strategic rocket forces, the Air Force, or the Navy) accounted for the fourth. The three top leaders, their *Chegets* linked through the Kavkaz national-leadership network, had to act together to generate one combined code. That code in turn had to be combined with a code keyed into the system down the line by at least one of the three commanders in chief (CICs). A concurring CIC could authorize the alerting of only his own forces in concert with the top leadership. If he decided not to do so, then no authorization code would be generated for those forces.

"Under the conditions present during the coup," Blair told the subcommittee, "the top leaders could not have bypassed these senior commanders. . . . I think it is fairly widely known that all three of the senior commanders decided among themselves to disobey any launch orders from the coup plotters. . . . And so this decision on the part of the three senior commanders categorically ruled out the possibility of a Soviet strategic attack." Gennady Yanayev, the drunken vice president, could not have used Gorbachev's *Cheget,* which required for its operation a personal identification code number that only Gorbachev knew. Nor did Yanayev seek a *Cheget* of his own on his presumed authority as Gorbachev's successor; the coup was focused on politics internal to the Soviet Union, not on the wider world. Had Yanayev done so, Blair said, the officers of the general staff, who were loyal to Gorbachev, would probably not have provided him with one. Indeed, once Gorbachev's *Cheget* was deactivated, the other two *Chegets* in the hands of Yazov and Moiseyev were useless, since all three were necessary to key a code; the general staff had therefore followed protocol and deactivated them as well.

So the worldwide concern that the coup leaders had stolen Gorbachev's codes and thus taken control of the Soviet nuclear arsenal was misinformed. Ironically, Gorbachev himself seems to have started the rumor when he complained to the Russian delegation that rescued him that the plotters had taken his *Cheget.* They hadn't, of course. They had cut him off from communication with it, after which the teams that operated it on his behalf, following protocol, had shut it down and erased its memory. Pavlov, speaking of the coup, acknowledged "that the situation that occurred had not been simulated before the system was set up." Nevertheless, he said, it prevented "an unauthorized use of nuclear weapons."

One other action, by the CIC of Soviet strategic rocket forces, General Y. P. Maksimov, served to alert U.S. intelligence that Soviet nuclear forces were under control during the coup: Maksimov ordered his SS-25 mobile ICBMs driven from their forest deployments back into their sheds, lowering their level of combat readiness. *The Washington Post* reported at the time, citing government sources, that the garrisoning of the SS-25s "was a significant source of reassurance to the Bush administration during the three-day Kremlin power struggle." Bruce Blair told me he learned about the SS-25s "in virtually real time from a source at NSA"—the U.S. National Security Agency. "Together we surmised that returning the missiles to garrison was a normal security measure associated with any emergency situation that didn't involve an external threat of imminent attack." Blair believes the lowering of alert status "almost certainly" also applied to all Soviet strategic rocket forces, including silo-based missiles. That change, however, would not have been detectable from overhead as moving the SS-25s was.

The Soviet nuclear command-and-control system incorporated much more security than the four-key protocol at the top. If it was designed to centralize control of the Soviet nuclear arsenal to a much greater degree than its American counterpart, it was also structured to limit control by any single individual or faction, reflecting the political reality that power in the old Soviet Union was distributed across the Politburo, the Party, the military, and the military-industrial complex, and was acquired and lost not by democratic process but by violence and coups d'état.

For the Senate subcommittee, Pavlov reviewed how the several levels of the Soviet control system worked together:

Let me describe . . . one possible scenario of attack under the conditions of the coup. The early warning system detects a missile attack and sends signals to the subsystems that assess the threat. It is a process that immediately involves the president of the country, the minister of defense, chief of the general staff and the commanders in chief of the three branches of strategic nuclear forces.

Then the chief of the general staff and commanders in chief of strategic nuclear forces form a command and send it down to the subordinate units. In essence, this command is meant to inform troops and weapons systems about a possible nuclear attack, and this command is called a preliminary command.

The preliminary command opens up access by the launch crews to the equipment directly controlling the use of nuclear weapons and also gives them access to the relevant special documentation. However, launch crews do not [yet] have the full right to use the equipment of direct control over the use of nuclear weapons.

As a more accurate assessment of the situation is made, a message is received from the early warning systems confirming the fact of nuclear attack, and the decision to use nuclear weapons may be made at that point. It can be carried out according to a two-stage process.

The first stage of this two-stage process, Pavlov continued, once again involved the top leadership in a political decision—whether or not to generate a "permission command" that would be sent to the CICs. Then, during the second stage, the CICs and the chief of the general staff would decide as military leaders whether or not to generate a "direct command" ordering launch crews to fire their weapons. Even then, the direct command had to pass through an ordeal of what Pavlov called "special processing by technical and organizational means to verify its authenticity." Each of these actions had time limits, and if the time for an action expired, the blocking system that normally prevented weapons from being launched automatically reactivated.

Cumbersome as the Soviet system seemed from their descriptions, Blair pointed out, it was "actually devised . . . to streamline the command system to ensure that they could release nuclear weapons within the time frame of a ballistic missile attack launched by the United States, that is to say, within 15 to 30 minutes." And despite its complexity, Blair added, a nuclear launch by the coup leaders might still have been possible had they persuaded the general staff to issue Yanayev a *Cheget* and had one or more of the CICs gone along. "There is an important lesson here," Blair concluded. "No system of safeguards can reliably guard against misbehavior at the very apex of government, in any government. There is no adequate answer to the question, 'Who guards the guards?' "

THE SECURITY OF THE entire Soviet nuclear arsenal worried Nunn as he returned to Washington from Moscow in the days after the coup. The unguarded guards would multiply if the Soviet Union fractured into individual republics, which it appeared to be on the verge of doing, and if those governments took control of the nuclear weapons on their soil. Ukraine declared its independence on 24 August, Belarus the next day, Moldova two days after that. Other republics soon followed. Of some twenty-seven thousand total Soviet nuclear weapons—bombs, warheads, and artillery shells—the majority were bunkered in Russia. But in Ukraine, besides a small fleet of bombers with bombs and cruise missiles, there were 176 missile silos housing intercontinental ballistic missiles (ICBMs) loaded with a total of 1,240 half-megaton warheads, each capable of destroying a large city. Belarus deployed 81 mobile ICBMs with single half-megaton warheads—"sufficient to eradicate Europe and the United States," the country's first president, Stanislav Shushkevich, told me. In Kazakhstan 104 silo-based ICBMs carried 10 half-megaton warheads each; Kazakhstan also had forty bombers. Tactical nuclear weapons were stored in most of the Soviet Union's republics—more than 2,000 in Belarus alone. Ukraine and Kazakhstan would each inherit more nuclear weapons than those in the arsenals of either Britain, France, or China. The Democratic senator from Georgia had work to do.

SIX MANY LITTLE MONSTERS

S AM NUNN'S GRANDFATHER fought in the Civil War. People find that hard to believe, he says, but his father, Samuel Augustus Nunn, Sr., was fifty-one when Sam was born, in 1938. Nunn senior was a lawyer and part-time farmer who had trained and worked as a pharmacist to pay his way through night law school. He'd been a member of the state board of education and a Georgia legislator, and for the first eight years of Sam's life he was mayor of the small town of Perry, Georgia, Sam's birthplace, one hundred miles southeast of Atlanta. Samuel Augustus Nunn grew peanuts, cotton, soybeans, corn, pecans, and sorghum on his farm, but his great love was purebred cattle, a hobby among Southern gentlemen in those days—"We never made any money on them," Sam Nunn notes. Sam grew up around farming, lawyering, politics, and small-town life. He participated in 4-H, the Future Farmers of America, and Scouting, and played high-school basketball well enough to be offered scholarships to several small colleges around the state. He preferred Georgia Tech, which had an accelerated undergraduate program for students going on to professional schools, and when the Tech coach encouraged him he registered there without a scholarship and played freshman basketball.

"My father was in very bad health by then," Sam Nunn recalls, "and I knew the clock was ticking. I wanted to be a lawyer. I wanted to get my military service done as quickly as possible because I wanted to go to law school, and I also wanted to go to Washington." Nunn's great-uncle was Carl Vinson, who had been a member of the U.S. House of Representatives since 1914 and for many years was chairman of the House Armed Services Committee. "He had said to me that if I ever wanted to come to Washington to work for him for a few months or a couple of years to let him know, so I had that very much on my mind." Nunn finished Georgia Tech in three years, trained for six months in the Coast Guard Reserve, and got back to Georgia in time to start law school at Emory University in early 1960. In those days student lawyers took their bar exams before they graduated; when Nunn finished law school, in June 1962, he was ready to look into Washington.

His Washington experience, as a young lawyer on the staff of the House Armed Services Committee, only lasted nine months, because by then his mother needed help with family affairs, but it set him on the course of working on military issues, particularly nuclear policy, which he pursued throughout his Senate career. One day in October 1962 the committee counsel asked if Nunn would replace him at the last minute on an Air Force–sponsored tour of NATO installations. Nunn at twenty-four had never been out of the country and jumped at the chance. The first week of the tour was uneventful. The next two weeks were consumed by the Cuban Missile Crisis:

Everybody at NATO, including me, had Top Secret clearances, so we were briefed every day by the Air Force, shown pictures every day. Right at the peak of the crisis, when it looked like the world was going up in smoke, at a dinner with top-ranking Air Force people at Ramstein Air Base in Germany, I happened to be sitting next to the commander of U.S. Air Forces Europe. His responsibilities included what's called forward-based air, the first planes that would deliver a nuclear package against the Soviet Union in the event of war. The Soviets knew that, so the planes and their bases were also the first Soviet targets. In the course of the dinner, he told me that he had something like a minute and a half to get the planes off the ground if he got the orders. He had all the pilots sitting in their planes; they knew their mission would be one-way. That made a permanent impression on me. I recognized how serious it was, I realized the importance of warning time and the absence of warning time and the terrible, terrible stress of short decision times when the whole world is at stake.

Nunn practiced law in Perry through the 1960s. In 1968 he won election to the Georgia state legislature. He intended to run next for the U.S. House, but the death of Georgia's Senator Richard Russell, in 1971, opened up one of Georgia's Senate seats and Nunn won it in 1972, when he was thirty-four. "I said to the people of Georgia even during the primary that my goal was to get on the Senate committee on armed services. When I won the primary, I asked Uncle Carl, who had retired in 1965, to go to Washington with me. He was about ninety-three then. He didn't like to fly. So we got on the train and went up to Washington and we called on several of the senators he knew. They all said they would help me get on the Senate committee, which they did."

A second trip to NATO, this time as a freshman senator, left a further imprint on Nunn of concern about nuclear command and control. The chairman of the Senate committee on armed services, John Stennis, asked the young senator in 1972 to inspect NATO for the committee. Nunn focused on storage and deployment sites for the thousands of tactical nuclear weapons that the U.S. shared with its NATO allies in Europe. "I remember very well," he said later, "visiting with U.S. generals who explained to me that all of our tactical nuclear weapons were secure. Everything was wonderful. We had perfect security. There was no problem." Unfortunately for the generals, a sergeant in one of the bunker complexes where the weapons were stored surreptitiously passed Nunn a note when they shook hands. Nunn pocketed the note and read it afterward in private. It asked the senator to meet the sergeant at his barracks that evening. Nunn did. "He and three or four of his fellow sergeants related a horror story to me, a story of a demoralized military, a story of drug abuse, alcohol abuse, a story of U.S. soldiers actually guarding tactical nuclear weapons while they were stoned on drugs. The sergeants thought that it would take no more than a group of six to eight well-trained terrorists to gain control over one of our tactical nuclear compounds in the middle of Western Europe. The horror stories went on and on for over two hours. I came out of that session thoroughly shaken and determined to do something about the matter."

What Nunn did about the matter was to take it up with President Gerald Ford's secretary of defense, James Schlesinger. Demoralization wasn't the only problem Nunn had found in Europe; another was the forward positioning of NATO's tactical nuclear weapons. Nunn was concerned that NATO would ask that the weapons be released for use at the outset of even a conventional conflict with the Soviet Union—so that they wouldn't be overrun by Soviet forces and because the NATO leadership assumed a presidential authorization would take three or four days. The solution Schlesinger proposed for both problems was reducing the number of forward-based tactical nuclear weapons in Europe. According to the American diplomat James Goodby, however, Henry Kissinger (at that time Ford's national security adviser) judged that "withdrawal of significant numbers of nuclear weapons from the Federal Republic of Germany would leave so few deployed there that they would become an easy prey for antinuclear activists seeking to make West Germany a nuclear-free zone." Ford agreed; he found Schlesinger condescending and difficult in any case, and soon asked for his resignation, replacing him with the hawkish Donald Rumsfeld. The tactical weapons, all seven thousand of them, stayed in Europe.

Nunn's tour of NATO left him convinced, he said, that "we had a major problem, one that grew out of the psychological trauma of the Vietnam War, and it was a problem that was not being acknowledged." He worked the problem of a deeply demoralized military further in the eight years after Vietnam when he chaired the Armed Services' manpower subcommittee. That experience, in turn, prepared him to recognize the even deeper demoralization that he saw in the Soviet military in the aftermath of the August 1991 coup. "The problems we had," he told me, "were based on Vietnam and getting out. The problem they had was that their whole way of life, the system they had believed in for seventy-four years, had come apart. I had spent all that time on the manpower subcommittee understanding that when the military has been demoralized, not only conventional capabilities are at risk but also nuclear capabilities. The two were connected." When he returned to Washington from Moscow in early September, he concluded that the Soviet Union was in great peril. "In particular, I believed that we needed to do everything we could to help the Soviet authorities gain control and keep control over their nuclear weapons."

While Nunn was in Moscow, his counterpart in the House of Representatives, Wisconsin Democrat Les Aspin, an economist and the chairman of the House Armed Services Committee, had publicly proposed allocating a billion dollars from the Defense Department budget to help feed the Soviet people that winter. "Civil war in a country with thirty thousand nuclear weapons," Aspin announced to the media on 28 August, "is too grim a prospect to contemplate." He called his humanitarian aid package "another form of defense spending. It is defense by different means." Secretary of Defense Dick Cheney disagreed. He called the proposal "foolish" and "a serious mistake." Cheney said he didn't foresee a situation, "certainly [not] under current circumstances, where we would be prepared to write out large checks or send large amounts of cash to the Soviet Union." President George H. W. Bush called the Aspin proposal "premature." He wasn't going to "cut into the muscle of defense of this country," he told the press at his compound in Kennebunkport, Maine, on

2 September, "in a kind of an instant sense of budgetary gratifi-
cation so that we can go over and help somebody when the needs
aren't clear and when we have requirements that transcend historic concerns about the Soviet Union."

Nunn felt the same urgency about helping the Soviets secure
their nuclear arsenals as Aspin did about preventing social
chaos. They got together. To prepare the way, Nunn published
an op-ed in *The Washington Post* on 15 September laying out
his proposal "to assist the Soviet Union and the republics to
dismantle the Soviet military-industrial complex and apply its
vast resources to civilian needs." Aspin, for his part, released a
white paper that reviewed his argument for immediate humanitarian relief. (It also offered the earliest statement I have seen of
the idea that nuclear terrorists might not be deterrable the way
nations are believed to be, an idea that would emerge to importance after the World Trade Center and Pentagon terror attacks
of 11 September 2001.) The problem for their joint effort, Nunn
explained, was that "both the House and the Senate had already
passed the defense authorization and appropriation bills. Our
committees were already in conference on our respective defense
authorization bills. Les and I decided to do something very
unusual. We decided to try to put his humanitarian aid package
and my concerns about weapons of mass destruction together
in a conference initiative, even though nothing of this nature
appeared in either the House or the Senate bill."

IN THE MEANTIME, Bush had decided on an alleviation of his
own, a unilateral initiative that may have been the finest act of
his presidency. He recognized its importance and called it "the
broadest and most comprehensive change in U.S. nuclear strategy since the early 1950s." During a discussion among principals
at a National Security Council meeting on 5 September 1991,
Cheney, National Security Adviser Brent Scowcroft, and the Joint
Chiefs of Staff chairman, Colin Powell, each contributed ideas

for reducing the U.S. nuclear arsenal in response to the diminished threat that the beleaguered Soviet Union seemed to present. Afterward, Scowcroft refined the ideas into a package.

"Cheney's distaste for negotiated arms control," he recalled, "together with several issues relating to tactical nuclear weapons, gave me an idea. Perhaps we could take advantage of the situation to solve a number of tactical-nuclear-weapons questions at the same time." NATO tactical weapons on German soil were now superfluous as well as dangerous, since East and West Germany had reunited. The presence of tactical weapons aboard U.S. Navy ships caused problems with countries such as Japan and New Zealand that refused to allow nuclear-armed ships to enter their ports. And although South Korea wanted the U.S. to withdraw its nuclear weapons, Scowcroft had been reluctant to recommend doing so without the camouflage of other such removals, "concerned that the North might take our actions as the beginning of a U.S. withdrawal." (One analyst would call the Korean removals "largely a gesture," since U.S. nuclear submarines could always stand offshore with their devastating arsenals of ballistic missiles.) The sum of all these issues, Scowcroft concluded, "led me to suggest that we unilaterally declare we were getting rid of all tactical nuclear weapons (except air-delivered ones)."

Bush liked the idea but asked Scowcroft to review it with Cheney. Cheney was predictably skeptical. He signed on only when Scowcroft agreed that a large share of the tactical weapons to be withdrawn would not be dismantled but kept in reserve. Across September, Cheney and Powell moved the new initiatives through the Pentagon. When they were ready for public presentation, Bush sent Gorbachev a letter about them and followed up with a phone call. He announced them from the Oval Office in a speech to the nation on the evening of 27 September.

With the changes in the Soviet Union, Bush said, he was "directing that the United States eliminate its entire worldwide inventory of ground-launched short-range, that is, theater nuclear weapons." Nuclear artillery shells and short-range ballistic-missile warheads would be shipped home, although air-delivered nuclear weapons would remain in Europe because they were "essential to NATO's security." The U.S. would withdraw all tactical nuclear weapons from its surface ships and attack submarines and from land-based naval aircraft. Tomahawk nuclear cruise missiles would come off ships and submarines, as would bombs from aircraft carriers. "The bottom line," Bush said, "is that under normal circumstances, our ships will not carry tactical nuclear weapons." Many of the withdrawn weapons would be destroyed, the president added, but Cheney would get his reserve: "Those remaining will be secured in central areas where they would be available if necessary in a future crisis."

There was more. The Strategic Air Command would immediately stand down its fleet of bombers, grounding a potent symbol of the high Cold War. ICBMs destined for destruction under the Strategic Arms Reduction Treaty (START) that Bush and Gorbachev had signed in July 1991 would be taken off alert as well and destroyed under an accelerated schedule once START was ratified. The huge U.S. Peacekeeper missile, seventy feet long and weighing almost two hundred thousand pounds, capable of carrying ten warheads and delivering them with unparalleled accuracy on ten different targets, would be cancelled in its mobile mode, although the silo-based model would continue to be deployed. Bush also asked "that the U.S. and the Soviet Union seek early agreement to eliminate from their inventories all ICBMs with multiple warheads," which he called "the single most unstable part of our nuclear arsenals." A nuclear short-range attack missile then under development would be cancelled. Command-and-control systems, then duplicated by each service, would be combined into a new U.S. Strategic Command. To all these proposals, Bush added appeals to the Soviet Union for a comparable response. A week later, Gorbachev responded enthusiastically with proposals of his own. "There were some differences in our positions," Bush wrote, "but on balance it was very positive and forthcoming."

One reason for eliminating U.S. tactical nuclear weapons was to give Gorbachev cover for removing at least tactical weapons from the increasing number of Soviet republics that were declaring their independence in the wake of the August coup. By the time of the coup, tactical weapons had already been quietly removed to the Soviet Union from Eastern Europe. Removing the weapons from former Soviet republics to Russia would take longer, until summer 1992. Bruce Blair described the process:

> Prior to shipment to Russia, each warhead was mechanically disabled to preclude the possibility of a nuclear explosion, and no more than two warheads were carried in each rail car. When trucks were used, each vehicle was loaded with one warhead. A convoy was heavily guarded using air cover and armored personnel carriers between each truck; public roads were closed when more than three warheads were transported. By all accounts the general staff custodians who have supervised the transfer experienced no lapses of security and suffered no serious accidents.

A U.S. government security analyst told Blair that disabling "involved removing tritium bottles from each warhead before shipping them to Russia. . . . The arming and fusing mechanisms on the warheads also could have been readily disabled in the field." (Tritium, a hydrogen isotope, is used to boost the yield of fission weapons; without tritium boosting, the weapons would have low-single-digit kiloton yields.) The care with which the warheads were handled indicates both their value and their great destructiveness. Only by comparison with city-busting strategic weapons are tactical nuclear weapons considered low-yield.

"WE RAN INTO A BUZZ SAW," Les Aspin reports of his and Nunn's unorthodox effort to draw off a billion dollars from the defense budget in conference. "When it was brought up," Nunn told me, "most people were against it." The chairman of the House budget committee, California Democrat Leon Panetta, opposed the amendment out of concern that it would violate the budget agreement then in effect between Congress and the administration. Other legislators feared that drawing on defense money for nondefense purposes would empower Aspin's committee. A special Senate election in Pennsylvania delivered the killing blow: Democrat Harris Wofford, campaigning under the slogan "It's time to take care of our own," successfully upset the expected favorite, the Republican former governor and U.S. attorney general Richard Thornburgh. "The results of that election," Aspin wrote, "were heard in Washington like a thunderclap. . . . Overall, a climate was created in which it was tough for anything that smacked of foreign aid, especially aid to the same people we've been preparing to fight for a couple of generations." Public and private appeals to the Bush administration "for a sign . . . that it supported and would use this authority and these funds" got nowhere; "There was no sign." In mid-November, rather than sink the entire defense budget, Nunn and Aspin withdrew their amendment.

An important influence on Congress's awareness of nuclear-proliferation challenges was a psychiatrist, David Hamburg, who at that time was the president of the Carnegie Corporation, one of the preeminent American private foundations. Hamburg's father, the son of Latvian Jews, had forgone pursuing a career in medicine to work at bringing other family members to America. He was horrified by the Holocaust, which manifested itself in Latvia in mass shootings by S.S. killing squads. Such childhood exposure to violence and rescue motivated Hamburg to study the biology and psychology of stress during his years of research and teaching at Stanford University; when he moved to the Carnegie Corporation, in 1983, he directed its work particularly toward programs for conflict resolution, arms control, and nuclear nonproliferation. It was Carnegie that had sponsored the Aspen Institute conference in Budapest that Sam Nunn had been attending during the August coup.

One day shortly after Nunn and Aspin withdrew their amendment to the defense budget, Senator Richard Lugar, an Indiana Republican interested in arms control, invited Nunn to an informal briefing that Hamburg had arranged. Among those attending were William Perry, a Stanford mathematician and former under secretary of defense for research and engineering, and Ashton Carter, a physicist, Rhodes Scholar, and government adviser who was then the director of the Center for Science and International Affairs (CSIA) at the John F. Kennedy School of Government at Harvard University. Carter and three of his CSIA colleagues had just completed a study for Carnegie, titled "Soviet Nuclear Fission," about controlling the Soviet nuclear arsenal as the country disintegrated. Carter led the briefing. Both senators were impressed with the CSIA's findings. "My response to the Soviet crisis had been a gut instinct," Nunn says. "I hadn't done an analytical product, and Ash had actually done an analytical product. That was enormously helpful."

The great virtue of the CSIA report—Nunn's "analytical product"—was its comprehensiveness. It answered questions about Soviet nuclear command and control—Blair had been a consultant to the study—and proposed approaches to increasing nuclear security, but it also explored which nascent republics would inherit strategic weapons (Russia, Ukraine, Belarus, and Kazakhstan) and explained why only Russia would be prepared to secure them (because "none of the other three republics . . . would alone possess anything like the [Russian] complement of warning systems, command centers and communications systems to perform the key functions of warning, attack assessment and survivable control considered necessary for 'strategic stability' . . . during the Cold War"). It dealt as well with the probable dilemma of nuclear scientists and engineers, of which the Soviet Union had thousands, going unpaid in their isolated secret cities, who might be tempted to sell their services to would-be nuclear powers such as Libya or

Iran: "Like the German rocket scientists who moved west to the United States or east to the Soviet Union [after the Second World War] to staff the new superpower missile programs, technical personnel associated with the Soviet nuclear weapons program may look outside the Soviet Union's territories for the money, status and reputation to which they are accustomed." It even answered a cynical question that Scowcroft and Cheney both had raised: why allowing one large nuclear power to fracture into multiple small nuclear powers would not be to the United States's advantage (because multiple nuclear powers would be a danger to global peace and stability, in which the U.S. had a strong interest; they would increase the risk of nuclear use spilling over into Europe; individual countries might be willing to transfer weapons to other settings "such as the Middle East"; and they might directly challenge the U.S. itself). In *Soviet Nuclear Fission,* Carter and his colleagues at Harvard had provided Nunn and Lugar with a detailed guide to containing the nuclear arsenal of a failing superpower.

"I told Lugar, 'I've got to have a strong Republican horse here,' " Nunn recalled of that first meeting. "There had been protests against the earlier effort on both sides, but seventy-five percent of it was Republican. So Lugar and I joined together and said, 'How can we reconstruct this? How can we put this back together?' " They agreed to work together to revive the program of support that had failed to pass muster as a conference amendment. Aspin agreed to work toward legislation on the House side as well.

The two senators decided to expose their colleagues to Carter's authoritative presentation. Invitations went out to twenty senators for a breakfast meeting with Carter on Thursday, 21 November, one week before Thanksgiving. Sixteen senators showed up. "There was a remarkable consensus," Lugar told the Senate the following Monday, "that we needed to rise above the so-called thirty-second sound bite mentality and work to initiate emergency legislation to deal with the nuclear dangers associated with the disintegration of the Soviet Union." Twenty senators had collaborated through the weekend to write the legislation; Nunn and Lugar introduced it that morning as an amendment to an unrelated bill. The senators had scaled down their funding request to $500 million and had made the funding discretionary: Bush could authorize spending it as he saw fit.

Aspin in the meantime collaborated in the House with Missouri Democrat Richard Gephardt and Indiana Democrat Lee Hamilton to move a similar measure through to timely passage. Aspin's primary concern continued to be humanitarian aid, he told a press conference:

> Basically, what we're looking for is to transport food. We've got some food. The U.S. military's got some food. You ought to know what the U.S. military's got in food. The U.S. military, in preparation for Operation Desert Storm, bought six months' worth of food and medicine. The war lasted five weeks. I mean, have we got food and medicine available. All we need is the authority to move it. . . . MREs [meals ready to eat]. MREs. This will be the real test of how hungry they are. The real test of how severe the winter is in the Soviet Union will be to see whether they eat those damn MREs.

The Senate passed the Soviet Nuclear Threat Reduction Act late on Tuesday afternoon, 26 November, by a vote of 88 to 8. Compared to the defeat of his earlier effort, Nunn told me proudly, he'd never seen so many Senate votes reversed so quickly. The House passed a similar measure the same day, and the two versions were reconciled on Wednesday, just before the Thanksgiving recess. The act provided for allotting $400 million from the fiscal year 1992 defense budget for dismantling nuclear and chemical weapons and $100 million for humanitarian relief, primarily military transportation of food and medicine. It was "a start," Aspin faintly praised the commitment in a speech on

16 December, "a lot better than nothing," but he worried that it fell far short of the Soviet Union's needs in both areas.

ONE BUSH ADMINISTRATION OFFICIAL who did not share the prevailing executive branch reluctance to provide hospice care to the Soviet Union in its final days and support to its disoriented survivors was Secretary of State James Baker. At the Middle East Peace Conference in Madrid in late October 1991, Baker had taken the measure of the Soviet Union's terminal condition in Gorbachev's uncharacteristic disorganization. The Soviet leader, Baker thought, "was as unfocused as I had ever seen him. It wasn't his mind; that was as sharp as ever. Rather, it was the overwhelming complexity of the multiple challenges beating down on him. Gorbachev would begin discussing the Middle East, but then would quite naturally become distracted by his own internal problems and veer off to talk about them. . . . He seemed like a drowning man, looking for a life preserver. It was hard not to feel sorry for him."

A key test of the impending breakup was a popular referendum endorsing Ukrainian independence scheduled for 1 December. In a controversial speech to the Ukrainian Supreme Soviet on 1 August, before the coup, Bush had warned the legislators about breaking away from Moscow. "We will maintain the strongest possible relationship with the Soviet government of President Gorbachev," Bush had said. "Freedom is not the same as independence. Americans will not support those who seek independence in order to replace a far-off tyranny with a local despotism. They will not aid those who promote a suicidal nationalism based upon ethnic hatred." The columnist William Safire had dubbed it the "Chicken Kiev speech," much to Bush's annoyance. Later, when I came to know one of the key players in the Soviet Union's final days, Stanislav Shushkevich, the chairman of the Belarusian Supreme Soviet, I asked him about it. "I think Bush was realizing that the nuclear monster could split up into many little monsters," Shushkevich told me. "I also was an admirer of Gorbachev, but he had done everything he could do by then."

By late November a vote endorsing Ukrainian independence was considered a near certainty. In meetings to discuss whether and when to award the new nation U.S. diplomatic recognition, Baker wrote, Cheney pushed for immediate recognition, because "Dick wanted to see the Soviet Union dismantled, felt Ukraine was the key and, moreover, believed that [if the United States got in] 'on the ground floor' with recognition, the Ukrainian leadership would be more inclined to a positive relationship with us." Baker's position was more nuanced. "I wanted to be sure the Soviet Union was dismantled *peacefully,* and that meant, above all, preventing a Russian-Ukrainian clash." Recognition was also a powerful card to play, Baker thought, "and I wanted to play this card only when we had received specific assurances from each republic on issues such as nuclear command and control." Baker's nightmare, frequently expressed, was what he called "Yugoslavia with nukes," referring to the messy and ultimately bloody breakup of the Yugoslavian composite state into warring components.

The Ukrainian referendum went as expected; more than 90 percent of Ukrainian voters chose independence. By then Bush had decided on delayed recognition, Baker writes, "though we all agreed that meant weeks, not months." As the end neared, events accelerated. At a hunting lodge near Brest in western Belarus on 8 December, Shushkevich, Boris Yeltsin, and the newly elected Ukrainian president, Leonid Kravchuk, met and decided without Gorbachev's knowledge to dissolve the Soviet Union and replace it with a new entity called the Commonwealth of Independent States. Kazakhstan's leader, Nursultan Nazarbayev, was insulted when he learned he'd been left out of the discussion, but after appropriate apologies he joined the new commonwealth. To Gorbachev it felt like another coup. By then Shevardnadze and Gorbachev's close adviser Alexander Yakovlev, out of friendship and respect, had returned to his side after their earlier resignations. "Shevardnadze would leave his apartment at night," Baker wrote of that final month, "and go spend long hours with Gorbachev, just to talk."

A speech Baker delivered at Princeton University on 12 December, intended to be a statement of American foreign policy in relation to the new republics, thus became something of an elegy for a reformed adversary dying from a mortal wound. Baker declared that the two nations had become "partners, no longer competitors, across the globe." They had been partners in facilitating the reunification of Germany, he said, partners in freeing up Central and Eastern Europe, partners in reducing both conventional and nuclear weapons, partners in ending regional conflicts all over the world, in reversing the Iraqi invasion of Kuwait and promoting peace in the Middle East, "partners, in short, in ending the Cold War."

In his State of the Union address, Baker's boss would soon claim, "By the grace of God, America won the Cold War." With more delicacy, Baker praised the farmer's son who had initiated the transformation and opened his country to the world: "These achievements were possible primarily because of one man: Mikhail Gorbachev. The transformations we are dealing with now would not have begun were it not for him. His place in history is secure, for he helped end the Cold War peacefully, and for that, the world is grateful and respectful."

But the Cold War, Baker continued, "left tens of thousands of weapons littering the Soviet Union, and it created a massive military-industrial complex. We must work with Russia, Ukraine, Kazakhstan, Belarus, the other republics, and any common entity to help them pursue responsible security policies. And that means first and foremost destroying and controlling the most dangerous vestiges of the Cold War: weapons of mass destruction." Exchanges had already begun "between our experts on nuclear weapons safety, security, and dismantlement and their Soviet counterparts," and the process would accelerate in the coming weeks. The administration was "prepared to draw upon the $400 million appropriated by Congress" to assist in the demolition. ("The President is a little late," Aspin critiqued Baker's declaration a few days later. "If he had embraced these notions three or four weeks ago when we were struggling in Congress, he would have come out with twice as much money and much more flexibility for action on his part. But better late than never.")

Traveling to Moscow three days after his Princeton speech, Baker met separately with Yeltsin and Gorbachev and quickly understood that the Soviet military had shifted its allegiances to Yeltsin. Yeltsin assured Baker that the nuclear weapons dispersed across the fracturing empire would remain under central command. To that end, after a meeting on 21 December in Alma-Ata, the capital of Kazakhstan, where seven other new republics—Armenia, Azerbaijan, Kyrgyzstan, Moldova, Tajikistan, Turkmenistan, and Uzbekistan—added their weight to the new commonwealth, the four initiators of the breakup were connected into the Kavkaz national leadership network—but three of the four would only be observers. "We received the equipment that was called 'Metal,'" Shushkevich told me, "which would connect those people, and there was always a man around us carrying it. We only tried it once and it worked. But it was all a farce—it was all hypocritical—all those weapons of course were controlled by Yeltsin, which we understood. And you Americans also understood it was a pretense."

While the president of Russia was to be first among equals in controlling the former Soviet Union's strategic nuclear weapons, the weapons themselves were physically distributed across the four new republics and would become their legal property when Soviet sovereignty dissolved at the end of the year. In his Princeton speech, Baker had called on the new states to ratify and implement the START agreement and adhere to the Nuclear Non-Proliferation Treaty as non-nuclear-weapons states, but how could they meet the requirements of the treaty with nuclear weapons in their possession, based on their soil, regardless of who controlled them? It was soon obvious to Baker that the only practical solution to the problem was that Belarus, Ukraine, and

Kazakhstan should give up their nuclear arsenals to Russia. Making that happen was a problem of diplomacy, and in those final days, before the new states shouldered free from the cracked shell of the old Bolshevik despotism, Baker prepared to set to work.

IT WOULD HAVE HELPED Baker's cause had Dick Cheney's Department of Defense welcomed mutual verification. Both the United States and the Soviet Union had pledged to dismantle thousands of nuclear weapons. In previous arms-control agreements, a suspicious United States had demanded "effective verification" that Soviet weapons were actually being destroyed. This time around, the Bush administration seemed prepared to sidestep the issue and take the new republics on trust. Bush had not mentioned verification in his unilateral-weapons-reduction speech of 27 September, and a fact sheet the Defense Department released the next day had announced plainly, "We do not envision any formal verification regime, although we are willing to discuss confidence-building measures with the Soviets." This omission seemed distinctly odd to two staff members of the American nonprofit Natural Resources Defense Council (NRDC), researcher Christopher Paine and physicist Thomas Cochran, who had already begun meeting with Soviet scientists and leaders concerned with the problem. "The administration was suggesting," they wrote of the fact sheet's dismissal of verification, "as the Soviet Union fell apart, that a mere 'exchange of information' would suffice to establish the whereabouts and eventual elimination of about 15,000 nonstrategic Soviet nuclear weapons . . . deployed throughout the republics."

In Moscow in mid-December, just as Baker was passing through, Paine and Cochran participated as members of a team representing the NRDC and the Federation of American Scientists in discussions with a small crowd of former Soviet Union (FSU) and Russian officials to explore how dismantling could be verified without exposing any secrets of weapons design. From Moscow, the team, which included current and former weapons scientists from three U.S. national laboratories, went on to Kiev to hold similar discussions with the Ukrainians.

The Americans had come prepared to discuss methods of securely tagging and sealing warheads to prevent their diversion from a dismantling facility, including "fingerprinting" the unique markings on an arbitrary area of the warhead casing using cellulose tape, applying super-adhesive bar codes and tamper-revealing sealing tape, and locking the warhead casing with fiber-optic seals. They also outlined a method of determining if a specific warhead's fissile materials, which are slightly radioactive, had been removed by recording each warhead's unique radiation signature and comparing it to the radiation signature of a standard reference warhead. To demonstrate the technologies, Cochran, keeping up a running commentary in his flat Virginia drawl, fingerprinted the back of his Timex watch and simulated rapid bar-code scanning of a warhead casing from several feet away using a handheld bar-code scanner.

If my personal experience of carrying American technology into the FSU six months later is relevant, Cochran's scanning equipment would have been intriguing even to the scientists among the FSU representatives watching his demonstrations. I delivered a laptop computer to my Russian research assistant, a geologist, in June 1992 to facilitate communicating with him by e-mail; dazzled, he characterized the obsolete laptop as "science fiction" and said neither he nor his many scientist friends had ever seen one. I also gave him a printer and a fax machine; we searched all over Moscow for fax paper before we found a roll at a new office-supply store on the outskirts of the city. Thereafter my assistant, who lived with his wife and small daughter in a single room in a communal apartment, kept his office equipment hidden under his bed, fearing he would lose his life at the hands of thieves intent on stealing such rare and valuable machines.

Whatever the other delegates thought of Cochran's presentations, the general in charge of maintaining and securing what was still formally the Soviet nuclear arsenal, Sergei Zelentsov, insisted adamantly that only designated Soviet military personnel would be allowed near his nuclear weapons. The Ukrainians, including the deputy chairman of the Ukrainian parliament, were willing to consider tagging and sealing the soon-to-be Ukrainian weapons they would ship to Russia for dismantling, but only if the United States was prepared to reciprocate by allowing U.S. weapons designated for dismantling under the START agreement and the Bush-Gorbachev unilateral agreements to be tagged and sealed in the presence of Ukrainian inspectors. The executive summary of the report the NRDC subsequently issued berated the Bush administration for choosing secrecy over arms control:

> Throughout its first three years, the Bush Administration has sought to shield the U.S. nuclear establishment from rigorous inspection by adopting a posture approaching benign neglect toward the disposition of the Soviet Union's nuclear stockpile and production complex. We are paying for that posture today, as one need only reflect on how different the current situation would be if the Reagan-Bush administrations had heeded the congressional call, beginning in 1983, for a verified fissile material production cutoff followed by verified warhead dismantlement and demilitarization of the removed fissile materials under international safeguards.
>
> Today there would be hundreds of U.S. and international inspectors all over the republics of the FSU; Soviet plutonium production reactors would be shut down; tritium* production reactors would be closed under bilateral safeguards; fissile material components of weapons retired without replacement would be stored under bilateral safeguards; and all civil reactors, nuclear fuel cycle facilities and civil stocks of fissile material would be under international safeguards.

*Multistage thermonuclear weapons ("hydrogen bombs") use plutonium, highly enriched uranium (HEU), tritium, and solid lithium deuteride-tritide (LiDT) as their nuclear fuel. Plutonium fuels and tritium boosts the yield of the primary stage, which is essentially a small atomic bomb; HEU and LiDT fuel the secondary stage—the hydrogen fusion component.

Throughout the 1990s, as post–Cold War states moved toward reducing and eliminating their nuclear arsenals, the resistance of the U.S. government to submitting its nuclear-weapons complex to the same transparency standards that it demanded of other states complicated and delayed the great disarming that ought to have followed the resolution of the superpower conflict.

When the American delegation had arrived in Moscow, its members had learned to their embarrassment that their in-country expenses had been covered by the International CHETEK Corporation, "a private venture set up to market nuclear explosions for waste disposal," in the words of the NRDC report. It had been too late to change the arrangements, but the Americans had resented being put in the position of seeming to endorse a private organization that was linked to senior officials of the Soviet Ministry of Atomic Power and Industry (MAPI) and senior weapons scientists at one of the U.S.S.R.'s two major weapons-design laboratories, Arzamas-16.

The notion of nuclear explosives and weapons-design knowledge in private corporate hands, whatever their program, was abhorrent to the Americans. They listened skeptically as Yuri Trutnev, the deputy scientific director of Arzamas-16, described a CHETEK-sponsored scheme to dispose of the three-kilogram plutonium cores that would be removed from the FSU's thousands of nuclear weapons:

> Trutnev . . . presented a plan for using a 100-kiloton deep-underground nuclear explosion to vaporize 20,000 nuclear weapons cores ("pits"), thereby distributing some 62 tons of plutonium in a much larger volume of molten rock. This rock would then vitrify as it cools, immobilizing the plutonium (in theory at least) 2,000 feet below the surface for many thousands of years. Regarding the disposition of the commercially valuable highly-enriched uranium (HEU) components of these "destroyed" warheads, a Russian weapons scientist stated that it would be "a simple matter" to "unscrew" the uranium sec-

ondary stage of the weapons from the plutonium primary stage
before blowing up the latter.

Undetermined in Trutnev's scheme was whether or not so
much vaporized plutonium might solidify in supercritical con-
figurations that would then fission to produce further uncontrolled nuclear explosions, possibly breaching its underground
confinement. The Trutnev proposal was shaped in the old heroic
Soviet mold, except that its main purpose appeared to be to
enrich CHETEK and the government officials allied with it.

Sam Nunn, on the occasion of his visit to Moscow immediately after the August coup, had been invited by his friend
Andrei Kokoshin to meet with what Kokoshin called the
"chambers of commerce" of the various new republics.
According to Nunn, Kokoshin drove him, "in his little tiny
car," to a dacha "way back in the woods" on the outskirts of
Moscow: "I looked out and all these limousines are pulled
up outside. So I go in there and it looked like something out
of Damon Runyon. I mean cigar smoke everywhere, whiskey
bottles everywhere, long-legged women everywhere, and these
guys were all in there *negotiating*. It was the people who were
conducting private enterprise and illegal activities all over the
Soviet Union—technically illegal. Illicit and illegal. This was
the beginnings of the business community in Moscow. The
people who knew about business were the people who had been
doing it, and all of a sudden they could do it legally. We spent
about two hours out there. They wanted to hear from me, but
we mainly listened to them. It was an uneasy meeting, because
all these guys had armed security around them." I asked Nunn
what they told him. "That they were going to do business,"
he said. "The shackles were off. They said, 'We're going to be
unbridled, we're going to do business.' This was, in effect, the
Mob. Kokoshin realized it as the meeting went along. We were
both ready to get the heck out of there." Like Nunn, the American delegation on verification had been offered a glimpse of

the rowdy new Russia that would tumble out of the ruins of the old Soviet Union.

MORE INTERESTING THAN Trutnev's plutonium-disposal nightmare was the question of what to do with the leftover HEU in the thermonuclear weapons, some fifteen kilograms per weapon. Diluted from its weapons-grade enrichment of greater than 90 percent uranium-235 to the enrichment appropriate for commercial power reactors, from 3 to 5 percent, the estimated four thousand thermonuclear warheads that would soon come under Ukraine's ownership and control would be worth about fifteen thousand dollars per kilogram of HEU, or nearly a billion dollars.

The Ukrainians, the American delegation was shocked to learn, were unaware of the treasure of tritium and HEU in their weapons; according to the NRDC report, "one senior official said he had been told that the warheads being removed from Ukraine contained no materials of commercial value." At the Commonwealth of Independent States meeting in Alma-Ata on 21 December, Ukraine, like Belarus and Kazakhstan, had agreed to allow its tactical nuclear weapons to be shipped to Russia for dismantling; Ukraine's 2,200 were supposed to be removed by 1 July 1992, and the Russian Army began removing them before the end of 1991. Five years previously, in April 1986, Ukraine had been the victim of the worst nuclear-reactor explosion in history. The nation was still suffering from the immense burden of cleaning up the Chernobyl disaster, which had strongly influenced Ukrainian public opinion against remaining a nuclear power. When the Ukrainian parliament had first declared its sovereignty, in July 1990, the declaration included a pledge "not to accept, not to produce and not to acquire nuclear weapons." Kravchuk went further at a CIS summit on 30 December 1991 and agreed also to allow the strategic nuclear weapons on Ukrainian territory to be removed to Russia by 31 December 1994, a date the Russian military determined based on its capacity for moving and storing the weapons.

At no time during these various discussions did anyone mention compensating Ukraine for the value of the special materials in the weapons, and Kravchuk and his advisers knew so little about nuclear weapons that they never raised the issue. As the members of the Rada—the Ukrainian parliament—came to learn how valuable the weapons actually were, they realized that the Russians had already swindled Ukraine out of the seven tons of plutonium in the tactical nuclear weapons that Kravchuk had essentially given away (assuming that the plutonium would not be destroyed but would be reserved for eventual civilian use in commercial power reactors). That realization in turn raised parliamentary hackles at the thought of also giving away Ukraine's strategic arsenal with its more immediately marketable HEU. Which may explain Ukraine's rapid turn, across the first months of the new year, from enthusiasm for abandoning its nuclear arsenal to determination to keep it—or, at least, to bargain for its value before allowing it to leave Ukrainian control.

One of the Americans invited to the verification meetings in Moscow and Kiev in mid-December was Thomas L. Neff, a blond, somber MIT physicist who was a specialist in nuclear fuel markets. Neff had watched the Soviet Union's downward spiral with increasing concern for the security of the Soviet nuclear arsenal. "It was immediately apparent," he said later, "that a potential outcome was that the weapons and personnel could be transformed in short order from a well-controlled force to a major weapons-proliferation threat to the world." Sam Nunn had characteristically responded to the crisis by pursuing legislation; Neff responded, he recalled, by looking for a way "to motivate and finance post-Soviet control of nuclear weapons, fissile material and personnel in a country where central authorities might not have the power to do so. It occurred to me that the HEU in surplus weapons has a high value when blended down to enrichment levels usable in civil power reactors. The destruction of weapons and fissile material could be a self-financing process, without cost to the U.S. taxpayer." The U.S. officials he briefed on the idea

Special envoy Donald Rumsfeld met with Iraqi dictator Saddam Hussein in 1984 in an effort to improve relations; arms deliveries followed. (Television image.)

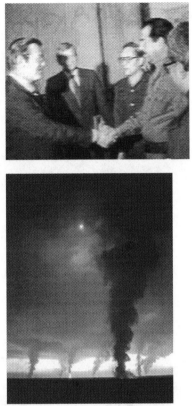

Above: U.S. F-117A Stealth fighter-bombers, nearly invisible to Iraqi radar, led a barrage of new high-tech weapons in the 1991 Persian Gulf War.

Right: Retreating from attacking Kuwait in 1990, Iraqi forces ignited 792 Kuwaiti oil wells that burned out of control for eight months.

With improved weapons and digital and satellite communications, coalition forces pushed kill ratios from 100:1 to 1,000:1—a thousand enemy dead for each coalition soldier killed—heralding a revolution in war.

U.S. bombing of suspicious buildings at the outset of the war destroyed a major Iraqi uranium-enrichment facility.

After the war, U.N. and IAEA inspection teams found evidence of a full-blown Iraqi atomic-bomb program, including the iron core of a large electromagnet used for enriching uranium.

When IAEA inspectors identified the primary Iraqi nuclear-weapons facility at Al Atheer in 1992, they oversaw its complete destruction.

After the dissolution of the U.S.S.R., U.S. diplomat Thomas Graham, Jr., assisted presidents George H. W. Bush and Boris Yeltsin in treaty negotiations. Later he would travel the world negotiating successfully to make the Nuclear Nonproliferation Treaty permanent.

American weapons labs led the way in helping their Russian counterparts secure Soviet nuclear weapons. At their first meeting, Arzamas director Yuli Khariton (left front) told Los Alamos director Sig Hecker, "I've been waiting for this moment for forty years."

Above: With U.S. support, former Soviet states Belarus, Ukraine, and Kazakhstan relinquished their nuclear weapons to Russia and destroyed their missile silos.

Right: In the late 1980s, outcast South Africa secretly built a small arsenal of uranium gun bombs that it stored disassembled in bank vaults.

The South African bombs fitted into ballistic casings for delivery by aircraft

Above: North Korean extraction of plutonium from its Yongbyon nuclear reactor precipitated a crisis with the United States in 1994. (On a later visit, shown here, Sig Hecker, center, inspected the spent-fuel storage pool.)

Left: The 1994 conflict nearly led to war on the Korean peninsula. Former president Jimmy Carter defused the crisis by visiting North Korea and meeting with its leader Kim Il-sung.

Iraq secretly destroyed its nuclear infrastructure but kept no records. Its resistance to inspections intensified after 1995. At the U.N., IAEA head Hans Blix (left) explored the challenge with his 1998 successor, Mohamed ElBaradei.

Before shepherding the Comprehensive Nuclear Test Ban Treaty through U.N. approval, Australian ambassador Richard Butler (right, with foreign minister Gareth Evans) led a 1996 commission on eliminating nuclear weapons. "We could do it in a morning," he said.

Above: Iraqi expulsion of IAEA inspectors in 1998 led to crisis meetings at the U.N. American bombing ended IAEA access, leaving the question of Iraqi nuclear progress seemingly unanswered.

Right: India conducted a series of five nuclear weapons tests in May 1998. Shakti-1, shown here, was supposed to be a hydrogen device, but according to a U.S. study, its hydrogen secondary stage failed to ignite.

Left: Pakistan responded to the Indian tests with a series of six tests in late May; one bomb, detonated in a tunnel, ventilated an entire mountain. (Television image.)

Below: President George W. Bush first received news of planes crashing into New York's World Trade Center during his visit to a grade school in Sarasota, Florida, on the morning of 11 September 2001.

The World Trade Center burning: New York City, 11 September

In the Situation Room at the White House on 11 September, Vice President Dick Cheney worked the phones while National Security Adviser Condoleezza Rice and other staff members advised.

In the rubble of the World Trade Center, President Bush called the nation to arms. Although regime change had been on the table for years, he had not yet decided to invade Iraq.

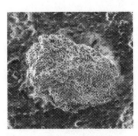

Letters to Congress containing weaponized anthrax spores (magnified here) and a contamination scare at the White House helped change Bush's mind.

Secretary of State Colin Powell highlighted anthrax in presenting to the U.N. the Bush administration's case for invading Iraq.

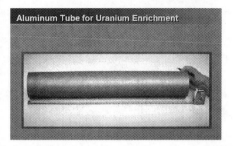

Aluminum Tube for Uranium Enrichment

To win support for its war, the Bush administration spuriously claimed Iraq was developing nuclear weapons. It cited as evidence aluminum tubes, which were supposedly imported to make centrifuges. They were actually casings for artillery rockets.

Left: At the end of formal hostilities, President Bush landed on an American carrier off the coast of California and spoke in front of a banner announcing "Mission Accomplished." Insurgent conflict in Iraq would continue to rage for years.

Below: In Prague in the spring of his presidency, Barack Obama pledged to pursue the elimination of nuclear weapons. "As the only nuclear power to have used a nuclear weapon," he said, "the United States has a moral responsibility to act."

showed little interest. Frustrated by the lack of response, Neff went public in October 1991 in an op-ed essay in *The New York Times*, proposing an exchange: trade former Soviet HEU, diluted down to fuel grade before shipping, for U.S. food and other essential goods. Fissioned in U.S. commercial power reactors, the former Soviet warhead material would never again be available to make weapons. "If the material in each nuclear weapon had commercial value on the order of a half million dollars," Neff explained, "not only would it be watched carefully, but the destruction of it and the uranium fissile material would be expedited. The highly capable scientists and engineers would continue to be supported, reducing the likelihood that they would be forced to sell their talents to other national or sub-national groups."

The MAPI deputy minister Viktor N. Mikhailov, the heavyweight among the various Soviet officials who met with the American delegation in Moscow, had noticed Neff's proposal and explored it with the MIT physicist on a previous visit to Washington. A sardonic, chain-smoking theoretical physicist and imperious Russian nationalist, Mikhailov had come to Washington primarily to sell the idea of U.S. support for a large-scale plutonium-pit storage facility. "We have spent too much just to throw this plutonium away," Mikhailov told the delegation in Moscow in December, dismissing the CHETEK/Trutnev explosive-disposal scheme. "Mikhailov said that the weapons storage depots in Russia were filled to capacity," the NRDC report notes, "and that trains carrying weapons to the depots had been stopped en route." He wanted the entire first Nunn-Lugar appropriation of $400 million for pit storage. Between $10 million and $100 million dollars of the appropriation "would probably be needed for local authorities to spend on civic improvement to ensure acceptance of the plutonium storage facility by the affected population. In contrast to the facility construction itself, a strict accounting of these local funds would be more difficult to maintain, he suggested." Building millions of dollars of bribes and possible kickbacks into his proposal was characteristic of Mikhailov's boldness. Cochran is blunt about Mikhailov. He calls him a crook. Others who came to know the Russian science bureaucrat in the following years believe he saved the Soviet nuclear complex from dangerous and proliferative breakdown. The two characterizations are not necessarily mutually exclusive.

THE FORMER SOVIET UNION was not the only superpower facing the obsolescence of its nuclear-production complex at the end of the Cold War. U.S. Secretary of Energy James Watkins, an admiral and a protégé of the legendary nuclear-submarine pioneer Hyman Rickover, had assumed responsibility for the U.S. production complex in 1989 after Bush recruited him with the blunt question, "Jim, can you clean up this mess?" At a press conference in Washington in December, a policy scholar reported, "Watkins finalized decisions to consolidate the [U.S.] nuclear weapons complex from what was now fifteen production facilities in ten states (itself a diminution from the seventeen sites in twelve states Watkins had inherited) to four production plants in four states (South Carolina, Tennessee, Texas, and Missouri) and a test site in Nevada. . . . 'Nobody likes nuclear bombs,' Watkins told [the] press conference in discussing the post–Cold War DOE. 'We want to get rid of the nuclear complex to the extent we can.' " The statement shocked the U.S. military, the defense industry, and conservative congressmen, who were committed to continuing U.S. nuclear-weapons production. As it turned out, getting rid of the nuclear complex would be easier said than done.

MIKHAIL GORBACHEV DISSOLVED the Soviet Union on Christmas Day 1991, resigning as its president on national television and giving up control of the *Cheget* to Boris Yeltsin. "When I became head of state," the exhausted reformer told the Soviet people, "it was already obvious that there was something wrong in this country." He continued:

We had plenty of everything: land, oil, gas and other natural resources, and God had also endowed us with intellect and talent—yet we lived much worse than people in other industrialized countries and the gap was constantly widening. The reason was apparent even then—our society was stifled in the grip of a bureaucratic command system. Doomed to serve ideology and bear the heavy burden of the arms race, it was strained to the utmost. . . . The country was losing hope. We could not go on living like this. We had to change everything radically.

He had shepherded radical change, he said, dismantling the totalitarian system, breaking through to democratic reforms, introducing a pluralistic economy and land reform, moving toward a free market. Most of all, he reminded the millions who watched him, "An end has been put to the 'Cold War,' the arms race and the insane militarization of our country, which crippled our economy, distorted our thinking and undermined our morals. The threat of a world war is no more."

After his speech Gorbachev called Bush, who described the conversation in his diary:

A second call confirmed that the former Soviet Union would disappear. Mikhail Gorbachev contacted me at Camp David on Christmas morning of 1991. He wished Barbara and me a Merry Christmas, and then he went on to sum up what had happened in his country: the Soviet Union had ceased to exist. He had just been on national TV to confirm the fact, and he had transferred control of Soviet nuclear weapons to the President of Russia. "You can have a very quiet Christmas evening," he said. And so it was over.

The Cold War at least was over. The aftermath—chasing down and securing the weapons and fissile materials left behind, scattered across the eleven time zones of a vast former empire—would demand a long commitment of labor and treasure.

WHEN THE SOVIET UNION broke up into fifteen new states, one nuclear power fragmented into four nuclear powers, each with formidable numbers of strategic nuclear weapons. Russian forces continued to guard and control the weapons, but their legal ownership devolved to the new countries where they were based: Russia, Belarus, Ukraine, and Kazakhstan. Each could keep them or give them up to Russia— or sell them elsewhere. In December 1991, a Kazakh journalist reports,

> Yasser Arafat, leader of the Palestine Liberation Organization, suddenly appeared in Alma-Ata to test the leader of the world's first "nuclear Muslim country." He offered [President] Nazarbayev the role of leading arbiter in the Middle East. Arafat also told Nazarbayev that the war in the Middle East could spread to new countries at any moment, and that Israel's bombs would then fall on the Middle East and Kazakhstan.
>
> Arafat's ambition was transparent: Nazarbayev would gain control of the nuclear arsenal and aim it in whatever direction Arafat desired. But Nazarbayev was not buying; he stressed that although he supported the Palestinians in their struggle to create an independent state, he did not approve of the use of force.

The following month, Iraq also made overtures to Kazakh-stan, requesting permission to send an Iraqi parliamentary leader to meet with the Kazakh parliament. The new government pointedly ignored the request. Nazarbayev told an American diplomat as well that several Middle Eastern countries had offered to buy the 1,040 half-megaton warheads on the 104 SS-18 ICBMs that Kazakhstan had inherited. Nazarbayev had turned down the offers, but they added to his second thoughts about his earlier decision to give up Kazakhstan's share of the former Soviet Union's nuclear arsenal without compensation.

He had announced that decision on 29 August 1991, following a debate in the Kazakh parliament about closing down the main Soviet nuclear test site near Semipalatinsk in northeastern Kazakhstan, where 456 nuclear tests, 116 of them above ground, had severely polluted a large area of the steppe lands. (The test site itself covered seven thousand square miles, an area about the size of Connecticut and Rhode Island together.) "With the support of the nation," Nazarbayev would write of his decision, "we proclaimed a unilateral ban on the inhuman testing of nuclear weapons . . . and declared that our country would always be a territory free of nuclear arms and their testing. . . . It was one of the first independent steps of an independent Kazakhstan." But Kazakhstan, a big country with a small population, lay between Russia on the north and China on the east, a potentially dangerous neighborhood that it was possible to believe a nuclear arsenal might make more secure. And who would pay the millions it would cost to ship all those warheads to Russia and clean up Semipalatinsk? There was even one unexploded warhead lodged in a borehole deep underground at the test site where it had been positioned for a test when Gorbachev declared a moratorium; who would dig the thing out and cart it away?

Of the four new nuclear republics that the dissolution of the Soviet Union had created, only Belarus under Stanislav Shushkevich was fully committed at the outset to nuclear disarmament. All four needed financial help to secure their nuclear arsenals.

In mid-December 1991, U.S. Secretary of State James Baker had flown from Moscow to Alma-Ata to swap U.S. assistance for Kazakhstan's accession to the Nuclear Non-Proliferation Treaty. "If the international community recognizes and accepts Kazakhstan," Nazarbayev had assured him, "we will declare ourselves a non-nuclear state." Baker would learn later, he writes, "that Nazarbayev could . . . string out negotiations for any and every advantage he could find." Next Baker flew to Minsk, where "Shushkevich was at pains to emphasize that Belarus would accept anything we wanted on nuclear weapons. Having lived through the trauma of Chernobyl, Shushkevich felt it was essential to get all nuclear weapons off Belarus territory.* He eagerly sought U.S. expertise for disabling and dismantling purposes, and I pledged that we would supply such." On to Kiev, where, Baker says, "Kravchuk was similarly cooperative." He may have been, but privately the Ukrainians were hatching other plans.

Baker, a shrewd man, grew up with his lawyer father's favorite saying drummed into his head: "Prior preparation prevents poor performance." In mid-January 1992 he sent an interagency delegation led by his under secretary of state for international security, Reginald Bartholomew, on a round-robin mission from one capital to the next, Moscow to Kiev to Minsk to Alma-Ata and back to Moscow, to negotiate with the new governments. Among about twenty participants, general counsel and ambassador Thomas Graham, Jr., a tall, soft-spoken Kentuckian experienced in arms negotiations, represented the U.S. Arms Control and Disarmament Agency. "Our mission," Graham told me, "was to tell these governments that President Bush meant what he said when he said that American recognition depended upon them accepting their international obligations, particularly in the arms-control field, particularly in the nuclear-weapons field." General John Shalikashvili, who held the disarmament

---

*See chapters one and two of my book *Arsenals of Folly* for a description of the Chernobyl disaster and its effect on Belarus.

portfolio at the Pentagon, represented the Joint Chiefs of Staff. The office of the secretary of defense sent Stephen Hadley, then assistant secretary of defense for international security. Douglas MacEachin, a senior official at the CIA, spoke for that agency.

It was frigid midwinter across the FSU, the new states were barely fledged, and triple-digit inflation had impoverished them. (In Moscow a few months later I would find the apartments of retired senior weapons scientists, the men who gave the Soviet Union the atomic and hydrogen bombs, stocked with half-empty gunny sacks of moldy potatoes because the scientists' fixed pensions had become nearly worthless; during that brutal inflation a dollar would flag down a driver and private car—or even a government limo—for a trip across the city.) At the Bartholomew delegation's first stop, in Moscow, Graham writes, "There was not much disagreement between the sides." While Russia would be the legal successor to the Soviet Union for the NPT, the United States wanted the other three new nations to sign the treaty as well. Which country or countries would take on the START agreement would have to be negotiated, as would succession to the 1990 Conventional Armed Forces in Europe Treaty (CFE), which had established equal limits to NATO and Warsaw Pact tanks and other heavy arms.

The Ukrainians balked at the U.S. delegation's terms, Graham recalls, despite Kravchuk's representations to Baker:

> Early on they indicated their ambition to be considered a nuclear power; they wanted to be a START nuclear state and they had problems with joining the NPT as a non-nuclear weapons state. One Ukrainian official said that Ukraine wanted to be the France of the East and France has nuclear weapons. It was clear to me that we would have a long road to travel with Ukraine.

Minsk was easier, and Shushkevich put up the delegation in Leonid Brezhnev's old hunting lodge outside the city—"deep snow everywhere," Graham remembers, "very beautiful." While

Bartholomew's flying squad was meeting with Belarusian officials, Bartholomew heard from his advance man in Alma-Ata that the Kazakhs would not refuel the State Department jet unless he arrived with twenty thousand dollars in small bills to pay for the jet fuel. Moscow banks, it seemed, took a 10 percent cut of any credit-card charges, and the Kazakhs weren't prepared to pay it. "They were very desperate," Graham recalls. "They said they'd allowed Secretary Baker to give them a check but they weren't going to let us do that." A few nights later Graham was standing beside the delegation's plane on the tarmac at the Minsk airport next to Bartholomew, waiting to do a red-eye to Alma-Ata. "All of a sudden I see this small plane land and taxi over and a man gets out with a black satchel. I recognized him as one of our ambassadors. He walked up to Reg and without comment handed him the satchel. That's the twenty thousand dollars. For a moment I wasn't sure if I was doing disarmament or running drugs."

In Alma-Ata, having surrendered the satchel, Bartholomew went off to confer with the prime minister before meeting with Nazarbayev. Graham and the others called the foreign ministry to arrange to discuss the treaties they wanted the Kazakhs to sign. No one at the ministry was prepared to conduct discussions, they were told; such authority was the province of only the president and the prime minister. "Kazakhstan, of course, had never been an independent state," Graham noted, "and was then about two weeks old." Eventually the flying squad held substantive talks. At a traditional banquet to mark that first visit, the foreign minister accorded Bartholomew the honor of distributing the eyeballs, ears, tongue, and other delicacies of the celebratory roasted sheep. Appropriately, one eyeball went to the spy among them—MacEachin of the CIA—who then gallantly accepted the other from a member of the group who lacked the stomach even to sample hers.

The large questions of treaty commitments with the four new states that the Baker flying squad had explored depended in turn on mutually agreed solutions to practical problems, Bartholomew told the Senate Armed Services Committee not long after the squad's return. Inevitably, Viktor Mikhailov's proposed "new and very expensive facility" for storing plutonium had come up in the discussions; Bartholomew told the committee chairman, Sam Nunn, that his experts had "real questions about [it]." More mundane proposals looked more promising:

> Let me describe some of the potential projects we are looking at. One would be to send to Russia a set of United States containers, nuclear weapons containers, for the safe transport and storage of nuclear weapons and materials for their examination. This could lead to production of containers based on U.S. technology for Soviet weapons and materials.
>
> We are also considering provision of U.S. safe, secure rail cars that we no longer use and have in storage, together with assistance from the United States in converting these rail cars to Russian track gauge. We are looking at the provision of Kevlar blankets, a large number of Kevlar blankets, to protect weapons in transit from small arms fire.

The need for refurbished weapons containers and railcars and Kevlar blankets to shield Russian nuclear warheads from the potshots of disgruntled citizens underscores the former Soviet Union's economic collapse in the first year after its breakup.

SEPARATELY AND INDEPENDENTLY, a small delegation from the two primary United States nuclear weapons laboratories, Los Alamos and Lawrence Livermore, traveled to Russia in late February 1992 to initiate a program of support for the FSU scientists and engineers isolated in their counterpart secret nuclear cities. Arzamas-16 (in Sarov), 250 miles southeast of Moscow, and Chelyabinsk-70 (in Snezhinsk), in the southern Urals another 550 miles farther along, were effectively company towns with no employers other than the Russian government, which had all but ceased paying salaries. Their triple barbed-wire fences enclosed several hundred thousand people whose working lives had been spent almost entirely within the Soviet military-industrial complex. The CIA director, Robert Gates, told a Senate committee in mid-January that at least one or two thousand of those people had the skills necessary to design nuclear weapons; across Russia, another three to five thousand had worked in uranium enrichment or plutonium production. "The brain drain problem is the area that causes us the greatest concern," Gates specified, "more than the loss of materials or weapons." He said that the breakdown of food networks supplying the secret cities had aggravated the problem, which the U.S. labs hoped to address.

The route that led the directors of two U.S. weapons laboratories to the gates of two secret cities that had only recently been restored to the Russian map was circuitous, but like so many transformations in the final years of the Cold War, it began with Mikhail Gorbachev and Ronald Reagan.

In the slow, frustrating process of forcing the nuclear genie back into its bottle, one approach that the United States arms-control community had pursued since the 1950s was limiting nuclear testing. Because new designs for smaller, more powerful, more deliverable nuclear weapons required testing at full yield in those days to demonstrate if they worked, limiting nuclear testing slowed the development of new weapons systems and encouraged doubts about the reliability of old ones. An early success had been the Limited Test Ban Treaty (LTBT) signed by the United States, the Soviet Union, and the United Kingdom in 1963. The LTBT prohibited testing nuclear weapons in the atmosphere, in outer space, or underwater, essentially eliminating the radioactive fallout from atmospheric and underwater testing that had roused the fears of ordinary people everywhere during the 1950s. While the treaty was an environmental and public-health triumph, it was also at least a partial victory for its signatories' nuclear-weapons establishments, which were allowed to continue unlimited nuclear testing underground, out of the public eye. Of a U.S. total of 1,054 nuclear tests conducted between 1945 and 1992, for example, 70 percent were fired underground.

The next step in confining the nuclear genie was to limit the yield of the underground tests allowed by the LTBT. In negotiations between the United States and the Soviet Union in 1974, the United States proposed that such tests be limited to yields of no more than 150 kilotons, about ten times the yield of the Hiroshima bomb. "The United States judged that such a limit would not hinder its basic program to support nuclear deterrence," Tom Graham writes, "and would limit the Soviet Union's high-yield programs [of testing] associated with their very large, or 'heavy,' ICBMs." Limited or not, the Soviets promptly signed the Threshold Test Ban Treaty (TTBT) and began observing its restrictions.

The TTBT provided for exchanges of information about test yields, to allow each side to calibrate its long-range seismic measurements so that treaty compliance could be determined without intrusive on-site inspections, which neither side wanted. U.S. neoconservatives, however, always on the lookout for ways to defeat arms-control treaties, seized on purported Soviet cheating on yield limits to justify Senate resistance to treaty ratification. (There were never more than ten tests in question, and a thorough 1988 U.S. Office of Technology Assessment study exonerated the Soviet program, but the cheating issue served to delay TTBT ratification until 1990.)

In 1984, speaking in New York at the annual opening of the United Nations General Assembly, Ronald Reagan offered to break the TTBT impasse by turning the problem over to the scientists. "I propose that we find a way for Soviet experts to come to the United States nuclear test site," he said, "and for ours to go to theirs, to measure directly the yields of tests of nuclear weapons. We should work toward having such arrangements in place by next spring. I hope that the Soviet Union will cooperate in this undertaking and reciprocate in a manner that will enable the two countries to establish the basis for verification for effective limits on underground nuclear testing." Reagan's proposal was not as generous as it seemed, since the Soviet Union was traditionally opposed to on-site inspection of its nuclear facilities. The proposal languished until September 1987, when the U.S. secretary of state, George Shultz, and the Soviet foreign minister, Eduard Shevardnadze, revived it. Reagan and Gorbachev formally endorsed it at their June 1988 Moscow summit meeting; the two sides agreed to pursue a program of joint verification experiments (JVEs) with "the ultimate objective of the complete cessation of nuclear testing as part of an effective disarmament process."

Preliminary visits had already taken place by then, with Soviet and American scientists touring installations they had known previously only from intelligence briefings. Donald Eilers, an associate group leader at Los Alamos, recalls landing at Semipalatinsk in January 1988 in "a rip-roaring snowstorm" after flying down from Moscow with his team. They were the first Americans ever to set foot on the site. A big man, calm and thorough, Eilers was a coinventor of the CORRTEX verification system, which the U.S. planned to use.* The hotel where the U.S. delegation stayed on the test site was surrounded with armed guards, he remembers; it took the intervention of the Soviet general who commanded the site to allow the visitors to walk more than fifty yards along the Irtysh River for exercise. "The nights were cold, about thirty degrees below zero, and the days were filled with trips to the test site where we and our equipment would be housed. It was out there in the middle of nowhere, on a very cold day with the wind howling at fifty miles per hour, when they brought us into a double-walled tent and hosted a great feast for us. We were very impressed."

---

*CORRTEX is an acronym for "Continuous Reflectometry for Radius versus Time Experiments." The system involves stringing a coaxial cable down the test-weapon borehole or down a nearby borehole, where the expanding shock wave from the explosion progressively crushes and shorts out the cable, giving a direct readout of shock-wave radius as a function of time, which can then be converted to a yield. The Soviets had two comparable systems, Miz and Contactor.

Eilers vividly recalled meeting Mikhailov for the first time on that trip. "He was then the director of the Scientific Research Institute of Impulse Engineering in Moscow, the institute responsible for many types of nuclear testing diagnostics. He certainly appeared to be leading their technical group, and I thought, 'Boy, what an intense guy.' He exuded self-confidence and pride. It was quite obvious that he was well-respected, and everybody and his brother listened to him." Later, when Eilers had worked with the Soviet physicist long enough for a friendship to develop, Mikhailov revealed that he sat on a committee for targeting U.S. cities. "Then he said, 'Don, it makes a big difference now that I can place faces at those targets.' He meant the job would be much more difficult." The Soviets had treated the Los Alamos delegation to an evening at the Bolshoi Ballet before it flew out to Semipalatinsk; when the counterpart Soviet delegation arrived to tour the Nevada Test Site sixty-five miles northwest of Las Vegas, the Americans introduced them to a typical shopping mall. "They were absolutely flabbergasted," Eilers says, laughing. "They thought it was all put up just for them, to fool them."

Mikhailov brooded more than once on the ironies of nuclear targeting as he crossed the United States in the summer of 1988 to lead the team that would observe the first JVE. "When we walked around Washington, New York and Las Vegas," he wrote in a memoir, "I could not imagine, even in a flight of scientific and technical fancy, those wondrous cities as 'military targets.' Sometimes those thoughts simply terrified me and made me shudder." The two months Mikhailov spent at the Nevada Test Site that summer added history to his rich impression of America:

In contrast to our test site . . . the Nevada Test Site has a marvelous swimming pool and a restaurant. Frankly, it would be very difficult to compare our living conditions. . . . We adapted quickly to the harsh climate of Nevada, and our American colleagues enlivened our stay with weekend trips to Las Vegas. The city makes an indelible impression in the daytime and at night. I think of it as a pearl in the State of Nevada. The temperature sometimes rose as high as 50 degrees Celsius [122° F.] in the shade, and the blue sky was absolutely cloudless. In my heart I had the greatest admiration for the pioneers who tamed the "Wild West" two hundred years ago. That took real courage!

In mid-August at the test site, after two months of preparations, the Soviet scientists closely inspected a steel canister containing an American nuclear weapon before the cabled assembly was lowered into its borehole, a two-thousand-foot hole ten feet in diameter that was then filled with rock and plaster of Paris. The canister had been painted red, white, and blue, which someone from the Soviet delegation pointed out drily were the colors of the deceased Russian royal family. At ten a.m. on 17 August 1988, with Mikhailov and his team in the control room and the Americans holding their breath—a dud would have been a great embarrassment—the United States exploded the weapon buried below the Nevada desert. The soil bulged around the borehole plug, but there was little ground shock in the soft rock. A Soviet seismic station set up near the Nevada-California border nevertheless picked up a signal from the blast, as had the U.S. and Soviet instrument cables at the site. Both verification systems agreed that the *Kearsarge* test achieved its design yield of 150 kilotons. The Soviet *Shagan* test recorded similar results using comparable instruments less than one month later at Semipalatinsk.

Improving verification was a political game more than a technical necessity, intended on the one hand to thwart the neocons who raised claims of Soviet cheating, serving on the other hand to introduce further delay in ratifying the TTBT. Despite its politics, the JVE project produced tangible returns, the contemporary director of Los Alamos told me; "the side product was, the scientists got to talk to each other." Siegfried S. Hecker, known as

Sig, a tall, lean, voluble Austrian-born plutonium metallurgist, was appointed Los Alamos's fifth director in 1985. "I was in the *Kearsarge* control room with Victor Mikhailov when we set that off," he said. "I'll never forget talking to the director of Chelyabinsk-70 at the steakhouse where we celebrated afterwards; he said the JVEs were boring, that there really wasn't any science in them and we did them because some politicians wanted them done. What we should really do, he said, since nuclear explosions take you into a space of physics you can't approach any other way, is use nuclear tests for joint scientific experiments. So even at the beginning of our exchanges, the scientific camaraderie took over. It happened with people working side by side, getting to know how much we shared. We working for our country, they working for theirs. This wasn't Reagan and Gorbachev any more; this was us. It had turned real."

After the two JVEs, both sides settled down in Geneva to hammer out the technical details of the Threshold Test Ban Treaty. Mikhailov ran that negotiation as well, and though in basic orientation he was a hard-line Russian nationalist, he and his allies in the Soviet nuclear establishment recognized that working with the American labs would give them credibility within their own country and help them get funding. "Our guys came back from Geneva in 1990 and said the Russians were ready to talk to us," Hecker recalled. "They're really serious, they'd like to get together and they'd like you to come over there. So I went to the Department of Energy and said we were picking up a lot of feelers that the Russians wanted to talk, that I thought we could get inside the fence [of the Soviet labs]."

The DOE wasn't interested. "It was too radical, and government bureaucrats aren't rewarded for their ingenuity. How could we possibly send people with knowledge of how to design nuclear weapons into enemy territory? It took a long time for us to get over the intelligence mode and into the outreach mode. The Russians made that transformation sooner than we did. DOE just didn't see what there was to gain." Hecker blames himself in part for not making the case. "My thoughts weren't that well developed. I mostly thought that we were spending millions for intelligence that we could get for free, as we did during the JVEs. We had a lot to learn and a lot to gain just by going over there and meeting these people. None of it took hold until the August putsch. Then people understood, some people, that potential disasters could come from the dissolution of the Soviet Union. But I still couldn't get through the bureaucracy. Nunn-Lugar was a totally separate initiative."

The breakthrough came indirectly from George H. W. Bush. The president had called his Cabinet together in mid-December 1991 to explore how to respond to the imminent breakup of the Soviet Union. As Gates would emphasize, Bush was particularly concerned with brain drain from the FSU nuclear-weapons complex and asked for ideas about keeping former Soviet scientists at home. A few days later, Hecker told me, at a retreat for DOE lab directors in Leesburg, Virginia, the secretary of energy, Admiral James Watkins, brought up Bush's worries. "He said Bush is concerned about what's going to happen to their scientists. Are they going to Iraq, Iran, and North Korea? What can we do to keep those guys at home? I'm asking you guys for input—what can we do?" After a short discussion Hecker raised his hand. "I said, look, Admiral Watkins, I'm a lab director and I worry all the time about losing our scientific talent. I'm sure that the Russian lab directors are sitting there thinking exactly the same thing—'The place is coming apart; how in the world do I keep these guys at home?' They probably have lots of ideas. Why don't we go ask them?" Hecker's question, writes a colleague, was "an astonishing suggestion for the time given the tight secrecy surrounding anything related to nuclear weapons." Watkins immediately responded, "Why don't you?"

Two months later, Hecker did, along with his Livermore counterpart John Nuckolls and two staff members from each lab. On 23 February 1992, when their plane landed at the Arzamas-16 airport, one of the leaders waiting to greet them in heavy coats and ear-flapped mink *ushankas* was Yuli Khariton, eighty-eight years old, who had established the weapons laboratory there under the sponsorship of Igor Kurchatov in 1946 and had served ever since as its scientific director. A small, sturdy man with jug ears and a prominent nose, Khariton extended his hand to the Americans and said, "I've been waiting for this moment for forty years."

Hecker was electrified. His scientific training had been technical, he told me, not philosophical, and until he became lab director at Los Alamos he had not given much thought to the larger political authority that lay latent in relations among scientists, who share common standards of logical clarity, honesty, and respect for evidence that transcend national boundaries. Coincidentally, the vehicle through which he explored those ideas had been my book *The Making of the Atomic Bomb,* particularly the discussion in it of the Danish physicist Niels Bohr's ideas about how the value system of science and the personal relations of scientists might serve as a model for improving international security. Reading my book, he had understood Bohr's argument intellectually, but it struck him with great emotional force when he shook Yuli Khariton's hand. "Then it was just born instantly," he told me. "All of a sudden I realized exactly the power that you wrote about. With scientists the respect is there already, on the table. The trust takes a little longer."

Khariton was the Soviet Oppenheimer, the man who directed the building of the first Soviet atomic bomb. "From the moment we stepped off the plane," Hecker said, "the offer of friendship was obvious." Before dinner on that first day in Arzamas-16, Khariton invited the Americans to the House of Science, a meeting place for the lab's science community, and talked there about the history of the atomic project in the U.S.S.R. "He addressed us in excellent English," Hecker recalled in a memorial lecture in 1999 (Khariton died in 1996), "with a decidedly British accent picked up during his graduate studies at Cambridge in 1926 to 1928." Oppenheimer and Khariton had both been graduate students in Ernest Rutherford's Cavendish Laboratory at Cambridge

University during those years, though they had not known each other.

As he did later in my own communications with him, Khariton took pains with the American lab directors to emphasize the quality of his lab's work, Hecker said:

> Academician Khariton told us that Klaus Fuchs, the German-born scientist who joined the Manhattan Project as part of the British mission, delivered detailed diagrams and descriptions to Soviet intelligence officials of the American device tested at Trinity on July 16, 1945. He told us that he and other Soviet officials made the decision to build a copy of the American device (although in the spirit of making scientists work hard and learn in the process, only a few of his co-workers saw the American diagrams). With great pride, he stated that by August 1949 they had actually developed a much superior design themselves right here in Arzamas-16. The Soviet design weighed half as much and was demonstrated to be twice as powerful when it was tested in 1951.

Hecker couldn't resist asking Khariton why he didn't test the superior Soviet design first. "He said it was very simple—they knew the American design worked. Given the tensions between the Soviet Union and the United States at that time, failure was not an option." Khariton and Igor Kurchatov had met with Stalin, the Arzamas-16 scientific director went on, and told the Soviet dictator they'd gone over the espionage information in great detail and believed they could do much better. Stalin had looked him in the eye and said coldly, "The cost of failure will be proportional to your rank in the establishment." Both scientists understood that Stalin was threatening them with execution if the first test failed. Stalin's threat was probably the basis for what Khariton called the "folklore" that the prizes awarded to the scientists after the successful test inverted Stalin's threat, that in Hecker's words, "those who in case of failure would have been shot were to receive the title of Hero of Socialist Labor, those who would have been given the maximum prison term were to be awarded the Order of Lenin, and so on down the list."

Hecker realized on that first visit that the Russian laboratories represented "an oasis in a third-world country: superb people, very well educated, very patriotic, very dedicated, but totally demoralized. They'd gone from privilege to hardship—late paychecks, still living in closed cities, nowhere to go. Superb schools, but not even the simplest medicines such as aspirin for their children and the aged." His Russian counterparts shared a broad view of the value of science for opening up the world. "We found scientists eager to work with us, to show their own country how good they were. Working with us, they thought, would help them with their own government and within their scientific community." The most immediate problem was security of their nuclear materials—the plutonium and HEU that the Soviet nuclear establishment had manufactured in such prodigal abundance over the decades of the Cold War. "The problem wasn't 'loose nukes,' " Hecker reflected. "Those things have serial numbers on them so you can track them. They're something you had to worry about, but it turns out they took good care of them. But the materials were a whole different story. The Soviet program created huge amounts of weapons-usable materials, close to fifteen hundred metric tons, enough for fifty thousand to one hundred thousand weapons. It was everywhere, at a hundred different sites across the FSU, in every imaginable form—weapons, scrap, acid solutions, waste ponds, waste dumps, fuel for reactors, experimental assemblies. No one knew exactly how much was produced, and it only takes a few kilograms to make a bomb."

In Soviet times, materials as well as weapons had been protected by what Hecker learned his Russian counterparts had called "the system of grave consequences." Los Alamos came to call it "guns, guards, and gulags." Hecker explained: "There was a good second line of defense. Everything in the country was closely controlled; Big Brother was watching everything in

Soviet society. The borders were virtually impervious and the social system didn't make it easy for someone to profit from illegal transactions." By 1992, these safeguards had broken down. "The gulags went away, the borders opened up, movement within the country became easy, the guards were demoralized and were paid only occasionally, the free-market economy took over (including a strong element of organized crime that rushed in to fill the vacuum left by the oppressive Communist Party) and everything was for sale."

Hecker saw the need immediately. "I started talking to the Russians right away about working together to see if we could help them protect their materials. Because we had experience. Our borders had never been closed, so we'd had to develop ways to control nuclear materials in a milieu much more like what the Russians now had to deal with." On the second leg of their visit, at Chelyabinsk-70, the Americans negotiated a tentative agreement on the work the two nations' labs would undertake together. "The list of topics for collaboration began with scientific experiments," Hecker recalled, "and then went down through nuclear-materials control, nuclear safety and security, and various arms-control-related things. We promised to take it back to Admiral Watkins for approval, and they said they would take it to Mikhailov."

After a final dinner in Moscow with Mikhailov, who was already complaining about the lack of action and lack of money, the two American lab directors stopped in Washington on their way home and presented Watkins with the tentative agreement they had negotiated at Chelyabinsk. "Just about instantly he gave us the go-ahead to do the scientific collaboration," Hecker says. "He also said that all the other topics needed to be approved and worked through the same government interagency process that all Nunn-Lugar programs were subject to. So he could not approve nuclear-materials control and accounting or even the environmental topics." In fact, the Bush administration's National Security Council balked at allowing the U.S. weapons laboratories to collaborate with the Russians on nuclear-weapons safety and security without interagency oversight. However urgent the need, foreign policy trumped nuclear-materials security, and approval would have to be negotiated among the NSC, Defense, State, and other interested agencies.

Where the resistance came from is not hard to work out. It revealed itself in congressional testimony even prior to the lab directors' trip to Russia. During a hearing before the Senate Armed Services Committee in early February 1992, Senator Trent Lott told a witness that he had a list "from Secretary Cheney" of Russian strategic-modernization programs "that are still under development and going forward. . . . Here is a country . . . that is still producing very sophisticated new programs. . . . Do they have the technical capability to do what needs to be done [to secure their nuclear material]? Or are they just saying, Hey, the Americans will pay for this [and] we can go do something else?" So Dick Cheney was feeding information to sympathetic Republican senators about Russian military developments, developments he interpreted to mean that the Russians might use American dollars to repair their broken nuclear complex while spending their own money on strategic modernization. Cheney's key involvement shouldn't be surprising; he had resisted aiding the FSU from the beginning, believing that it should be allowed to crumble into ruin, and Nunn-Lugar money in particular was coming out of his defense budget.

Hecker wisely opted to move cautiously. If protecting materials was still too controversial, the labs would do scientific experiments together, lab to lab, to support the Russian scientists while building a record of successful collaboration. Soon after his return from Russia Hecker appointed Stephen Younger, a physicist who had designed nuclear weapons at Livermore before moving to Los Alamos in 1989 to work in senior management, to coordinate the collaboration. With others from Los Alamos, Livermore, and the Sandia National Laboratories, the U.S. lab responsible for ordnance engineering and stockpile maintenance, Younger traveled to Russia in May 1992. One of the Russians with whom he had already discussed a joint experiment, Alexander Pavlovskii, surprised him with a list of proposed topics of collaboration. "I was not the head of the delegation nor an expert on Russian science," Younger told a Los Alamos roundtable in 1996, but "Pavlovskii singled me out and said, 'I want to give you a list of proposed topics of collaboration, and I want you to write comments on it and give it back to me in the morning.' I was later told that the Russians at Arzamas-16 had picked me as their principal representative in the United States." Younger marked up the list, crossing out large numbers of topics "because some of them were very sensitive and others were outright classified. . . . Our response to many of their proposals was that we weren't allowed to talk about many of the things on their list, but there were some topics that were real possibilities."

On a second visit a month later, they worked out a specific agreement. "During that trip," Younger noted, "we became acutely aware that many of the scientists were facing financial catastrophe. And I'm not using that word lightly. It's one thing not to be able to replace the TV if it breaks. It's quite another not to be able to buy insulin for your kid who is diabetic and who is going to die unless you find some money. That's the kind of financial pressure they were facing." The administrative director of Arzamas-16, Vladimir Belugin, raged at Younger over what he considered to be delays in delivering aid. "I'm tired of Americans coming to the Institute and making promises and not delivering anything," Younger quoted him. "Americans talk, talk, talk but never do anything. Unless this meeting results in something substantive, this will be your last visit to Arzamas-16." An agreement emerged to work on two experiments in pulsed-power generation using explosives, Pavlovskii's specialty and an interest of Younger's. Back in Los Alamos, Hecker agreed to release discretionary laboratory funds to support the joint research even though, he says, "we were on extremely thin ice" in doing so.

Younger was aware of high-level opposition to the lab-to-lab endeavor. "There were many people in the United States who didn't want us to work with the nuclear institutes," he says. "They were afraid we might be working on nuclear weapons and giving away secrets. Or maybe we were all spies, or maybe all the money we spent would go to the Communist Party." His own feelings toward the Russian scientists and their labs warmed as he traveled back and forth, much as Mikhailov's had:

> Prior to my first trip to Moscow, I bought a travel guidebook, complete with a foldout map of the city. What struck me immediately was that there were no target circles on the map—most of my experience looking at maps of the Soviet Union involved thinking of it as the enemy. This impression faded with time as I recognized that being at the Russian nuclear-weapons laboratories was somewhat like looking into a mirror. Russian scientists had the same dedication to their country that I had to mine, the same attention to security and the same concern about the potential proliferation of nuclear weapons to other countries.

Younger had been as belligerent as Mikhailov in the high days of the Cold War, telling new recruits at Los Alamos not that nuclear weapons were weapons of last resort but that they were "intended to prevent other countries, other states, other national entities from doing something that really isn't in America's national interest," that "you get people's attention when you threaten the existence of their nation." The reification of human beings into an enemy fed such democidal arrogance on both sides of the Iron Curtain; opening up the weapons complex, as Bohr had predicted, opened up more than a few hardened hearts.

SAM NUNN LED A Senate delegation to Russia and Ukraine in mid-March 1992, including Republicans Richard Lugar of Indiana and John Warner of Virginia and Democrat Jeff Bingaman of New Mexico. Besides Senate staff, three independent experts accompanied the senators: Ashton Carter, David Hamburg, and Bill Perry, the former under secretary of defense for research and engineering who had sponsored the development of the first Stealth aircraft. Perry was a professor at Stanford at that time and codirector of its Center for International Security and Arms Control (CISAC). Bad weather at the Minsk Airport prevented a planned stop in Belarus. The delegation met with high-level Russian and Ukrainian officials and toured a nuclear risk-reduction center and a defense plant undergoing conversion.

Defense conversion—converting industries dedicated to military production into industries producing consumer goods—was one of the delegation's central concerns. It was also Perry's specialty at that time, the subject area in which he worked and taught at Stanford. "The success of these countries in moving from totalitarianism to democracy," the trip report observed, "is squarely in our national interests, as is their success in demilitarizing the large portion of the military-industrial complex that is excessive to their legitimate defense requirements." The scale of the challenge was staggering; the Soviet military-industrial complex had employed more than ten million people, directly or indirectly supporting about one-fourth of the Soviet population. So far, very little in the way of defense conversion had been accomplished, largely because the Russian government's approach to the problem was "to generate funds for the later conversion of their defense industry by first promoting sales of arms to other countries." The senators offered a long list of recommendations, but they acknowledged in their trip report that conversion in the FSU "will be very difficult at best."

In the meantime, no Nunn-Lugar funds had yet been expended, because Bush had not yet certified to Congress that the new states had met the act's conditions. Evidently Mikhailov's and Belugin's impatience with American talk was justified.

In Kiev the four senators received "strong hints that Ukraine might assert a claim to the strategic nuclear missiles and warheads remaining on its soil." Two days after the delegation returned to the United States, on 12 March 1992, Kravchuk announced that he was suspending shipments of tactical nuclear weapons to Russia, though he still supported ridding Ukraine of nuclear arms. He was being "assailed by nationalists in the Rada," writes the foreign-policy analyst Leon Sigal, "who realized that Ukraine was getting nothing in return for handing over the nuclear arms to Russia.... Kiev began demanding compensation for giving up the warheads. Some in the Rada wanted this as a ploy to get Ukraine's share of Nunn-Lugar aid for dismantling. Russia had been promised $400 million; Ukraine as yet had none. It was receiving some U.S. humanitarian assistance, and it had high hopes for more. Others wanted compensation for the highly enriched uranium Russia could extract from the warheads. Still others . . . feared that, bereft of its nuclear inheritance, Ukraine would be left alone with its collapsing economy to fend off its overbearing neighbor." Ironically, unknown to Kravchuk and the Rada nationalists, the Russian military quietly continued shipping tactical nuclear weapons from Ukraine back to Russia. By 6 May all the weapons had been transferred.

Nunn and his colleagues thought a large part of the problem was "an almost exclusive [Bush] administration focus on Russia to the exclusion of other new countries." Their concerns found support in what Nunn and Lugar would call "a potent memo" from former president Richard Nixon to Bush that was leaked to the media on 10 March after circulating privately around Washington for a week. The memo, titled "How to Lose the Cold War," caused a sensation. It was all the more potent for appearing in the midst of a presidential campaign, with Bush courting conservatives and preparing for a fight against Arkansas's governor, Bill Clinton. Nixon's primary focus (besides reestablishing his foreign-policy credentials at Bush's expense) was supporting Boris Yeltsin, but he excoriated U.S. and Western aid to the FSU as "a pathetically inadequate response." The "hot-button issue in the 1950s," Nixon wrote bluntly, "was, 'Who lost China?' If Yeltsin goes down, the question of 'who lost Russia' will be an

infinitely more devastating issue in the 1990s." Though Bush
pretended he and Nixon were in agreement, he was stung.

Nunn recognized the value of the Nixon memo to his cause
and alluded to it indirectly in one of his first interviews after he
returned from Russia. "The place in history of President Bush
will be judged by what happens in our own government in treating this as a priority over the next several months," he said. When
the senators met with James Baker on their way up the ladder to
Bush himself, Nunn and Lugar write, "Baker indicated that he
had asked his staff to pull together the basic elements of a Russian assistance package." Bush feigned detachment at the outset
of his meeting, but soon came around:

> The president opened the meeting by noting that he was luke-
> warm about the idea of trying to get a major assistance pack-
> age for Russia through the Congress in an election year. After a
> thorough vetting of the [trip] report's findings and recommen-
> dations and Secretary Baker's comments on the State Depart-
> ment's review of basic components of an assistance package,
> however, the president decided that this opportunity to assist
> the reform process in the states of the former Soviet Union
> should not be missed. He asked the secretary to put together a
> comprehensive legislative aid proposal for consideration by the
> Congress. The president also said he would give strong personal
> support to the proposal.

Out of this political jockeying came the Freedom Support
Act, passed in April, which incorporated many of the recommendations the four senators had formulated, particularly
military-to-military contacts and aid for defense conversion. To
support these purposes the act provided another $400 million
in aid. The appropriation was hardly adequate, but how much
might be enough for the United States' shattered and corrupted
former enemy was a hard question; the FSU had swallowed
up $44 billion in world aid in 1990 and 1991, an NSC staffer

reported in mid-March, adding, "And no one is sure where it went."

Determined to wring binding commitments to nuclear disarmament from the three FSU states other than Russia that had inherited portions of the Soviet nuclear arsenal, James Baker set to work in April to sell the idea of a protocol to the START agreement to Belarus, Ukraine, and Kazakhstan. Belarus's Shushkevich was cooperative as always. Nazarbayev, Baker wrote, "was rather cagey, thanking me and noting that he hoped our 'special relationship' would continue." The Kazakh president was angling to become at least a temporary nuclear power under the NPT, whatever that meant—the treaty recognized no such entity. Baker understood that the United States needed to supply recognition and endorsement to Kazakhstan as well as Ukraine to win both states to his protocol, and he arranged for Nazarbayev and Kravchuk to meet with Bush in Washington in May, before Yeltsin arrived for a summit in June.

Ukraine dug in its heels. With Kravchuk's foreign minister, Anatoliy Zlenko, Baker "haggled over the protocol and the side letter of assurances that would go along with it" in eight phone conversations between late April and early May. Zlenko wanted international supervision of the disarming process, something the START agreement didn't provide, and Baker refused, pressing Zlenko by reading him a *New York Times* editorial that recommended withholding political and economic support from Ukraine until it signed. "Finally Zlenko got the message," Baker writes, just in time for Kravchuk's visit to Washington on 5 May.

Kravchuk played good cop during his visit, agreeing to Baker's terms. That agreement in turn put pressure on Nazarbayev, who on his visit to Washington on 18 May agreed to Baker's protocol and his plan that the three countries would sign "side letters" specifying that they would give up their nuclear arms. "The START protocol was done," Baker writes, "and we would sign it that weekend in Lisbon, where all the states involved were meeting for the conference on assistance to the former Soviet Union.

I breathed a sigh of relief. Three months of negotiating were over—or so I thought."

Tom Graham went ahead to Lisbon to organize the conference, taking with him one of only two known U.S. Kazakh linguists to translate the texts of the START protocol and the side letters. "In Lisbon I made the rounds of the delegations," Graham recalled. "Belarus was no problem. When I finally found the Kazakhs, they were not a problem either. . . . The Ukrainians were another matter. I had three meetings with them on Thursday and Friday, and they said that maybe they could sign, maybe they could not, and they were unsure about providing a signed copy of the Kravchuk letter."

Frustrated, Graham finally called London, where Baker was staying overnight, and spoke with Baker's assistant James Timbie. "Early the next morning," Graham wrote, "Jim [Timbie] called me at my hotel in Lisbon. He said Ukraine was going to be all right. The previous night he had relayed my message to Baker in his hotel room. Baker was sitting there in athletic attire, having just come from the exercise room. He promptly telephoned Ukrainian Foreign Minister Zlenko and Jim said, 'I will tell you later what he said, but suffice it to say that I have never heard one man speak to another in quite that way.' "

Baker didn't characterize his speech, except to say he was "infuriated" and had slammed down the phone. "There's nothing worse in a negotiation," he wrote later, "than to have an interlocutor who you begin to feel can't be trusted."

Graham, delegated to brief the participants, including Baker, on the protocol of the signing ceremony, gathered them together in a small holding room off the hall where the documents were waiting, "explained how each was to enter the room, where to sit, what documents would be passed for signature in what order, and finally what would indicate the conclusion of the ceremony. Baker interjected at that point 'and then you will all leave'; he did not want any Ukrainian or Russian speeches." Baker had locked Zlenko and the Russian foreign minister, Andrei Kozyrev, into a room and refused to let them out in order to force their last-minute agreement. "Finally," wrote the secretary of state, "at 8:10 p.m., I filed into the Winter Garden Room of the Ritz Hotel with representatives from Belarus, Kazakhstan, Russia and Ukraine. In an austere, wordless ceremony—we didn't want a shouting match—the protocol was signed, the letters were exchanged and six minutes later, we had reached our goal: there would only be one nuclear power on the territory of the former Soviet Union."

Baker's optimism notwithstanding, Ukraine had not yet finished bargaining, but the burden of persuading the Ukrainians to disarm would fall next to the Clinton administration and to Bill Perry. A happier outcome that summer of 1992 was a joint understanding between Bush and Yeltsin to reduce their two nations' strategic arsenals by a further 50 percent, from six thousand warheads and bombs down to between three thousand and thirty-five hundred, and to eliminate multiple warheads on strategic missiles. They might have gone lower; the Russians were willing to cut their arsenal to twenty-five hundred, and so were the U.S. Joint Chiefs of Staff. Dick Cheney balked and the levels stayed at between three thousand and thirty-five hundred, more than the Russians could afford to maintain. The agreement, which became START II, would meet years of resistance in the legislatures of both nations.

Everyone has his own marker of when the Cold War ended. For Tom Graham it was the signing of the Conventional Forces in Europe Treaty in 1990, reducing the forces of NATO and the Warsaw Pact so that neither side could sustain an offensive war. For some of the Los Alamos and Livermore scientists who traveled to Russia to meet their long-hidden counterparts it was entering the gates of secret cities that had been black boxes for forty years. For millions around the world who watched the events on television it was the opening of the Berlin Wall, East Germans crowding through narrow checkpoints into West Berlin like prisoners released from their cells by a siege.

The breakdown of the Soviet Union and its re-formation into a swarm of new states ended the long, ill-considered, profoundly dangerous nuclear-arms race between two nations that shared no common borders and ought to have found less hazardous ways to compete. Fortunately or unfortunately, the end of the Cold War also cast loose a crowd of client nations from the security of their alliances with the superpowers. Some would relinquish their nuclear ambitions across the next decade; some would renew them. And even as moderates moved to restrain nuclear arsenals further, the ideologues and warhorses of the Cold War cast about for new enemies to justify continuing the politics of threat inflation into the new age.

PART THREE

COMING IN
FROM THE COLD

NUCLEAR WEAPONS, which men and nations had sworn were guardians of their survival during the Cold War, depleted to commodities in its aftermath. Ukraine and Kazakhstan were prepared to trade their plentiful inventories back to Russia if the United States paid them for their trouble and promised to protect them. "Our deputies don't care where these things are aimed," a member of the Ukrainian parliament declared cynically in January 1992. "They know that they must get something for them." By that summer, having returned more than two thousand tactical nuclear weapons to Russia without compensation, Ukraine at least was feeling sufficiently mistreated to reconsider the bargain it had struck in Lisbon in May. But since the Soviet successor states outside Russia had not developed the weapons in the first place and lacked the codes necessary to launch them, the determined American pressure to see them consolidated under one nation's command eventually overcame any residual prestige or deterrent value they might have had.

One leader who never perceived his nation's nuclear arsenal as munitions to be sold was Stanislav Shushkevich of Belarus, chairman of the Belarusian Supreme Soviet, the nuclear physicist and university provost whose disgust at Moscow's mishandling of the Chernobyl reactor disaster had led him into politics in the years of the Gorbachev reforms and who became his country's first head of state when Belarus declared its independence in August 1991. I met Shushkevich a decade later, after his efforts at reform had earned him a vote of no confidence from the reactionary Belarusian parliament and he had retired to private life. He was my host on a visit to Belarus when I was researching the mass killings of Jews there by special forces of the Nazi S.S.; he made a special point of taking me as well to visit the site on the Minsk ring road where in 1988 the archeologist Zyanon Paznyak had uncovered the mass graves of tens of thousands of Byelorussian victims of prewar Stalinist repression. He and his physicist wife, Irina, were my houseguests in turn when they visited Northern California in 2004.

"I was active in denuclearizing Belarus," Shushkevich told me proudly. "I consider it my greatest achievement. We have a population of ten million, living on two hundred two thousand square kilometers of land. The nuclear weapons in place there were a danger. Belarus had more than two thousand tactical nuclear weapons. We had eighty-one mobile missiles, of which nine were MIRVed—sufficient to eradicate Europe and the United States. But whom were we defending ourselves from? So I thought that the sooner they were out of the country, the happier we would be." I asked him if the Belarusian military had agreed. "Who asked them?" he answered sharply. "Our military was the Soviet military, and they were happy to have their missiles returned. We saved money as well."

Alyaksandr Lukashenka, who followed the liberal Shushkevich as the president of Belarus and turned the country into a Stalinist-style dictatorship, allied himself closely with Moscow. Shushkevich's loyalty lay with Belarus first of all. When I arranged for him to speak at Yale University on one of his visits to the United States, he apologized to his audience for speaking in Russian. "But this is the result of the old Soviet system," he said, "that I speak Russian but not English." In 1918, he wrote me once, "Byelorussian patriots resolved that Belarus should be an independent state. At about the same time, Ukraine, Lithuania, Latvia, Estonia and Finland also announced the formation of independent states. This actually worked for some of them (Finland, for example), but not for others. Later on, people who had had these sorts of impulses were relentlessly destroyed by the Bolsheviks. The Bolsheviks exterminated almost the entire Belarusian intelligentsia. We came back to the idea [of independence] only in 1990." From Shushkevich's perspective, nuclear weapons were a burden and a curse for a small independent state, especially if it hoped to turn westward to Europe and America. He signed the Lisbon Protocol enthusiastically, pledging in an accompanying letter to George H. W. Bush to eliminate "all nuclear strategic offensive arms located on [Belarusian] territory . . . during the seven-year period as provided by the START Treaty."

Like Gorbachev but even more directly, Shushkevich had been powerfully affected by Chernobyl. At the United Nations' Earth Summit in Rio in June 1992 he estimated the disaster's monetary damage to his country at 206 billion rubles, sixteen times Belarus's annual budget. And the cost in rubles did not include the moral and social costs, he said. When Belarus signed a Nunn-Lugar agreement with the United States in October 1992, the largest single item on the list was a provision of $25 million for environmental cleanup. Returning Belarus's eighty-one SS-25s to Russia was agreed at the same time. In January 1993, while expressing his approval of the signing of the START II treaty in Moscow earlier that month by Bush and Boris Yeltsin, Shushkevich confirmed publicly, "We want to get rid of the nuclear arsenals on our territory as soon as possible." Belarus, he added, wasn't looking for any special benefits in return. In that it was different from Ukraine and Kazakhstan, both of which expected substantial payments for nuclear disarming, although Kazakhstan's leader, Nursultan Nazarbayev, pursued funding more subtly than the unruly Ukrainians, by feigning indecision and delaying.

Shushkevich certainly hoped the West might help his despoiled and impoverished country—a Marshall Plan for the FSU might have prevented much of the robbery and reversion to authoritarianism that followed—but he understood we might not trust our former enemies. "You wouldn't have to give us money," he told me. "Give us bulldozers and paving machines and let us build a highway from Minsk to Moscow so that we can transport and sell our goods." Ukraine, in contrast, wanted security guarantees, assistance for dismantlement, and compensation for the weapons themselves.

I asked Congressman Lee Hamilton of Indiana once why the United States didn't support a Marshall Plan for the FSU. He considered for a moment and said, "We were so used to thinking of them as the enemy, we just couldn't turn our heads around that fast."

Under Shushkevich's leadership, Belarus ratified START I in February 1993 and acceded to the NPT as a non-nuclear-weapons state. By summer it had returned all its tactical nuclear weapons to Russia. In December it received $76 million in Nunn-Lugar funds to facilitate moving its strategic nuclear arsenal as well, and by September 1994 it had transferred forty-five SS-25s to Russia, leaving thirty-six still to go. But Lukashenka had been elected president of Belarus by then. Lukashenka allowed another eighteen SS-25s to be returned as he consolidated his power over the Belarusian Supreme Soviet, rigged elections, and arranged for his presidential term to be extended from four to seven years. In July 1996 he tried to suspend shipment of the last eighteen SS-25s, arguing that his predecessor had made a mistake in giving them up, but pressure from Russia, with which he sought reunion, brought the final transfers in late November, whereupon Belarus became in fact the non-nuclear-weapons state that Stanislav Shushkevich had believed it should be.

Russia was an apparent exception to the commodification of the FSU nuclear arsenal: It considered itself the successor to the Soviet Union so far as nuclear weapons were concerned. As such, it received weapons from its detached former parts, increasing the size of its arsenal. The increase was only temporary, however; the weapons Russia received were not added permanently to its arsenal, an expansion which the economically challenged country could not in any case afford, but were stored—stacked all over the place, in fact—until they could be dismantled, and the dismantling was paid for in large part with American funds. Paying for the dismantling of a former enemy's most destructive weapons was such a bargain compared to building defenses against them that Bill Perry coined a name for it: preventive defense.

And it worked, Perry and Ash Carter wrote in 1999:

When we took office in 1993, it seemed to us entirely unlikely that Ukraine, Kazakhstan, and Belarus would all stay on the path to become nuclear-free states; that Russia would continue to safeguard and dismantle weapons amidst its titanic social upheaval; that somewhere, sometime, there would not be a sale, diversion, theft, or seizure of these weapons or nuclear materials by disgruntled military officers or custodians somewhere across the eleven time zones that had been the Soviet empire. Every morning we would open the daily intelligence summary fearing to read that nukes had broken loose and hoping that at least U.S. intelligence sources would have detected the break. But so far, nukes have not broken loose. Much of the credit must go to Sam Nunn and Dick Lugar and their timely vision of Preventive Defense.

This acknowledgment was generous, but the program follow-through was Perry's. It was Perry, before and after he succeeded Les Aspin as secretary of defense in February 1994, who won over a recalcitrant Ukraine as its parliament wrestled with the issue of delivering its formidable arsenal of nuclear weapons to a Russia that was both hostile and predatory. In late 1993, during a meeting between Vice President Al Gore and Russia's Prime Minister Viktor Chernomyrdin, Deputy Secretary of State Strobe Talbott proposed sending a joint mission to Kiev that would negotiate a resolution to Ukraine's dogged resistance to arming Russia with nuclear missiles it considered to be its own. Gore asked Perry to head up the effort. "With Bill Perry leading our delegation," Talbott writes, "we quickly reached broad agreement on a complex deal that would result in Russia getting the warheads along with American money to help with their dismantlement and Ukraine getting various forms of assistance from the U.S. as well as debt relief from Russia and international assurances on its sovereignty."

Yet it was particularly difficult to bring the Ukrainians around, Talbott wrote, when Ukraine and Russia were hostile to each other:

> Through the fall [of 1993], the U.S. had conducted quiet but arduous shuttle diplomacy between the two sides. For me, the short hop between Moscow and Kiev was like passing through the looking glass. From the Russian perspective, everything the Ukrainians did was stupid, childish, reckless, ungrateful and proof that their country had no business being independent. As the Ukrainians saw it, everything Russia did was malevolent, menacing and unfair, and validated hanging on to "their" missiles. From our own standpoint as go-betweens, both sides were doing just about everything they could to make a reasonable compromise impossible.

The United States had made a bad beginning, U.S. arms negotiator Linton Brooks told me, especially with Ukraine, "because we started out with a model that we would convert the [START] treaty [between the U.S. and the Soviet Union] into a U.S.-Russia treaty and treat the other three successor states as if they were basing states—the analogy was, like the states in Europe that had American tactical weapons in them. A terrible mistake, but we quickly got by that." Brooks was responsible for the final preparation of the START I and START II treaties in 1991 and 1992. "It was very surprising to us how little the nuclear aspect mattered at that point in the East-West relationship," he recalled. "It wasn't central the way it was during the Cold War. During the Cold War it was one of the chief venues of what passed for dialogue. But as the Warsaw Pact started to collapse and all that happened, it just became not very important in any kind of visceral way. So it changed the dynamic a lot."

Elizabeth Sherwood-Randall, Perry's deputy assistant secretary of defense for Russia, Ukraine, and Eurasia, points to the Clinton administration's deliberate effort to move beyond purely nuclear issues as the key to converting the FSU successor states to the American view. "It required a reduction in focus on nuclear weapons—denuclearizing the agenda—to resolve the situation with Belarus, Ukraine and Kazakhstan," she recalled. Ukraine, and to a less obvious extent the other new states, had concluded that the United States was only interested in seeing them disarmed of their nuclear arsenals, after which it would abandon them to their fate. They had reason to be concerned. Talbott reported Clinton getting just such advice from Congress and even some of his own advisers. "You listen to those folks," Clinton told him, "and what they're saying comes down to: Write that place off. It's going down. Step back so we don't get sucked in."

Rather than invoking their disdain, the notion of a former Soviet Union armed with tens of thousands of nuclear weapons collapsing into ruin and civil war ought to have sobered Clinton's critics. Even under the difficult but not yet ruinous conditions of the postcollapse period, the real point of consolidating FSU nuclear weapons in one successor state was less to prevent proliferation than to forestall terrorism. "It was all called nonproliferation," Linton Brooks clarified, "but the overwhelming majority of it had nothing to do with nonproliferation. It had to do with counter-terrorism. If you secure the Russian arsenal, if you secure Russian nuclear material, you've done nothing about proliferation, because if they decide they want to give it to somebody, they still can. What you've done is to make nuclear terrorism more difficult. For all that we bragged about very large expenditures on nonproliferation, most of those expenditures were on things that really were securing arsenals."

Which explains a troubling paradox of post-Soviet assistance: why we promoted and facilitated the removal of thousands of nuclear weapons back to Russia, where even under Boris Yeltsin there were powerful factions still hostile to the United States. Viktor Mikhailov, for example, Russia's minister of atomic energy, vigorously opposed almost every United States–led effort at mutual security and cooperation. In 1993, over strenuous U.S. objections, Mikhailov tried to sell Iran a nuclear reactor. In 1994 and 1995, Talbott wrote, the Russian nationalist was "bypassing his own government's export controls, blocking adoption of new and better ones and cutting deals with Iran that would accelerate its development of a nuclear weapon. His latest move in that direction was to offer the Iranians gas centrifuges, which they would unquestionably use to produce weapons-grade uranium," and *four* nuclear reactors. Yeltsin quickly quashed Mikhailov's rogue initiative at Clinton's behest, but it illustrates the complexities of FSU threat reduction.

The Russians had every reason to secure their nuclear weapons against diversion: They were surrounded by potential enemies, including breakaway regions like Chechnya, with which Russia fought a brutal war between 1994 and 1996. But they were not immediately convinced that the nuclear materials distributed across the country in laboratories and storage sites were similarly at risk.

A Los Alamos scientist, Ron Augustson, recalled participating in a government-to-government program beginning in 1992 to design and build a storage facility for retired Russian nuclear warheads. "Progress on the storage facility was extremely slow," Augustson said. "Meetings were held through 1992 and 1993, but everything was bogged down in the politics and administrative requirements of working with the [U.S.] Department of Defense. There was no money to pay the workers in Russia to build the facility and no money to buy Russian materials and equipment. The DoD wanted all the money to be spent here in this country.

On the other side, the Russians did not admit the importance of our particular interests, which were safety analysis and protecting materials from insider threats. It was all very discouraging."

Protection from insider theft had not been incorporated into the Russian nuclear-safety culture. The Soviet Union had been "a 'concentration camp' state," a Ukrainian nuclear safety official commented in an interview. "The system of protection in such a camp is designed so that those inside the camp cannot get out and flee. So the system of physical protection of nuclear material [did] not meet the standards that currently exist elsewhere in the world." A Russian official at the Ministry for Atomic Energy told Jessica Stern, an NSC fellow, "Nobody even considered the possibility of workers stealing nuclear materials."

"As [our] contacts grew," Augustson continued, "not only with the folks from Arzamas but with others as well, we learned that the Russians have a tremendous system of paper records, but nobody checks those records, and they were never meant to be used to draw an inventory. The emphasis was on putting product out, making a certain number of weapons from a certain amount of material. If they had a good process, they'd have more plutonium than they needed and they'd put that aside in case they ever had a need for it. After awhile, they would lose track of where they put the stuff. Through the fall of 1992 and into 1993, we were definitely getting the picture that they didn't have a good idea of how much plutonium or highly enriched uranium they had at any given location." Saving plutonium for a contingency sounds odd, but hoarding production was a standard subterfuge in Soviet industry, where benefits and promotion depended on fulfilling and overfulfilling quotas set annually by central planners. If production problems reduced output below quotas, the prudent manager could add the hoarded material to current output to make up the difference.

The program to buy blended-down Soviet warhead HEU as fuel for American power reactors that the MIT physicist Thomas Neff had initiated in 1991 slowly came to fruition. "I do not know who ultimately approached whom (both sides remember it differently)," Neff wrote, "but by August of 1992, the US and Russia were in serious discussion of a framework for an HEU purchase agreement. On August 31, President Bush announced that the US and Russia had agreed in principle for the US to purchase fuel products from produced Russian HEU." The two countries signed a bilateral agreement in February 1993: The United States would buy five hundred metric tons of HEU, "the quantity contained in roughly 20,000 nuclear weapons," and the proceeds, expected to be about $12 billion, would be divided among the four FSU successor states. ("Used for making fuel," Neff noted, "a kilogram of HEU is worth about $24,000, about twice the value of gold.") The HEU would be blended down to reactor-level enrichment—less than 5 percent U235—and converted to uranium oxide in Russia, then shipped to the United States and sold to U.S. utilities, which meant that the program would pay for itself. "This process," wrote James Timbie, a senior U.S. government adviser to the program, "would ensure that substantial amounts of fissile material would never again be used for nuclear weapons, would no longer require elaborate protection and accounting, and would never fall into the wrong hands."

There were problems along the way, including Russian concerns that U.S. monitoring of the blend-down process might reveal nuclear-weapon-design information, and efforts by the small U.S. uranium-production industry and its plant workers to block the importation of Russian-made fuel under fair-trade rules, but each problem in turn was laboriously resolved. As of 1998, when Neff spoke of his experience, Russia had dismantled more than half its Soviet-era nuclear weapons, making available four hundred metric tons of HEU. In 2010, uranium from Soviet nuclear-missile warheads was generating about 10 percent of U.S. electricity. The program was scheduled to be completed in 2013.

THE HIGHEST-PROFILE FSU threat-reduction project may have been Sapphire, the covert retrieval of 1,278 pounds (581 kilograms) of highly enriched uranium from a warehouse at the sprawling Ulba Metallurgical Plant outside Ust-Kamenogorsk in far eastern Kazakhstan, about a hundred miles southeast of the main Soviet nuclear-weapons test site at Semipalatinsk. Besides affording the Clinton administration a welcome antiproliferation success story, the Sapphire operation—or, rather, a Hollywood version of it involving a stolen nuclear weapon—was dramatized in a 1997 thriller, *The Peacemaker,* starring Nicole Kidman and George Clooney.

The real story was thrilling enough. A new, small, elegantly streamlined Soviet submarine turned up one day in 1969 at a quay on the Neva River reach of the Leningrad Sudomekh submarine shipyard. Across the next decade, extensive CIA and naval intelligence collection and analysis led to the conclusion that the submarine, given the NATO designation Alfa, was an advanced new nuclear-attack submarine with a titanium hull, a Soviet first. The Alfa was the world's smallest military submarine and at burst speeds of forty-five knots—more than fifty miles per hour—one of the fastest. To deliver high power from a small power plant, the Alfa carried a molten-lead-cooled nuclear reactor fueled with highly enriched uranium. The uranium, in the form of uranium oxide–beryllium oxide ceramic fuel rods, was produced at the Ulba plant, which manufactured most of the Soviet Union's military and civilian reactor fuel.

The Alfa never made it into fleet operation, and Ulba stopped producing submarine fuel in the 1980s. A considerable quantity of leftover fuel and precursor materials remained in insecure storage at the plant, prodigally forgotten, when the Soviet Union dissolved, in December 1991. "The Kazakh government had no idea that this material was there," Kazakh officials later told Harvard's Graham Allison, a national-security analyst. "The facility director discovered the material and said, My goodness, here we have a thousand pounds of highly enriched uranium." Its presence only became an issue when Kazakhstan began working with the IAEA early in 1993 to introduce the IAEA safeguards system into its civilian nuclear program. "By mid-1993," wrote the nuclear historian William Potter, "Kazakhstan's leadership appears to have decided that it would be prudent either to upgrade national safeguards at Ulba or, alternatively, remove the HEU from the plant." Kazakhstan had committed itself by then to signing the NPT as a non-nuclear-weapons state—the Kazakh Supreme Soviet would ratify this commitment in December 1993—and President Nazarbayev chose removal. He contacted the United States government through its ambassador, William Courtney, in August 1993.

Unfortunately, everyone who might be expected to follow up on Nazarbayev's request for help securing enough HEU to make at least thirty-five atomic bombs was busy dealing with North Korea, which had expelled IAEA inspectors from its reactor complex at Yongbyon and was threatening to reprocess the reactor's spent fuel to extract its plutonium. It was February 1994 before an engineer from the U.S. Department of Energy's Y-12 uranium enrichment plant at Oak Ridge, Tennessee, Elwood Gift, traveled to Kazakhstan to inspect the Ulba material. Gift described his inspection to journalists Andrew and Leslie Cockburn:

> He found himself in a vault about twenty feet wide and thirty-five feet long. From the twenty-five-foot ceiling the dim bulbs shone on hundreds of steel cans of differing sizes, most of them about the size of quart cans of tomato juice, stacked everywhere. Some were on wire shelves, some sat on the floor. Others were on plywood platforms. There were no windows, which Gift thought was just as well . . . but there was another door at the opposite end—unguarded.
>
> The next door opened to a similar sight, and the next. Gift had no idea how many hundreds of cans he was looking at. No one had been here for a long time and the dust lay thick on the shelves.

The plant officials accompanying the Oak Ridge engineer allowed him to pick out sample cans for a random assay. In the plant laboratory, technicians dissolved four uranium samples from the cans in nitric acid and assayed the dissolved material in a mass spectrometer. As claimed, it was 90 percent U235. Gift estimated that he had 360 cans. He collected several more samples, shipped them back to the United States via diplomatic pouch from the U.S. embassy in Almaty, the newly renamed Kazakh capital (formerly Alma-Ata), and returned home.

With confirmation that the cache of submarine fuel was HEU, and with Kazakhstan's formal accession to the NPT as a non-nuclear-weapons state at a signing ceremony in the White House on 14 February 1994, the U.S. government finally took the Ulba uranium problem seriously. Word came as well that Iranian officials had visited the Ulba plant, ostensibly interested in buying beryllium and low-enriched reactor fuel but presumably also exploring the possibility of an HEU buy. In June, Vice President Al Gore cleared the proposed removal with the Russian government through his ongoing collaboration with Viktor Chernomyrdin. Elwood Gift's boss at Oak Ridge, a senior engineer named Alex Riedy, was assigned to lead the technical team, and to see what he was getting into, Riedy traveled to Kazakhstan at the beginning of August with eight other Oak Ridge experts. He was shocked to discover that Gift had underestimated the number of fuel containers by almost 300 percent: There were 1,050 cans in the Ulba vault, not 360. Riedy had been thinking of a fourteen-person team, two weeks of repackaging, and a single shipping container. He scaled up his plans accordingly.

Back at Oak Ridge, he put out a call for volunteers. Twenty-seven Department of Energy contractors from Oak Ridge and Nevada signed on—nuclear, chemical, and industrial engineers; health physicists; industrial hygienists; packaging experts; criticality safety engineers; and maintenance technicians. The DoD supplied a military coordinator and three interpreters, and an Oak Ridge doctor rounded out the thirty-two-person team. The team members' job, a government official explained later, "was to assay the material, to make judgments as to its stability, and to determine whether it required processing." Once they had done so, they would package the material in standard IAEA-approved steel containers. The packaging would have to be done in chemical protection suits with respirators because even a single exposure to inhaled beryllium dust can cause berylliosis, a chronic, debilitating lung disease. Riedy had a portable glove-box unit—a "hood line" used for handling dangerous materials—built at Oak Ridge that would fit inside the Ulba vault; the team spent the late summer of 1994 doing what Riedy called "emergency drills and dry runs."

Washington had set up a Tiger Team—a special, one-off group of experts from a number of different U.S. departments and agencies—within the DoD to coordinate the Sapphire operation. "I was running the meetings," Jessica Stern told me of her work that autumn and winter. "It was pretty exciting." The national security bureaucracy had debated whose budget would carry Sapphire as well as compensate the Kazakh for the uranium. That debate continued through the summer, with the responsibility finally assigned to the Nunn-Lugar program. "By fall," Stern said, "who was going to pay was settled. That's when we started the operation." Clinton signed off on Project Sapphire on Friday afternoon, 7 October 1994; the Sapphire team flew out of McGee-Tyson Air National Guard Base, near Knoxville, early the next morning on one of three black C-5 Galaxy heavy transports, with a share of 130 tons of equipment in the cargo hold and the team members seated facing backward on the troop-carrier deck above.

For the next six weeks, Riedy's team worked twelve-hour days, six days a week, processing and canning the Ulba HEU. "It was a very big endeavor," the engineer said later. "We had about 1,050 nuclear containers to empty. . . . There were also about 6,000 sample bottles that we had to empty that the Kazakh officials at the Ulba plant unloaded and put in a form that we could repackage." The 581 kilograms of HEU that was the object of the team's effort wasn't pristine; it was incorporated into a total of 2.37 metric tons of material stock, including uranium metal, uranium oxides, uranium-beryllium alloy rods, uranium oxide–beryllium oxide rods, uranium-beryllium alloy machining scrap and powder, uranium-contaminated graphite, and laboratory salvage. Everything but the kitchen sink, that is, and some of it "wet," in semiliquid form, which Riedy asked the Ulba technicians to dry. "But it came back not in powder form," the Cockburns report, "as they had expected, but caked into hard lumps. Now the workers on the hood line had to spend hours breaking it into small pieces before they could pack it up."

While the canning went on at the Ulba plant, Bill Perry was working with Kazakhstan's defense minister, Sagadat Nurmagambetov, to further the country's nuclear disarmament in other realms. In an exchange of messages with the secretary of defense on 13 October, Nurmagambetov reported nuclear warheads and SS-18 ICBMs formerly based in Kazakhstan being moved to Russia. Missile silos and launch-control centers would soon be closed down, he added, with destruction scheduled to begin before the end of the year.

During the same period, Ukraine as well moved toward compliance; on 16 November the Ukrainian parliament voted 301 to 8 to endorse Ukraine's accession to the NPT. The Ukrainians had been impressed by the implicit threat of a Russian preemptive first strike in the event of a military conflict, a threat Russia had emphasized, wrote the international relations specialist William Martel, "when it pledged not to attack signatories of the NPT." So Ukraine came to recognize that its nuclear arsenal was more a danger than a shield, capable of drawing down the lightning.

On their one day a week out of the canning room, Riedy's chemists and engineers took up humanitarian work. Secretary of Energy Hazel O'Leary described it at a press conference afterward:

The team, I want to tell you, worked ten to twelve hours every day, six days a week. On the rare seventh day when they were off, their colleagues working there at the site simply took them sightseeing around the area. The USA team asked, "Is there anyone nearby who needs some assistance?" They were told about the orphanages and a pension home. . . . From that one question the team on the ground adopted an orphanage and later decided on their own that they would like to collect funds so that the youngsters living in two orphanages there would receive milk and other food and clothing for the cold winter. They then called back to the States, discussed with their colleagues both at Martin Marietta and at the Defense Department and in the Department of Energy the further need for other equipment to get citizens through the winter. That phone call led to a follow-on of the $1,800 that the team on the ground put together for the youngsters in the orphanage, and then the delivery of some 30,000 pounds of equipment that went in with the transport plane that brought out the material.

That November, the Republican Party won a landslide victory in the Clinton midterm elections, the first Republican legislative majority in forty years. Democrats lost fifty-four seats in the House of Representatives. Newt Gingrich, the new House speaker, announced his Contract with America. The new crowd of representatives brought a highly parochial perspective to government, Christian Alfonsi noted:

Many of the new Republicans on Capitol Hill were young enough to have avoided Vietnam entirely; and most of those who had not been young enough had received deferments. Never before had the American people elected a congressional majority so few of whose members had served in the military. Perhaps the most striking attribute of the new House membership, though, was its startling lack of familiarity with the world outside America's borders. Fully a third of the new Republican House members had never set foot outside the United States. In the main, many of them considered that a good thing; or if not, then certainly not a deficiency to be rectified. The deep suspicion of the UN reflected in the Contract with America was an accurate reflection of these individuals' deep distrust of the foreign, in all senses of that term.

Gingrich, no international sophisticate himself, was sufficiently concerned about his colleagues' parochialism that he considered "putting together an orientation program," Alfonsi added. "When the possibility of discussing foreign policy with the staff of the Clinton White House was raised in caucus, the House Republicans angrily kyboshed the very notion."

The Sapphire team finished recanning the Kazakh HEU around 18 November 1994, six days before Thanksgiving that year. Criticality is an issue with HEU; too much HEU in any one place can result in a massively explosive and radioactively deadly chain reaction. The 1,050 Ulba cans had yielded 1,299 smaller, IAEA-approved cans of material. Acquiring it cost the United States between ten million and thirty million dollars (the actual amount is classified) and a warehouse of goods: eight police cars, five minivans, eight pickup trucks, and four buses as well as cameras, computers, printers, scanners, software, photocopiers, and medical supplies. The cans were loaded into 447 special fifty-five-gallon drums for secure transport and planes were summoned from America.

Five C-5s left Dover Air Force Base, in Delaware, on the Sunday of Thanksgiving week, but blizzard conditions forced them to turn back. A second group of four C-5s tried again on Monday. This time three were diverted and one made it through. The lone C-5, braving the icy, washboarded nine-thousand-foot runway, landed at four a.m. on 22 November. It happened to be the plane that carried the thirty thousand pounds of supplies that Tennesseans had donated for the Ust-Kamenogorsk orphanages, which may have been what inspired its crew to fight past the sleet and snow that had forced the other crews to divert.

Working with local authorities, a Sapphire military liaison had traced out a truck route from the Ulba plant to the airport. With the arrival of the first and so far the only aircraft, Kazakh security forces now took up positions lining the route that the truckloads of barreled HEU would follow. The crew unloaded the orphanage supplies as it waited for the delivery. At the plant, the shipment, too much even for a Galaxy, was sorted into two allotments. Twelve trucks, heavily guarded, delivered the first allotment to the airport by midmorning and a forklift loaded the barrels into the big aircraft's capacious hold, its three loadmasters strapping down the multimillion-dollar cargo.

The runway appeared impassible, thick with ice and snow. But heroic solutions to impossible problems were part of the Soviet heritage, and a large, battered truck now rolled onto the runway with an aircraft jet engine bolted onto its bed beside a tank of fuel. A team fired up the engine and it screamed to life. "The joke was on the Americans," the Cockburns reported, "because within seconds the roaring jet exhaust began to blast away the thick layer of ice. Massive chunks flew through the air. The airmen laughed at this 'brute force deicing,' but it was working." The Galaxy, six stories high, needed deicing as well. For that the Kazakhs ordered up an Ust-Kamenogorsk fire truck with high-pressure pumps that hosed deicing fluid over the wings and tail. By then, alerted to the landing of a second C-5, the only other plane that got through, the second convoy set out from the Ulba plant with the remainder of the barreled HEU.

The first C-5 departed while the second was loading; they could coordinate by radio across the twenty-hour flight back to Dover, sustained by five aerial refuelings. The last of the Sapphire team departed on the second plane. Colonel Mike Foster, in command of the mission, recalled afterward that he and his crew "were sitting there in the cockpit writing Tom Clancy novels in our heads about what would happen if we had to go down." From Dover, four three-truck convoys delivered the HEU to Oak Ridge to be blended down for reactor fuel.

TWO WEEKS LATER, on 7 December 1994, the major nuclear powers meeting together in Budapest signed the Memorandum on Security Guarantees for Kazakhstan, guaranteeing its independence and territorial integrity and pledging conventional and nuclear nonaggression. The United States, Russia, Belarus, Kazakhstan, and Ukraine exchanged instruments of START I ratification at the same conference; Ukraine deposited its instrument of accession to the NPT as well. In February 1995, China also weighed in with security assurances for Kazakhstan. The new nation officially announced that it was free of nuclear weapons in May 1995.

"Under the Cooperative Threat Reduction program," Bill Perry summarized in *Foreign Affairs* the following year, "the United States has helped Russia, Ukraine, Belarus, and Kazakhstan remove over 4,000 nuclear warheads from deployment and dismantle more than 800 bombers and ballistic missile launchers. . . . All nuclear weapons were removed from Kazakhstan last year, and by the end of 1996 Belarus will be rid of nuclear weapons. Nunn-Lugar funds also help the former Soviet nuclear states secure the weapons and materials to keep them from finding their way into the global marketplace."

In January 1996, Perry would recall, "I joined my Russian and Ukrainian counterparts in personally demolishing an SS-19 silo at the Pervomaysk missile complex in Ukraine. Pervomaysk was the crown jewel of the former Soviet ICBM system, housing 700 nuclear warheads aimed at targets in the United States. By June the missile field was a sunflower field (the flowers are a cash crop in Ukraine) and Ukraine had become nuclear-weapons-free."

For Sig Hecker, removing the weapons from Belarus, Ukraine, and Kazakhstan was "the single most important accomplishment of the 1990s."

NINE LEAVING THE *LAAGER*

NOT ONLY FORMER Soviet states found it prudent to disarm as the Cold War came to an end; so also did states on the periphery of the long conflict. Brazil and Argentina abandoned their arms race well short of building any actual bombs. France and China belatedly signed the Nuclear Non-Proliferation Treaty; China's strategic arsenal was minimal in any case, while France eventually stopped testing bombs and reduced its nuclear stockpile by half. The most notable of the converts was South Africa, the only nation in the world with an indigenously produced nuclear arsenal that has voluntarily disarmed.

In June 1944, in the midst of the Second World War, when only the United States and Britain were yet fully committed to the development of nuclear weapons, the two allies agreed to set up an organization called the Combined Development Trust for the ambitious purpose of acquiring and controlling all known world resources of uranium and thorium ore.* At that time, Winston

---

*Thorium, element 90, atomic weight 232, is fertile but not fissile; it can be irradiated in a nuclear reactor to produce uranium-233, which has fissile properties similar to plutonium (its bare critical mass equals 16.13 kilograms compared to 10 kilograms for plutonium and 47.53 kilograms for U235), although its intense gamma radiation (from an impurity, U232) makes it more difficult to fabricate into bombs. The United States tested a composite U233/plutonium-core implosion device during the *Teapot* series at Yucca Flats, Nevada, in April 1955; the 800-pound device yielded 22 kilotons.

Churchill asked the South African prime minister, Jan Smuts, to conduct a survey of his country's uranium-ore resources. They proved to be substantial at low concentrations, and South Africa became the primary supplier of uranium for American and British weapons; the two allies paid $450 million for forty thousand tons of South African uranium-oxide concentrate in the early years of the Cold War, when the Afrikaner-dominated nation was installing the official form of racial segregation known as apartheid. "The secret income flows were a windfall for the South African mining industry," wrote the South African economist David Fig. "They helped to resolve the infrastructural bottlenecks in transport and steel production which plagued the country after the war, and the resulting boom served to stabilize and consolidate the apartheid government." The United States also trained a generation of South African nuclear physicists, chemists, and other specialists in the new technology of nuclear energy.

Under the Eisenhower administration's Atoms for Peace program, the United States and South Africa in July 1957 signed a fifty-year agreement for nuclear collaboration. Since South Africa ranked only eighty-fifth in the world in recoverable oil reserves but fourth in uranium, it committed itself to nuclear-power development, and in 1961 the U.S. licensed the export to its primary uranium supplier of an Allis-Chalmers swimming-pool-type twenty-megawatt research reactor fueled with four kilograms of highly enriched uranium; the South Africans christened it Safari-1.

The world began to isolate South Africa in the aftermath of the Sharpeville massacre of 21 March 1960, when a large but peaceful demonstration against the South African pass laws, which limited the movements of non-whites, came to bloodshed after the Sharpeville police fired into the crowd to disperse it. Sixty-nine people were killed, including women and children—many shot in the back—and more than 180 injured. The U.N. Security Council condemned the massacre, and the following year Britain forced South Africa out of the British Commonwealth. Successive

U.S. administrations continued to cooperate with South Africa in nuclear-energy development, anti-Communism trumping antiracism, but schemed to avoid media coverage. Thus a U.S. National Security Council staff member wrote President Lyndon Johnson's national security adviser McGeorge Bundy on 17 August 1964 proposing to keep quiet a shipment of Safari-1 reactor fuel until after the November 1964 presidential election:

> South Africa has imported an Allis-Chalmers experimental reactor which is due to go critical this winter. . . . A private US supplier will ship the fuel in the next several months. These events will be publicized in South Africa, which will unquestionably kick up a nice propaganda storm elsewhere about US nuclear cooperation with South Africa. . . . I propose to ask AEC to insure, quietly, that there is no fuel shipment or other cause for publicity until December.

Bundy approved the proposal.

South Africa began working secretly on uranium enrichment in the early 1960s and demonstrated an indigenous uranium-enrichment technology at laboratory scale in 1967. The aerodynamic technology involved blowing a mixture of gaseous uranium hexafluoride and hydrogen at high velocity through a tapered vortex tube to separate higher-U235 fractions from natural uranium by centrifugal force—in effect, a stationary centrifuge. Construction of a pilot-scale enrichment plant using vortex-tube technology began in 1969 at a site called Pelindaba, fourteen miles west of Pretoria. Since vortex-tube technology was capable of enriching uranium to weapons grade, South Africa's technical preparation for secretly developing nuclear explosives can be dated from that time.

The country has claimed that its intentions in developing nuclear explosives were benign, that a mining country might have use for such technology, and that it took its inspiration from the U.S. Plowshare Program. Plowshare, championed by the Lawrence Livermore National Laboratory director Edward Teller, sought to develop peaceful nuclear explosives (PNEs) for mining, harbor dredging, and underground gas and oil liberation. The U.S. Atomic Energy Commission conducted thirty-five PNE tests between 1957, when the program began, and its termination in 1973. Teller and his lab were "proselytizing the PNE worldwide" during that period, a nuclear official told the journalist Mark Hibbs. The only important difference between a peaceful and a military nuclear explosive, however, is its target. Significantly, South Africa began secretly supplying Israel with uranium yellowcake in 1961, with a first shipment of ten tons, and by 1972 it was negotiating the first of many secret agreements with its Middle Eastern ally.

Waldo Stumpf, a metallurgical engineer who was the general manager of the South African Atomic Energy Corporation (AEC) from 1987 to 1989, characterizes his country in the 1970s as beleaguered, increasingly isolated both politically and technologically, and essentially backing into weapons development:

> During the 1970s and especially during the latter half of that decade, the international security situation around South Africa deteriorated markedly. This was mainly due to its own racially-based internal policies but was also exacerbated by Portugal's withdrawal from its African colonies of Mozambique and Angola and the uncertainties about the true intentions of the Warsaw Pact countries and especially the Soviet Union, in the light of their openly declared expansionist policies in Southern Africa. The strong buildup of Cuban surrogate forces in Angola from 1975 onwards and which eventually peaked at 50,000 foreign soldiers reinforced a strong perception within the Government of international isolation should South African territory be under threat.

> Increasing international restrictions on the supply of conventional arms against South Africa, primarily due to its internal policies, also made the argument that the country virtually had no alternative but to develop its own nuclear deterrent to coun-

ter an external threat probably convincing to the Government of the time.

Stumpf cites as particularly egregious affronts the Carter administration's 1976 decision to block further shipments of fuel for Safari-1 (while pocketing the payment that the South Africans had made), and the U.S. Congress's passage of a non-proliferation act in 1978 that forbade the transfer of nuclear technology to countries not party to the NPT. "This pressure by the USA," Stumpf writes, "was viewed very negatively by South Africa. . . . These actions strained US-South African relations in the nuclear field severely at that time." South Africa was denied a seat on the IAEA board of directors in 1977, Stumpf complains further, and barred from participating in an IAEA conference held in India in 1979 despite the fact that India itself had tested a "peaceful" nuclear explosive in 1974.

The problem with all these complaints is that South Africa had been pursuing nuclear-explosives development since at least the early 1960s, and probably even earlier, in the mid-1950s, like many other countries (e.g., Sweden, Norway, Yugoslavia, and Switzerland) in the years before the NPT provided a treaty-based alternative to nuclear arms. "South African scientists demonstrated the feasibility of uranium enrichment at the same time that the country began to experience increased threats from enemies in the region and throughout the world," two historians of the South African nuclear program pointed out. "The concept of 'encirclement,' or perceptions of heightened threats from all quarters—at home, in the region and abroad (the *laager* complex)*—figured prominently in the minds of senior South African political and military officials." The historians continued:

Senior South African politicians, members of the ruling Afri-kaner elite, and scientists, engineers, and military officers

---

*A *laager* is an encampment made by circling the wagons.

involved in defense research and development shared a sense that they had been abandoned by the United States after it intervened in Angola in the mid-1970s. The sense of betrayal and abandonment was fueled further by escalating violent opposition at home, increased pressures from international anti-apartheid opponents, and a recognition by leaders of governments, the political Afrikaner elite, and the wider defense-establishment elite that time was not on their side. As both a strategic rationale and a rationalization, former apartheid leaders viewed weapons of mass destruction as a form of insurance and political leverage to guarantee Western involvement in the event that the apartheid regime found itself "up against the wall facing an overwhelming communist threat" at home and in the region.

By 1976, South Africa was preparing a site at Vastrap Weapons Range, a military testing ground in the Kalahari Desert about four hundred miles west of Johannesburg, for an underground nuclear test. Its enrichment plant had not yet enriched enough uranium, but the bomb-design team had constructed a first massive uranium gun bomb. The design was similar to the Little Boy gun bomb that was exploded over Hiroshima. Little Boy fired a hollow, cylindrical uranium "bullet" up a cannon barrel where it seated itself around a uranium target post to form a cylindrical supercritical mass. The target in both devices was surrounded with a tungsten tamper to reflect neutrons back into the core and to hold the explosion together for a few milliseconds longer, allowing the chain reaction to proceed through a few more exponential generations and thus produce a higher yield. Little Boy had yielded 13.5 kilotons; the yield of the South African design was estimated to fall between 10 and 18 kilotons. The South African target assembly is reported to have been spherical rather than cylindrical, however, with a blind hole into which a solid uranium bullet seated itself.

The gun assembly system, while technically the most straightforward method of detonating a nuclear weapon, is still difficult to design. "In comparing a gun device with an implosion device," a U.S. expert told Hibbs, " 'If you had to rely on the open literature, you would get the impression that the gun bomb was easier.' But engineering problems in the gun device would 'later arise which would not be apparent on the basis of the design itself.' " Hibbs explored the engineering problems with a spokesman for Armscor, the South African government's weapons manufacturer:

LITTLE BOY CROSS SECTION
(COURTESY OF JOHN COSTER-MULLEN)

In fact, when engineering work got started, South African experts soon ran into trouble. "Many areas of development and production were problematic during the early years of the program," Armscor said.

South Africa had problems in assuring that the velocity for the HEU projectile in the gun barrel—which experts said would be about 700 meters [2,300 feet]/second—could be repeatedly attained with accuracy and reliability. If the speed is not carefully controlled, one U.S. expert said, "injection of neutrons into the highly supercritical system can happen too late. If so, the 'bullet' will feed on the target and burst into pieces." Timing problems, another weapons expert said, could be solved only by "experimental investigation. You set it up, fire it over and over, and record what happens with cameras and timing equipment. Then you look at the result and find out where the problems are."

"Projectile velocity was a critical factor" in the early days of the program, Armscor said. "Special propellants and igniters were developed and matched to give the desired accuracy." Doing this was very challenging, since "the team had to develop everything in-house due to the security requirements of the program."

Armscor also had problems with the "symmetry requirements when the projectile is injected." Experts clarified that this pointed to difficulties in getting the uranium "bullet" to travel predictably and seat properly into the uranium target during firing tests. Some problems were caused by variations in temperature. South Africa had to "qualify" the design "to make sure that the 'bullet' didn't wobble in the barrel and that the device would work in conditions of heat and cold."

South Africa also experienced problems in demonstrating the reliability of arming devices. These problems, according to one U.S. expert, are "common to all nuclear weapons development efforts."

In 1975, the South Africans began drilling three deep boreholes in the ground at Vastrap, abandoning one because of bad geology, completing the other two in 1977. They planned first to cold-test a uranium gun with a depleted uranium core (which would therefore not chain-react) to assess the performance of its nonnuclear components, instrumentation, and telemetry. Then, when their enrichment plant had produced enough HEU, in late 1977 or 1978, they would test a second gun at full yield. Since India had tested Smiling Buddha, its so-called peaceful nuclear explosive, underground in 1974 without irreparable damage to its international relations, the South Africans did not expect any large outcry.

On 3 and 4 July 1977, however, a Soviet Cosmos 922 surveillance satellite photographed the test-preparation activities at Vastrap. The film returned from that mission alarmed Soviet intelligence sufficiently that it launched a Cosmos 932 low-orbit close-look satellite on 20 July. That film convinced the Soviets that a South African test was imminent, and on Saturday, 6 August 1977, coincidently the thirty-second anniversary of the atomic bombing of Hiroshima, the Soviet embassy in Washington hand-delivered a message to Jimmy Carter's White House from Soviet leader Leonid Brezhnev asking for Carter's help in preventing a South African test. The appeal was an exemplary but far from unique example of Cold War cooperation between the two supposedly implacable enemies.

Within hours, the White House ordered U.S. aircraft and satellite surveillance of the Kalahari site. The next day, wrote the analyst Jeffrey Richelson, "an unmarked light aircraft flew over the borehole sites, the instrumentation and cable trenches, the area that would house the instrumentation trailers, the office and the accommodation block." The South Africans failed to identify the plane, Richelson added, which "belonged to the U.S. military attaché's office in Pretoria and was equipped with suitable cameras." In the days ahead at least one, and possibly two, U.S. reconnaissance satellites—one capable of returning imaging data in near-real time—were repositioned to keep watch over Vastrap.

Tass, the Soviet news agency, broke the story on Monday, and the next day South Africa began scrubbing the site even as it issued contemptuous denials of the Soviet Union's "romantic notion about a Kalahari Test Site." Brezhnev wrote to the British prime minister, James Callaghan, on Monday as well, pointing out that Britain had "the necessary channels and possibilities to exercise direct restraint in respect of [South Africa]." Callaghan, surprised and out of the loop because British intelligence had missed the call, spoke to Carter on 14 August, suggesting that the Germans might be involved. Carter told Callaghan drolly, the conversation notes report, "that although he knew that the Germans were involved, he had considered the US and the French were the two main culpable parties." Carter responded to Brezhnev that day as well, agreeing with the Soviet assessment. He sent an ambassador to France with satellite photographs to win the French government's support.

"The United States and other governments exercised concerted pressure," Richelson concluded, "which reportedly included France's threat to break diplomatic relations and terminate its assistance in constructing the nuclear power plants that it had sold South Africa—a sale for which the French had taken some flak. The United States followed by sending to Pretoria a precise statement of the assurances it wanted. 'We were pretty severe in private,' one U.S. official noted." South Africa capitulated on Sunday, 21 August, and Carter announced its prevaricated pledge at a press conference the following Tuesday: "South Africa has informed us that they do not have and do not intend to develop nuclear explosive devices for any purpose, either peaceful or as a weapon." He knew better, having seen an interagency assessment on 18 August that identified a "long-standing [South African] program to develop a nuclear weapon" but could postulate no circumstances under which the South Africans could be forced to desist. Though he had just asserted that South Africa had no program, Carter went on to say that the United States would "continue to monitor the situation very closely."

A problematic consequence of doing so appeared two years later, in September 1979. In the interim South Africa had filled the Vastrap boreholes with sand, capped them with concrete, and dismantled and abandoned the site. It had continued producing HEU and had designed and built a one-ton gun bomb to replace the three-ton behemoth of the Vastrap era. According to analysts Helen Purkitt and Stephen Burgess, the U.N. Security Council's passage of a resolution in 1977 calling for a mandatory South African arms embargo had perversely emboldened corporate South Africa, which thereafter celebrated the day "as the onset of the growth of the South African military-industrial complex." (The share of its weapons budget that South Africa spent domestically increased from 29 percent in 1977 to 85 percent by 1982.)

Most significantly, the prime-ministership had passed from B. J. Vorster to P. W. Botha, a right-wing white supremacist who for a decade previously had been minister of defense and who continued to hold the defense portfolio as prime minister. Upon taking office in 1978, Purkitt and Burgess reported, Botha had articulated a brutal program of "total strategy" to defend the

Afrikaner regime, including "assassinations, torture, and smuggling as well as forgery, propaganda, and subversion. All were defined as legitimate weapons against the 'total onslaught' of communist and black nationalist forces." Botha also gave "unconditional support to the development of advanced weapons projects, including weapons of mass destruction. . . . Covert nuclear warheads and an arsenal of different types of missile systems came to be viewed as essential force multipliers for a military stretched thinner and thinner by operational demands at home and along the border, which included South West Africa (Namibia) and Angola."

As part of his "total strategy," Botha assigned Armscor, the South African Defense Force, and the Atomic Energy Board to develop a nuclear-weapons-research program; the committee thus formed was authorized to look beyond heavy gun bombs to "studies of implosion and thermonuclear technology" that might produce weapons more adaptable to delivery by missile. In the summer of 1978, Armscor took over production of nuclear weapons, inheriting from the Atomic Energy Board the one-ton gun bomb, charged with about 60 kilograms of 80-percent-enriched uranium.

On 22 September 1979, an aging and ailing U.S. Vela satellite orbiting sixty thousand miles above Earth picked up an intense double flash of light in the South Indian Ocean. No natural phenomenon is known to produce such a double flash; its only known source is a nuclear explosion.* The time between the

---

*Most of the energy of a nuclear explosion is released in the first one-millionth of a second, before the fireball has had time to expand beyond the volume of the physical bomb itself. This energy-dense early fireball radiates ten-million-degree X-rays, which cook up so much ozone and nitrous oxide in the surrounding air that the fireball radiation is veiled; this initial opacity marks the low starting point on the left side of the graph. As the fireball continues to expand, a shock front of heated air forms around it that engulfs cold air and cools to visibility. At the graph's first peak, the temperature of the shock front is about 10,000° C, the temperature of intense blue-white light. The shock front is still opaque to the fireball inside, but it becomes increasingly transparent as it continues to expand and cool. Within a few ten-millionths of a second after deto-

peaks of the double flash gives a direct measure of the yield, and in this case the yield measured between two and four kilotons, too low for one of South Africa's uranium-packed gun assemblies, which in any case hardly needed testing.

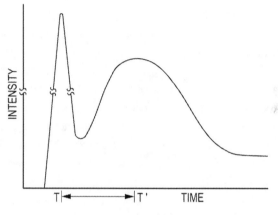

GRAPH OF NUCLEAR EXPLOSION DOUBLE FLASH

President Carter, National Security Adviser Zbigniew Brzezinski, Secretary of State Cyrus Vance, and other officials gathered at the White House within twenty-four hours of the flash report to hear from CIA and Defense Intelligence Agency representatives that the Vela signals almost certainly indicated a nuclear test. Carter wanted two questions answered: Was it really a nuclear test? And, if so, whose was it?

A panoply of investigations followed. Multiple missions of military aircraft—twenty-five sorties totaling 230 flight hours between 22 September and 29 October—searched the remote

---

nation the shock front has cooled to about 3000° and the interior fireball—still radiating beyond the range of visible light—shines through. This is the first minimum on the graph. Now the fireball itself cools to visibility—the second peak of light, with a temperature of about 7000°. From that point the decline in brightness simply registers the progressive loss of energy as the fireball continues to cool with expansion.

ocean regions southeast of the southern tip of Africa and collected samples of air and dust. Data was reviewed from U.S. military satellites, as were recordings of underwater acoustic signals picked up by U.S. navy hydrophones. An all-sky camera at Japan's Showa Base, in Antarctica, revealed a suddenly brightened patch of aurora tens of kilometers in diameter northward of the base at exactly the time of the double flash. The Arecibo radio telescope in Puerto Rico detected an upper-atmosphere electromagnetic disturbance moving southeast to northwest early on the morning of 22 September. Corroborative data would come later from New Zealand—radioactive fallout in rainwater samples collected between the beginning of August and the end of October—and from western Australia, where low but measurable levels of radioactive iodine-131 in sheep thyroids were registered.

All such measures that were directional pointed toward a pair of isolated islands, Prince Edward and Marion, two seamounts located twelve hundred miles southeast of the southern tip of Africa and fifteen hundred miles north of Antarctica in a region of wind and bad weather where ships rarely sail or aircraft fly and where clouds shield the islands from visual satellite coverage an average of 288 days per year. Significantly, they were South African possessions.

While its investigations were ongoing, the Carter administration kept the Vela information secret. By 23 October, at a meeting of the National Security Council's Special Coordination Committee (SCC), the State Department was prepared to report that "the Intelligence Community has high confidence, after intense technical scrutiny of satellite data, that a low yield atmospheric nuclear explosion occurred in the early morning hours of September 22 in an area comprising the southern portions of the Indian and Atlantic Oceans, the southern portion of Africa, and a portion of the Antarctic land mass." If this information became public, the report continued, "most observers will assume that South Africa tested a nuclear device." The debate then focused on what to do about it.

Far from advancing the United States' antiproliferation efforts, the State Department argued, this discovery of a clandestine test actually threatened those efforts. If South Africa were called out and further isolated, it "might then support nuclear weapons programs in other politically isolated states, such as Israel and Taiwan." Public exposure would lead to a more stringent United Nations arms embargo that would probably go beyond what "Western members of the Security Council could accept." It would "come at a bad time for efforts to achieve settlements in Rhodesia and Namibia." It could interfere with "efforts to deter proliferation elsewhere, e.g., Pakistan and India." Perhaps more to the point, the State Department acknowledged, "the South Africans have the capability to retaliate against sanctions with some effect. . . . The UK, for example, receives something more than 50 percent of its uranium from South Africa. . . . The West Germans look to South Africa for nearly half their uranium, the Japanese would view with alarm any major dislocation in the world uranium supply market, and a number of other countries would be affected to varying degrees." Not mentioned in the NCC discussion was the fact that the following year, 1980, was an election year in the United States, and that the Carter administration already had its hands full dealing with a revolution in Iran; the day before the NCC meeting, Carter had reluctantly admitted the deposed Shah, Mohammad Reza Pahlavi, into the United States for treatment of pancreatic cancer, a decision that led directly to the long hostage crisis that began on 4 November and would plague Carter's final year as president.

The solution the administration found to its problem was denial. When the story of the test broke, on 25 October, Cyrus Vance informed a press conference that it was "not clear that there has been a nuclear detonation" and that the U.S. didn't know "that anything has happened in South Africa." Curiously, the South Africans took a similar line, a CIA document noted: "On 26 October, immediately following the announcement in Washington of the Vela indication, Jacobus de Villiers, President of South Africa's Atomic Energy Board, told the press, 'If there was anything of the sort, my first reaction would be that some other power might have undertaken a test, but it was definitely not South Africa.' " The CIA was suspicious, however, of a comment Botha had made three days after the Vela flashes. In a speech to a provincial congress, the South African prime minister said his country's enemies ought to watch out, or they "might find out we have military weapons they do not know about."

To obfuscate the evidence of a nuclear test, the Carter administration appointed an outside ad hoc panel of scientists to consider if the evidence could have derived from natural phenomena. Led by Jack Ruina, an engineering professor at MIT and the former head of the Defense Advanced Research Projects Agency, the panel of nine included the physicist Luis W. Alvarez of the University of California at Berkeley, a Manhattan Project veteran, Nobel laureate, and skilled scientific detective. The panel met three times between 1 November 1979 and early April 1980. It concluded that the Vela signals came not from a nuclear explosion but from a micrometeorite dislodging material from the satellite body that reflected sunlight into the Vela's sensors as it spun past—a sequence of unlikely coincidences to which a January 1980 Stanford Research Institute study gave odds of between one billion and one hundred billion to one.

As it happened, I worked with Alvarez a decade later helping him edit several thousand pages of dictation into his popular memoir *Alvarez: The Adventures of a Physicist*. A tall, ruddy, California-born ice blond despite his Spanish name, the Berkeley physicist was stubbornly independent, politically conservative, and not likely to have participated in a cover-up for a Democratic administration (or a Republican one, for that matter). The challenge of finding an explanation for what he called a "zoo-on," meaning an event so rare that it belonged in a zoo, evidently overcame his usual good sense. When I knew him, he and his geologist son Walter had recently parlayed the curious absence of fossils in a layer of otherwise fossiliferous sedimentary rock that

Walter found in Gubbio, Italy, into a theory, controversial then but now strongly supported, that an asteroid impact sixty-five million years ago induced an "asteroid winter" across the world that led to the extinction of the dinosaurs. If Alvarez had personally investigated the Vela event, my guess is he would have concluded that it registered a nuclear test. The ad hoc panel, in fact, began its deliberations assuming that the satellite had seen the double flash of an atomic bomb. It then listened to various expert presentations, in the course of which the panel members changed their minds, dismissing a great deal of corroborative evidence in order to do so. Ruina understood that his assignment was deliberately narrowly framed. "My mandate was to only look at technical data," he told the journalist Seymour Hersh in 1991. "We didn't include any political data—like are the Israelis interested in nuclear weapons? That was not in our charter."

An important clue to the origin of the 22 September 1979 test was the modest scale of the explosion—unlikely for a gun bomb overloaded with HEU as South Africa's bombs were. A U.S. interagency intelligence memo prepared for the NSC in December 1979, after reviewing evidence of South African naval activity on 22 September and systematically eliminating other candidates, proposed that the Vela event might have been "a secret test by Israel":

The Israelis might have conceivably foreseen needs for more advanced weapons, such as low-yield nuclear weapons that could be used on the battlefield. Or they might have considered desirable a small tactical nuclear warhead for Israel's short-range Lance surface-to-surface missiles. Israeli strategists might even have been interested in developing the fission trigger for a thermonuclear weapon. If they were to have developed reliable nuclear devices for any of these weapons without access to tested designs, moreover, Israeli nuclear weapons designers would probably have wanted to test prototypes. A low-yield nuclear test conducted clandestinely at sea could have enabled them to make basic measurements of the device's performance. . . . Indeed, of all the countries which might have been responsible for the 22 September event, Israel would probably have been the only one for which a clandestine approach would have been virtually its only option.

Conducting a clandestine nuclear test off South Africa's shore and allowing its ally to take the blame, however, was "not consistent with Israel's policy or attitude toward Pretoria," the interagency memo argued. That conclusion raised the possibility that the test had been conducted jointly by South Africa and Israel:

> If the South Africans had considered testing Israeli designs in exchange for Israeli technical assistance, the benefits of cooperation would have been carefully weighed by both parties against the security risks inherent in such joint operations. On the one hand, the Israelis would have calculated that South Africa, as a pariah state in need of reliable friends, would have had every reason to preserve security and to remain silent in the face of inevitable speculation about its complicity with Tel Aviv. The Israelis also could have counted as a high probability that responsibility for any nuclear test in the area under investigation would be attributed to South Africa. . . . Israelis have not only participated in certain South African nuclear research activities over the last few years, but they have also offered and transferred various sorts of advanced nonnuclear weapons technology to South Africa. So clandestine arrangements between South Africa and Israel for joint testing operations might have been negotiable.

A joint test of an Israeli nuclear-artillery shell or the primary stage of a thermonuclear device would explain the discrepancy between the brute-force South African gun bombs and the low yield of the 22 September event. A joint test of an Israeli weapon would also account for Jacobus de Villiers' comment that "some other power might have undertaken a test, but it was definitely not South Africa" and Botha's warning to his country's enemies to watch out. In these and other comments, the South Africans appear to have been toying contemptuously with the announced nuclear powers that maintained their own large stockpiles of nuclear weapons but punished South Africa's efforts to acquire such weapons when it believed itself to be surrounded and at mortal risk.

And a joint South African–Israeli test, as it turned out, was indeed what the U.S. Vela satellite had recorded on 22 September 1979. Seymour Hersh broke the story in his 1991 book *The Samson Option,* quoting "former Israeli government officials" who told him "that the warhead tested that Saturday morning was a low-yield nuclear artillery shell." The Vela satellite event, his sources also told him, "was not the first but the third test of a nuclear device over the Indian Ocean. At least two Israeli Navy ships had sailed to the site in advance, and a contingent of Israeli military men and nuclear experts—along with the South African Navy—was observing the tests. 'We wouldn't send ships down there for one test,' one Israeli said. 'It was a fuck-up,' he added, referring to the capture of a test by the Vela satellite. 'There was a storm and we figured it would block Vela, but there was a gap in the weather—a window—and Vela got blinded by the flash.' "

A well-informed but anonymous source told me that only one weapon was tested, however, despite Israeli claims to Hersh, and that South Africa's participation was limited to supplying the island test site. The weapon was, indeed, an Israeli artillery shell, the source said.

BY THE MID-1980S, Israel's military and security association with South Africa had become an acute embarrassment in a world increasingly active in opposing apartheid. Besides the 1979 nuclear test, the two countries had collaborated on developing a variety of conventional arms and other military materiel. "We created the South African arms industry," Alon Liel, a former Israeli ambassador to South Africa, told the British journalist Chris McGreal in 2006. "They assisted us to develop all kinds of technology because they had a lot of money. When we were developing things together we usually gave the know-how and they gave the money. After 1976, there was a love affair between the security establishments of the two countries and their armies. We were involved in Angola as consultants to [the South African] army. You had Israeli officers there cooperating with the army. The link was very intimate." The Israeli security establishment resisted Israel's mid-1980s withdrawal. "When we came to the crossroads in '86-'87," Liel told McGreal, "in which the foreign ministry said we have to switch from white to black, the security establishment said, 'You're crazy, it's suicidal.' They were saying we wouldn't have military and aviation industries unless we had had South Africa as our main client from the mid-1970s; they saved Israel. By the way, it's probably true."

Israel's withdrawal from cooperation was less painful for South Africa than it might have been. Since the late 1970s, even as the number of South Africans drafted into military service doubled— a measure of the country's perception of internal and external threats—the apartheid state had been restaging its nuclear ambitions. While it researched implosion and boosted-fission weapons, which would require higher-enriched uranium as well as tritium, the country had given immediate priority to developing a minimal deterrent that would work, uniquely, not only by threatening South Africa's enemies but also by challenging her nominal allies, the United States in particular, to come to the pariah country's aid.

In July 1979, when South Africa decided to build seven gun bombs, it had turned the gun-bomb program over to Armscor for development. The nuclear analyst David Albright has speculated that South Africa limited its nuclear arsenal because it realized that using nuclear weapons "would have been akin to committing suicide." But the fact that it was actively researching more advanced implosion systems and had purchased tritium from Israel at great expense to investigate boosting yields* argues

---

*Heated to forty million degrees at the center of a nuclear explosion, tritium, an isotope of hydrogen, fuses into helium with the release of high-energy neutrons which greatly increase the efficiency of a nuclear chain reaction.

for another, hedged scenario: build a few gun bombs first as a deterrent or as weapons of last resort (prodigal as they were of HEU) while developing smaller, more efficient tactical nuclear weapons for war-fighting in the event deterrence failed.

This scenario would explain South Africa's willingness to risk censure or worse to host the September 1979 Israeli test of a nuclear artillery shell—exactly the sort of weapon that South Africa itself might want to add to its arsenal eventually but that was currently beyond its technical means. It would explain why South Africa in 1977 and 1978 had exchanged fifty tons of yellowcake uranium for thirty grams of Israeli tritium, supplied in 2.5-gram capsules over a period of months. It would explain why Israel and South Africa collaborated extensively in the 1980s on missile development. It is supported in part by something Armscor officials told Albright in 1993: that Armscor had planned to "replace the seven cannon-type devices with seven upgraded devices when [the gun bombs] reached the end of their estimated life by the year 2000." The upgrade, Albright understood, would involve switching from gun assembly to implosion.

South Africa's deterrent strategy, AEC chairman de Villiers said in 1993, had involved three phases:

> Phase 1 called for strategic ambiguity: internationally, the government would neither confirm nor deny whether it possessed a nuclear weapons capability. If the country were threatened militarily, Phase 2 required South Africa covertly to reveal its nuclear capability to leading Western governments, principally the United States. Should Phase 2 fail to persuade the international community to intervene to alleviate an armed attack from outside South Africa's borders, Phase 3 required Pretoria publicly to disclose its nuclear arsenal, either by official acknowledgement or an underground nuclear test.

There was an unspecified Phase 4 to the South African strategy: actual use of the arsenal against an enemy. Armscor designed its gun bombs to be airdropped by bomber if no other country came to South Africa's aid. But beyond even that phase of nuclear strategy, wrote Los Alamos's Frank Pabian, "the questions that must be answered are: Why did the South Africans go to the added expense of constructing a second generation nuclear weapons manufacturing complex [at Pelindaba] when they already had a 'credible' deterrent, and why did South Africa complete the infrastructure for building 3,000-kilometer-range ballistic missiles designed for delivering nuclear weapons?"

South Africa never answered these questions. Its claim of having built only seven gun bombs, like its claim not to have exploded a nuclear weapon on 22 September 1979, is evidently a half-truth. The whole truth is that its small cache of gun bombs was a picket guard in advance of a full-scale nuclear arsenal, with means of delivery that would have included everything from atomic artillery to ICBMs—the ICBMs to hold Soviet cities at risk, a "Samson option," as Hersh calls it, that Israel had already implemented. Deliverable nuclear weapons equalize the capacity of smaller powers to do unacceptable harm even to superpowers, however invulnerable those superpowers may imagine themselves to be—which is why superpowers have, or ought to have, a fundamental security interest in eliminating nuclear weapons from the arsenals of the world.

Given South Africa's belligerence and dogged determination, why did it turn around at the end of the 1980s and dismantle its arsenal under IAEA supervision? It did so primarily because its security needs had been met. The decision, Pabian points out, "was due in large part to the removal of the external military security threat brought about by the Angolan/Namibian peace settlement and the collapse of the Soviet Union. As President F. W. de Klerk stated [later], 'In these circumstances, a nuclear deterrent had become, not only superfluous, but in fact an obstacle to the development of South Africa's international relations.'"

An uglier reason was Afrikaner determination not to allow nuclear weapons to pass into the hands of the inevitably approaching South African black-majority government. Waldo Stumpf admitted as much in an interview with a *Washington Post* correspondent in 1991. When "questioned about the reasons behind the change of government thinking about the objectives of its nuclear program," the *Post*'s David B. Ottaway wrote, "Stumpf said that the prospect of black-majority rule in the 'New South Africa' within a few years was a major consideration." This consideration explains, at least in part, the Armscor/AEC joint effort, beginning in 1990, to eliminate not only the seven gun bombs in storage at Pelindaba but also to destroy all the program's documentation.

De Villiers describes the stark dénouement:

> The Y Plant was closed on February 1, 1990. The working group reported that it would need about 18 months to fully dismantle the country's nuclear deterrent capability, and Armscor and the AEC were jointly entrusted with this task. They studied the problem for five months before beginning in July 1990. An independent auditor, directly responsible to de Klerk, was charged with overseeing the dismantlement of the six assembled nuclear devices and ensuring that the HEU from each, as well as from the incomplete seventh device, was removed from Armscor's custody and returned to the AEC. He was also to confirm that all technology and hardware were destroyed. The entire process was completed by early July 1991.

On 10 July 1991 South Africa signed the NPT. De Klerk, to avoid the kind of intrusive inspections ongoing at the time in Iraq, waited until 1993 to announce his country's nuclear disarming to the world. However racist South Africa's domestic purpose was in disposing of its nuclear arsenal, its fundamental reason for doing so was to increase—not decrease—its security. It not only came in from the cold of international pariahdom; it also set a unique and instructive example for the world.

TEN A MILLION AND A TRILLION

R EMEMBERING HANS BLIX'S hesitations in Iraq in 1991, Bob Gallucci was amazed at the IAEA director's bulldog tenacity the following year in North Korea. Gallucci said it taught him that the IAEA "could dramatically adjust to new circumstances. It was just a cruel trick of fate that I should go through this experience with Iraq and then, just a very short period of time afterwards, be confronted with an IAEA that was over the top about a need for special inspections in North Korea." The IAEA's ability to learn and adapt has already become an important question in the context of nuclear elimination, since it is the likeliest candidate to serve as monitor and inspector against the risk of nuclear breakout in a world without nuclear weapons—the risk, that is, that a nation might attempt to rebuild its nuclear arsenal.

The need for special inspections in North Korea arose in the second half of 1992. In April of that year, North Korea had ratified a safeguards agreement with the IAEA to complete its accession to the Nuclear Non-Proliferation Treaty. As part of the safeguards process it had submitted a nuclear-materials declaration—an account of its holdings of uranium and plutonium, if any. In May, Blix and three IAEA experts had traveled to the North Korean capital of Pyongyang and then fifty-two miles due north to Yongbyon, a nuclear-research complex set within a meander on a fork of the Chongchon River, to begin assessing the accuracy and completeness of the North Korean declaration. The discrepancies the IAEA inspectors gradually uncovered indicated that North Korea might be reprocessing spent reactor fuel to extract plutonium for atomic bombs.

The North would not be the first of the two Koreas to pursue nuclear weapons. South Korea had studied going nuclear in the early 1970s, after Richard Nixon withdrew twenty thousand U.S. troops from the country—the entire 7th Infantry Division—as part of his plan to wind down the Vietnam War. Henry Kissinger, then Nixon's national security adviser, had to threaten president Park Chung Hee with U.S. withdrawal from the peninsula to force the South Korean government to give up its nuclear-weapons work.

If the South felt vulnerable to a U.S. withdrawal, the North had felt continually threatened by the U.S. presence on the peninsula since the brutal years of the Korean War (1950–1953), a civil war between left- and right-wing dictatorships in an artificially divided country poisonously subrogated to early Cold War hostilities. Besides suffering the bloody back-and-forth of the three-year ground war, the Democratic People's Republic of Korea had been battered by the United States in a vast, unrelenting, but little-known campaign of strategic bombing. "The air war . . . leveled North Korea and killed millions of civilians before the war ended," wrote the historian Bruce Cumings. "By 1952 just about everything in northern and central Korea was completely leveled. What was left of the population survived in caves. The North Koreans created an entire life underground, in complexes of dwellings, schools, hospitals and factories. . . . Korean and Chinese forces built massive underground installations because they had lost control of the air and because of well-grounded fears of nuclear attack."

Cumings writes with a barely controlled sense of outrage at such indiscriminate mass destruction, but even a military historian, Conrad Crane, has concluded that with few North Korean military or industrial targets left in the third year of the war, the U.S. Far Eastern Air Force (FEAF) was reduced to bombing flood-control dams:

> Destroying the last major target system in North Korea would be hard to justify to world opinion as "solely military." . . . In March 1953, the FEAF Formal Target Committee began to study the irrigation system for 422,000 acres of rice in the main agricultural complexes of South Pyongan and Hwanghae. The deployment of North Korean security units to protect key reservoirs from guerrillas during the growing season indicated the importance of those targets to [FEAF intelligence officer Gen. Charles] Banfill. His staff estimated that denying the enemy the rice crop from the area would cause a food shortage, tie up transportation routes with the necessity of importing rice from China, and require the diversion of troops for security and repair efforts. [Far East commanding general Mark] Clark advised the [U.S. Joint Chiefs of Staff] that in case of a prolonged recess in the peace talks, he planned to breach twenty dams to inundate the two areas and destroy an estimated one-quarter million tons of rice, "thereby curtailing the enemy's ability to live off the land and aggravating a reported Chinese rice shortage and logistic problem."

An odor of atrocity lingers to this day over these derelict plans to attempt once again to prove that wars could be won by air power alone, the U.S. Air Force's perpetual Grail quest. FEAF's commanding general Otto Weyland, a former fighter pilot, pronounced himself "skeptical of the feasibility and desirability" of the irrigation-system attacks, concerned that their brutality might alienate allies and compromise truce negotiations then under way, but he authorized dam bombings anyway, ostensibly to flood downstream airfields. "North Korea decried 'barbarous raids on peaceful agricultural installations,' " Crane wrote, "or attacks on water reservoirs that were not military objectives, but no one seemed to notice." One reason no one noticed was that targeting rice crops went unmentioned in FEAF dispatches, while "in accordance with Far East Command and JCS desires, the dam attacks were also not highlighted in UN communiqués."

The last meetings of the Formal Target Committee, Crane notes, "were dominated by discussion about how best to exploit the possibilities of the dam attacks." Weyland and Clark rationalized them as interdiction raids—that is, raids intended to interrupt the delivery of supplies—but "neither their planners nor the Communists perceived them that way." The attacks on the Toksan and Chasan Dams "did flood two key rail lines and many roads, but they also inundated nearby villages and rice fields. The flash flood from Toksan 'scooped clean' twenty-seven miles of river valley, and both raids sent water into the streets of Pyongyang." People lived in that river valley, of course, but since they grew the rice that fed North Korea, Air Force doctrine counted them among the enemy.

In the end, there was little left above ground in North Korea to target; "eighteen of twenty-two major cities had been at least half-obliterated," Crane wrote, five of them above 90 percent. Pyongyang was 75 percent destroyed. In aerial photographs North Korea's most damaged cities look like the burned and blasted landscapes of Hiroshima and Nagasaki. The armistice signed at Panmunjom on 27 July 1953 ended three years of hostilities but brought no peace. The United States froze the North Korean assets it held and placed embargoes on almost all commercial and financial transactions between the two countries. The North Korean people, whose leaders had fought a long guerrilla war with Japan through the 1930s and the Second World War, emerged from their caves and tunnels to rebuild their country. For the next forty years North Korea operated on the realistic assumption that it must remain perpetually alert for an attack from South Korea and the United States, with which it was technically still at war.

"They are prepared for war," a visiting Hungarian delegation heard from North Korean military and diplomatic briefers in 1976. "If a war occurs in Korea, it will be waged by nuclear weapons rather than by conventional ones. The DPRK is prepared for such a contingency as well. The country has been turned into a system of fortifications, important factories have been moved underground . . . and airfields, harbors and other military facilities were established in the subterranean cave networks. The Pyongyang subway is connected with several branch tunnels which are currently closed, but in case of emergency they are able to place the population there." The briefers, unwilling to admit their vulnerability, also claimed that their country possessed nuclear warheads and the missiles to deliver them.

It did not, but it wanted to. Documents found in Hungarian diplomatic archives from the 1960s report repeated North Korean requests to Soviet officials for information about and access to nuclear-weapons technology. Thus the Soviet ambassador to North Korea wrote his superiors in 1963, "Our specialists reported that the Korean uranium ore is not rich and is very scarce. The mining and processing of such ore will be extremely expensive for the Koreans. But from conversations with the Korean specialists they learned that the Koreans, despite all odds, want to develop the mining of uranium ore on a broad scale." The Soviet Union provided the North with a small HEU-fueled research reactor in 1965. The next year the North Korean premier, Kim Il Sung, visited the U.S.S.R. incognito and met with Soviet leaders Leonid Brezhnev and Alexei Kosygin, who rejected his request for a nuclear-power plant. They did so partly because the North Koreans had kept their Soviet benefactors in the dark about their research-reactor operations.

Much of the North's electrical generating capacity, about half of which was hydroelectric, had been destroyed by FEAF bombing attacks during the war; the Soviet ally therefore sought turnkey nuclear-power reactors to generate electricity even as it sent its young people off to East Germany and the Soviet Union to learn nuclear physics and engineering. For their part, Soviet leaders repeatedly pressed the Koreans to accede to the Nuclear Non-Proliferation Treaty and conform to its requirements, pressure the Koreans resisted. "The Soviet side asked the Korean comrades," a 1969 Hungarian report said, "whether they thought that it would be a good thing if, for instance, Japan—which possesses the required industrial and technical capacity—obtained nuclear weapons. In this concrete case the Korean comrades naturally acknowledged that nuclear nonproliferation was justified, but in general they did not (by which they actually give veiled support to the Chinese position)." The Chinese opposed the NPT, denouncing it when it was opened for signature in 1968 as a "conspiracy concocted by the USSR and the US to maintain their nuclear monopoly," and resisted signing it until 1992.

North Korea compromised in 1974 by joining the IAEA without acceding to the NPT. Having thus conformed to Soviet demands, in 1976 it again sought Soviet nuclear power technology, the Hungarians reported:

> The DPRK side . . . made a request for the construction of a nuclear power plant. For various reasons—primarily military considerations and the amount of the investment—the Soviet side declared that this [request] was now inopportune, and proposed to come back to it only in the course of the next [five-year] plan. The Korean side was very reluctant to accept this Soviet decision and the rejection of a few other investment demands.
>
> Particularly in the course of negotiations over credit, but also in other issues . . . the head of the Korean delegation—Deputy Premier Kang Chin-t'ae—behaved in an extremely aggressive way, definitely crude and insulting in certain statements vis-à-vis his Soviet counterpart. . . . He declared several times that if the Soviet Union was unwilling to make "appropriate" allowances for the "front-line situation" of the DPRK and did not comply entirely with the Korean requests, the DPRK would be compelled to suspend her economic relations with the Soviet Union.
>
> It was only after his visit to Comrade Kosygin that Kang Chin-t'ae changed his conduct. . . . Comrade Kosygin, among others, firmly rebuked him, declaring that the Soviet Union did

not accept ultimatums from any country and did not let anyone behave in such a way.

"Until the 1960s," a Library of Congress country study reported, "North Korea's economy grew much faster than South Korea's. Although Pyongyang was behind in total national output, it was ahead of Seoul in per capita national output, because of its smaller population relative to South Korea. For example, in 1960 North Korea's population was slightly over 10 million persons, while South Korea's population was almost 25 million persons. Phenomenal annual economic growth rates of 30 percent and 21 percent during the Three-Year Plan of 1954–56 and the Five-Year Plan of 1957–60, respectively, were reported." The reports were not fraudulent, the Library of Congress investigators explain; rather, "during the reconstruction period after the Korean War, there were opportunities for extensive economic growth—attainable through the communist regime's ability to marshal idle resources and labor and to impose a low rate of consumption." By the mid-1970s, however, the two Koreas were reversing positions economically, although their per capita incomes remained about equal up to 1976. After that time the North fell progressively further behind the rapidly industrializing South, particularly in fuel resources and transportation infrastructure, with the North diverting a crushing share of its income—above 30 percent—to defense.

The North always counted electricity generation as a vital part of its nuclear-development program. In 1976, when the obstreperous Kang Chin-t'ae asked the Soviet Union for a nuclear-power plant, the Soviets denied the request on the grounds that they had long-term commitments to construct such plants elsewhere. Kang then asked for help enlarging one of his country's thermal-power plants. That request was also denied. Kang withdrew, and the following day, according to a Hungarian observer, his replacement admitted "that the DPRK was in a difficult economic situation and needed immediate assistance from the socialist countries, including the Soviet Union. His concrete request was the following: 200,000 metric tons of oil and 150,000 metric tons of coking coal, as early as this year [in addition to more than a million metric tons of oil and 1.2 million metric tons of coal already supplied that year]. . . . In the opinion of the Soviet diplomat who told me this information, there is very little likelihood of fulfilling the request. To his knowledge, in the case of Korea the Soviet Union will not satisfy unexpected demands in the future either." The "difficult economic situation" that Kang's replacement reported was partly the result of a prolonged drought, which had severely limited hydroelectric generation. Nevertheless, said the Hungarian informant, the Soviets took every opportunity to make the Koreans understand that the countries of its predominately Eastern European economic alliance, COMECON, had priority.

The lesson of Soviet rejection of North Korea's humiliating appeals cannot have been lost on the D.P.R.K. leadership: If you want something from someone and have nothing to trade in return, you may need a plausible and dangerous threat to force him to provide it.

Failing to win Soviet support, in 1979 North Korea turned to Czechoslovakia for help, asking for uranium-mining equipment and a 440-megawatt nuclear-power plant. "If we compare the output of electric power generation that South Korea plans to reach by the end of 1986 with that of the DPRK," the Hungarian ambassador Ferenc Szabó reported that year, "the South Korean output is about three times that of the DPRK. This may explain why from [1979] on, but also earlier, the DPRK strongly urged the socialist countries—for instance, Czechoslovakia, the Soviet Union, Yugoslavia and China—to provide it with equipment for nuclear power plants or even to build a nuclear power plant. She tries to make up for her lag behind South Korea in this way, with the hidden intention that later she may become capable of producing an atomic bomb."

Szabó's speculation about North Korea's hidden intentions was timely. While seeking energy assistance throughout the

Communist world, Kim Il Sung had also begun pursuing an indigenous nuclear-weapons capacity through the cadres of nuclear scientists and engineers he had sent abroad to be trained. A Russian historian named Alexandre Mansourov, who served in the Soviet Embassy in Pyongyang, wrote that in the late 1970s "Kim Il Sung is believed to have authorized the DPRK Academy of Sciences, the Korean People's Army (KPA) and the Ministry of Public Security to begin the implementation of the North Korean nuclear program design, including rapid expansion of the nuclear-related facilities and development of the infrastructure for a nuclear weapon program in Yongbyon." A uranium mine had been commissioned at Yongbyon, Mansourov adds, as well as "a mill for concentrating the uranium ore into 'yellowcake,' a plant to purify the material, a nuclear fuel rod fabrication plant and a storage site."

Deng Xiaoping, who emerged to power in China after Mao's death in 1976, encouraged the proliferation of nuclear-weapons technology to the Third World as a counterweight to Western dominance. "In the 1980s and with the coming of Deng Xiaoping in China," wrote the American nuclear experts Thomas Reed and Danny Stillman, "serious nuclear weapon developments began to appear [in North Korea], such as high-explosive craters in the sand [from implosion experiments] and the construction of a [five-megawatt] nuclear reactor at Yongbyon.* The latter went critical in April 1986. Construction of a reprocessing facility began, in secret, in 1987."

North Korea lacked facilities for enriching uranium; the five-megawatt reactor, adapted from an early British design, graphite-moderated and air-cooled, worked with unenriched natural uranium metal. As it had been for the British, it was an ideal dual-use system, capable of producing weapons-grade plutonium as well as electricity. Yet when the East German chair-

---

*A fifty-megawatt reactor, for which construction began around 1984, remains unfinished and abandoned at the Yongbyon site.

man Erich Honecker visited North Korea in October 1986, the same month as the historic summit meeting between Mikhail Gorbachev and Ronald Reagan in Reykjavik, Kim Il Sung "affirmed that the DPRK does not intend to attack South Korea, nor could it. More than 1,000 US nuclear warheads are stored in South Korea, ostensibly for defense, and it would take only two of them to destroy the DPRK. The DPRK supports the proposals [for nuclear disarmament] made by Comrade Gorbachev in Vladivostok and Reykjavik. Many problems could now be solved with South Korea. Progress in relations between the Soviet Union and the US would also help resolve the Korea problem." If Kim Il Sung was being candid—and his assessment of South Korean defenses is accurate—it would follow that the modest nuclear arsenal he had begun pursuing by 1980 could hardly be more than a regional deterrent, if that. Certainly his small and increasingly impoverished country had no capacity to match the U.S. nuclear arsenal in South Korea, or the extended U.S. arsenal worldwide.

The North Koreans had long felt massively threatened by the United States's South Korean deployment; with the exception of Jimmy Carter, U.S. leaders throughout the Cold War had been uniformly hostile to the durable Communist regime. Encouraging the removal of the American arsenal became a central goal of North Korean foreign policy, along with increasing the country's supply of electricity, preferably with nuclear power. The Soviet Union had been the North's grudging patron in the years since the Korean War. The relationship grew progressively worse in the later 1980s as the North's economy declined and it was unable to meet its trade obligations. At some point along the way, Kim Il Sung began looking for a new patron.

As early as 1986 the North's "Great Leader" was already encouraging his government officials to reach out to the United States, which he evidently identified as a potential new patron despite the long and bitter history of dispute between his country and the Western superpower. A Stanford University Asia scholar,

John W. Lewis, visited North Korea as a private citizen on many occasions over the years and heard the appeal repeatedly. "The long-term goal of the Democratic People's Republic of Korea," Lewis told a Stanford audience in 2006, "one that was first stated to me in 1986, is to have a normal, positive relationship with the United States. That's their strategic goal. They want that because they are 'little shrimp,' as they put it, surrounded by all these whales that have been very nasty to them in history. The Chinese, the Japanese, the Russians have all caused them problems over the millennia. They believe that a fair and balanced relationship with the United States would be a long-term asset. They're realistic; they talk about the balance of power in terms that sound like Henry Kissinger."

To that end, North Korea acceded to the NPT in December 1985, although it was not yet prepared to admit safeguard inspectors to Yongbyon, which it was supposed to do within eighteen months. (The Soviet Union, which had encouraged the North Korean commitment, was also supposed to provide light-water reactors in return, but that arrangement foundered on the North's delay in following through with safeguards until after the Soviet Union's demise.) A key North Korean requirement for improving North-South relations was the withdrawal of U.S. nuclear weapons from South Korea. George H. W. Bush found a way to meet that demand after the failed August 1991 anti-Gorbachev coup in the Soviet Union, when he announced the unilateral U.S. withdrawal of all ground-launched tactical nuclear weapons throughout the world, a withdrawal that included U.S. nuclear weapons, both ground and (in a secret codicil) air-launched, in South Korea. The action was palatable to Republican congressional hawks because American naval ships and nuclear submarines armed with nuclear weapons still patrolled the Pacific and the Sea of Japan.

On a visit to North Korea in December 1991, the New York congressman Stephen Solarz pressed Kim Il Sung about the North's nuclear program. The North Korean leader's response, which was consistent with his response to Erich Honecker three years previously, endorses John Lewis's understanding of Kim's strategy for transferring fealties. "What's the use of a few nuclear weapons?" Kim asked Solarz. "In ten thousand years' time we couldn't have as many nuclear weapons as you. Assume that we are producing nuclear weapons and have one or two nuclear weapons. What's the point? They'd be useless. If we fire them, they will kill the Korean people." Threatening the United States or its South Korean ally with a few nuclear weapons would be suicidal, but a nuclear-weapons program could be traded away as a bargaining chip in D.P.R.K.-style high-risk negotiations.

Selig Harrison, a former Northeast Asian bureau chief at *The Washington Post*, learned later from North Korean contacts of a bitter debate at that time in D.P.R.K. leadership circles about whether or not an opening to the United States was feasible:

> It became increasingly clear to the reformers that the nuclear issue was the principal obstacle to normalization [of U.S.–North Korean relations] and thus to a liberalization of foreign economic policy. In December 1991, they forced a showdown over nuclear policy in the Workers Party Central Committee and won a significant victory. With Kim Il Sung's blessing, the committee gave the go-ahead for the inspection of North Korean nuclear facilities by the International Atomic Energy Agency, then a key U.S. demand. North Korean informants have subsequently told me of the bitterness that marked the intra-party debate over the IAEA issue. The reformers argued that economic survival required an economic opening to the United States, Japan, and South Korea. Hard-liners ridiculed the idea that Pyongyang would get any help from Washington, Tokyo, and Seoul, insisting that they wanted to bring about the collapse of North Korea.

As a result of the reformers' victory, the North signed a joint declaration with South Korea at the end of December 1991 on the denuclearization of the Korean Peninsula that proscribed even the production of plutonium and HEU, a restriction that exceeded NPT requirements. The North was then prepared to sign its IAEA safeguards agreement as soon as the U.S. certified that all nuclear weapons had been removed from the Korean Peninsula. Certification followed in early January 1992, and the safeguards signing took place in Vienna at the end of the month. Russia's announcement in March that it was canceling technical and financial assistance for North Korean nuclear-power-plant construction (it had ceased exporting nuclear equipment and fuel to North Korea the previous year) underlined the urgency of the North's transition from Russian to American patronage. In April it officially ratified the IAEA safeguards agreement and began compiling its safeguards declarations. Those arrived in Vienna at the beginning of May in the form of a detailed and surprisingly revealing 150-page inventory. Blix and his three-man team of experts, who had been briefed extensively by U.S. intelligence, traveled to Yongbyon on 11 May for an initial six-day visit, to be followed by IAEA inspections, and the confrontation between North Korea and the IAEA began.

"SO I WAS THERE and it was all sunshine," Hans Blix told me with irony. "They took us to Yongbyon, they took us to see a two-hundred-megawatt nuclear power plant under construction, they took us to a place where they were milling uranium in a mine. But they didn't want to take us into the laboratory at Yongbyon. They called it a 'radiochemical' laboratory. I said, 'Now, you've been opening everything so well, and you must realize that if you say no to this, then I have to report it.' So eventually they took us to the lab. It had glove boxes"—for handling radioactive materials—"but they were not linked together in a line, and they had only installed about half of the equipment. Even so, we were suspicious that it might be a reprocessing plant." For a laboratory supposedly making radiochemicals, which are typically used in small quantities for medical and industrial diagnostics, the building was impossibly large, six hundred feet long and six stories high. Blix asked his attendants about the purpose of their "radiochemical" laboratory. "They said they wanted to have breeder reactors in the future so they were learning to reprocess spent fuel. I found what they said very odd. I thought, if they had said that they wanted to reduce the volume of waste, then, yes, reprocessing would have been plausible, but a breeder reactor was not very plausible." Even the French, with years of experience designing and operating nuclear reactors, had trouble during this period developing advanced breeder reactor technology; for a country such as North Korea, at the outset of its nuclear-power development, to advance directly to building breeders was unlikely in the extreme.

The North Koreans told Blix that they had separated about a hundred grams of plutonium, some three ounces, as a scientific experiment, and they gave him a sample—in powder form in a single-walled glass vial, not the safest way to transport powdered plutonium.* The plutonium, they said, came from several damaged fuel rods they had removed from the five-megawatt reactor in 1990. The IAEA director reserved his judgment of that claim pending detailed tests.

More significantly, in light of what followed, North Korean officials sought Blix's help in acquiring light-water reactors to ease their country's energy shortage—the same request they had made previously of the Soviets. They offered to abandon fuel reprocessing in exchange. Since light-water reactors require enriched uranium, which the North lacked the facilities to produce and would have to buy internationally, it was essentially offering to give up its indigenous nuclear program. That offer ought to have rung bells in Washington and elsewhere, but the George H. W. Bush administration's mind-set on North Korea

---

*Plutonium, contrary to popular opinion, is relatively harmless to handle as solid metal or oxide—it radiates weak alpha particles, which a sheet of paper or even bare skin can block—but plutonium powder is hazardous to inhale.

was baleful. A "senior Defense Department official deeply involved in monitoring the North Korean effort" crowed to *The New York Times*'s David Sanger, who broke the story, "They are moving toward an admission that they have had a bomb project underway, but they are trying to save face. It tells you that the pressure is working."

In late May, in July, and again in September 1992, IAEA inspection teams swabbed and sampled the operations at Yongbyon, set up surveillance cameras, and installed seals. By September the inspectors had identified discrepancies in the North Korean declarations. "Our inspectors went into the nuclear waste at the site and took samples," Blix told me; "that was when they found that the isotopic composition of the pure plutonium the Koreans had given us and of the waste was not the same."

In the idiom of metallurgy, the word "campaign" refers to the period during which a furnace is continuously in operation—by analogy with military campaigns, which are "a distinct period of activity." (The science of metallurgy evolved from the craft of making weapons.) In nuclear metallurgy, the furnace is a nuclear reactor. The plutonium bred in the uranium fuel in the course of a single campaign of reactor operation should contain the same proportions of various plutonium isotopes (e.g., Pu-239, Pu-240, Pu-241) as the traces of plutonium in the liquid waste left behind from its purification. The plutonium powder that the North Koreans had given Blix turned out to be highly homogeneous, indicating that it had been produced in a single campaign, just as Blix had been told. Not so the waste in the tanks that the inspectors had sampled. That waste revealed plutonium concentrations indicative of three distinct campaigns. Since plutonium-241 decays fairly rapidly (it has a half-life of 14 years) to americium-241, measuring the amounts of americium-241 in the waste dated the three campaigns successively to 1989, 1990, and 1991. The North Korean story—that they had undertaken only one reprocessing campaign between March and May 1990 as a proof test of their as-yet-unfinished laboratory—was evidently false.

Other measurements found discrepancies between the claimed and actual amounts of plutonium reprocessed.

The North Korean scientists were shocked to have been caught in a deception. They had been careful to adjust the volume of their liquid waste to levels appropriate to the single reprocessing campaign they claimed to have run. They were apparently unaware of more recent technologies for measuring minute amounts of radioisotopes picked up as swab samples. "So I began to press the North Koreans to admit that they'd had more than one campaign," Blix told me, "and so there must be more plutonium, and they said, 'No, no, no, we only had one campaign.' I had the North Korean minister in my office and I remember saying to him, 'Look, if you have overlooked something, it's much better that you tell us now than that we find out.' And he said, 'No, we have not overlooked anything.' They made the most strenuous efforts to try to frustrate us, but our inspectors were quite clear that they had seen the numbers and there was no credibility to the claims."

What the North Koreans had actually done was more difficult to determine. One scenario that the IAEA developed led to the conclusion that only a few grams of plutonium had been separated. The other scenario, however—that more irradiated fuel rods had been removed from the five-megawatt reactor than Yongbyon had admitted—implied that several kilograms had been separated, which would have put the D.P.R.K. well along the road toward its first plutonium implosion bomb—assuming they had mastered implosion.* The North Koreans raised further suspicions by refusing to allow the inspection of two sites at Yongbyon that the IAEA believed contained undeclared nuclear waste—another sign of unacknowledged reprocessing.

Having learned boldness from the IAEA's efforts in Iraq, Blix in February 1993 formally requested special inspections of the

---

*The plutonium implosion bomb (called Fat Man) that the United States exploded over Nagasaki on 9 August 1945 was built around a solid plutonium core that weighed less than six kilograms.

two suspicious sites. Also that month, with the newly inaugurated Bill Clinton determined to cast himself as tough on proliferation, General Lee Butler of the new U.S. Strategic Command announced the retargeting of U.S. strategic nuclear weapons from Russia onto several countries with which the U.S. had conflicts, including North Korea, and the CIA director James Woolsey described North Korea as "our most grave current concern." Clinton also reinstated the annual large-scale Team Spirit joint military exercises with South Korea that his predecessor had canceled in 1992, exercises which the North considered to be a screen for a possible U.S. nuclear surprise attack. (For the same reason, a comparable NATO exercise in Europe in 1983, Able Archer, had nearly prompted a Soviet preemptive attack on the United States.) If North Korea was the worst threat the United States faced in the winter of 1992–1993, then America was secure indeed. Colin Powell, the chairman of the Joint Chiefs of Staff, had implied as much two years earlier when he told a reporter for the *Army Times,* "I'm running out of demons. I'm running out of villains. I'm down to Castro and Kim Il Sung." But even if the U.S. concern for the security of its South Korean ally was warranted, the North also had the misfortune to have been caught bargaining with the nuclear devil at a time when the U.S. military-industrial complex and its allies in Congress and the intelligence bureaucracy were conjuring demon villains to rationalize resisting major cuts in the defense budget that many thought the end of the Cold War more than justified.

Rather than allow special inspections, and responding to the opening of Team Spirit '93 on 9 March, North Korea on 12 March announced its intention to withdraw from the Nuclear Non-Proliferation Treaty as provided in the treaty's Article X if a signatory "decides that extraordinary events, related to the subject matter of this Treaty, have jeopardized the supreme interests of its country." North Korea was the first NPT signatory ever to do so. Withdrawal required three months' notice, so D.P.R.K. withdrawal would not take effect until mid-June.

Three American participants in the ensuing events—Bob Gallucci, Joel Wit, and Daniel Poneman—wrote at length in a subsequent memoir about what they called "the first North Korean nuclear crisis." In their analysis, the IAEA's demand for special inspections had presented Kim Il Sung's son Kim Jong Il, then fifty-two years old, with "his first major foreign policy crisis since assuming most of his father's responsibilities." Kim Jong Il had replaced his father as chairman of the D.P.R.K. National Defense Commission—as military leader of his country, that is—just prior to the NPT withdrawal announcement, Gallucci and his colleagues noted:

> The recent example of Iraq loomed large in the minds of North Korea's leaders. Pyongyang had closely studied U.S. military operations during Desert Storm, but also the broader political implications of the Gulf War, concluding that Saddam Hussein may have maintained his grip on power [after the war], but Iraq had lost its independence of action because of measures taken by the international community. For the North Koreans, such a fate would be intolerable, perhaps fatal. They vowed never to let the United States turn their country into another Iraq. Yet that was precisely the danger Pyongyang perceived.

If North Korea's withdrawal from the NPT was a crisis for that country, it was perhaps an even more exigent one for the United States. With the NPT up for review in 1995, the withdrawal of a state while in violation of its NPT agreements, a state that was believed to be advancing steadily toward acquiring nuclear weapons, would at the very least seriously undercut that crucial vote. It might even destroy the treaty. Worse, wrote Gallucci and his colleagues, given the danger to South Korea and Japan of a nuclear-armed North Korea, "it was clear to all that, if the North's plutonium production program could not be stopped by negotiations, the only real alternative was military action. Perhaps the United States could strike and destroy Pyongyang's nuclear facilities from the air without suffering retaliation, but that was not the assessment of the U.S. intelligence community or its military leaders." Both sides, then, had reason to hurry into negotiations before the mid-June opening for North Korean withdrawal from the NPT.

Hans Blix, in the meantime, was looking for a way to limit the North's access to the plutonium bred in the Yongbyon five-megawatt reactor, which was approaching the end of its most recent operating campaign and was due for shutdown and refueling in early May. The surveillance cameras his teams had installed were still operating, but would soon need new batteries and film. If they ran down, the IAEA would be blind to North Korean removal of the irradiated fuel, which might be diverted for plutonium extraction. (If the entire fifty metric tons of fuel rods in the reactor core were removed and the eight thousand fuel rods reprocessed, about 9.5 kilograms of plutonium could be extracted, enough for a bomb and a half or possibly two.) Creatively, Blix decided to adapt an existing stipulation in the IAEA-D.P.R.K. safeguards agreement to the new conditions. "In a telex to Pyongyang," wrote Gallucci and his colleagues, "he proposed an inspection to maintain 'the continuity of safeguards information.' " Inspections had never previously been limited to replacing batteries and film. Nevertheless, the North Koreans agreed, the IAEA inspectors arrived in Yongbyon on 10 May for four days of work, and the cameras continued to record.

Much political maneuvering between the United States and North Korea, South Korea, and the United Nations ensued before Gallucci, who had become assistant secretary of state for political-military affairs, sat down in the conference room of the American mission to the United Nations in New York on the morning of Wednesday, 2 June 1993, opposite the North Korean first vice-minister of foreign affairs, Kang Sok Ju—"a short, stocky man" in Gallucci's recollection, "who displayed a mixture of earthiness, bluster and unexpected candor." Gallucci's exposure to the Koreas was so limited—"I knew that the North was on the top and the South was on the bottom," he told me—that he had to be taught beforehand how to pronounce Kang's name.

He wasn't in the language business, however. "I'd been to Korea, but I wasn't a regional specialist. I was in this because the North Korean nuclear-weapons program was an issue of crisis proportion for the Clinton administration at that time. Not because they had a million-man army fully deployed, not because they had a ballistic-missile program. They'd had the army for a long time, and they could have all the ballistic missiles they wanted which had CEPs"—circular error probable, a measure of missile accuracy—"the size of Ohio, because if they didn't have nuclear weapons, who cared? Not even the South, you know, because with North Korea that close, the artillery would reach. Let's keep our eye on the ball here: the ball is the nuclear-weapons program, and all I need to be interested in, in this negotiation, if I'm going to do my job, is the extent to which I can stop that program. And if it's not a permanent stop, then I've got to make sure that we are always better off with any deal we make than without it at whatever point the deal ends. So that we aren't snookered, so they don't get something and get ahead. I can't have long-term confidence in this deal, I just need to be constantly evaluating, putting us in a better position than if we didn't have the deal. It's a very incremental, small-steps-for-little-feet kind of deal."

By custom, as the head of the visiting team, Kang spoke first. "Not surprisingly," Gallucci and his colleagues wrote, "he portrayed his country as the injured party." Kang went on in that vein for some time. "You want to strangle us," Gallucci remembered Kang saying. As Gallucci interpreted Kang's opening statement, "they felt threatened by the trajectory of their economy, their state and the South Korean economic miracle, by the South Korean alliance with the United States and the disappearance of their alliance with Russia. Those things all led them to feel as though they were extremely vulnerable, and the only thing that would prevent them from being overrun was the ability to deter. So they were interested in a reliable deterrent in the interest of defending themselves and their sovereignty." Kang then offered the argument that both Kim Il Sung and his son Kim Jong Il had made routinely in recent months in conversations with visitors:

> Now, according to the chief delegate, his country faced an important decision: whether to use its reactors to produce nuclear weapons or electricity. Kang said Pyongyang had the "capability" to build such weapons, but going that route made little sense since the United States had a large nuclear arsenal. "We make one, two, three or four but what is the use," he shrugged. His government's decision, however, hinged on the outcome of this meeting. Switching to English for emphasis, Kang proposed a deal. If the United States stopped threatening North Korea, his country would commit itself never to manufacture nuclear weapons.

That afternoon, Kang made his offer concrete: He proposed the old trade that the D.P.R.K. had sought first from the Soviet Union, then from Russia, then through the good offices of Hans Blix: light-water reactors in exchange for dismantling the D.P.R.K.'s several gas-graphite reactors, the one in operation and the two under construction, and ending reprocessing of spent fuel. Unfortunately, the Americans were so focused on keeping the North in the NPT that they missed the offer, and the North Koreans inexplicably let it go.

This first round of talks continued through 11 June, when the two sides issued a joint statement agreeing to give "assurances against the threat and use of force, including nuclear weapons," to principles of "peace and security in a nuclear-free Korean Peninsula," to "support for the peaceful reunification of Korea" and to continue talking. In exchange for the U.S. agreements, North Korea unilaterally suspended its withdrawal from the NPT for "as long as it considers necessary" and agreed to allow safeguards inspections again.

The two teams next met in Geneva in mid-July. Gallucci had

hinted to Kang that the North Korean negotiator might want to bring up the reactor deal again, and two days into the meetings, at a luncheon at the D.P.R.K. mission, Kang did so, formally introducing what he called his "bold new instructions": North Korea was willing to trade its gas-graphite reactors for light-water reactors. Since the United States insisted that the D.P.R.K. reestablish itself under the NPT before discussing such a trade, the ensuing days of discussions were brutal, with Gallucci even pounding the table at one point and Kang musing threateningly that without agreement, the North Korean military would "remove the fuel rods and declare to the world they would make bombs." The best Gallucci could tell the press afterward was that the meetings were a small step forward.

The vulnerability model that Gallucci described to me as one version of why the North Koreans might want nuclear weapons was what he called "Model One, the happy model." He had another, competing model in mind as well during the negotiations. "Model Two is that they are ideologically, psychologically, and politically forever committed to unifying the peninsula under their regime. That they have no hope of doing this except by force, and the only way to succeed by force is if they are able to fracture the [South Korean–American] alliance. And by fracture I mean to deter us, on the assumption that we aren't willing to trade Los Angeles for Pyongyang. And therefore their interest in the nuclear program was for deterrence, but in the service of offense."

With the first model in mind, Gallucci went on, "You could actually believe that if we succeeded in buying off their nuclear-weapons program with light-water reactors, fuel oil, and a smile, it could be a genuine trade in which the North Koreans were persuaded that they were gaining a relationship with the United States, which no longer made it politically plausible for us to join the South in an invasion. That they would in a sense achieve a sort of détente with us and with the South. Model Two, unfortunately, would lead one to believe that they wouldn't be interested in really giving up a nuclear-weapons capability and would look on an agreement to freeze their program as a sort of rental agreement. They might 'rent' or 'lease' these weapons or potential weapons for awhile, but they would never really give them up because that would mean giving up their dream of dominating the peninsula. I mean, you can have other models but these were two."

Either way, Gallucci and his colleagues wrote, "in making the proposal the North Koreans created a precarious tightrope for both negotiators. At the core of the proposal was a sensitive argument over self-reliance versus dependence on the outside world"—because the D.P.R.K. would have to rely on the outside world to supply it with enriched uranium fuel for the light-water reactors. "That issue went to the heart of a decade-long debate between 'conservatives' and 'realists' in North Korea. . . . Accepting the new reactors meant accepting dependence." Since the North had organized itself around the principle of *Juche*—proud self-reliance—dependence would require a realist victory in the intra-party debates. Much of the confusion and conflict of this period of relations between the United States and the D.P.R.K. appears to have derived from confusion and conflict within North Korea itself about how the country should proceed in the new post–Cold War world. Of course the same could be said of the United States, Russia, and several other nuclear and near-nuclear nations as well.

Gallucci couldn't agree to the United States's giving North Korea reactors; U.S. export laws made doing so impossible even if the price had not been billions of dollars. He identified a potential alternative during a lunch that summer with James Laney, a Methodist minister and former college president who had lived in Korea, spoke Korean, and was the incoming ambassador to Seoul. Laney "suggested that the United States put together a consortium to build the new reactors," Gallucci and his colleagues reported, "using Japanese money earmarked for the North should the two countries normalize diplomatic relations."

At about the same time—August 1993—Tom Graham, who had become acting director of the Arms Control and Disarmament Agency (ACDA) at the beginning of the year, led a delegation of ACDA staff out to Omaha for a day of briefings by officers of the U.S. Strategic Command (STRATCOM). The new organization, which had replaced SAC, operated the entire U.S. strategic triad: ICBMs, strategic bombers, and nuclear submarines. General Lee Butler was commander-in-chief, and the highlight of the day, Graham wrote, "was a full hour-long presentation by the CINC himself, in which he briefed us as to how nuclear weapons really could be, safely and effectively, drastically reduced and eventually prohibited someday in the future under appropriate verification and enforcement arrangements. And the enforcer could be STRATCOM, North Korea could be a type of test case, and we were fortunate that the first breach of the nonproliferation regime was by a country as reprehensible as North Korea. It was a brilliant presentation."

The Clinton administration pursued diplomatic discussions with North Korea directly, and indirectly through the IAEA, during the summer and fall of that year. Blix reluctantly accepted North Korean limitations on his inspectors' access at Yongbyon, deeming "continuity of safeguards" a lesser evil than the alternative; at least it allowed him to make sure that no fuel gravid with plutonium—or, at least, no more fuel—would be diverted. "Clearly," wrote Gallucci and his colleagues, "the consequences of declaring continuity of safeguards broken weighed heavily on Blix. 'If I announce that continuity is lost, then what?' he would later ask the South Koreans." For their part, the North Koreans made sure the IAEA inspectors could at least change the tapes and batteries in their instruments before they failed.

But conservative Republican pressure on Clinton drove him at the same time to explore a military solution to the North Korean challenge. On the NBC television program *Meet the Press* in early November he painted himself into a corner by announcing, "North Korea cannot be allowed to develop a nuclear bomb.

We have to be very firm about it." As far as he knew, North Korea might already have done so; the following month, a Special National Intelligence Estimate concluded that a D.P.R.K. nuclear weapon or two was "more likely than not."

General Gary Luck, a Kansan who had commanded the 18th Airborne in the Persian Gulf War, was now commander of U.S. forces in Korea. Luck returned to Washington that fall, officially to consult on war preparations, but his personal mission was to make sure that Clinton and his advisers understood the stakes they were playing for with the North Koreans. "If we pull an Osirak," he told Daniel Poneman, likening an attack on Yongbyon to the 1981 Israeli attack on Iraq's nuclear reactor, "they will be coming south." (Poneman was the National Security Council's senior director for nonproliferation at the time.) Luck reported the results of a recent war game that produced between 300,000 and 750,000 U.S. and R.O.K. military casualties and an equivalent or greater number of casualties among South Korean civilians as well. He requested a battalion of Patriot missiles to shield his forces from North Korean Scuds.

The CIA and the Defense Intelligence Agency raised the stakes further in late December with an estimate that North Korea had separated at least twelve kilograms of plutonium, enough for at least two implosion bombs, adding to the pressure on Clinton. Separating plutonium and building a reliable implosion weapon are two very different challenges, but Clinton and his advisers had been badly rattled by the "Black Hawk Down" incident in Somalia in early October, when a U.S. Special Forces unit in Black Hawk helicopters pursuing renegade Somali political leaders in Mogadishu was shot down and surrounded, with eighteen Americans killed and eighty-three wounded; some of the bodies were dragged through the streets. The incident led directly to Defense Secretary Les Aspin's resignation on 15 December. (Fortunately, his replacement would be Bill Perry, the Stanford mathematician whose advanced weaponry had transformed the 1991 Persian Gulf War.) To add insult to injury in that miserable season, General Merrill McPeak, the U.S. Air Force chief of staff, told reporters with impolitic disappointment, "We can't find nuclear weapons [in North Korea] now except by going on a house-to-house search." Nor was South Korea happy so far with the United States' diplomatic initiatives.

Despite the stakes Luck had described, Clinton and his advisers judged North Korea to be bluffing in rejecting inspections; White House officials told *The Washington Post* in late January 1994 that the D.P.R.K.'s "bellicosity" was "more of a negotiating tactic than a genuine threat to peace on the peninsula." Ironically, that description fit Clinton's bellicosity rather better than it did North Korea's. Sanctions were the answer, Clinton now argued, even though the North had threatened to go to war rather than allow itself to be strangled with sanctions as Iraq had been. (By one careful contemporary estimate, sanctions would cost the D.P.R.K. up to 8 percent of its GNP at a time when it was suffering from an economic decline so severe that it was asking its population to reduce its food intake to two meals per day. On the other hand, 8 percent of its GNP was a high price to pay for a few atomic bombs.) The clear deadline was 22 February 1994, when the IAEA would hold its next board meeting, a point beyond which Blix felt it was dangerous to extend his continuity-of-safeguards certification.

When *The New York Times* broke the story of Luck's Patriots on 26 January—Clinton was said to be "likely" to approve the general's request—the North Koreans managed a surprisingly muted response. In discussions in Vienna with the IAEA they were actively working to avoid being denounced to the IAEA board and the U.N. Security Council. They came to agreement on a comprehensive list of safeguard inspections on 15 February, just in time. The problem with their cooperation, of course, was that it fed the belief of Clinton and his advisers that the D.P.R.K.'s threats were idle. After the 15 February deadline, relations deteriorated progressively as the three interested parties—the United States, North Korea, and South Korea—fell out of sync.

An IAEA inspection team was admitted to Yongbyon on 1 March 1994 to conduct what the DPRK believed would be only a continuity-of-safeguards inspection. That is, in the words of an 18 March D.P.R.K. memorandum, "all the activities in the DPRK's nuclear facilities as specified in the Vienna agreement of February 15, including the reloading and servicing of containment and surveillance devices, the verification of the physical inventories, examination of a number of records and documents, verification of the design information, sampling and measurements." The inspectors replaced several dozen seals, the North Koreans reported in a second memo, read tank levels, did fresh- and spent-fuel measurements, did limited gamma mapping (detecting gamma rays in order to locate and identify any traces of radioisotopes from clandestine reprocessing), and conducted thirty-five destructive-assay samplings (in which samples are altered by testing) and smear tests. The inspectors "thanked us for our cooperation on several occasions," the North Koreans claimed. They may have, but Yongbyon's refusal to allow thorough inspection of the big reprocessing building, where the inspectors were shocked to discover that a second reprocessing line was nearing completion, prompted three separate telexes from Vienna—from Blix, that is—threatening to report "that the Agency is not in a position to verify non-diversion of nuclear material."

When the inspectors returned to Vienna on 15 March, Blix did just that, the very next day, and on 21 March the IAEA board of directors voted to refer the North's refusal to the U.N. Security Council as a serious violation. A few days later at Panmunjom, on the 38th parallel, which divides the two Koreas, the South's Song Young Dae raised the possibility of U.N. sanctions. The North Korean negotiator raged, "We are ready to respond with an eye for an eye and a war for a war. Seoul is not far from here. If a war breaks out, it will be a sea of fire. Mr. Song, it will probably be difficult for you to survive." It was the first time in more than forty years that the North had explicitly threatened war. The South Korean leadership, as ready as its northern counterpart to cast blame, put the threat, which had been surreptitiously taped, on national television.

FINALLY, IN APRIL, the Clinton administration stopped dithering. At the beginning of the month it formed a senior policy steering group on Korea and made Bob Gallucci its chairman, with ambassadorial rank and authority to coordinate overall U.S. policy toward North Korea. Gallucci quickly allied himself with the new secretary of defense, Bill Perry. Both Gallucci and Perry believed that freezing the North's present nuclear-weapons capacity was more important than punishing it for its past. Asked about the possibility that the North already had one or two nuclear weapons, Perry told *Time* on 11 April, "We don't know anything we can do about that. What we can do something about, though, is stopping them from building beyond that."

The two men bonded on a five-day visit to Seoul in mid-April during which the first delivery of three Patriot missile batteries—twenty-four launchers and eighty-four Stinger antiaircraft missiles to defend the Patriots—arrived by ship at Pusan and Kim Il Sung, having just celebrated his eighty-second birthday, disavowed his Panmunjom negotiator's "sea of fire" threat, calling it "out of place." He added, "Actually, we don't want any war. Those who like war are completely out of their minds." The North Korean leader also said pointedly, "The only way that the nuclear problem on the Korean peninsula can be solved is through direct talks with the United States." There had been direct talks in the past, but not at the national leadership level. "Except for . . . one senior-level session during the Bush administration in 1992," wrote the U.S. career diplomat Marion Creekmore, Jr., "and . . . two during the Clinton administration in 1993, all contacts between the United States and North Korea had been conducted by lower-policy-level officials with North Korean diplomats assigned to the North Korean mission in New York." Evidently Kim Il Sung wanted talks only at the highest level; in May, when senior U.S. senators Sam Nunn and Richard Lugar volunteered to undertake the mission, the North denied them visas.

Since Gallucci's negotiations the previous summer with Kang Sok Ju, the North's first vice foreign minister, the two diplomats had stayed in touch by exchanging messages and letters. Leaving Seoul, Gallucci heard from Kang that the North had decided to unload the fuel from the five-megawatt reactor—the first step toward reprocessing. Gallucci and his colleagues call this message "a bombshell." The reactor had been operating long enough to have bred sufficient plutonium in its eight thousand fuel rods, Perry would estimate, to make "four or five nuclear bombs." If Perry and Gallucci had decided to focus on the present and the future of D.P.R.K. nuclear-weapons progress rather than the past, here were the present and the future staring them in the face.

The challenge then was to persuade the North Koreans to allow IAEA inspectors to observe the unloading operations. On 2 May, Gallucci warned Kang that unloading the reactor in the absence of IAEA inspectors would end the United States–North Korean dialogue. Perry followed up in a speech to the Asia Society in Washington the next day:

> If North Korea were to break the continuity of safeguards—for example, by refusing to allow adequate IAEA monitoring of the spent fuel rods it will remove from the 5-MWe reactor—the issue would return to the United Nations, where the U.S. and others would consider appropriate steps, including sanctions. . . .
>
> We believe this response would be commensurate with the problem posed by North Korea's refusal, and it would be done with no intention of being provocative. However, North Korea has stated that the imposition of sanctions would be equivalent to a declaration of war. This is probably another example of excessive North Korean rhetoric, but, as Secretary of Defense, I have a responsibility to provide for the adequate readiness of U.S. military forces in the face of such threats.

The North's pointed rejoinder, starting around 10 May, was to begin unloading the five-megawatt reactor. Essentially a large block of graphite drilled through with a lattice of multiple vertical channels for fuel rods and gas-coolant circulation, the reactor was built below a floor—a biological shield of thick concrete—with a corresponding lattice of holes for fuel-rod insertion and retrieval. An unloading machine would pull the rods out of the core one at a time while shielding the operators from their intense radiation, and transport them to a nearby cooling pond, where distilled water would remove their heat and shield their radiation as their accumulation of short-lived fission products decayed to less radioactive, longer-lived elements.

Blix expected the unloading to take about two months to complete, based on the use of one unloading machine operating during normal work hours. He sent off his inspectors from Vienna on 15 May, with Dimitri Perricos in charge. When they arrived at Yongbyon, they found that the Koreans were using two unloading machines and running them both twenty-four hours a day. By 20 May they had already unloaded fourteen hundred fuel rods, and they were making no effort to identify where in the reactor core the rods had been positioned—information the IAEA required if it hoped to determine how many campaigns the reactor had run. Blix dispatched more inspectors to deal with the around-the-clock defueling operation, but the Koreans only allowed them to watch.

"They just dumped the fuel rods into baskets in the spent fuel pool," Sig Hecker, who visited Yongbyon at a later time, told me. "They made an incredible technical mess because the fuel rods were clad in magnesium alloy, and water and magnesium don't mix well. The only way you can put magnesium in water is to very carefully control the pH, which they didn't do. The rods were a little over half a meter long and an inch and a half or so in diameter, forty to a basket, and they just dumped them." Perricos called the unloading "a big mess" and told the journalist and historian Don Oberdorfer that he'd "concluded that this disarray was deliberate. On reflection, the struggle over the fuel rods reminded him of a poker game in which Pyongyang's ace was the outside world's uncertainty about how much plutonium it possessed. He believed that a political decision had been made, probably at the very top, that Pyongyang would not give up its high card."

In Washington, the Clinton administration was advancing rapidly toward requesting United Nations sanctions despite the D.P.R.K.'s threat that it would consider the imposition of sanctions to be an act of war. "You think of the United Nations as neutral," Kang Sok Ju warned Gallucci. "But they were the belligerent opposite us in the Korean War. So a sanctions resolution in the United Nations would be a violation of the armistice of 1953."

Perry understood, Gallucci and his colleagues wrote, that "the United States could not fight a war in Korea without Japan. Bases in that country would be critical to support forces on the Korean Peninsula." At the same time, Japan recognized "the possibility of North Korean attacks [on Japan] using chemical or biological weapons or attempts to destroy the twenty-five nuclear reactors [on the Japanese coast] along the Sea of Japan, vulnerable to North Korean commando operations and missile attacks."

At a meeting with Clinton and his senior advisers on 19 May, Perry, Luck, and the Joint Chiefs' chairman, John Shalikashvili, gave a tough-minded assessment of a war they believed they could win at great cost—without mentioning the cost. "When asked by the president at a different briefing whether the United States would win the war," Gallucci and his colleagues wrote, "General Luck replied, 'Yes, but at the cost of a million and a trillion.'" The million were military and civilian casualties killed or wounded; the trillion was the loss in dollars to the South Korean economy of a second Korean War. Standing against these grim statistics, Hecker pointed out, was the reality that the entire North Korean plutonium capability was still concentrated at Yongbyon, so that "at that time they still would have had the chance to destroy it all. If they bombed the reactor or bombed the reprocessing facility or bombed the spent fuel pool they would destroy the fuel rods, and the plutonium would be gone."

Why taking out or defending a plutonium-production facility in a country which had not yet tested a bomb would be worth thousands of American, hundreds of thousands of South Korean, and an unspecified number of North Korean and perhaps Japanese lives, no one in the several governments involved has yet satisfactorily explained. Perry, with his former assistant secretary of defense Ashton Carter, attempted to do so in 2003 when another crisis mounted on the Korean Peninsula. The only reason the two former Pentagon officials could adduce, nine years later, that the North "must not be allowed to produce a series of nuclear bombs" was that "nuclear weapons might embolden [North Korea] to believe it could scare away the United States from defending the South, making war more likely." That was a repetition of Gallucci's "Model Two" argument, which of course depended entirely on how easily the United States, a superpower with more than ten thousand nuclear weapons in its arsenal, could be intimidated.

The other justification Perry and Carter gave for threatening war over their hypothetical was the familiar Vietnam-era claim that "the North's nuclear program could set off a domino effect of proliferation in Asia and around the world." It could, but it also might not, and sufficient unto the day is the evil thereof. Nor was it likely that it would, because the U.S. nuclear umbrella would remain in place, and if the American arsenal was adequate to deter a Soviet nuclear attack on Europe and the United States for four decades, why would it not be adequate to deter a North Korean attack on the South, or even on Los Angeles? The risks inherent in the red line that the U.S. drew across the defueling became more evident at the beginning of June 1994 when Blix, faced with the fact that Yongbyon had unloaded more than 60 percent of the five-megawatt reactor's fuel rods, finally abandoned his Trojan-horse "continuity of safeguards" ruse and reported to the U.N. Security Council that the loss of information about the reactor's previous operations was irreversible. The North's response, on 5 June, was to threaten that "sanctions mean war, and there is no mercy in war."

ELEVEN GREAT LEADERS

A T LEAST ONE PERSON was alive in that time of crisis on the Korean Peninsula with the perspective necessary to see beyond the mutual folly of the U.S.–North Korean dispute. Former U.S. president Jimmy Carter had followed the enlarging confrontation closely through the winter and spring of 1994, and beginning in June, against the Clinton administration's strong resistance, he moved to intervene. North Korea had been trying for three years to convince Carter to visit Pyongyang. The obvious thing to do was to pick up the invitation.

Before he did so, Carter wanted to be thoroughly briefed and to coordinate his efforts with Clinton. He called Clinton on 1 June and warned the president that sanctions could lead to war. Clinton was noncommittal. He offered to send someone to brief Carter on the state of play. That became a comedy of errors when the person assigned—the NSC's Poneman—sought a few days' delay because his wife had just given birth. To placate an angry and impatient Carter, the White House substituted the all-purpose Gallucci, who met with the former president and his wife Rosalynn at their home in Plains, Georgia, on Sunday morning, 5 June.

Gallucci had never met Carter before. The former president explained at the outset of their conversation why he was considering personal intervention: because the North Koreans had appealed to him to help. "I spent over three hours with President Carter," Gallucci told me, "going through the intelligence on why we were concerned about the North Korean program. Then where we were in the negotiations, why we had reached this impasse, why we had left the negotiating table when they discharged fuel from the reactor. What our concerns were about the gas-graphite reactor, the problems it presented in terms of the corroding fuel cladding and reprocessing, et cetera, et cetera. And therefore the crisis and our intent to proceed next to the Security Council."

Present at the discussion was Marion Creekmore, Jr., the former career diplomat, now a Carter aide and adviser. Creekmore reported Gallucci expressing his personal view "that North Korea wanted to make a deal. He thought that Kim Il Sung wanted enough investment to strengthen the [North Korean] economy and so protect the country during the political transition from his rule to that of his son."

"President Carter's capacity to see something from the other person's perspective is truly remarkable," Gallucci told me. "He immediately started devil's-advocating, asking what right we had to determine the North Koreans' choice of fuel cycle." Reprocessing spent fuel is allowed under the Nuclear Nonproliferation Treaty, although the North had agreed not to do so in its 1992 South-North Joint Declaration on the Denuclearization of the Korean Peninsula. "And I said, 'Well, if you recall 1977, you made quite a thing about the American position on reprocessing. We haven't liked it when other countries reprocess. Even when it's France, never mind North Korea.' Obviously he knew all this, but he made me work my way through it." It was the defueling of the five-megawatt reactor to reprocess the fuel, which the North Koreans had insisted was long overdue, that had precipitated the current crisis. Ominous in the background was what the Clinton administration was calling the Osirak option, the option of a preventive attack on Yongbyon. Gallucci told Carter, he and his colleagues wrote, "that the United States became 'very flexible' at this point, in part because Secretary of Defense William Perry, after reviewing the surgical strike option and its possible adverse consequences, favored a negotiated settlement."

The North had no intention of tolerating a U.S. buildup of forces in the region as Saddam Hussein had done after invading Kuwait. A North Korean colonel, Oberdorfer reported, had said as much to an American officer at Panmunjom in May: "We are not going to let you do a buildup." An American general "with access to all the available intelligence" told Oberdorfer, "I always got this feeling that the North Koreans studied [the 1991 Persian Gulf War] more than we did almost. And they learned one thing: you don't let the United States build up its forces and then let them go to war against you."

Carter responded to Gallucci's briefing with his own assessment of what the root cause of the standoff might be, Creekmore wrote:

> Carter emphasized his strong view about how to deal with Kim Il Sung. He said that despite Washington's understandably negative view of him and his record, Kim Il Sung must be treated with respect and honored as a senior statesman if the crisis was to be resolved peacefully. Unfortunately, the administration had moved in the opposite direction. It was proposing sanctions that, even if not implemented, would be a "tangible and official branding of [Kim Il Sung] as a criminal and outlaw." He insisted that the passage of a sanctions resolution by the United Nations Security Council would likely cause North Korea to leave the NPT permanently. The act of imposing sanctions, whether done in one or more stages, would be for North Korea "an act of war."

Carter flew to Washington on 10 June for further briefings, including a full-scale presentation by government experts whose conventional wisdom Carter systematically challenged by asking if they had ever been to North Korea, and if not, how did they know? Tony Lake, Clinton's national security adviser, tried to tell the ex-president what he could and could not say to Kim Il

Sung and was similarly rebuffed. Clinton would authorize Carter to visit North Korea only as a private citizen, not as an official representative of his administration. The young president was afraid to associate himself too closely with Carter, Creekmore wrote, citing two Clinton administration officials as his authority; "too close an identification with Carter would undercut the image of toughness in international affairs that he was trying to project. . . . [He] regarded Carter as a loser and did not want to appear to be close to him . . . out of his fear of being categorized as 'another failed Southern governor.' " Gallucci had a very different view of the former president. "Carter is a man of strong views," he said, "and he is also a man of real political calculation. The idea that he is a sort of neophyte in political terms and not up to the job is complete nonsense."

While Carter hacked his way through the Washington thicket that day, the IAEA board of governors in Vienna voted to suspend technical aid to North Korea. The amount involved was modest, only $250,000, but the insult registered; three days later the North pointedly withdrew from membership in the international agency.

By then the Carters had arrived in Seoul. Creekmore was traveling with them. The thriving South Korean capital, in the west of the Korean peninsula just twenty-three miles southeast of the demilitarized zone that divided North from South, was in ferment. "With rumors of shortages floating widely," Creekmore wrote, "constituents deluged members of the South Korean National Assembly with phone calls asking whether they should stockpile basic foodstuff. Most acted without advice, cramming into stores to buy quantities of dried noodles, rice, and candles. The Seoul stock market plunged 25 percent between June 13–15."

"I know a lot of people," Gallucci told me, "who said they didn't believe we were close to war. I can tell you that the strike planning had been done. The decision to call up the reserves had been made, a limited call-up. I mean, we didn't do any of it, but it was essentially the front end of a war plan that we were putting in place. The most provocative thing we were doing was starting NEO planning—non-combatant-evacuation operations, which means essentially that you evacuate the embassy and take the Americans out. And that's really provocative, because then the North Koreans can see that you are getting ready to do something. Well, we were headed that way." Some eighty thousand Americans lived among ten million Koreans in the crowded capital, within range of North Korean artillery. Evacuating them would be no easy task. Other foreign embassies in Seoul were also struggling with the question of when to evacuate their nationals.

The Carters crossed into North Korea at Panmunjom on Wednesday morning, 15 June, at about eleven a.m., walking past a crowd of media from the South to the North Korean side of the border. Carter found the experience eerie.

"The crossing at Panmunjom was a bizarre and disturbing experience," he wrote in a report completed immediately after returning from Korea, "evidence of an incredible lack of communication and understanding. For more than forty years, the Koreans and Americans have stared across the demilitarized zone with total suspicion and often hatred and fear. We were the first persons permitted to cross the DMZ to and from Pyongyang—since the armistice was signed in 1953!"

Carter, an engineer by training, next noticed the party's two-hour drive to Pyongyang "over an almost-empty four-lane highway" and in Pyongyang itself "a superb mass transit system . . . with an especially beautiful subway system more than three hundred feet underground." The system's depth, of course, had been determined by its dual purpose as a shelter against atomic bombing. Rosalynn Carter saw a "beautiful" countryside "with mostly rich-looking crops (some poor-looking corn), trees, rivers, and mountains," and in Pyongyang "roses in full bloom, on bushes along the streets and trailing over fences along the sidewalks . . . stretches of hollyhocks . . . ginkgo trees and weeping willow." Then the great bronze statue of Kim Il Sung loomed up, sixty-five feet high, reaching forth his hand.

Carter did not meet Kim that first day. Instead, Creekmore wrote, the ex-president and his party had to sit through a tedious seventy-five-minute speech by the North Korean foreign minister, Kim Yong Nam, "that spelled out, in a taxing and repetitive manner, the hard-line position of his country." Carter responded, says Creekmore, by focusing on achieving four major goals: "To persuade the North Korean leadership to keep the IAEA inspectors in place, to stop North Korean actions that could lead to nuclear weapons development, to facilitate U.S.-North Korean negotiations to resolve the outstanding nuclear issue, and to make the imposition of UN sanctions unnecessary." He projected "the image of a trusted neutral seeking to help [the two countries] find a peaceful and mutually productive resolution of their differences." But when Carter "probed for possible North Korean flexibility," the foreign minister responded by emphasizing the red line of U.N. sanctions: "We strongly affirm," he said, "that any sanctions enacted by the UN Security Council would be seen as a declaration of war."

The North Koreans wanted another round of talks with the U.S. before offering any concessions; the U.S. wanted concessions before any more talk. Carter made a note to himself: "Tell Wash. Sanctions will have *no* effect here except as an insult to an aging deity. Advise Gallucci schedule 3rd Round [of talks], maybe in Panmunjom *now*. It's a society like the religious group at Waco."* That night, after a banquet featuring ginseng liqueur, side dishes of fiery kimchi, lengthy toasts, and a strolling female band strumming guitars and singing "Oh Susannah" and "My

---

*The religious group to which Carter referred, the Branch Davidians, was a schism or "branch" of the Davidian sect of the Seventh-Day Adventist church, organized by a charismatic but sociopathic leader named David Koresh. Koresh and seventy-five of his followers had been killed the previous year when the U.S. Bureau of Alcohol, Tobacco, and Firearms attempted to serve a search warrant on the sect's compound near Waco, Texas—the Davidians violently resisted and a fifty-one-day siege of the compound culminated in a devastating fire from which only a few of Koresh's followers escaped.

Darling Clementine," Carter awoke at three a.m. agonizing over the clear possibility that his mission might fail and the United States and North Korea blunder into war. He roused Creekmore, who joined him and Rosalynn Carter in the garden of their guesthouse, out of range of hidden microphones, and spent the next two hours walking and talking about the problem. They decided that Carter might be getting a good-cop-bad-cop routine and that his meeting in the morning with Kim Il Sung might bring something better than the current bleak standoff. In case it didn't, Carter wanted Creekmore to return to Panmunjom in the morning with a confidential message from Carter to Clinton—they lacked secure communications in Pyongyang—which he would only transmit to Washington if Carter sent word. The message asked Clinton to authorize a third round of talks without prior North Korean concessions.

That Thursday morning, 16 June 1994, Creekmore found no one in authority south of the DMZ who believed Carter's appeal would carry the day in Washington, where Clinton was under siege. "We are heading toward catastrophe," Ambassador Laney told him. "Carter must persuade the North Koreans to make a tangible gesture of good faith to save Clinton's face. Kim Il Sung has to decide on a bold new initiative." Laney, wrote Creekmore, was worried about a White House meeting scheduled for ten a.m. in Washington, eleven p.m. Korean time, "over which President Clinton would preside, [when] the administration would decide whether and by how much to increase American troops and equipment in and around South Korea as a precaution against a possible military thrust by North Korea." Two freight trains—U.S. military deployment and the Jimmy Carter–Kim Il Sung diplomatic effort—were racing for the crossing.

Carter sat down with Kim Il Sung at his palace in Pyongyang at ten in the morning with Rosalynn Carter and their translators. The North Korean leader looked like his son Kim Jong Il but with a lower hairline and ruddier complexion. At eighty-two his legs were bandied; otherwise he was plump, vigorous, and alert. He still smoked. His son was not present. Kang Sok Ju, Gallucci's counterpart, joined the meeting at his Great Leader's side along with several other officials, in a conference room with a vast wooden table along which the two delegations lined up on opposite sides.

Kim clearly wanted a direct connection to the United States, a new patron to replace the Soviet Union and help with his country's failing economy, and a U.S. guarantee against nuclear attack. "We must have a way to live," he told Carter. "We need electricity, and if we cannot fulfill our electric power needs, our economic development efforts will be harmed." Carter wanted the IAEA inspectors to be allowed to remain in Yongbyon, the five-megawatt reactor and spent-fuel pool kept under their surveillance, and the nuclear program frozen until the next round of talks. "The central problem is that we lack trust," Kim said at another point, "and creating trust is our most important task. The distrust comes from the lack of contacts between us."

But Kim returned repeatedly to his need for light-water reactors, which was evidently, after a U.S. guarantee against nuclear attack, his bottom line:

> If the U.S. had helped us acquire a lightwater capability [following the Gallucci-Kang talks in 1993], even if from a third country, we could have avoided the current problem, and we would have reached a point of greater confidence, and we would now enjoy improved relations. If the U.S. would agree to hold a third round of talks, and to help us get lightwater reactors, then there will be no problems. . . . We announced that we are withdrawing from the IAEA, but we have not withdrawn completely from the NPT; if we get lightwater technology, we can take care of these things. . . . We need to build confidence, so your country can help us get lightwater reactors, and then we could do away with our existing reactor. If we can solve this problem, we intend to return fully to the NPT regime . . . [and] immediately freeze all our nuclear activities.

Carter summarized Kim's offer in his post-mission report:

He accepted all my proposals, with two major requests. One was that the United States support the acquisition of lightwater reactor technology, realizing that the funding and equipment could not come directly from America. . . . This is something we want the North Koreans to have, because the enriched fuel will have to be acquired from foreign sources, and the production of weapons-grade plutonium is not so easy as in their old graphite-moderated reactor that can use refined uranium directly from their own mines. His second request was that the United States guarantee that there will be no nuclear attack against his country. He wanted the third round of United States–North Korean talks to be resumed to resolve all the outstanding nuclear issues. He was willing to freeze their nuclear program during the talks, and to consider a permanent freeze if their aged reactors could be replaced with modern and safer ones. . . .

I assured him that there were no nuclear weapons in South Korea or tactical weapons in the waters surrounding the peninsula, and that my understanding is that the United States desires to see North Korea acquire lightwater reactors. He agreed with me that the entire Korean peninsula should be nuclear-free.

At that point Carter saw that he had achieved his goals in the negotiation. Through an aide he passed word to Creekmore to stand down and return to Pyongyang. Carter still had to run the gauntlet of an afternoon session with Kang Sok Ju. Kang pressed Carter to give up some of his gains, but Carter was far too shrewd to be manipulated. When Kang pushed, the former president "asked him each time if he had a different policy from his 'Great Leader,' [whereupon] he would back down."

After dinner, Carter called Gallucci on an open line to brief him on the breakthrough. It was eleven p.m. Friday evening in Pyongyang, ten a.m. Friday morning in Washington, and Gallucci was at the White House participating in the urgent meeting of Clinton administration principals. The meeting included Clinton, Vice President Gore, Secretary of State Warren Christopher, Perry, the Joint Chiefs chairman John Shalikashvili, the C.I.A. director James Woolsey, the U.N. ambassador Madeleine Albright, and Tony Lake. Clinton had authorized a push for U.N. sanctions at the beginning of the meeting; the discussion concerned what military preparations should follow. The president was still smarting from the October Somalia debacle, which he was widely accused of having botched by dispatching too few troops to protect the mission.

"The North Koreans had virtually told us that we could expect a violent response even to a sanctions resolution," Gallucci recalled, "never mind an attempt to implement sanctions. Secretary Perry was presenting a force-enhancement package that Christopher and Shalikashvili had signed off on at breakfast earlier that morning. And right in the middle of the meeting, as Perry was presenting the options, the door opened and the person at the door said, 'President Carter is on the telephone.' The president started to get up and the person said, 'No, no, it's for Bob Gallucci.' Remember, I had briefed Carter twice; he'd probably called my office and they'd patched him through to the White House. So I kind of slunk out, not on all fours, but I slunk out and talked to Carter. He told me that they had made a deal that we could go back to the table and the North Koreans wouldn't reprocess any of the fuel that they had offloaded into the pond. I said, 'Okay, I'll report that.' He said, 'What do you think?' I said, 'Well, the President's in the other room; I don't know if what I think matters very much right now. I think I'd better report this.' He said, 'You can also report that I'll be describing this on CNN.' I said, 'Okay.' He said, 'So give me a call.' I said, 'Actually, you'll have to call back, we aren't allowed to call North Korea.'"

"So I got off the phone," Gallucci continued, "and went back in and told them President Carter had worked out a deal with the North Koreans. If we were to accept it, then they would not reprocess and we could go back to the bargaining table. Someone said, 'That's not new. This is where we were before,' and there was moaning and grousing. Then I said, 'Oh, and he's going to go on CNN and say this.' Tony Lake said, 'You did tell him not to do that, didn't you?' I started to answer. I was sitting next to the secretary of state. His eyebrows went up and he said, 'You did tell him not to do that?' Then the president said, 'What did he say when you told him not to do that?' So I had the national security establishment of the United States after me. I said, 'Actually, I didn't tell him not to do that. I didn't think it would have much impact.' 'But you did try, didn't you?' 'No, no I didn't.' So I thought that this was the end of what had up until then been a pretty successful career for me. But before we went any further, someone said, 'Let's go into the next room and watch it on TV.' Which we did." The principals crowded into the adjoining reception area, filling the available chairs or standing. A few sat on the floor. Gallucci retreated to a corner behind Gore and sat against a credenza, making himself inconspicuous.

The interview that the White House watched on CNN was the second that Carter had given that night. It crossed the Pacific on radio circuits rather than television. After Carter's television interview, he had returned to his government guesthouse and undressed for bed and some much-needed sleep, when CNN knocked apologetically on his door to report that the North Korean television station whose satellite uplink CNN had expected to use had shut down for the night; the network now wanted to do a live radio interview to fill in. Irritably, Carter had changed back into his day clothes and submitted to the interview, which was broadcast live on CNN television with a still photograph of Carter for a visual. Creekmore said the former president agreed to the second interview because he was concerned that Kim Il Sung's advisers might persuade the North Korean leader to renege on his commitments. But Carter may have been at least as concerned about forestalling rash U.S. action as he was about restraining North Korea; his first words to Creekmore after the television taping had been, "That killed the [United States's] sanctions resolution. The Chinese will never permit it to get out of the Security Council now."

CNN's Wolf Blitzer and Judy Woodruff interviewed Carter at length. Carter called Kim Il Sung's commitments "a very important and very positive step toward the alleviation of this crisis." What was needed now, he said, was "a very simple decision just to let the already constituted delegations from North Korea and the United States have their third meeting, which has been postponed. That's all that's needed now, and all the North Koreans are addressing." After the radio interview was broadcast, the earlier television interview was archived and never run.

In Clinton's eyes, Carter had preempted the White House's authority and prerogatives. Gore moved to bandage the presidential wound. "The outcome of that," Gallucci told me, "was that the vice president said, 'We've got lemons, go make lemonade—go make this a good deal.' " Gallucci got the thankless task of drafting the Clinton requirements. "We said, 'Well, let's raise the bar. Let's say they can't restart the five-megawatt reactor. So that would be our deal. It wouldn't be Carter's deal, it would be Clinton's deal. And then I went out to face the press, and the first question, after I told them what had happened, was, 'Did you tell President Carter not to go on CNN?' I said, 'Tell President Carter not to go on CNN? Of course not.' They said, 'Really? You didn't try to discourage him?' I said, 'Absolutely not.' So when I went back in, Tony Lake said, 'You are a lucky son-of-a-bitch.' "

Carter was predictably furious to be second-guessed, but Kim Il Sung wanted the deal enough to go along with the additional terms. The crisis ended there, only days short of what might have been a second Korean war even more brutal than the first.

GALLUCCI MET WITH Kang Sok Ju in Geneva for the first of the third-round talks on 8 July 1994. The next day, Kim Il Sung died of a heart attack. There was mass lamentation in North Korea, but the death of the Great Leader hardly slowed the negotiations. "We postponed that round just a little bit," Gallucci said, "and then ultimately we had a round. I've never been able to identify an impact on the negotiations. We were heading in a direction and we just kept going in that direction."

The two sides resumed the delayed negotiations on 15 July. They discussed the curious option of shipping an unfinished power reactor from Washington State to North Korea. The Washington Public Power Supply System, WPPSS, had two white-elephant reactors—the "whoops" reactors, people called them derisively, punning on their acronymic names—that had been cancelled when the bottom dropped out of U.S energy demand in the wake of the 1973–1974 Arab oil embargo. The cancellation, wrote Gallucci and his colleagues, "occasioned the largest municipal-bond default in American history. Ever since then, the desperate owners had sought some alternative use for the reactors to recover at least part of their investment."

Eventually Kang and Gallucci agreed on two new reactors, implicitly South Korean reactors although not named as such, to be supplied by a new multinational consortium called the Korean Peninsula Energy Development Organization (KEDO).* In October, the two sides completed four months of negotiations by adopting an agreed framework. North Korea agreed to freeze and eventually to eliminate its nuclear complex by dismantling its Yongbyon reactor and the two larger reactors under construction elsewhere in the country. It agreed to allow the IAEA to conduct special inspections and the Americans to can the five-megawatt reactor's eight thousand spent fuel rods and ship them out of the country. In exchange, KEDO would finance and supply the D.P.R.K. with two light-water reactors. Until they were finished and operating, their equivalent energy, two thousand megawatts,

---

*Originally the Korean Energy Development Organization. Gallucci liked the acronym and kept it after the change in name because he and his son were studying aikido, the Japanese martial art.

would be made up by annual shipments totaling five hundred thousand tons of heavy fuel oil.

Congressional Republicans bitterly criticized the Agreed Framework, calling it appeasement. It had not been an easy sell. When Gallucci came back from Geneva to push the agreement through the interagency process, he told the *Atlantic Monthly* some years later, he was confronted by people such as Kenneth Adelman, the neoconservative former director of the U.S. Arms Control and Disarmament Agency, who had opposed negotiating with the D.P.R.K. "They hated the idea of trying to solve this problem with a negotiation," Gallucci said. "And I said, 'What's your—pardon me—your fucking plan, then, if you don't like this?'

" 'We don't like—'

"I said, 'Don't tell me what you don't like! Tell me how you're going to stop the North Korean nuclear program.'

" 'But we wouldn't do it this way—'

" 'Stop! What are you going to do?'

"I could never get a goddamn answer. What I got was, 'We wouldn't negotiate.' "

Gallucci and his colleagues disagreed with conservative assessments of the Agreed Framework:

From the standpoint of American taxpayers, [it] left them a good deal safer at a relatively small cost, *even if the North Koreans eventually broke the freeze or did not dismantle their nuclear program.* In other words, the Agreed Framework did not deprive the United States of any future options. One way to think of the U.S. contribution to the Agreed Framework was as term insurance; for a small yearly premium, the United States avoided an increment of tens of new bombs' worth of plutonium being separated in North Korea over the same twelve-month period. . . . And, obviously, if the North broke the terms of the Agreed Framework, the United States would stop paying its yearly premium [of heavy fuel oil].

Despite troubles and setbacks, the Agreed Framework held together, just barely, through the remainder of Clinton's second term. The U.S. relaxed its sanctions on North Korea in June 2000, allowing trade and investment, and the North reciprocated by reaffirming its moratorium on missile tests, the new bone of contention between the two countries. (At a dinner following a meeting between Kim Jong Il and South Korean president Kim Dae-jung in the summer of 2000, a South Korean newspaper publisher asked Kim Jong Il why he was spending so much money on ballistic missiles. "The missiles cannot reach the United States," the Dear Leader answered, "and if I launch them, the U.S. would fire back thousands of missiles and we would not survive. I know that very well. But I have to let them know I have missiles. I am making them because only then will the United States talk to me.")

Secretary of State Madeleine Albright visited North Korea in October 2000. She was preparing the way for a visit by Clinton in December, and the D.P.R.K. was near an agreement to eliminate its missiles and end its missile exports, but the visit was cancelled when Clinton decided he had to remain in the United States during the dispute between Al Gore and George W. Bush about who won the 2000 presidential election. When George W. Bush was determined to have won, his administration backed away from the Clinton administration's grand bargain with North Korea. Thereafter, relations between the two countries progressively worsened. Bush administration observers quipped with gallows humor that the rule in the new Bush White House was to study what Clinton had been doing and then do the opposite.

TWELVE

THE CORNERSTONE OF PEACE AND STABILITY

I N AUGUST 1994, while Bob Gallucci was negotiating with Kang Sok Ju over light-water reactors, Tom Graham, the ambassador and U.S. arms negotiator, had occasion to visit, with a State Department colleague, the workshop where South Africa had assembled its uranium gun bombs. The bombs were gone and their highly enriched uranium components melted down and stored, but the building where Armscor had crafted them remained, as did the ten bank vaults lined up behind false doors where their separated barrels and breeches had been secured. "Look around you," Graham's hosts told him as he entered the workshop. "Nothing has changed."

"There was nothing there that you would not find in a high-school machine shop," Graham recalled. "They showed us the cases they used to move the weapons around, so we had an idea of their size; one would have easily fit in the back of a panel truck. 'We built six weapons,' they said, 'and were working on a seventh when we shut the program down. Nobody knew about it. We never had more than one hundred fifty people involved, including the janitor. We spent twenty-five million dollars. We used gun-barrel technology so we didn't need to test—we knew the weapons would work.' They were showing us their operation, they said, because they wanted us to understand that if a country, or even a subnational group, can acquire the nuclear material, the rest is really easy. You don't need an infrastructure. You just need a few skilled scientists and engineers and the HEU."

Graham had visited South Africa to solicit its vote on the indefinite extension of the Nuclear Non-Proliferation Treaty. After his work in the early 1990s encouraging the new states of the former Soviet Union to consolidate their nuclear arsenals in Russia and join the NPT, the accomplished Kentuckian had been appointed acting director of the U.S. Arms Control and Disarmament Agency. When a new permanent director was confirmed in November 1993, Graham asked to be appointed special representative of the president for arms control, nonproliferation, and disarmament, with responsibility for the NPT. Graham considered the treaty to be "the centerpiece of international efforts to control the spread of nuclear weapons." As the 1995 stand-or-fall vote on its indefinite extension approached, the NPT was under siege from signatories who felt that the nuclear powers had failed to sustain their part of the nonproliferation bargain; Graham wanted to represent the United States in the fight to save it. "Although few agreed," he wrote, "I believed that [indefinite extension] was achievable if we remained optimistic, were creative and never wavered."

It had been customary in previous NPT negotiations to meet with diplomats at the perpetual Conference on Disarmament in Geneva or at the United Nations in New York, catch-as-catch-can. Graham decided instead to make the case for NPT extension in person to national foreign-policy leaders in capitals around the world. Between 1993 and 1995 he visited more than forty capitals in North and South America, Europe, Africa, Asia, and the Pacific. "I traveled all over the world looking for votes," he said later. "It was a little bit like a political convention." He went to South Africa because it was a key vote, a swing vote. "They had the possibility of bringing in a lot of nonaligned countries who were opposed to us, to support our view that the NPT should be permanent."

His basic argument in all his presentations, Graham told

me, was that there would be only one chance—the 1995 review and extension conference—to make the NPT permanent: The twenty-fifth anniversary vote had been preapproved when the original treaty was ratified, but any further votes would require new parliamentary ratification by a majority of NPT member states, which Graham called "an impossibility in today's world." The NPT, he declared, was "the cornerstone of international peace and stability and the base on which all other arms control and nonproliferation agreements are built." If the nonnuclear states wanted the nuclear powers to disarm, the nuclear powers would need the protections of the NPT to do so. If they wanted the commercial benefits of what he called "peaceful nuclear cooperation," meaning support for the development of nuclear power and other nuclear technologies, the NPT was the "best basis." For example, he argued, "a nuclear power reactor requires ten years to build and thirty years to operate, and the spent fuel has to be safeguarded forever"—to ensure that it isn't reprocessed for its plutonium. "For the appropriate economic decisions to be made, there must be assurance that the IAEA safeguards which flow from the NPT will not expire."

Graham found significant resistance to making the NPT permanent, especially among the member states of the Non-Aligned Movement (NAM), which includes many countries in Africa, the Middle East, South America, and the Caribbean. One of his reasons for working state by state, visiting the key capitals, was to forestall the NAM from opposing the treaty en bloc. In exchange for their votes, he wrote, "many countries stressed the importance of a CTBT"—a comprehensive test-ban treaty that would ban all nuclear testing. (A test ban was the next obvious step forward in limiting nuclear-weapons development and proliferation, because only the simplest and bulkiest weapon designs, unsuited for missile delivery, could be devised indigenously without testing.) "Some also emphasized the need for updated and legally binding negative security assurances—pledges by the nuclear-weapon states not to attack non-nuclear-weapon states with nuclear weapons (most of the NAM wanted this) and positive security assurances—pledges by the nuclear-weapon states to come to the aid of non-nuclear-weapon states threatened or attacked with nuclear weapons (Egypt wanted this). Some countries, primarily in the Middle East, underscored the problem of Israel not being an NPT party."

Before he could sell the NPT to other countries, Graham had to line up support at home. The NPT itself was not a problem, since limiting the proliferation of nuclear weapons had always been to America's advantage and therefore a U.S. priority. But he understood early on that the price of making the NPT permanent would be U.S. commitment to a CTBT—and the U.S. weapons labs and the Pentagon were resisting such a ban.

More was at stake for the labs than their ability to test new weapon designs or assess the safety of old ones. Their future might be at stake and the careers of their scientists and engineers, many of whom had never known any other line of work. Sig Hecker was still director of the Los Alamos National Laboratory at the time of the internal U.S. debate over ending weapons testing. A fundamental issue, Hecker told me, was how to balance the loss of certainty about the performance of the U.S. nuclear arsenal against the increased security that would result from eliminating nuclear testing throughout the world.

The dissolution of the Soviet Union in December 1991 had brought unprecedented changes to the U.S. nuclear-weapons complex. The Strategic Air Command furled its colors and stood down on 31 May 1992. George H. W. Bush and Boris Yeltsin agreed at a June 1992 summit to cut their nuclear arsenals to between 3,000 and 3,500 deployed strategic warheads by 2003. (Counting their strategic reserves, each side's remaining numbers would actually be around 10,000.) They would limit submarine-launched ballistic missiles to 1,750 warheads while scrapping all their multiple-warhead ICBMs. Yeltsin had proposed mutual reductions to 2,500 strategic warheads each, but Secretary of Defense Dick Cheney successfully opposed the lower number, Graham writes, "and the Russians eventually accepted the [higher] 3,000–3,500 [limit], a level they could not [financially] support for their own services." Despite Cheney's sabotage, diplomat James Goodby rightly called the agreement "the greatest disarmament program in the history of the world."

Cheney resisted reductions in the U.S. nuclear arsenal because he was then in the process of formulating a new post–Cold War defense policy that he considered more appropriate to the new status of the United States as the world's only remaining superpower. (Russia, according to the conventional wisdom, had receded to the status of a Third World country with nuclear weapons.) An early version of the 1992 Defense Planning Guidance (DPG), wrote the policy experts Derek Chollet and James Goldgeier, "laid out very clearly how America should think now that the Cold War was over: 'Our first objective is to prevent the re-emergence of a new rival, either on the territory of the former Soviet Union or elsewhere, that poses a threat on the order of that posed formerly by the Soviet Union. This is a dominant consideration underlying the new regional defense strategy and requires that we endeavor to prevent any hostile power from dominating a region whose resources would, under consolidated control, be sufficient to generate global power.' " Cheney, the two policy experts concluded, "wanted the United States to remain the pre-eminent world power by keeping others at bay and bending the world to its wishes." The names of those on Cheney's staff who worked on the document would become familiar in the post-2000 administration of George W. Bush: Paul Wolfowitz, Zalmay Khalilzad, Lewis "Scooter" Libby, Stephen Hadley, Eric Edelman. In the last year of the administration of Bush's father, the DPG draft was not well received. "That was just nutty," George H. W. Bush's national security adviser Brent Scowcroft told Chollet and Goldgeier. "I read a draft of it. I thought, 'Cheney, this is just kooky.' It didn't go anywhere further. It was never formally reviewed." But of course it did go further, after the interregnum of the Clinton years.

Despite Cheney's resistance, the U.S. nuclear-weapons-production complex was downsizing, partly in response to uni-lateral and negotiated arms reductions, partly because public concern had caught up with its environmentally abandoned ways. The FBI had actually raided the Department of Energy's plutonium-production facility at Rocky Flats, in Colorado, in 1989, looking for evidence (which it found in abundance) that the DOE and Rockwell International, a contractor, had violated environmental-protection laws. In September 1992, Secretary of Energy James Watkins cancelled plans for a new reactor to make tritium for nuclear weapons; with thousands of weapons to be removed from the arsenal from which tritium could be canni-balized, existing stocks of the yield-boosting gas would serve until at least 2012.* "The September decision was a climax in the transition of the DOE weapons complex," wrote the historian W. Henry Lambright, "from an enterprise whose principal mis-sion was weapons-making to one whose primary role would be weapons research and development and environmental cleanup. Almost half of the entire $12 billion budget of DOE [in 1992] now focused on nuclear cleanup."

The most radical challenge, however, came in October 1992, when U.S. senators Mark Hatfield, James Exon, and George Mitchell supported and Congress approved a bipartisan amend-ment to an appropriations bill mandating a ten-month morato-rium on U.S. nuclear-weapons tests, after which the U.S. could conduct no more than fifteen tests over a four-year period before a comprehensive test-ban treaty was negotiated, and those tests were only to be for assessing the safety and reliability of U.S. nuclear weapons. The Hatfield-Exon-Mitchell amendment responded to a challenge moratorium instituted by France the previous April. It was designed to position the United States favorably to campaign for a CTBT, and it set a deadline for

---

*With a half-life of only 12.3 years, tritium has to be replenished at the rate of about 5.5 percent per weapon per year as it decays into helium.

achieving such a treaty of 30 September 1996. George H. W. Bush signed the appropriations bill, with its subversive amendment, with great reluctance, but the bill included money for a huge particle accelerator, the Superconducting Super Collider, to be built in Texas, a plum that Bush considered important to his reelection. An underground nuclear test fired at Yucca Flat, Nevada, on 23 September 1992, was thus the last of 1,125 weapons tests the U.S. had fired since 1945. A moratorium on U.S. nuclear tests would impose a de facto moratorium on Britain as well, since the British no longer maintained a test site themselves but tested exclusively at the Nevada range.

George H. W. Bush lost his bid for reelection that November (and the Superconducting Super Collider was subsequently abandoned unbuilt) to Bill Clinton. Sig Hecker was dismayed, as were many of his colleagues. "It was a whole different world," he told me. "Just a bunch of young people in the White House. Many of them had no idea of what the nuclear-weapons business was about. Right from the beginning, Clinton and Gore made it clear that it would be very difficult to convince them that we should do any of these Hatfield-Exon-Mitchell tests. And then we got Ms. Hazel O'Leary as secretary of energy. We went from a four-star admiral, Admiral Watkins, to Hazel O'Leary. And now she had responsibility for nuclear weapons."

O'Leary, a lawyer, former prosecutor, and utilities executive, fifty-six years old in 1993, was the first African-American woman to serve as secretary of energy. She was a Virginia native, the daughter of two physicians who had made a point of sending her to summer camp in Massachusetts and high school in New Jersey, where she lived with an aunt, to shield her as much as possible from the spirit-breaking ugliness of the segregated South. Partly as a result, O'Leary grew up to be a smart, attractive, gregarious, hugely self-confident woman with a gift for cutting through the bureaucratic underbrush and getting to the point.

She got to the point quickly enough in numerous meetings that winter and spring of 1993 with Hecker and other managers of the nuclear-weapons complex, Hecker recalled. "She said, 'You guys have done a thousand tests. I don't see what else you're going to learn with a dozen more.'" Hecker thought her point oversimple, but he understood it wasn't irrational. "She listened to a number of folks who were pro–arms control—which I consider myself to be—but who were also anti-testing. They felt strongly that testing really was one of the main things that drove the arms race." Sidney Drell, a vigorous, no-nonsense Stanford theoretical physicist and a founding member of the legendary JASON defense advisory group, was one of O'Leary's advisers. Sixty-seven in 1993, Drell had been a member of the Clinton transition team on matters related to defense, nuclear in particular. "Sid had just been an enormous advocate of stopping testing," Hecker told me, "I think since the late 1950s. But he was also a very wise man. He understood the defense world. And without ever saying it directly, he really made me feel the responsibility I had as lab director to give the government the best advice we could possibly give. Without being driven by any of the side issues. And that the reputation of our institution depended on it. I had a strong sense of responsibility anyway, but he made me feel it even more so."

Tom Graham came into the debate as well, in May 1993, when the questions of extending the nuclear moratorium and of negotiating a CTBT had worked their way up to the Cabinet-level National Security Council Principals Committee. "Reliability testing is not something that had been done very often historically," Graham wrote later. "There was no demonstrable purpose in doing the testing except simply to have nuclear tests. . . . This did not seem to me to be sustainable. Further, and more important, in about two years we were going to seek to extend the NPT, we hoped, indefinitely." Graham was concerned as well with the difficulty the U.S. was having at that time in convincing Ukraine to turn over its nuclear arsenal to Russia. "How were we going to persuade Ukraine to give up the nuclear weapons on its territory if we were emphasizing the usefulness of nuclear weapons with a test program?" Before the principals' meeting, he had tried to confer with O'Leary at DOE. "I had not been able to see [her], but I spoke with her deputy, and he said that it was their view that there is a time for an end to everything, and that nothing should just continue on forever with no rationale. I was cheered by these words."

Among those attending the principals' meeting besides Graham were Clinton's national security adviser, Tony Lake; Lake's deputy, Sandy Berger; Hazel O'Leary; the CIA director, James Woolsey; the White House science adviser, John Gibbons; Colin Powell, the chairman of the Joint Chiefs; Secretary of State Warren Christopher; and Secretary of Defense Les Aspin. Other nuclear issues dominated the first forty-five minutes of the one-hour meeting, after which Lake asked, "Who will speak for the moratorium?" Graham was ready:

> I raised my hand and gave the speech that I had used in [a previous] meeting, stressing NPT extension and also Ukraine. I argued that if the United States resumed testing (and having the British tests in Nevada), Russia and China likely would discontinue their moratoria. Indefinite extension of the NPT in 1995 against a backdrop of all five nuclear weapon states testing likely would prove impossible. I further argued that the tests were not necessary and should not jeopardize NPT extension if they were not.

The question went around the room. Powell cautioned great care; America's nuclear weapons, he said, were its "crown jewels." Christopher and Aspin thought the U.S. should run the fifteen tests that the Hatfield-Exon-Mitchell amendment had authorized, since that was the deal Congress had struck. Gibbons agreed with Graham that the U.S. should continue its moratorium. Then O'Leary almost casually finessed the debate and took control, Graham wrote:

> Hazel, however, to the annoyance of Tony [Lake], stopped the show. She said she was a new kid on the block and that she had not really had time to study the issue and consult her experts.

She wanted to put off any discussion of this issue for two weeks so that she would have time to study and understand it. This created something of a furor, but she stuck to her guns. When asked about the position of DOE at lower levels that opposed the moratorium, she noted that she was the secretary. Grumpily, Tony announced that there would be no decision, no outcome to send to the president, and that the principals would meet again on this issue in two weeks' time.

The next time Graham saw O'Leary, in her DOE office a few days before the second principals' meeting, they were joined by Victor Reis, the Pentagon's shrewd and influential director of defense research and engineering, a mechanical engineer with degrees from Rensselaer Polytechnic, Yale, and Princeton and decades of government experience. "It was an inspirational meeting," Graham writes. "Hazel said that she was with us and that stopping testing was the right way to go." O'Leary qualified her endorsement, however, telling Graham, "It would require a lot of laboratory support to maintain the weapons without testing." Reis, Graham comments, "made no dissent and seemed happy." The second principals' meeting, in late May, was divided on the moratorium extension, Graham wrote:

> Hazel brought with her, among others, two senior lab experts to give a briefing on the status of the nuclear weapon stockpile. They explained how, for at least ten years, even if we were to do nothing, there was no problem with the safety and reliability of the stockpile. After that period of time they could not be so certain, but they were confident that any problems could be addressed successfully through means other than testing. After a lengthy discussion on this Tony went around the room on the moratorium issue.

O'Leary had evidently struck a deal with Reis. There was still resistance from some of the principals to banning testing, but on

O'Leary's recommendation, on 3 July 1993 Clinton resolved the dispute by announcing that the United States would continue to observe the nuclear-testing moratorium until September 1994, provided that no other state tested. Clinton said that the moratorium would then be renewed year by year under the same terms until successful negotiation of a comprehensive test-ban treaty, a process that would begin in January 1994.

WHAT VICTOR REIS'S DEAL with O'Leary might be began to reveal itself that summer, when Reis left Defense at the beginning of August to join the DOE under O'Leary as assistant secretary for defense programs. Reis told Hecker that his fundamental assignment from O'Leary was to cut the nuclear-weapons budget. The new assistant secretary had a more positive goal in mind: to figure out what the nuclear-weapons complex needed to maintain the U.S. arsenal without testing and then to make it available.

"Vic knew nothing about nuclear weapons," Hecker told me, "so he started to learn. He had this wonderful technique of bringing in lots of people from different sides of the business. Bringing them together in workshops, brainstorming ideas, working things through. He'd have a few of his department people, the lab directors, even people from the Office of Management and Budget, because in the end, if you don't have those guys supplying the money, you don't have anything. He had congressional staff and people from the regulatory agencies. These people all said nuclear weapons were still important, still the cornerstone of our defense strategy for the security of the country. But, they said, we don't want to make any new ones. We just want to make sure that those we have are safe, secure, and reliable. And then that meshes in with the direction of our negotiations with the Russians for arms reductions.

"So that summer of 1993 we started strategizing the future," Hecker continued. "Vic was unquestionably the driving force. We'd called the weapons program R, D & T in the past, for 'research, development, and testing.' We lost the testing, so we called what we were doing R & D. But that wasn't what people wanted. They didn't want more R & D on nuclear weapons; the whole idea now was that the world had changed. So we tried to find a way to describe what it was that we were now supposed to do, and we came up with the idea of stockpile stewardship."

Reis defined the concept succinctly at a congressional hearing in 1999 from a perspective six years along. "Stockpile Stewardship," he said then, "consists of two interlocking parts: restoring and modernizing the production capability of the [nuclear weapons] complex, and being able to perpetually certify the reliability, safety and security of the nuclear weapons in the stockpile." Given the state of the production complex in 1993, Reis testified, "This was, and is, an extraordinary challenge. . . . Rocky Flats, the only facility capable of producing plutonium pits, was permanently closed. Oak Ridge Y-12, the nation's uranium factory, was soon to shut down for safety concerns, and there was no source of tritium and no money in the budget to develop a new source. And to top it off, the weapons laboratories were being strongly encouraged by the DOE to turn their attention to non-defense missions and they were doing so. Frankly, it was not a pretty picture, and few gave the program much chance for success."

The nuclear-weapons complex could either reinvent itself or fall apart, and under Reis's leadership and with full budgetary support from Congress the effort to slim down and modernize succeeded. By 1999, Reis could testify in operational terms to what stockpile stewardship had meant:

> For three years running we have been able to certify to the President and the Congress that the stockpile is safe and reliable. We have been able to modify and deploy a version of the B61 [hydrogen] bomb to replace the very old and very large B53. We have started deliveries of a refurbished W-87 [nuclear warhead] to the Air Force; Y-12 [the primary uranium enrichment facility at Oak Ridge, Tennessee, which had been shut down for safety

violations] is up and running. We have re-established neutron generator manufacturing at Sandia, tritium gas bottles at Kansas City, and are on schedule to produce tritium with the TVA and Savannah River and plutonium pits at Los Alamos. Savannah River is operating the new tritium refill facility, and since 1990 we have safely dismantled over 10,000 weapons at the Pantex Plant [in Amarillo, Texas].

There had always been a price to pay within the U.S. defense bureaucracy for arms-control treaties and particularly for arms reductions. The price for the bureaucracy's support had been money for new weapons systems, or, failing that, money for modernization of the weapons systems that remained. In that regard it was not much different from the defense bureaucracy of the old Soviet Union. "A very large part of the [Soviet] military budget," wrote William Odom, the U.S. general who directed the National Security Agency during Ronald Reagan's second term, "went to the [Soviet Military Industrial Commission] for constant modernization of weaponry." What Reis, Hecker, and others in the U.S. nuclear-weapons complex organized in the second half of the 1990s was a physically leaner complex appropriate to a smaller nuclear arsenal. So many weapons were being dismantled in response to U.S.-Russian arms negotiations that the remaining weapons could be maintained from dismantled parts.

A more serious problem, however, was manpower. Without the experience of designing new weapons and testing them, new recruits to the national laboratories would acquire little of the personal knowledge that was vital to their work. Science and engineering both require not only book learning but also craft skills, and craft skills grow from hands-on experience. Under the new, leaner regime that Reis was building for the Clinton administration, where would that personal knowledge come from?

"We did some planning exercises as we went into 1994," Hecker told me, "trying to lay out the requirements within the DOE defense complex depending on what the force structure would look like and on whether or not the START II treaty went into effect. Those are significant differences in terms of how much tritium you need, for example, what sort of construction capacity you need, how many people you need. So Vic not only did workshops; he also did very specific studies. And from that emerged his variation on the Clinton election mantra 'It's the economy, stupid.' Vic said, 'It's the labs, stupid.' He meant, you really have to start with the labs and then you build the complex around that." Hecker explained:

> Better than anyone else, he was able to articulate the link between stewardship and no testing. He said, look, maybe the country doesn't need us to develop new weapons, but it needs us for stewardship. We're being asked to take cradle-to-grave responsibility for an incredibly complex mechanism. And as these weapons age, they change, and now we have to maintain them without testing.
>
> Every organization needs a major goal. What he helped us to see was that the goal was no longer the next great bomb, but doing something that had never been done before. Vic kept reminding us that nuclear weapons were still officially in the supreme national interest. If so, he said, then our leaders had to have confidence that they would work. How do we have confidence if we can't test? We do it by building a program that ensures that confidence in the absence of testing.

Ironically, Reis and the U.S. laboratories were reaching this conclusion even as others in the defense bureaucracy had concluded that continued testing was the answer. Hecker told me:

> It seemed to us that the proponents of testing were pushing toward a world where we would get a few tests a year to ensure ourselves that the bombs we still had in the stockpile would work. I felt very, very strongly that taking one out every now and then and testing it was the wrong way to go, a vulnerability the

United States couldn't afford. As Vic had said, the more important plan was to keep the intellectual capacity of our laboratories. Make the laboratory such that it still attracted the smartest people in the country to think about these issues and about what other defense issues there might be. I was afraid that if you did a test now and then and you finally had a problem, the laboratory would have become the Jiffy Lube of the nuclear-weapons business—an oil change and a lube job at best. And the people doing it would know just that much and no more. They wouldn't have the ability to really sort things out if the going got tough. Vic said, Sig, do you believe the Israelis have bombs? I said, Well, yes, of course. He said, Do you think they ever tested their bombs? I mentioned the 1979 test, but if they did that one, it was probably not a very big one.

He said, Do you think their bombs work? I said, Yes, sure. He said, Why do you say that? And I said, Because they've got smart people.

I thought about that conversation many times.

Reis also believed that each laboratory needed a major scientific facility to attract the best people. "He called it the Nordstrom Mall concept," Hecker recalled. "He said, You can have a lot of boutiques, but if you don't have a major department store anchoring it, you don't have a mall. It's a simple point, but it was very effective. He said, The way we'll do this is, Livermore will get the lasers and Los Alamos will do the neutrons. Meaning, Los Alamos would build the next big accelerator and Livermore would build the next big laser."

Hecker defends the multibillion-dollar investments the U.S. made in its weapons laboratories in the years after 1993. The lab directors sign an annual letter certifying that the U.S. nuclear-weapons stockpile is safe and reliable and that testing is not required. Hecker signed two of those letters to the president before he left the Los Alamos directorship in 1998. "There's nothing else that I've ever done," he told me, "that caused me to think more and pause more and worry more than the responsibility I felt when I did that. It's easy to be a critic on the outside and say you don't need this or that, you don't need this budget. In the end, though, the president can only go with the judgment of the lab director. He has no other way of judging. But unless the lab director has faith in his system and his institution, he can't certify the nuclear weapons. If you still consider the weapons to be important to the future of the country, you have to take that seriously."

AT THEIR FIFTH SUMMIT MEETING, in September 1994, Bill Clinton and Boris Yeltsin agreed to continue the testing moratorium and to support both indefinite extension of the NPT and a worldwide ban on fissile-material production—a fissile-material-cutoff treaty.* In December, Tom Graham flew to Israel to discuss the concerns of NPT member states about Israel's refusal to become a signatory. "Israeli officials regarded the NPT as important," Graham writes. "Several officials said that when Israel could be assured that Iran and Iraq were not threats to acquire nuclear weapons, they would consider the NPT, but not before."

As Graham continued making the rounds of national capitals, the United States continued promoting the NPT. In a speech celebrating the twenty-fifth anniversary of the treaty's entry into force, 5 March 1995, Clinton announced that he was ordering two hundred tons of plutonium and HEU permanently withdrawn from the U.S. stockpile. "None of that material will be used to build a nuclear weapon ever again," Graham wrote. "The president decided that this bold disarmament gesture was an appropriate way to emphasize the commitment of the United States both to Article VI and to the NPT in general." Article VI, the treaty requirement that the nuclear powers work seriously toward eliminating their nuclear arsenals, continued to be a source of contention with the nonnuclear signatories.

*Still unnegotiated in 2010.

Graham reported a revealing mix of motives among the treaty parties for and against indefinite extension. Egypt's foreign minister told Graham that Egypt "could not live forever with a huge, unconstrained nuclear arsenal on its border," meaning Israel's. Egypt wanted concrete steps on Israel's part toward its accession to the NPT. A Jordanian diplomat told Graham he thought Egypt "was misguided, that Israel would eventually join the NPT not as a result of confrontation but only after a long evolutionary period in which Israel's security could be assured." Mexico had been horrified by the 1962 Cuban Missile Crisis, which would have irradiated it along with Cuba and the United States had nuclear weapons been used, as they very nearly were. "Mexico was determined that it never be caught up again in such a crisis," Graham wrote. "This had been the motivation for the Treaty of Tlatelolco, the Latin American nuclear-weapon-free zone treaty," signed in 1967. Argentina, which had signed the NPT only a few months before the NPT extension conference after a decade when it raced Brazil partway to a bomb, confessed through its representative that it "had kept open the nuclear option, thinking it would add to their security, but it only served to cut them off from the countries with which they wished to be associated." After its military dictatorship fell it was free to end its nuclear program. "Countries began to join the NPT more rapidly as the conference approached," Graham reported. Peru, Chile, Ghana, Kenya, the Philippines, Ivory Coast, Togo, Argentina, El Salvador, Belize, all signed on. "And thus the 160 NPT parties in 1993 became 177 parties at the conference . . . raising a simple majority from 81 to 89."

THE NPT REVIEW and Extension Conference began on Monday, 17 April 1995, at the United Nations building in New York. It would continue in session for almost a month, until 12 May. A popular Sri Lankan diplomat named Jayantha Dhanapala was elected president. Extending the NPT indefinitely only required a majority vote, but because a sharply divided outcome would undercut the treaty's authority, Dhanapala—and Graham—worked for extension by consensus. And as if to drive home the stakes involved in limiting the worst of all weapons of mass destruction, on the third day of the conference a truck bomb loaded with four thousand eight hundred pounds of nitrate fertilizer and fuel oil exploded outside the Alfred P. Murrah Federal Building in Oklahoma City, shattering the building and killing 168 people, including nineteen children playing at a day-care center on the second floor.

The Non-Aligned Movement states (NAM),* none of them nuclear powers, were deeply skeptical of indefinite extension. The nuclear-weapons states, the NAM delegates argued, had never taken seriously their Article VI obligation to work toward nuclear disarmament. "Several important NAM ambassadors made this point to me privately," Graham wrote, "emphasizing that the NPT created two classes of member states, and they were only willing to remain second-class states under the NPT temporarily as negotiated disarmament proceeded. They were not willing to be second-class states on a permanent basis." Vice President Al Gore addressed this mistrust in the opening U.S. national statement. "The treaty did not create a permanent class of nuclear-weapons states," Gore asserted. "What the treaty did create was a requirement that those who already possessed nuclear weapons did not help others to acquire them, coupled with a binding legal obligation in Article VI to pursue good-faith negotiations on nuclear arms control and disarmament. By extending the NPT indefinitely, non-nuclear states will ensure that this obligation remains permanently binding and create the conditions for its ultimate achievement."

*The NAM includes among its members Afghanistan, Algeria, Bangladesh, Belarus, Bolivia, Cambodia, Chile, Egypt, Ethiopia, Ghana, Guatemala, Indonesia, Iran, Iraq, Jordan, Kenya, Kuwait, Libya, Malaysia, Namibia, Niger, Nigeria, Pakistan, Panama, Peru, Philippines, Saudi Arabia, Senegal, South Africa, Sri Lanka, Syria, Tanzania, Thailand, Tunisia, Venezuela, Vietnam, Yemen, Zambia, and Zimbabwe.

Making an obligation permanently binding that had so far been largely ignored was a damp squib so far as the Australian ambassador Richard Butler was concerned. A rawboned, vigorous man of clear intellect and strong opinions, fifty-three years old in 1995, Butler believed as deeply as Graham in the importance of the NPT; it was, he would write, one of "the principal elements of the post–World War II international architecture" along with the U.N. Charter, the Universal Declaration on Human Rights, "and possibly the Nuremberg Trial principle of individual responsibility for crimes against humanity." The norm established in the NPT, Butler argued, "is that no state or person should possess nuclear weapons."

Butler and his government hoped to see the NPT indefinitely extended, but he no more wanted the free ride of the nuclear powers to continue than the NAM states did. "The treaty had served the purpose of maintaining their exclusive club brilliantly," he wrote, "in spite of the fact that they had never kept their side of the treaty bargain. . . . Their problem [now] was that they needed the agreement of those they had steadfastly rejected or ignored—the non-nuclear-weapon states." Their initial strategy "was to behave as bullies, [but] the bullying hit the wall; it did not work. So another solution had to be found." Butler played a central part both in formulating that solution and in negotiating it. He and his delegation developed a conceptual outline for what became "a series of documents on nuclear disarmament and what could be simply described as a prescription for generally better behavior, in the future, by the nuclear-weapon states."

The idea of supplementing the NPT with a further agreement among the treaty parties emerged from the Australian government's concerns that Israel's nuclear status might become a central and fatal issue at the conference (even though Israel was not, of course, participating). To forestall such a disaster, his government asked Butler to visit Israel several months prior to the conference "to seek its cooperation." As he described it, "I spent two days in Jerusalem in a series of talks at the Israeli foreign ministry. At the end, I obtained agreement that, in conjunction with the conference, Israel would issue a statement that it supported the objectives of the treaty." Butler had his brainstorm on the way out to the Middle East:

> It was during the long flight to Israel that I, along with one of my colleagues from Canberra, designed the concept of documents on future work under the NPT, separate from the extension decision, but to be adopted with it as a means of solving the overall 1995 extension problems.
>
> We subsequently handed this package to the South African delegation in New York and asked them to promote it, if they agreed with the approach. We judged that their influence would be considerable because of their new post-apartheid and post-nuclear-weapons status. South Africa agreed and then played a major role in the subsequent negotiations.

After three weeks of hard negotiating by twenty countries including the five declared nuclear-weapon states, Butler wrote, "the possible final form of these documents was emerging, but the countries were by no means agreed." Butler decided to pull together a core group somewhere outside the oppressive U.N. basement where the conference had been meeting (the group included Graham and Dhanapala):

> At the request of others, that move, on the second to the last night of the conference, was to the dining room of my apartment at Beekman Place, the residence provided to me by the Australian government. . . .
>
> I invited sixteen key players: the five nuclear-weapon states, the leaders of the non-aligned movement, some Western non-nuclear-weapon states, and Iran. Dinner started late, well after 9 p.m., fueled by not excessive quantities of Australian wine. The table conversation moved slowly from the periphery of the issues to the core. It established, above all, that the

moment was serious. The nuclear-weapon states would have to agree to the draft documents or the NPT would not be extended without a vote [i.e., it would not be agreed upon by consensus]. If there was a vote, the extension would almost certainly go through, but the vote would be seriously divisive, the numbers would be poor. . . .

We moved from the table into the sitting room where I had set out sixteen comfortable chairs and, of course, coffee. At about 2 a.m., agreement was reached. All would agree to the package of documents. All would implement them faithfully. We would all pass the word around next day, and twenty-four hours later, when the documents were printed, meet in a formal session of the whole conference to adopt them.

Graham summarized succinctly what was included in the package that acquired the official name "Statement of Principles and Objectives for Nonproliferation and Disarmament" when it was adopted late on the last day of the conference:

- a CTBT by 1996, a fissile material cutoff treaty, and reaffirmation of Article VI commitments;
- continued pursuit of nuclear weapons reductions leading toward eventual elimination;
- additional NWFZs [nuclear-weapons-free zones], including one in the Middle East;
- enhanced verification; and
- universality of NPT membership.

An NWFZ in the Middle East and universality of NPT membership were obvious allusions to Israel, but also perhaps to Iraq, which was still resisting complete disclosure to the IAEA and suffering under sanctions as a result. And for all the NPT members, these commitments were political, not legal, meaning that a state could terminate them when its political circumstances determined it to do so. At least they prevented a state from claiming that the matter was purely domestic. "Though [political commitments] do not give rise to legal responsibility," a textbook of international law explains, "they may . . . have a significant bearing on the international legal rights and obligations of the states concerned."

As both Graham and Butler, from their differing perspectives, had hoped for and worked to achieve, the 1995 NPT Review and Extension Conference came to consensus on indefinitely extending the Nuclear Non-Proliferation Treaty and attaching to that document the politically binding "Statement of Principles and Objectives" designed to hasten accomplishing its goals.

AS IF TO UNDERLINE the importance of the work advancing in Vienna and New York, a convoy of black Mercedeses crossed the border from Iraq into Jordan on the night of 7 August 1995 carrying Saddam Hussein's son-in-law Hussein Kamel, his immediate family, and a small crowd of relatives into exile. Kamel had been the general in charge of the Iraqi atomic-bomb program. Two weeks after his arrival in Amman, on the evening of 22 August, he met with a delegation of UNSCOM officials for a three-hour debriefing. UNSCOM's executive chairman, Rolf Ekéus, was present, as was the IAEA nuclear expert Maurice Zifferero, an UNSCOM chemical weapons specialist, and a representative of Jordan's King Hussein who served as an interpreter.

In the notes taken by the chemical weapons expert, Ekéus proposed to Kamel that the meeting begin with "the nuclear issue." Zifferero took over and asked Kamel first of all for his "explanations on the full abandonment of the nuclear weapon programme by Iraq. Original Iraqi documents indicated that the programme had been terminated in January 1991 due to damage by coalition raids." Kamel started with the Osirak reactor that the Israelis had bombed in 1981 and went on to describe both the subsequent electromagnetic isotope separation program and centrifuge-development efforts using both high-strength maraging steel and carbon fiber. He said they had studied "12 ton, then 9 ton and then 5 ton" implosion bomb designs; the "main aim," he added, "was to deliver [the weapons] by aircraft or missile." These "were only studies," he said. "All the time they worked to make it smaller but had never reached a point close to testing."

Zifferero was skeptical of Kamel's claim that only studies had been involved; he pointed out to Kamel that Iraq had invested a great deal of money in uranium enrichment. Without quite explaining the prodigality of the uranium program, Kamel repeated that "the reason for these studies was to use less uranium," adding, "they had only a few centrifuges so they could not produce a lot."

The discussion moved on to biological weapons, then missiles and then chemical weapons, all of which Kamel admitted Iraq had been developing. Then, late in the debriefing, as he was explaining why the Iraqi leadership had chosen not to use chemical weapons against coalition forces in the 1991 war—"They realized that if chemical weapons were used, retaliation would be nuclear"—Kamel said plainly what the administration of George W. Bush would later obfuscate and deny: "All chemical weapons were destroyed. I ordered destruction of all chemical weapons. All weapons—biological, chemical, missile, *nuclear*—were destroyed."

THE MOST IMMEDIATE major goal of the NPT extension conference's "Statement of Principles and Objectives" was the Comprehensive Nuclear-Test-Ban Treaty. That treaty had been under negotiation at the Conference on Disarmament in Geneva since January 1994 with the full support of the Clinton administration. Shortly after the NPT extension conference, and following the election of Jacques Chirac to the presidency of France in May 1995, France announced that it had stopped testing too soon and intended to conduct a series of eight tests in the South Pacific east of New Zealand. "This provoked a huge protest in Australia, New

Zealand, and Japan," Graham wrote. "In New Zealand, French restaurants changed their names; Australia cancelled some major defense contracts (and a national union of prostitutes announced that one could no longer speak of the French kiss). Japan threatened to cut off all trade. Chirac was quoted in the press as complaining to an aide, 'Why didn't someone tell me that this was the fiftieth anniversary of Hiroshima?' "

The French president reversed his country's policy early the following year, announcing a new posture of minimum deterrence that included ending tests and closing the French test site in the South Pacific, supporting a zero-yield CTBT, signing the third of three nuclear-weapon-free-zone protocols, halting production of HEU, and unilaterally reducing France's deployed nuclear arsenal by 15 percent. "In retrospect," Graham wrote, "the French tests were one of the best things that happened to the CTBT negotiation. As a result of this experience, the French really got religion. . . . They became one of the strongest supporters of the CTBT, having been one of the most recalcitrant."

There was a battle as well within the U.S. weapons and defense bureaucracies over allowing tests up to some yield limit—Perry proposed five hundred tons—but Clinton agreed to support stockpile stewardship with an initial budget of $4 billion in tacit exchange for zero yield. (Not everyone was happy with the quid pro quo. Graham visited Los Alamos and found a hostile if generally polite audience. "Several of them," he told me, "said the government had betrayed them. 'They made a deal with us,' one said, 'that we would be able to work on nuclear weapons for our entire careers and they betrayed us.' That didn't seem like a very rational argument to me. Right at the end of the questioning, Sig Hecker stood up and made a really gracious speech. He said, 'The CTBT is national policy, a moratorium is national policy, there are good reasons for it, and here's what they are and we should support it.' I went to lunch with him afterward and told him, 'You know, Sig, I strongly support the CTBT, but you may recall that a predecessor of yours, Harold Agnew, used to complain that people had forgotten what nuclear weapons are like because we don't have atmospheric tests any more. I wouldn't be against having an internationally supervised atmospheric test once every five years or so. To remind people how awful these things are.' Sig said, 'You know, I've been thinking the same thing.' ")

By July 1996, all the declared nuclear-weapons states had joined the testing moratorium, but negotiations had bogged down over Chinese, Russian, and British insistence that threshold nuclear states, India in particular (which had conducted its so-called peaceful nuclear test in 1974, its first and, in 1996, still its only), had to be necessary parties to the treaty for it to enter into force. The compromise the delegates found—requiring all states that were members of the Conference on Disarmament (CD) and had nuclear facilities on their soil to be signatories—would hold the treaty hostage to at least India's and North Korea's signatures. Both India and North Korea were still holdouts as late as 2010.

The entry-into-force compromise, Graham wrote, failed to placate the Indians, who announced in August "that they would break consensus and block the treaty from being sent to the United Nations to be opened for signature, as was the CD practice." Rather than allow the years of work on a comprehensive test ban to founder on India's resistance, reported Keith Hansen, a member of the U.S. negotiating team, "countries favoring the Treaty devised a plan to get it to the UN General Assembly in New York." Richard Butler went to work:

> For the subsequent month in New York, I held a recurring round of meetings with every member state of the United Nations to discuss and seek support for a procedural device I designed that would allow an identical treaty to the one negotiated in Geneva to be put as a resolution to the UN General Assembly. I met with member states three times in their regional groups, totaling some sixty meetings, before I was satisfied that the proposal would win.

Butler's "procedural device" involved submitting the *draft* resolution to the United Nations as a document for the General Assembly to consider, noting that it was, in Butler's words to the Assembly, "identical—identical—to that negotiated by the Conference on Disarmament." There was nothing that India could do, Hansen wrote, "other than to complain that the Treaty had been 'hijacked' out of Geneva and to try to defeat the Treaty in the General Assembly in New York, where only a majority of positive votes was required to adopt a resolution supporting the Treaty."

The Comprehensive Nuclear Test-Ban Treaty won that majority; it opened for signature at the United Nations in New York on 24 September 1996. Bill Clinton was the first to sign it. The American commitment gave Butler great personal satisfaction:

> I stood just feet away from President Clinton as he entered the first of what would be signatures by seventy-one states on the day the CTBT was opened for signature. I reflected on how twelve years earlier, a year after I had been appointed Australia's first ambassador for disarmament, the Reagan administration had privately approached the prime minister of Australia and asked that I be removed because of my strong advocacy for the CTBT. The then director of the U.S. Arms Control and Disarmament Agency, Kenneth Adelman, nicknamed me "Red Richard" during that period. . . . For the record, Australian Prime Minister Bob Hawke rejected the Reagan administration's demand.

By 2010 the CTBT had not yet entered into force, partly because the United States Senate in 1999 had voted against its ratification. U.S. politics took a radical turn to the right in 1994 with the election of Republican majorities in both the U.S. House and Senate for the first time since 1953. Congressional resistance to moving away from dependence on nuclear weapons paralleled renewed strategic insecurities between India and Pakistan in the final years of the last decade of the twentieth century.

THIRTEEN THE DOG ATE
MY HOMEWORK

I NDIA HAD RESISTED allowing the Comprehensive Nuclear Test-Ban Treaty draft to be forwarded to the United Nations in August 1996—the resistance that Richard Butler and his colleagues had channeled around—partly to preserve its option to conduct developmental nuclear-weapons tests, including both boosted-fission (in which a fusion reaction in the bomb increases the energy of the explosion) and thermonuclear designs. It had been prepared to test late in the previous year, with devices actually emplaced in boreholes at its Pokhran test site in the Thar Desert, about 350 miles southwest of Delhi, but the preparations at Pokhran had been imaged by U.S. intelligence satellites. Frank Wisner, the U.S. ambassador to India, had actually shown the imagery to senior Indian officials in December 1995 to persuade them to desist. They did so, but learned in the process how to conceal their test activity from overhead observation.

India abhorred the double standard built into the Nuclear Non-Proliferation Treaty—"nuclear apartheid," Indian political leaders called it. Prestige and international respect were important motives for Indian nuclear development. Acquiring a deterrent against both China and Pakistan was a powerful purpose as well, the more so since China had allied itself with Pakistan and supported it with bomb-design information and testing. China had conducted a nuclear test as recently as 15 May 1995 (four days after the consensus agreement on indefinite extension of the NPT), flaunting its status as one of the privileged original five nuclear powers. Only if the original five committed to time-bound negotiations for nuclear elimination was India prepared to abandon nuclear weapons.

With testing temporarily suspended in response to U.S. pressure, India's several political parties debated whether to remain a nation with an ambiguous nuclear status and a minimum deterrent or to move on to become a full-scale, declared nuclear power. The price of doing so would be burdensome U.S. sanctions that would interfere with the nation's ambitious program of economic development. Emphasizing how important the Indian defense establishment judged nuclear weapons to be, the hawkish Bharatiya Janata Party (BJP) produced a manifesto during the campaign for parliamentary elections in May 1996 declaring that if it won it would "reevaluate the country's nuclear policy and exercise the option to induct nuclear weapons."

The elections produced no clear winner among the parties, but the BJP won the largest number of votes. The Indian president gave the party fifteen days from the 16 May inauguration of its prime minister, Atal Bihari Vajpayee, to build a majority coalition. Vajpayee immediately ordered nuclear testing to proceed. At least one test device was lowered into a shaft at Pokhran, activity which the United States once again detected and protested. "The scientists wanted no delay, recalling the setback they suffered in late 1995," wrote George Perkovich, a historian of India's nuclear program. He went on:

> The situation was more urgent now that the test ban treaty [i.e., the CTBT] was nearing completion. The scientists feared that it would be effected whether India signed it or not and that the weight of the international community would then lean so hard on India that no government would authorize nuclear tests. They had high confidence in their designs for fission weapons that could be fitted on the Prithvi [missile] or still more easily

on the [larger] Agni. But what they really wanted was the opportunity to demonstrate to the nation and the world their great leap forward to thermonuclear capability and to conduct other explosive experiments that would provide data for long-term computer-aided design activities in case no further tests were to be allowed. They also wanted to test their capacity to use non-weapon-grade plutonium in weapons, a capacity that would significantly increase India's potential stockpile.

A round of nuclear-weapons tests in the midst of the CTBT negotiations that summer might have compromised those negotiations; it would certainly have brought down international condemnation on India. The Vajpayee government lost a vote of confidence on 28 May, however, and the new coalition prime minister, concerned about the economic consequences of sanctions, postponed the test round indefinitely. Immensely frustrated, the Indian defense establishment pulled the one loaded test device from its borehole, disarmed the other devices it had prepared to test, and impatiently bided its time until the BJP could build a majority and return to power.

HUSSEIN KAMEL'S AUGUST 1995 defection led Iraq to revert to a policy of cooperation with UNSCOM inspectors after having announced only weeks previously that it would cease cooperating entirely. Rolf Ekéus told an audience later that the defection had "profoundly shocked the Iraqi leadership, and UNSCOM benefited from significant Iraqi cooperation for several months; Iraq even surrendered important documents and explanations of Iraq's weapons-development strategies."

To explain their sudden turnabout, the Iraqis blamed Saddam's errant son-in-law; Hussein Kamel's deputy Amer Rashid, who remained loyal to Saddam, wrote Ekéus in New York in mid-August that Kamel "had been responsible for hiding important information on Iraq's prohibited programs" and asked the

UNSCOM chairman to return to Baghdad. After revealing discussions there which Ekéus complained were devoid of documentation, he was directed to the defector's chicken farm, on the road between Baghdad and the international airport, where he was advised he would find "items of great interest." As the journalists Andrew and Patrick Cockburn paraphrased him, "In a locked chicken shed, Ekéus found piles of metal and wooden boxes packed with over half a million documents as well as microfiches, computer disks and photographs. Almost all of this treasure trove carried an abundance of detail about the secret weapons programs, particularly the nuclear weapons effort."

Kamel repatriated to Iraq with most of his relatives in February 1997, lured improbably by Saddam Hussein's promises of forgiveness. "Do you think I could harm the father of my grandchildren?" Saddam had asked him ingenuously during one of their telephone negotiations. The world had not welcomed Saddam's son-in-law, except for intelligence debriefings, nor had the United States been willing to implement his plan to overthrow the dictator—in a CIA agent's contemptuous summary, "He would return to Baghdad behind the U.S. Army and Air Force. End of subject." At his sister's villa in Baghdad within days of his return, members of his clan loyal to Saddam sent in a carload of submachine guns to allow him to defend himself, then killed him in an extended gun battle.

Ekéus understood from Kamel's revelations that UNSCOM had been systematically deceived. He decided to switch his organization's efforts from inspections designed to ferret out WMD programs and facilities to inspections designed to unravel the Iraqi concealment system. "UNSCOM would be spying on Iraq," wrote its deputy chairman, Charles Duelfer, a trim, astute American brevetted to the U.N. commission from the CIA. "We would be using virtually every technical collection technique sophisticated countries used to obtain information about their opponents. The only area we ruled out was directly recruiting agents. The goal was to either peel back the layers of untruth ourselves or simply cause Iraq to decide to be completely forthcoming." The new strategy coupled surprise inspections, sometimes after hours, with monitoring of Iraq radio and phone transmissions and real-time overhead imaging via U-2 spy plane. "Since the U-2 could loiter over certain areas and flew very high," Duelfer explained, "it could provide very broad coverage. If inspectors triggered an Iraqi reaction in an adjacent area, we could pick it up with the U-2 imagery." The U-2, an old aircraft, had frequent mechanical problems, however, and the Iraqis could track it with their air-defense radar. Duelfer said he asked the CIA for a Predator UAV, "but in 1996–1997, there were only a couple, and those were committed to the Balkans. The U.S military also questioned their value. The Air Force hated them, because they had no pilots. For our purposes, a Predator would have been great. It would have allowed us to put aerial eyes on sites, with a very long loiter time. It was asking for too much, too soon."

In similar spirit, Dimitri Perricos organized what he called a "urinalysis of Iraq's rivers," a radiometric survey of samples of water from the Tigris and Euphrates conducted across ten days in April 1997. It showed "no indication of Iraq having carried out any proscribed nuclear activities," he reported to the U.N. Security Council, but it confirmed the sensitivity of the technology by detecting real radioactive urine from medical tests carried into the rivers by the Iraqi sewage system. By October 1997, the IAEA was able to report that it had carried out more than a thousand inspections in Iraq, including 250 since the previous April, for which there was "no indication of prohibited materials." That could mean that the Iraqis had dismantled their WMD programs, as they claimed, or it could simply mean that they had succeeded in hiding them. No one was prepared to take their word for it anymore, and they continued to withhold documents. Even the chicken-farm documents, one and a half million pages, had been purged. "There were no documents from the Ministry of Defense," Duelfer noted. "Not one. . . . This fact, and the clear evidence that these documents had been systematically retained and concealed, forced us to conclude that there was a government-directed system to retain WMD materials, if not weapons themselves. And the documents provided no clear evidence that the system was terminated." The missing documents and artifacts made Hussein Kamel's claim—Iraq's claim—that its WMD had been destroyed impossible to prove, Duelfer pointed out:

> The Iraqis had provided so many explanations over the years to explain their partial revelations that it became impossible for them to recreate a completely consistent and verifiable accounting of their WMD materials. Given the track record of past concealment and their reluctant admissions of key program elements, UNSCOM had no reason to give Iraq the benefit of the doubt. Moreover, we knew that Iraq's account was wrong at particular points and those points were more logically explained by a decision by Iraq to retain weapons than by the explanations Iraq offered, which were akin to "the dog ate my homework."

The third-highest-ranking Iraqi WMD official, Duelfer says, Dr. Amer al-Saadi, told UNSCOM that it was asking Iraq to "verify the unverifiable. . . . Nothing is left, it is obliterated." Duelfer added, from a post–Gulf War perspective: "It emerged that this was, in fact, the case. In the end, we had asked Iraq to prove the nonexistence of something—a task wholly dependent on trustworthiness. The Iraqis did not have WMD. But neither could we ever trust them." In that discrepancy lay the seeds of the second Gulf War.

ROLF EKÉUS LEFT UNSCOM in the summer of 1997 to become Swedish ambassador to the United States. To replace him, the U.N. secretary-general, Kofi Annan, chose Richard Butler, at that time the Australian ambassador to the United Nations. "Head of UNSCOM was certainly an appropriate job for me," Butler wrote.

"Having spent years learning about weapons of mass destruction and crafting treaties and procedures for controlling and limiting them, I found it exciting to consider taking on the challenge of physically eliminating them from one of the world's most troubled and important regions." Butler had questions about the job's feasibility, but in the end he accepted the challenge.

The Australian diplomat had been drawn to and involved with large issues of international peace and security, nuclear issues in particular, for most of his life. Born in 1942, the son of a landscape gardener, he grew up in Bondi, a working-class suburb of Sydney known worldwide for the quality of its surfing at Bondi Beach. Like most young people in the neighborhood, Butler body- and board-surfed his way through childhood. "I would sit on my surfboard out at the back of the waves at Bondi Beach," he told me, "and see the planes going from Sydney Airport off to America and off to Europe and I used to look at those and think, 'I'm going to be on one of those one day.'"

Bondi was filled with recent immigrants. "Half of my schoolmates were refugees," Butler wrote, "mostly Ashkenazi Jews, from Hitler's Europe. In talking and playing with them, I was introduced to the world beyond Australia, a world I realized was filled with armed conflict, political problems, and real beastliness by humans against one another. I became very interested in those things." High school brought further exposure to the world's beastliness, "the arrival of refugee kids from the Soviet invasion of Hungary [which suppressed the Hungarian revolution of 1956]. This again increased my interest in international relations." Butler majored in politics and economics at the University of Sydney, worked briefly for the Australian Atomic Energy Commission after his graduation in 1963, and the following year was one of fourteen candidates for the Australian diplomatic corps selected from among eight hundred who applied.

Although the atomic bombings of Hiroshima and Nagasaki when Butler was four years old had astonished and relieved Australia, which had faced Japanese invasion through much of the Pacific War, the Australian diplomat traces his interest in nuclear issues to his exposure to Jewish war refugees after 1945. He learned German as a result, read about the abortive German atomic-bomb program, and "really wanted to know more about where all this came from and where it was going to lead."

Another vivid experience that turned Butler toward nuclear issues was a 1965 visit to Australia by Alvin Weinberg, the director of the Oak Ridge National Laboratory and a prominent nuclear pioneer. Short, Jewish, and urban, Weinberg was an unlikely candidate for Butler's program of entertainment: Besides leading him on a weeklong tour of Australia's nuclear infrastructure, the junior officer took him bodysurfing at Bondi Beach.

"He was amazed at how strong the waves were and how they battered a person," Butler wrote. "I tried to teach him how to shoot a wave, how to catch one with his body. He was just fascinated by it all. He was also fascinated by the bikinis,* how natural it seemed to be for young women there to be wearing almost nothing and no one paid any attention. He found that quite extraordinary."

As a young diplomat, Butler was posted to the IAEA in Vienna from 1966 to 1969. He wrote a master's thesis during his time in Vienna on the IAEA safeguards system. "It was probably the most intensely productive period of my life, burning the candle at both ends, putting in fifteen-hour days and then coming home at ten o'clock at night and working on my thesis." Canberra summoned him home in 1969 and assigned him to the Africa–Middle East section to season him to bureaucratic routine, to which he has never taken kindly.

That year the Australian national security establishment was facing the fact that the NPT, opened for signature in 1968, would

---

*The bikini, still mildly scandalous in the United States in 1965, had been designed by a French engineer in 1946 and named after the exciting new sport of atmospheric atomic-weapons testing, initiated that year with U.S. tests in the air and underwater at Bikini Atoll in the Marshall Islands.

foreclose Australian access to British nuclear-weapons technology, which it had been maneuvering for a decade to acquire. To convince Australia to sign the treaty, the United States had to send over Secretary of State Dean Rusk, who reassured the Australian cabinet that the United States was willing to support Australian work on so-called peaceful nuclear explosives as well as a bomb program "to a point just short of final manufacture."

Australia finally did sign the NPT in 1970, reluctantly and with fine-print reservations. For Australian hawks, the only evident alternative to British collaboration was an indigenous program. To that end, the Conservative Party proposed building a natural-uranium-fueled nuclear-power reactor south of Sydney at Jervis Bay, a proposal enthusiastically endorsed by the Australian AEC chairman Sir Philip Baxter, a chemical engineer and nuclear-weapons enthusiast. Butler thought the proposal nonsensical. "Australia has more coal than most people have hot dinners," he told me. "Australia is rich in coal. It also has the world's largest stock of uranium, but even today a major export is low-sulfur, high-energy coal. We're one of the last countries in the world that needs to generate electricity by nuclear means."

The covert purpose of the proposal was to breed plutonium for weapons. Baxter, said Butler, had even begun saying in public "that Australia's security was threatened by Indonesia and others and that we needed to have a nuclear deterrent." Outraged at the idea of his country abandoning the NPT to become a renegade nuclear power, Butler barged in to complain to his superior, the deputy secretary of state. "He listened to me and said that he admired my passion and zeal and all that sort of thing but that I was way out of line. It would be best if I went back to the Africa–Middle East section and kept my nose out of these things."

Instead, Butler arranged to write an article on the subject for *The Bulletin,* the Australian equivalent of *Time* magazine. "In that article I compared Sir Philip Baxter to Dr. Strangelove and said that he was lying to the government and lying to the people. Jervis Bay was not about producing electricity, it was an attempt to bring Australia into nuclear-weapons status and it should be seen for what it was and utterly rejected." The reactor project and the implicit bomb program were cancelled in 1971, when the government changed. By then, Butler had found a mentor in the Australian ambassador to the United Nations and had moved to New York to work as one of eight diplomats managing the Australian mission.

In 1976 the Labor Party enlisted Butler to manage its national election campaign. "Australian elections are a blood sport played with take-no-prisoners intensity," he wrote. "In 1977, we hit the road, and for several weeks the polls looked promising. But our hopes were dashed in the last two weeks of the campaign. We lost." Labor had better luck in 1983, when Bob Hawke was elected prime minister and appointed his Labor Party predecessor, Bill Hayden, as foreign minister. Butler was then representing Australia at the Organisation for Economic Co-operation and Development in Paris. Visiting Paris for a ministerial meeting, Hayden used the occasion to sound out Butler about the nuclear unease then abroad in the world:

> He and I were walking together by the River Seine when he said to me, "Richard, I'm deeply concerned about the standstill in progress on nuclear disarmament that we've had since Reagan became president." Remember the atmosphere in those days. Reagan wouldn't even speak to the Russians during 1981 and 1982; he was talking about the "evil empire" and vowing an arms buildup against their perceived threat. As a result, the world was as worried about nuclear war as it had ever been; the film *The Day After* was released, scientist Carl Sagan and others were writing and speaking about "nuclear winter," and so on.
>
> Hayden said, "Richard, you're an expert on nuclear matters. What can we Australians do about it?" I said, speaking largely theoretically, that if we wanted to make an impact we would have to devote new and specific resources to the task. Hayden subsequently came up with the idea of creating an entirely new

diplomatic position, called Australian Ambassador for Disarmament, with a cabinet-level mandate to do whatever he could to move the world toward disarmament.

When Hayden announced the new position that June, he also announced that Butler would receive the appointment.

Since then the ambassador for disarmament had worked in many venues to reduce and limit the world's nuclear arsenals. Finishing the job of disarming Iraq, as he hoped to do, would add hands-on experience to his portfolio. "I've spent a lifetime *talking about* disarmament," he told Kofi Annan when he accepted the assignment—"passing resolutions, extending treaties, and so on. Now I'll be able to roll up my sleeves, get my hands on some weapons, and do some actual, physical disarmament. Everything I've argued for in the past compels me to do this real job." He would do it because Annan had asked him, he added, and because Ekéus had said he would have "real flexibility of operations."

He soon learned otherwise. "Butler came in at an extremely difficult time," Duelfer commented. "The Security Council was fracturing, and Iraq was losing patience. . . . The Iraqis set out to take advantage of him, if at all possible." Tariq Aziz plied Butler with Cuban cigars at their first meeting in Baghdad, and when Duelfer thought Butler seemed receptive, the American said, he wrote the new chairman a cautionary memo warning him that the Iraqis "would quickly take advantage of any perceived softness or weakness. 'You have to grab them by the throat,' " Duelfer quoted himself, " 'and feel the pulse of the carotid artery under your thumb. Apply pressure and don't let go.' " Whatever Butler thought of that vivid advice, Duelfer said he "quickly came to his own harsh assessment of the regime. . . . It did not take him long to become very antagonistic. In turn, the Iraqis treated him with disdain, painted him as under the control of Washington, and tried to undermine him in the Security Council via [their allies] the Russians and the French."

In September 1997 Butler organized a mass inspection designed, Duelfer wrote, "to flood Iraq with a large number of inspection teams, aiming to overwhelm Iraq's ability to monitor and control them all. We succeeded. There were several blockages and confrontations, which produced clear evidence of Iraqi deception activities—though again, we could not tell exactly what they were concealing." Iraq struck back at the beginning of November by refusing to allow American inspectors to enter the country. Butler countered by pulling all his inspectors, whatever their nationality, and referring the Iraqi challenge to the Security Council. The Council supported him, but Kofi Annan questioned him sharply about why he needed American inspectors and sent three U.N. diplomats to Baghdad to negotiate a compromise.

U.N. inspections went downhill from there, Butler wrote:

Iraqi propaganda began to have its effect at the UN Secretariat. Kofi Annan's senior staff increasingly argued that the source of the problem in regard to the disarmament process was not Iraq, or Saddam Hussein, or his weapons—but UNSCOM. It was argued that UNSCOM was run by a bunch of out-of-control cowboys, a posse bent on frontier justice. Annan's trio of envoys helped confirm this view. They returned with videotapes, provided by Baghdad, of UNSCOM staffers interviewing Iraqi officials, tapes edited to make our inspectors appear like latter-day inquisitors.

By January 1998 it was clear to Butler that Saddam Hussein had decided to block further inspections. "Saddam had every reason to believe," UNSCOM's last chairman noted, "that Russia, and possibly France and China, would support him vigorously within the Security Council." In addition, "Iraq was receiving signals from the UN secretary-general and the UN Secretariat that they would be amenable to some kind of diplomatic solution. Their motivation was to see sanctions come to an end and the political problem of Iraq dissolved; true disarmament was apparently of secondary concern." The United States and Britain began augmenting their forces in the Persian Gulf to support UNSCOM with bombing if necessary. In a speech on 17 January, Saddam demanded that sanctions be lifted within six months regardless of whether or not Iraq had been certifiably disarmed. Back in Bahrain on 21 January after eight and a half hours of harrowing negotiations with Tariq Aziz, Butler turned on the TV in his hotel room and "stood transfixed, watching the first reports from Washington about an alleged sexual affair between the president of the United States and a young White House intern named Monica Lewinsky." Butler's U.N. security guard stopped checking the room for bugs and watched with him. "Jesus, boss," the guard said finally, "it's *Wag the Dog*."*

Clinton hardly needed the Lewinsky affair to prompt him to take military action against Iraq. He had begun his second term the previous January with a high 60 percent approval rating and a NASDAQ gaining by double-digit percentages from year to year. "Many Republicans were frustrated and demoralized," wrote the analyst Christian Alfonsi. "The prospect of four more years out of power was a dreary and disquieting one to them. How to create the conditions for an eventual Republican restoration was the question of the hour. They could hardly fault the president on his stewardship of the American economy. They turned, then, to his stewardship of American foreign policy, and to the theme that the Clinton administration was failing to confront the emerging national security threats of tomorrow." Threat inflation had been the predominant Republican strategy of the Cold War years, holding Democratic president after president to single terms; Clinton was the first Democrat to win a second term since Franklin Roosevelt. If threat inflation worked so well with the Soviet Union, there was every reason to think it

---

*A film in which a president starts a war to distract the nation from a sexual affair.

would work again with Iraq—especially when even Butler and his UNSCOM/IAEA colleagues had been unable to determine definitively if Iraq had or had not completely destroyed its arsenals of WMD and the machinery of their manufacture.

Iraq, unable to prove a negative, and unwilling to reveal its weakness to the United States, Iran, or Israel, had decided to reject inspections even though it understood that the consequences might be renewed American bombing. American neoconservatives, for their part, had been clamoring for regime change in Iraq since as early as the late summer of 1996, when former under secretary of defense Paul Wolfowitz, writing in *The Wall Street Journal,* called for the United States to move "beyond containment":

> Saddam Hussein is a convicted killer still in possession of a loaded gun and it's pointed at us. Saddam is driven by a thirst for revenge in his personal struggles with individuals . . . as well as with countries. He never forgets and is determined to get his enemies, however long it takes. Should we idly sit by with our passive containment policy, and our inept covert operations, and wait till a man with large quantities of WMD and sophisticated delivery systems strikes out at us at a time of his choosing?

Since UNSCOM and the IAEA had failed to locate any such "large quantities of WMD and sophisticated delivery systems" across five years of hard-won inspections, it was pure chutzpah on Wolfowitz's part to invent them or exaggerate their quantity for his threat-inflated scenario. Even the language of his argument—"strikes out at us at a time of his choosing"—prefigures the language of the arguments that George W. Bush would eventually make to justify regime change in Iraq.

Après Wolfowitz, *le déluge:* The editor William Kristol and the Afghani RAND Corporation strategist Zalmay Khalilzad urged "deposing Saddam" in *The Washington Post* in November 1997. Kristol and the historian Robert Kagan, cofounders of the neo-con Project for the New American Century, extended the argument with an essay in Kristol's *Weekly Standard* claiming that "the only sure way to take Saddam out is on the ground. We know it seems unthinkable to propose another ground attack to take Baghdad. But it's time to start thinking the unthinkable."

Brent Scowcroft, who had been George H. W. Bush's national security adviser, responded immediately to the Kristol/Kagan argument with an op-ed in *The Washington Post,* associating it with Cold War–era threat inflation:

> The Kristol/Kagan analysis of containment as a policy (containment leads to detente, and detente leads to appeasement) calls to mind a debate that raged during the first half of the Cold War. Critics insisted that containment would merely provide the Soviets the time they needed to build up their forces to the point at which they could destroy us. These critics argued that since a war was inevitable and containment only served to strengthen the position of our enemies, we should attack them preemptively and destroy them while we could. Our victory in the Cold War proved these critics wrong, and provides a powerful case that a policy of containment—implemented with strength, determination and patience—can serve core U.S. national security interests. And if containment could produce a peaceful end to the Cold War on our terms, surely it can be sufficient to deal with threats posed by Saddam Hussein.

The following day, *Time* published an article by Scowcroft and the president he had served, called "Why We Didn't Remove Saddam." In it the two men predicted disastrous results of a cavalier invasion—results that in fact would occur:

> We would have been forced to occupy Baghdad and, in effect, rule Iraq. The coalition would instantly have collapsed, the Arabs deserting it in anger and other allies pulling out as well. . . . Going in and occupying Iraq, thus unilaterally exceeding the U.N.'s

mandate, would have destroyed the precedent of international response to aggression we hoped to establish. Had we gone the invasion route, the U.S. could conceivably still be an occupying power in a bitterly hostile land. It would have been a dramatically different—and perhaps barren—outcome.

One week after the news broke of the Clinton-Lewinsky affair, the Project for the New American Century sent the beleaguered president an open letter signed by Elliott Abrams, Richard Armitage, William Bennett, John Bolton, Robert Kagan, Zalmay Khalilzad, William Kristol, Richard Perle, Donald Rumsfeld, Paul Wolfowitz, James Woolsey, Robert Zoellick, and others who would be major players within two years in the administration of George W. Bush: "We may soon face a threat in the Middle East more serious than any we have known since the end of the Cold War," the letter began ominously. It asked Clinton "to enunciate a new strategy that . . . should aim, above all, at the removal of Saddam Hussein's regime from power." Containment was eroding, the signers argued; the U.S. could no longer depend on its Gulf War coalition partners; its ability to ensure that Iraq wasn't producing WMD had "substantially diminished" because of Iraq's resistance to inspections. Even if full inspections were to resume, "the lengthy period during which the inspectors will have been unable to enter many Iraqi facilities has made it even less likely that they will be able to uncover all of Saddam's secrets." That meant the United States would be unable to determine "with any reasonable level of confidence" whether or not Iraq possessed WMD. Spinning up from one hypothetical to the next, the letter added doom on doom:

Such uncertainty will, by itself, have a seriously destabilizing effect on the entire Middle East. It hardly needs to be added that if Saddam does acquire the capability to deliver weapons of mass destruction, as he is almost certain to do if we continue along the present course, the safety of American troops in the region, of our friends and allies like Israel and the moderate Arab states, and a significant portion of the world's supply of oil will all be put at hazard.

Given the magnitude of the threat, the current policy, which depends for its success upon the steadfastness of our coalition partners and upon the cooperation of Saddam Hussein, is dangerously inadequate. The only acceptable strategy is one that eliminates the possibility that Iraq will be able to use or threaten to use weapons of mass destruction. In the near term, this means a willingness to undertake military action as diplomacy is clearly failing. In the long term, it means removing Saddam Hussein and his regime from power. . . . Although we are fully aware of the dangers and difficulties in implementing this policy, we believe the dangers of failing to do so are far greater.

Here in brief, early in 1998, more than three years before the terrorist attacks of 11 September 2001, was the basic argument the administration of George W. Bush would use to justify starting a second war against Iraq in 2003 and forcing Saddam Hussein from power. It would be possible later to question if Iraq might have reconstituted its WMD during the five-year hiatus when the U.N. was barred from inspections; both Butler and Blix told me they had initially believed that Iraq had done so when the U.N. prepared to reenter the country for inspections in 2003. But the war had already been framed by its chief instigators in 1998, when years of inspections were just coming to an end, when all Iraq's nuclear materials and infrastructure had been discovered and destroyed, and when the relatively primitive state of Iraq's missile development was obvious—when, in other words, there was no threat to the United States to justify an invasion. The authors of the 1998 letter did not dare to make such a claim, but pointed instead to the supposed vulnerability of American troops *in the region,* of Israel, and of the supply of Middle Eastern oil.

A classic example of threat inflation, the neoconservative

assault on Clinton at a time when he was beleaguered by revelations of personal scandal was effective. It led him, the following September, to sign the Iraq Liberation Act, which provided support for "efforts to remove the regime headed by Saddam Hussein from power in Iraq and to promote the emergence of a democratic government to replace that regime." Since the act directed Clinton to designate "one or more Iraqi democratic opposition organizations" to receive assistance in deposing Saddam, it was not yet George Bush's full-scale war. It started the clock on that war, however, by setting regime change as "the policy of the United States" and assigning primary responsibility for achieving that policy to an organization that would soon prove itself incapable of doing so, Ahmed Chalabi's Iraqi National Congress. As with many government projects, from new fighter aircraft to Army Corps of Engineers dams, once the goals were defined and the funds invested, setbacks along the way then simply became reasons to redouble the effort. And since doing so cost more money, which only Congress could provide, new and more extreme threats had to be concocted to justify the added expense.

IN THE MIDST OF international maneuvering with and over Iraq that winter and spring of 1998, the Hindu nationalist BJP returned to power in India in late March as part of a minority coalition government, with Vajpayee again prime minister, and immediately began clandestine preparations to conduct a series of nuclear tests.

India had been one of only three states that voted against the Comprehensive Nuclear Test-Ban Treaty at the United Nations in September 1996—Bhutan and Libya were the other two, with Pakistan abstaining. At that time, wrote George Perkovich, "The government believed that India needed only the capacity to assemble and deliver quickly a nuclear retaliatory blow to an adversary, and such a capacity existed in the strategic enclave's undeclared possession of perhaps two dozen or more fission devices, which could be delivered by air force units that had by now practiced the necessary operations." The strategic debate continued in India, however, about whether air-delivered twenty-kiloton fission bombs were adequate to deter China and, more insistently, about what India required in order to be recognized as a great power along with the five NPT-acknowledged nuclear-weapons states.

The BJP was determined to resolve the argument in favor of full nuclear-power status, and made "inducting" nuclear weapons one of its campaign pledges (but did not define what "inducting" meant or specify a timetable). Mindful of its previous thirteen-day tenure, it moved to revive nuclear testing immediately after it won a vote of confidence on 28 March, despite the burdensome cost such testing would impose in the form of international sanctions, a cost the U.S. would estimate at $2.5 billion.

A coincidental event early in April hardened the BJP's decision: Pakistan tested its Ghauri missile, a design based on the North Korean Nodong (itself an adaptation of the U.S.S.R.'s Scud) developed by engineering affiliates of the Pakistani bomb-maker A. Q. Khan. With a 900-mile range and the capability of carrying a 425-pound warhead, the Ghauri for the first time put India's major cities under threat of a missile strike from Pakistan. One Indian commentator called the Ghauri trial "the last straw," and Vajpayee made the final decision to test three days after the launch. Bill Richardson, the U.N. ambassador and a Clinton troubleshooter, on a late-April mission to broaden and renew U.S. relations with India, encouraged the Indians not to respond hostilely to the Pakistani missile test. In a private conversation, Richardson asked the Indian minister of defense, George Fernandes, "George, there aren't going to be any surprises on testing, are there?" And Fernandes, a minor-party leader and self-described pacifist who had not been included in the nuclear-decision loop, responded, "Absolutely not." Richardson judged his mission a success. Only after the Indian tests did he realize that Vajpayee must have already committed to them at the time of Fernandes's reassurance, since they required a month or more to prepare.

The BJP had covered its tracks by announcing an extensive three- to six-month national-security review (and implying that any nuclear-testing decision would await the results) even as the country's nuclear scientists covered their tracks at Pokhran by burying test cables, moving equipment during coverage gaps of the two U.S. KH-11 Keyhole satellites that monitored the area, visiting the test site in disguise, and relying on shifting sand to conceal signs of activity.

Although U.S. intelligence was aware that India was moving toward testing, it failed to predict the timing of the tests themselves and was surprised and embarrassed when they occurred. India conducted five tests across two days, Monday and Wednesday, 11 May and 13 May 1998: three tests on Monday and two more on Wednesday. Each round of tests was fired simultaneously because the test devices were positioned only one kilometer apart. "We needed to make sure that the detonation of one did not cause damage to the other," the chairman of the Indian Atomic Energy Commission, Dr. R. Chidambaram, explained at a 17 May press conference, "since the shock wave has a time travel in milliseconds. So [we] went in for simultaneous detonation. It was also simpler—use one button to blow three. We had close-in seismic measurements and accelerometer data also." The AEC announced that the 11 May devices, exploded in test shafts 328 feet below the desert surface, had yielded 12 kilotons, 0.2 kilotons, and 45 kilotons. One of the scientists who observed the tests said afterward, "I can now believe stories of Lord Krishna lifting a hill."

The first two Indian test devices were fission designs. Chidambaram insisted at the press conference that the 45-kiloton device was a true two-stage thermonuclear design despite its low yield.

The 13 May tests yielded 0.5 and 0.3 kilotons. Chidambaram said that the yields had deliberately been limited to prevent damage to nearby villages, the closest of which was only about three miles away. The tests had actually been fired under sand dunes rather than in boreholes. The fissile material used was "completely indigenous," the AEC announced. (As of 2010, India had conducted no more tests.)

The U.S. intelligence community did predict the Pakistani follow-on tests of 28 and 30 May, but Pakistan essentially announced them in advance in its angry response to the Indian tests. During the debate before the Defense Committee of the Pakistani cabinet (DCC), A. Q. Khan argued that his Khan Research Laboratories (KRL) should conduct the tests rather than the Pakistan Atomic Energy Commission (PAEC). "Dr. Khan reminded the DCC," wrote a Pakistani journalist, "that it was KRL which first enriched uranium, converted it into metal, machined it into semi-spheres of metal and designed their own atomic bomb and carried out cold tests on their own. All this was achieved without any help from PAEC. . . . Dr. Khan went on to say that since it was KRL which first made inroads into the nuclear field for Pakistan, it should be given the honor of carrying out Pakistan's first nuclear tests and it would feel let down if it wasn't conferred the privilege of doing so." The PAEC, however, had built the test site in the Ras Koh Hills, at Chagai, in Balochistan, in the west of Pakistan wedged between Afghanistan and Iran, and Khan's bomb design had come from China. In the end both organizations were allowed to participate.

On 28 May, fifteen days after the last Indian test, Pakistan fired five devices simultaneously in a fishhook-shaped horizontal shaft drilled into a mountainside in the Ras Koh Hills. The announced yields were one device of 25 to 36 kilotons, one of 12 kilotons, and three of less than one kiloton each. The Southern Arizona Seismic Observatory (SASO), however, which recorded the seismic signals as they passed through the earth and around the world, estimated the total yield of all five 28 May tests at only 9 to 12 kilotons, and perhaps that was the reason that Pakistan fired the device on May 30 in the Kharan Desert, about ninety miles south of Ras Koh. It had an announced yield of 12 kilotons that the SASO estimated at only 4 to 6 kilotons. At the end of the series, one more fission device remained emplaced at the Kharan desert test site unfired. (As of 2010, Pakistan, like India, had conducted no further full-yield nuclear tests.)

Why did U.S. intelligence fail to anticipate India's nuclear tests in the spring of 1998? The CIA director George Tenet was sufficiently chagrined about the lapse to ask a retired former vice chairman of the U.S. Joint Chiefs of Staff, Vice Admiral David E. Jeremiah, to head a commission to investigate and report back within ten days. The Jeremiah Commission report has not been made public, but Jeremiah indicated at a 2 June 1998 press conference that one serious problem with Indian intelligence collection had been competition for resources. Asked if the lapse had been a U.S. intelligence failure or an Indian intelligence success, Jeremiah responded, "About equal. I guess I'd rather not say that it was a success on the part of anyone in keeping secrets from us. But, in fact, that happens, and some of that occurred here. And some of it was not putting enough assets against it and the competition for assets to deal with other things." The "other things" that the U.S. intelligence community had been dealing with had been Iraq, a CNN reporter noted after the Jeremiah press conference: "In retrospect, the U.S. might have overcommitted those resources to the Persian Gulf, where U.S. forces were massed against Iraqi president Saddam Hussein."

FOR THOSE IN THE United States and elsewhere who dealt with nuclear proliferation, the final years of the 1990s felt like pushing a heavy stone up a steepening hill. India and Pakistan had broken away. Bill Clinton had signed the CTBT, but the Republican Senate kept pushing new roadblocks into the path to its ratification. Iraq, having disgorged thousands of pages of documents following Hussein Kamel's defection in 1995, writhed like a desperate snake seeking release from U.N. sanctions and

IAEA intrusions, while the debate among American policy elites over how to deal with Saddam Hussein shifted toward regime change. Downsizing the U.S. arsenal and committing the United States to an international treaty banning testing were anathema to the new class of Newt Gingrich Republicans, who were parochial in background and generally suspicious of international agreements.

The CTBT, in Republican thinking, "was basically a Democratic issue," Keith Hansen told me. "It never really had bipartisan support." Along with maximum deterrence, the Republican Party had carved out an approach to dealing with the nuclear threat more suited to its unilateralist spirit: national missile defense. Ronald Reagan's space-based Strategic Defense Initiative had been cancelled in 1993 after a cumulative expenditure of $32 billion, with little to show for the investment. To replace SDI, the Republican Party's 1994 Contract with America proposed that the U.S. invent and build a ground-based national missile defense (NMD). (From 1996 through 2009, NMD swallowed another $90 billion without even demonstrating that it could reliably track and destroy a missile warhead.)

CTBT ratification became a divisively partisan issue in 1999, after North Carolina Republican senator Jesse Helms had kept the treaty locked away in the Senate Foreign Relations Committee for two years on the grounds that earlier treaties such as the Kyoto Protocol on global warming had to be delivered up first for slaughter, something the Clinton administration was loath to do. Beginning in the spring of 1999, Arizona Republican senator Jon Kyl quietly canvassed his party colleagues to solicit their votes against treaty ratification. "By the end of September," wrote the historian Terry Deibel, "Kyl and company had 42 out of 55 Senate Republicans pledged to vote against the CTBT, 8 more than were needed to defeat it."

When a Democratic senator, Byron Dorgan, then unwittingly staged a filibuster on the Senate floor to force a vote on ratification, the Republican majority leader, Trent Lott, on 30 September abruptly agreed to schedule the vote within a week under a unanimous consent agreement, "with no guarantee of hearings or committee reports, very restrictive conditions on amendments, and only ten hours of Senate debate." The Democrats realized too late that they had been outmaneuvered.

They were sandbagged as well by the Clinton administration's failure to campaign publicly for the treaty, largely because Clinton had been distracted while fighting off impeachment for perjury, obstruction of justice, and abuse of power following his affair with Lewinsky. (He was impeached by the House on 19 December 1998 but acquitted by the Senate on 12 February 1999.) "Clinton had not mounted a public campaign on the treaty's behalf," wrote Deibel, "he had not appointed a high-level official within the administration to lobby for its passage, and he had not recruited a senior Republican senator to work for the CTBT in the Republican caucus."

When the Democratic leadership found out what Kyl and his colleagues had done, they tried to have the Senate vote postponed. The Republicans blocked a postponement. Two weapons lab directors, Paul Robinson of Sandia and Bruce Tartar of Lawrence Livermore testified against the CTBT, as did the former Nixon administration secretary of defense James Schlesinger. Henry Kissinger, Deibel observed, after advocating postponement, "wrote on the day of the vote opposing approval." The vote fell out at 48 to 51, not only not the required two-thirds but not even a majority.

Beyond the obvious partisanship and factionalism, beyond the vindictive Republican desire to humiliate Clinton once more by rejecting what he had called "the longest-sought, hardest-fought prize in arms control history," the Senate's failure to ratify the Comprehensive Nuclear Test-Ban Treaty sounded the fundamental dissonance of the Faustian bargain that the United States and the other nuclear powers have made with nuclear weapons. We have feared them even as we have tried to convince ourselves that they protect us, and so we have found it possible neither to employ them nor to break them and throw them away. Deibel concludes:

> It would be a mistake to interpret the CTBT's defeat as a lesson only on the salience of politics, procedure, and partisanship. Substance also mattered, primarily because of the Clinton administration's decision . . . to go for a comprehensive ban on nuclear testing, one that prohibited all nuclear tests forever. The scope and finality of the commitment seemed to require near-certainty about a lot of things—the effectiveness of the stockpile stewardship program, the capabilities of monitoring and challenge inspections, even the future of deterrence and war itself—that were uncertain at best. By making the treaty absolute and permanent, the administration raised the stakes for the Senate, and it did so despite a lack of cooperation from significant numbers of the opposition. It thus presented the treaty's opponents with the opportunity to use their dominant legislative position to deny senators time to sort out their concerns about the treaty and satisfy themselves that its benefits were worth its risks. . . . The rushed procedure . . . made it difficult for senators to learn about the many highly technical aspects of the CTBT and to get comfortable with the political issues it posed. Lacking that knowledge and comfort, senators were unwilling to commit themselves and their country in perpetuity.

"It would be fair comment," Richard Butler wrote, "to declare all of this a circus, in every sense of that fine Latin word: something that simply goes around and around, or a tragicomedy with glitzy performers, none quite real. What has been and remains in play is raw power, massive and unequally distributed, the indelible, primary manifestation of which is the possession of nuclear weapons."

It follows, as Butler has also written, that "the problem of nuclear weapons is nuclear weapons"—the weapons themselves, that is, not the tangle of political disputes among the declared and undeclared nuclear powers. As ideological competition among nuclear powers lessened in the aftermath of the dissolution of the U.S.S.R., the irregular but unmistakable trend in international relations has been toward the reduction and elimination of nuclear arsenals. When all is said and done, more nations gave up their nuclear ambitions during the 1990s than sought to acquire those weapons of terror and mass death. That achievement was a promising sign of fundamental change, but few would recognize its implications until the United States resolved its conflict with Saddam Hussein's Iraq.

PART FOUR

AN INTOLERABLE THREAT TO ALL HUMANITY

FOURTEEN REGIME CHANGE

G EORGE W. BUSH CAME TO the presidency in 2001 already committed to regime change in Iraq should an *opportune casus belli* arise. In a 1999 conversation with his ghostwriter Mickey Herskowitz, candidate Bush told Herskowitz, "One of the keys to being seen as a great leader is to be seen as a commander-in-chief. My father had all this political capital built up when he drove the Iraqis out of Kuwait and he wasted it. If I have a chance to invade Iraq, if I had that much capital, I'm not going to waste it." In a primary-campaign debate that year Bush confirmed that he meant regime change: Asked what he would do if Saddam Hussein were discovered to have weapons of mass destruction, he said, "I'd take 'em out, take out the weapons of mass destruction." (Herskowitz also recalled Bush expressing a more general principle of executive action. "He said, 'All I've heard for years is, what has the boy done on his own?' So he said, 'I've got to make a clear distinction between myself and my father.' ")

Many were shocked when Herskowitz's story was reported in 2004, but Bush's Clinton-era commitment to regime change in Iraq was hardly original. Had Al Gore won the decision in the U.S. Supreme Court which resolved the disputed 2000 presidential election, he too would have been committed to regime change. Gore had first called for overthrowing Saddam Hussein in the wake of the Persian Gulf War—Bush's father's war—

writing in *The New York Times* in September 1991, "The only way we can hope for long-term relief from Saddam Hussein is if Saddam Hussein ceases to hold power." Gore did not propose preventive war, to be sure, but neither at the outset did George W. Bush. "In general," Gore wrote of Saddam, "the formula for deposing him involves these elements: blocking his access to international support, building up his opponents and cutting off resources for rebuilding his military machine." Gore had criticized Bush's father for stopping short of Baghdad: "We can no more look forward to a constructive long-term relationship with Saddam Hussein," he complained, "than we could hope to housebreak a cobra." The vice president reiterated his support for regime change in October 2000 during his second presidential-campaign debate with George W. Bush, as did Bush himself.

Many others had also been critical of the elder Bush's prudence, which his secretary of defense, Dick Cheney, had vigorously defended through much of the 1990s. But as the decade wore on and Iraq did its best to thwart the work of UNSCOM and the IAEA, the notion of regime change as the answer to the problem of the untamed cobra in Iraq grew in favor with the U.S. foreign-policy establishment. From 1996 onward it was heavily promoted by neoconservatives, the policy scholar Russell Burgos has pointed out, but it was endorsed as well by a broader consensus in Washington and in the media:

> From 1993 to early 1998 most advocates of regime change proposed to support an exile government tied to an underground army, like the French Maquis in World War II, promoting the existence of a rhetorical fiction they called the "Free Iraqi Forces"—thousands of regime opponents said to be waiting for the opportunity to take on the Republican Guard. With limited American military support, this "democratic opposition movement" would oust the regime by undertaking military operations from within the northern and southern safe

havens. Though he alone did not create it, this rather fanciful notion was often called the "Wolfowitz Plan," and it comprised the opening gambit in the ideational competition to redefine Iraq policy. . . . The United States would also formally recognize Ahmed Chalabi's Iraqi National Congress [INC] as a "Provisional Government-in-Exile," supporting the INC economically, militarily, and politically as it led the attack on what remained of rump Ba'athist Iraq.

Significantly for what followed, Burgos noted, this plan identified Saddam as the focus of the problem: "In the rhetorical contestation to redefine Iraq policy in the 1990s, Saddam Hussein had already been defined as a terrorist, a WMD threat, and a clear and present danger to U.S. national security." The plan implied that removing him would liberate a country eager to be liberated under exile leadership.

With Kuwait freed from Iraqi occupation in 1991 and Saddam pushed back—"kept in his box," Clinton's secretary of state Madeleine Albright liked to say—the only real point of contact between the United States and Iraq was the United Nations–sanctioned inspections, which the United States followed closely through its intelligence agencies. Iraqi resistance to providing a full accounting of its WMD across seven years of inspections seemed to confirm that it must be hiding some portion of those assets, which had included at least biological-warfare agents, nerve gases, and uranium-enrichment facilities if not yet atomic bombs. Iraq's claim to have secretly destroyed its WMD simply compounded the confusion, Richard Butler told the United Nations Security Council in June 1998:

> This unilateral destruction, in violation of resolution 687, has created a major problem for UNSCOM in the verification of Iraq's compliance.
>
> The unilateral destruction was conducted by Iraq in such a manner as to hide the existence of these weapons, and to some

extent to cover the level of achievement of its weapons programs. Iraq recognized this in a letter to the Security Council on 17 November 1997, which reads: "The unilateral destruction was carried out entirely unrecorded. No written and no visual records were kept, as it was not foreseen that Iraq needed to prove the destruction to anybody."

Thus at the end of October 1998, when Iraq gave the U.N. an ultimatum—lift sanctions, restructure UNSCOM, and remove Butler as UNSCOM executive chairman or it would refuse all further cooperation—the stage was set for the campaign of American bombing, called Desert Fox, that began on 16 December 1998. Even the bombing, which lasted only four days, failed to resolve the issue of Iraqi WMD. Of one hundred bombing targets designated to be hit by a thousand bombs or cruise missiles, wrote the intelligence analyst William Arkin, "only 13 targets on the list [were] facilities associated with chemical and biological weapons or ballistic missiles," while forty-nine targeted "the Iraqi regime itself: a half-dozen palace strongholds and their supporting cast of secret police, guard and transport organizations. . . . National security insiders . . . convinced themselves that bombing Saddam Hussein's internal apparatus would drive the Iraqi leader around the bend. 'We've penetrated your security, we're inside your brain,' is the way one senior administration official described the message that the United States was sending Saddam Hussein."

So few WMD targets were bombed, Arkin adds, because CENTCOM's commanding general, Anthony Zinni, had "insisted that the United States only bomb Iraqi sites that had been identified with a high degree of certainty." The journalist Fred Kaplan put it another way: "Iraq's nuclear and chemical materials were not attacked. Part of the reason might have been that nobody knew where these materials were." Arkin told Kaplan, "I think we're hitting a lot of empty buildings." The long Iraqi effort of obfuscation thus served not only to raise suspicions about hidden WMD but also to sustain and deepen them even after the Desert Fox bombing, which in any case was generally criticized as ineffectual. It escaped no one's notice that Clinton's impeachment was deliberated in the U.S. House of Representatives during Desert Fox. Who could disagree that the president was needed at the White House when bombs were falling on Iraq? The House could; it voted on Clinton's impeachment on the last day of the bombing campaign.

After the 1998 bombing, Charles Duelfer has reported, Iraq communicated its interest in beginning a dialogue with the Clinton administration. As Tariq Aziz explained to Duelfer later, "It would have been normal for governments to proceed with a dialogue. All governments eventually change. We could have been on a different path now." Doubtfully, Duelfer passed the offer along to Washington. "There was never any answer," he recalled. "The Clinton administration could not have a dialogue with Baghdad, even if it thought dialogue was a good idea. Clinton was in the midst of being impeached. A dialogue with the Saddam regime would have been used by the Republicans to shred the administration."

Scott Ritter, the former U.S. Marine intelligence officer and UNSCOM inspector whom Rolf Ekéus had appointed to head the UNSCOM concealment unit, came to a very different view of the state of Iraq's WMD before and after Desert Fox. Writing in June 2000, at the end of the Clinton years, Ritter noted first that Iraq had refused to cooperate with the new United Nations Monitoring, Verification and Inspection Commission (UNMOVIC) established in December 1999 under Hans Blix just as it had refused to cooperate with UNSCOM before, "on the grounds that this new inspection regime is merely a repackaged version of UNSCOM." Eighteen months had passed since the last inspection, Ritter continued; Iraq and the Security Council were deadlocked, and there was "no hope for the return of inspectors to Iraq anytime soon. With each passing day, concern increases over the status of Iraq's WMD programs because there are no inspectors in place to monitor them."

But did Iraq in fact have any functioning WMD programs? Ritter thought it highly unlikely, and explained why:

From 1994 to 1998 Iraq was subjected to a strenuous program of ongoing monitoring of industrial and research facilities that could be used to reconstitute proscribed activities. This monitoring provided weapons inspectors with detailed insight into the capabilities, both present and future, of Iraq's industrial infrastructure. It allowed UNSCOM to ascertain, with a high level of confidence, that Iraq was not rebuilding its prohibited weapons programs and that it lacked the means to do so without an infusion of advanced technology and a significant investment of time and money.

Given the comprehensive nature of the monitoring regime put in place by UNSCOM, which included a strict export-import control regime, it was possible as early as 1997 to determine that, from a qualitative standpoint, Iraq had been disarmed. Iraq no longer possessed any meaningful quantities of chemical or biological agent, if it possessed any at all, and the industrial means to produce these agents had either been eliminated or were subject to stringent monitoring. The same was true of Iraq's nuclear and ballistic-missile capabilities. As long as monitoring inspections remained in place, Iraq presented a WMD-based threat to no one.

Ritter proceeded to summarize each of Iraq's WMD programs to demonstrate that the country had been *qualitatively* disarmed, "a meaningful, viable capability to produce or employ weapons of mass destruction" eliminated, even if every last weapon, component, or "bit of related material" had not been accounted for—that is, even if "quantitative" disarmament was indeterminable. When he came to nuclear weapons, Ritter drew his conclusions from personal experience as an inspector in Iraq:

Responsibility for overseeing the disarmament of Iraq's nuclear weapons capability was given to the International Atomic Energy Agency (IAEA). Often overlooked in the debate about Iraq's nuclear capabilities is just how effective the IAEA was at destroying, dismantling, or rendering harmless Iraq's nuclear weapons capability. Despite every attempt by Iraq to retain some level of nuclear weapons capability, the massive infrastructure Baghdad had assembled by 1991 to produce a nuclear bomb had been eliminated by 1995. Al Atheer, the nuclear weaponization facility, had been destroyed—blown up under IAEA supervision—and all other major facilities related to Iraq's nuclear weapons program had either been dismantled or were subjected to one of the most stringent forms of ongoing monitoring and verification inspections ever implemented under a disarmament accord.

By 1996, the IAEA had established a seamless monitoring-based inspection regime that provided absolute certainty Iraq would not be able to reconstitute its nuclear weapons program short of acquiring a complete nuclear weapon abroad.

Mohamed ElBaradei, the Egyptian attorney who was Hans Blix's successor at the IAEA, took a similar view. "By December 1998," he would tell the U.N. Security Council—"when the inspections were brought to a halt with a military strike imminent"—i.e., Desert Fox—"we were confident that we had not missed any significant component of Iraq's nuclear program. While we did not claim absolute certainty, our conclusion at that time was that we had neutralized Iraq's nuclear weapons program and that there were no indications that Iraq retained any physical capability to produce weapon-usable nuclear material."

Yet further confirmation of Iraq's disarmed status had come to Charles Duelfer in the months before Desert Fox from the Iraqis he dealt with in organizing inspections:

From an Iraqi perspective, it was difficult to comprehend why the vaunted CIA did not know the diminished status of their WMD programs, especially after they had been forced to reveal so much and there were so many defectors. On several occasions, senior Iraqis would say something like, "Mister Duelfer, we understand you must know the true extent of the programs. They are obliterated, and your people must know this. Why must you keep denying that?"

Duelfer's confidants' confusion reflected the hall of mirrors that Iraq had become for both sides:

Our continued insistence that they might have WMD led to some strange questions that I would be asked, very confidentially. These questions suggested that even some very senior Iraqis thought that while *they* had absolutely no evidence that Iraq retained WMD, if the CIA was convinced that Iraq indeed had WMD, then maybe there was some very secret reserve that only Saddam and the CIA knew about.

To make an atomic bomb, Iraq would have needed natural uranium and the large-scale, easily detectable facilities drawing megawatts of power—centrifuges, EMIS magnets and tanks, gaseous-diffusion cascades—necessary to enrich it to weapons-grade. Alternatively, Iraq would have needed an operating nuclear reactor to breed plutonium and a reprocessing facility to separate it. Across the decade, the IAEA had either destroyed or removed all that Iraq had accumulated of such facilities and materials. Even if it acquired a new supply of uranium—and there was plenty of ore available domestically in Iraq—it lacked the equipment necessary to enrich it or use it to breed plutonium. Despite the absence of continuing inspections, that is, the world had little to fear from Iraq so far as the most dangerous weapons of mass destruction were concerned. It would have taken years for Iraq to reconstruct even such limited nuclear facilities as it had previously been operating, and the effort would have been obvious to overhead surveillance. Nor is it plausible that any other nation or subnational entity would have risked the world's wrath by supplying Iraq with plutonium or enriched uranium, much less a finished bomb.

Yet despite Scott Ritter's informed analysis and the IAEA's firm conclusion, the U.S. intelligence community, shamed by its failure to identify Iraq's WMD threat prior to the first Gulf War, convinced itself that the Middle Eastern nation was reconstituting its WMD. Robert Einhorn, Bill Clinton's assistant secretary of state for nonproliferation, summarized the Clinton administration's post-1998 view of Iraq in congressional testimony in March 2002:

> How close is the peril of Iraqi WMD? Today, or at most within a few months, Iraq could launch missile attacks with chemical or biological weapons against its neighbors (albeit attacks that would be ragged, inaccurate, and limited in size). Within four or five years it could have the capability to threaten most of the Middle East and parts of Europe with missiles armed with nuclear weapons containing fissile material produced indigenously—and to threaten U.S. territory with such weapons delivered by nonconventional means, such as commercial shipping containers. If it managed to get its hands on sufficient quantities of already produced fissile material, these threats could arrive much sooner.

The Middle Eastern dictatorship was a hollow threat after 1998, but the United States was both uncertain of that fact and no longer willing to tolerate Saddam's belligerence. If Clinton was exhausted from his personal battles, unwilling to spend much of the $97 million Congress authorized with the Iraq Liberation Act of 1998 to foment Saddam's overthrow, George W. Bush arrived fresh at the front lines, convinced that victory over Saddam would set him up for a triumphant presidency. This time the boy would do something on his own.

YET EVEN BUSH WAS skeptical initially of refighting the first Gulf War. Iraq was the subject of his first National Security Council meeting on 30 January 2001, ten days after his inauguration. Paul O'Neill, his treasury secretary, would recall the meeting in detail to the journalist Ron Suskind. As Suskind summed up O'Neill's recollection, "The opening premise, that Saddam's regime was destabilizing the [Middle East], and the vivid possibility that he owned weapons of mass destruction—a grainy picture, perhaps misleading, but visceral—pushed analysis toward logistics: the need for better intelligence, for ways to tighten the net around the regime, for use of the U.S. military to support Iraqi insurgents in a coup." Toward the end of the meeting, when Bush was handing out assignments, O'Neill recalled him telling Secretary of Defense Donald Rumsfeld and General Hugh Shelton, the chairman of the Joint Chiefs of Staff, that they "should examine our military options." Those would include, Suskind paraphrased, "rebuilding the military coalition from the 1991 Gulf War," but only in the context of "examining 'how it might look' to use U.S. ground forces in the north and the south of Iraq [i.e., under the no-fly zones] and how the armed forces could support groups inside the country who could help challenge Saddam Hussein."

If Saddam's destabilizing of the Middle East was one reason for regime change in Iraq, another reason, which Rumsfeld articulated at a second NSC meeting, was to make an example of the country, to demonstrate to minor states such as North Korea and Iran what would happen to them if they continued to pursue asymmetric power in the form of weapons of mass destruction. A Rumsfeld memo on the subject concluded, "The risk to US and Alliance security is increasing as the US fails to respond effectively and decisively to asymmetric threats likely to characterize the first quarter of the 21st century." But *how* to transform Iraq, how to force regime change, was not yet clear. "From the start," O'Neill told Suskind, "we were building the case against Hussein and looking at how we could take him out and change Iraq into a new country. And, if we did that, it would solve everything. It was all about finding *a way to do it.* That was the tone of it."

What solved everything was September 11, the attacks by Al

Qaeda on New York's World Trade Center and the Pentagon in Washington, using commercial jetliners, eight months into George W. Bush's first term. The attacks struck fear in the hearts of the president and vice president who were the nation's responsible leaders—fear that more were coming, then fear that they would be repeated, fear that the young administration's political capital would be laid waste. Bush had been told of the first attack just as he arrived that September morning at the Emma E. Booker Elementary School in Sarasota, Florida, for a photo-op appearance with a group of schoolchildren. The White House's Situation Room director, Deborah Loewer, a Navy captain and part of Bush's entourage, took a call from one of her assistants in Washington and passed the news personally to Bush as he emerged from his limousine that a plane had "impacted the World Trade Center."

In an interview two months later, Bush conflated his experiences before and after his classroom appearance. Though he had watched the first footage of the burning towers on a school television set before he left Booker Elementary (no footage of the planes themselves was broadcast until the following day), as he recalled it, "I was sitting outside the classroom waiting to go in, and I saw an airplane hit the tower—the TV was obviously on. And I used to fly myself, and I said, well, there's one terrible pilot. I said, it must have been a horrible accident. But I was whisked off there, I didn't have much time to think about it."

The first plane struck the north tower of the World Trade Center at 8:45 a.m. Eastern time; the second hit the south tower at 9:03, while Bush was in the classroom listening to the second-graders read aloud in singsong unison to the click of teacher Sandra Kay Daniels's baton beating time against her desk. The White House chief of staff, Andrew Card, whispered the news of the second attack into Bush's ear, but the president stayed in the classroom another ten minutes until the children finished their reading, and even allowed the excited scrum of media to depart the room first. Despite the possible danger—the school had been picked for its proximity to Sarasota-Bradenton Airport, to save the president time—he remained at the school long enough to watch the television coverage, begin making calls, and deliver a brief speech at a planned 9:30 a.m. press conference. "Today, we've had a national tragedy," he said. "Two airplanes have crashed into the World Trade Center in an apparent terrorist attack on our country. I have spoken to the vice president, to the governor of New York, to the director of the FBI, and I've ordered that the full resources of the federal government go to help the victims and their families and to conduct a full-scale investigation to hunt down and to find those folks who committed this act." Echoing his father's first public statement in reaction to Iraq's invasion of Kuwait in August 1990, he added, "Terrorism against our nation will not stand." Then he asked for a moment of silence, finishing with, "May God bless the victims, their families and America."

(Osama bin Laden found occasion to ridicule George Bush's dilatory comprehension of the attacks. "And for the record," bin Laden sneered in a videotaped speech broadcast by the Al Jazeera network just before the 2004 U.S. presidential elections, "we had agreed with the Commander-General Muhammad Atta, Allah have mercy on him, that all the operations should be carried out within 20 minutes, before Bush and his administration notice. It never occurred to us that the commander-in-chief of the American armed forces would abandon 50,000 [sic] of his citizens in the twin towers to face those great horrors alone, [at] the time when they most needed him. But because it seemed to him that occupying himself by talking to the little girl about the goat and its butting was more important than occupying himself with the planes and their butting of the skyscrapers, we were given three times the period required to execute the operations—all praise is due to Allah.")

The terrible sequence of events continued to play out through that bright, sun-filled September morning: The two World Trade Center towers burned like vast torches, their dense black smoke billowing southwest over New Jersey; American Airlines Flight 77, the third of four commercial jetliners entombed with passengers, crashed into the Pentagon; the World Trade Center south tower collapsed in an eruption of choking dust; United Flight 93 drove itself downward at full speed into an open field near Shanksville in Somerset County, Pennsylvania, shredding the aircraft and all the lives on board; the World Trade Center north tower imploded. Nineteen highjackers died in the attacks, as did 2,954 victims.

Speaking from the White House that night, Bush told the American people, "The search is under way for those who are behind these evil acts. . . . We will make no distinction between the terrorists who committed these acts and those who harbor them." Afterward, at a meeting of what would become his war cabinet, among the participants Vice President Dick Cheney, Secretary of State Colin Powell, Secretary of Defense Donald Rumsfeld, National Security Adviser Condoleezza Rice, and the CIA director, George Tenet, Bush called the attacks "a great opportunity." Cheney commented that Afghanistan, Al Qaeda's home base, lacked good targets after decades of war. Rumsfeld repeated Bush's observation in his earlier speech that countries that supported terrorism were as much a part of the problem as Al Qaeda.

Bush went to bed later than his usual early hour, around 11:30 p.m. Before then he dictated an entry in his sometime diary. "The Pearl Harbor of the twenty-first century took place today," the president dictated. "We think it's Osama bin Laden. We think there are other targets in the United States, but I have urged the country to go back to normal. We cannot allow a terrorist thug to hold us hostage. My hope is that this will provide an opportunity for us to rally the world against terrorism." In his speech earlier that night Bush had spoken of a "war on terrorism." The phrase was still taking shape. In a few days he would have it right.

D ONALD RUMSFELD HAD BEEN thinking about Iraq even as
the Pentagon burned, the *Washington Post* journalist Bob
Woodward has reported. "At 2:40 p.m. that day," Woodward
wrote of September 11, "with dust and smoke filling the [Pen-
tagon] operations center as he was trying to figure out what had
happened, Rumsfeld raised with his staff the possibility of going
after Iraq as a response to the terrorist attacks, according to an
aide's notes. Saddam Hussein is S.H. in these notes, and UBL
is Usama"—an alternative transliteration of bin Laden's first
name favored by the intelligence community—"bin Laden. The
notes show that Rumsfeld had mused about whether to 'hit S.H.
@ same time—not only UBL' and asked the Pentagon lawyer
to talk to [assistant secretary of defense] Paul Wolfowitz about
the Iraq 'connection with UBL.' " The next day, Rumsfeld raised
the question of including Iraq in the American response to September 11 in a meeting of the president's advisers, calling it an
"opportunity."

But Iraq had not yet taken priority over Afghanistan in the
president's mind. When Rumsfeld raised the question again
at a Camp David meeting on Saturday, 15 September, it found
little support. Even Dick Cheney worried, presciently, "If we go
after Saddam Hussein, we lose our rightful place as good guy."
The following morning on *Meet the Press,* the host, Tim Rus-

sert, asked the vice president if the U.S. would be reluctant to "go after" Saddam Hussein if it determined that he was "harboring terrorists." Cheney said no, adding, "In the past there have been some activities related to terrorism by Saddam Hussein. But at this stage, you know, the focus is over here on Al Qaeda and the most recent events in New York. Saddam Hussein's bottled up at this point, but clearly, we continue to have a fairly tough policy where the Iraqis are concerned." Russert then asked directly, "Do we have any evidence linking Saddam Hussein or Iraqis to [the September 11 attacks]?" Cheney answered, "No." That Sunday afternoon, Woodward reported, "Bush told Rice that the first target of the war on terrorism was going to be Afghanistan. 'We won't do Iraq now,' the president said, 'we're putting Iraq off. But eventually we'll have to return to that question.' "

Two months later, Bush had changed his mind, telling Donald Rumsfeld on 21 November, a few days before Thanksgiving, "Get Tommy Franks looking at what it would take to protect America by removing Saddam Hussein if we have to." Why Bush revised his priorities has not yet been fully explained. Attacking Iraq carried far more risks than pursuing Al Qaeda in Afghanistan, as subsequent events would demonstrate. What new circumstance convinced Bush that taking those risks was necessary?

Most analysis of the Bush administration's reasoning about invading Iraq has focused on the neoconservative campaign to reorder the Middle East by forcing regime change, first in Iraq and then in Iran. That campaign extended back to 1996, however, and envisioned an Iraqi exile insurgency, not another United States–led ground war. Nor had the idea of attacking Iraq along with Afghanistan been welcomed by Bush's advisers or Bush himself when Rumsfeld first floated it on 15 September. What happened to change the president's mind between the Al Qaeda attacks of September 11 and his 21 November order to Rumsfeld?

Once the question is posed that way, the answer leaps out from the cluttered background of post–September 11 activity: What happened was the multiple anthrax-letter attacks that frightened and paralyzed Washington and alarmed the rest of America beginning in early October. The first letters contaminated with *Bacillus anthracis* had been mailed on 17 or 18 September, only a week after 9/11. They failed to attract media attention because their first victims, at the *New York Post* and in the regional post office in Hamilton, New Jersey, thirty-five miles south of Manhattan near Asbury Park, suffered only skin lesions that were successfully treated with antibiotics. The first case of inhalation anthrax, a much more lethal form of the disease, afflicted a sixty-three-year-old British photo editor, Robert Stevens, at the tabloid newspaper *The Sun* in Boca Raton, Florida. Stevens began feeling ill on 30 September. Inhalation anthrax was confirmed on 3 October, and Stevens died two days later. Even he was first assumed to have acquired the disease naturally; people can be infected with anthrax through contact with contaminated raw wool, leather, meat, and other animal products, although there had been no U.S. cases since 1992.

A second case of inhalation anthrax emerged on 5 October in a seventy-three-year-old coworker of Stevens named Ernesto Blanco, a mail clerk. With aggressive antibiotic therapy, Blanco survived.

These first anthrax cases elicited a significant threat from Donald Rumsfeld on 9 October. Rumsfeld declared that the U.S. would directly attack Iraq if it proved to be connected to the Florida infections. The first case outside Florida, a skin lesion on a thirty-eight-year-old New Yorker named Erin O'Connor, who was an assistant to the NBC television correspondent Tom Brokaw, was reported the same day. The following Friday, 12 October, Cheney appeared on public television's *NewsHour with Jim Lehrer* to say that it was "reasonable" to link the anthrax attacks with September 11. "Maybe it is coincidence," he added, "but I must say I'm a skeptic." To justify his skepticism, Cheney cited Al Qaeda's terrorist training manuals, which he said teach "how to deploy these kinds of substances." He said that over the years bin Laden had "tried to acquire weapons of mass destruction." Most ominously, he cautioned, "we have to assume [a terrorist attack] will happen again."

Neither Cheney nor Rumsfeld was yet prepared to beat the war drums, at least not publicly. A paragraph from an analysis in the London *Guardian* accurately identifies the dilemma the Bush administration faced:

> In a sense, September 11 changed little as far as Iraqi policy was concerned. The US desperately wants to get rid of Saddam Hussein, as it has done ever since troops first began massing for Desert Storm in 1990. As a matter of dynastic honor, the president would dearly love to settle the business his father failed to finish. But there is no evidence that his administration has any more idea how to achieve that goal than its two predecessors. "I think the debate is over for now and I'm not even sure it went so far as to be a real argument in the first place," said Judith Kipper of the Council on Foreign Relations. "The truth is that nobody knows how to go after that regime and bombing won't do the job."

By mid-October twelve people had been exposed to anthrax, five of whom would eventually die. The U.S. government deployed military units nationwide to guard nuclear power plants, water supplies, oil refineries, airports, railroad terminals, the Empire State Building, the Brooklyn and Golden Gate bridges. Then a letter arrived at the Senate offices of the Democratic majority leader Tom Daschle containing not the low-grade form of anthrax included in the first round of letters mailed to Florida and New York but a highly purified, military-grade aerosolized powder that was ten times as deadly. The Senate shut down the next day, 16 October, the House the day after that. Twenty-eight staffers were found to have been exposed. The Senate office building attacks made front-page world news and sowed panic throughout Washington.

But something else happened that week in Washington that had an even greater impact on George Bush and Dick Cheney's thinking. Special sensors that detect chemical, biological, or radiological agents had been installed in the White House to protect the president. On Thursday, 18 October, they went off while Cheney and his aides were working in the Situation Room. "Everyone who had entered the Situation Room that day," the journalist Jane Mayer reported, "was believed to have been exposed, and that included Cheney. 'They thought there had been a nerve attack,' a former administration official, who was sworn to secrecy about it, later confided. 'It was really, really scary. They thought that Cheney was already lethally infected.' " Cheney had recently been briefed about the lack of U.S. defenses against a biowarfare attack, Mayer revealed. Thus, "when the White House sensor registered the presence of such poisons less than a month later, many, including Cheney, believed a nightmare was unfolding. 'It was a really nerve jangling time,' the former official said."

Cheney got religion. Within a week, Mayer writes, he "had convinced the President to support a $1.6 billion bioterrorism-preparedness program" and "argued that every citizen in the country should be vaccinated against smallpox," a prophylaxis that had fallen out of favor in the decades since the eradication of wild smallpox in 1977 because a small number of those vaccinated contracted systemic infections as a result. On 29 October Cheney literally went underground, moving to a nuclear bunker dug deep into bedrock near Camp David—the famous "secure, undisclosed location" of contemporary news references to his whereabouts. When he traveled to Washington, he traveled with a duffel stuffed with a gas mask and a biochemical protective suit beside him in his limo. The terror Cheney and his colleagues felt was palpable, Mayer wrote:

> Officials who worked in the White House and other sensitive posts with access to raw intelligence files during the fall of 2001 say it is nearly impossible to exaggerate the sense of mortal and existential danger that dominated the thinking of the upper rungs of the Bush Administration during those months.

"They thought they were going to get hit again. They convinced themselves that they were facing a ticking time bomb," recalled Roger Cressey, who then headed what was known as the Terrorist Threats Sub-Group of the National Security Council.

(I witnessed the government's residual panic six months later when I went to Washington to participate in a one-day discussion of terrorist psychology sponsored by the Defense Threat Reduction Agency. Our DTRA host welcomed us by congratulating us on our "courage" in daring to set foot in the nation's capital.)

Two Washington postal workers died of anthrax on 21 and 22 October. A New York hospital worker succumbed on 29 October. For the next three weeks, no new cases emerged, and it began to seem the attacks might have ended. Then, on 16 November, a ninety-four-year-old Connecticut woman, Ottilie Lundgren, was admitted to a Derby hospital suffering from an upper-respiratory infection and shortness of breath. Inhalation anthrax was confirmed on 20 November, by which time her breathing had worsened despite antibiotic treatment, and her kidneys had begun to fail. A story about Lundgren appeared in *The Washington Post* the next day, 21 November, the day she died.

Lundgren's death was a turning point. She had seldom left home and had no apparent link with the sources of anthrax infection identified earlier in Florida, New York, and Washington. Her case was actually an outlier, and a link through cross-contaminated mail was eventually identified, but an infection in rural Connecticut seemed to the beleaguered White House to mark the beginning of a wider epidemic, if not a national attack. If George W. Bush had not already been briefed on the Lundgren case, he would have known of it from the *Washington Post* story on the morning of her death. He probably discussed it with Cheney that morning, as he did with Condoleezza Rice. "I think the seminal event of the Bush administration was the anthrax attacks," someone close to the president told the journalist Jacob Weisberg. "It was the thing that changed everything. It was the hard stare into the abyss." What is certain is that Bush met with Donald Rumsfeld on the afternoon of 21 November and gave his secretary of defense the order to investigate removing Saddam Hussein.

ALTHOUGH NO REASON WAS as visceral, there were others besides protecting America from anthrax for going to war with Iraq. Bush had long thought his father should have finished the job in 1991; he would eventually insult the elder Bush by saying his administration had "cut and run early." Regime change had been the conventional wisdom in Washington for years. Paul Wolfowitz from the inside, Richard Perle and others from the outside, were vigorously promoting the neoconservative vision of remodeling the Middle East a little closer to their hearts' desire, and in time Bush would embrace it.

Most fundamentally, terrorism provoked the same dilemma that the development of nuclear weapons had provoked: the impossibility of defense. Rumsfeld discussed the problem with Bob Woodward four months after September 11, a discussion that reflected the debates within the Bush administration at the time. "The key thought about this," Rumsfeld said, "is that you cannot defend against terrorism. . . . You can't defend at every place at every time against every technique. You just can't do it, because they just keep changing techniques, time, and you have to go after them. And you have to take it to them, and that means you have to preempt them." The problem of the impossibility of defense against nuclear weapons had led the United States to seriously consider attacking the Soviet Union preemptively in 1954, before the Soviets had built up a nuclear arsenal sufficiently large to deter the United States from doing so. President Dwight Eisenhower had rejected preemption out of hand as un-American; the Japanese attack on Pearl Harbor was still a vivid memory. Now it had emerged again as a possible strategy for preventing further terrorist attacks on the United States.

There was yet another problem with tolerating the existing regime in Iraq, one that the independent scholar Christian Alfonsi first identified as a motive for Bush's decision to prepare for war: Saddam's propensity to cause trouble when it was most inconvenient politically. Alfonsi located an early discussion of this problem at the Bush team's Camp David meeting of 15 September 2001:

> Since the end of the Gulf War ten years earlier, Saddam Hussein had exhibited a consistent pattern of capitalizing on major crises involving the United States in order to challenge the will of the international community. Many in the room—including Vice President Cheney, Secretary Powell, and Wolfowitz himself—had had bitter firsthand experience of this during the summer of 1992, when Saddam Hussein capitalized on a White House distracted by the outbreak of ethnic war in the Balkans to mount an "across-the-board" challenge to the UN regime imposed on Iraq after the Gulf War. Now, in the aftermath of the worst attack ever on American soil, there was concern that Saddam might "take advantage" of the situation [whether he was involved in it or not]. . . .
>
> By the end of the day on September 15, the focus of the planning in the group had shifted entirely to al Qaeda and Afghanistan. Still, President Bush remained concerned about the possibility of Iraq taking hostile action at a moment of perceived American weakness.

STARTING A WAR WITH Iraq would require more justification than a handful of anthrax letters, however terrifying. In any case, by November 2001 the FBI was working on the theory that the letters had been sent by a domestic terrorist, not Al Qaeda or Iraqi infiltrators; the strain of anthrax in the letters identified the powder as an American product developed for U.S. biowarfare research. It was difficult to see how Iraqi or Al Qaeda terrorists hiding out in the United States, with minimal laboratory facilities at best, could have purified the low-grade anthrax used in the first round of mailings into the weapons-grade anthrax used in the second round of mailings in the short span of time between the two. Nor was the scale of the attacks consistent with state sponsorship; despite all the contamination and panic they caused, only seven letters had been mailed. A serious anthrax attack would almost certainly have involved distribution of the deadly organism by aerosol spray from aircraft, which could contaminate an entire city and produce casualties on the scale of the Hiroshima and Nagasaki atomic bombings.

Bush and his colleagues sent mixed signals at first of their new animus. In the White House Rose Garden on 26 November the president noted, "Saddam Hussein agreed to allow inspectors in his country, and in order to prove to the world he's not developing weapons of mass destruction, he ought to let the inspectors back in. Afghanistan is still just the beginning." On 9 December Cheney emerged from his bunker to appear on *Meet the Press* positing a connection between Iraq and Al Qaeda. Most notably and pointedly, Bush used the memorable phrase "axis of evil" in his State of the Union address on 29 January 2002 to link Iraq with Iran and North Korea as "regimes that sponsor terror." Significantly, Bush mentioned anthrax first in his list of particulars against Iraq, claiming that "the Iraqi regime has plotted to develop anthrax, and nerve gas, and nuclear weapons for over a decade." The would-be war president had begun to nail down his argument, adding, "This is a regime that has already used poison gas to murder thousands of its own citizens— leaving the bodies of mothers huddled over their dead children. This is a regime that agreed to international inspections—then kicked out the inspectors. This is a regime that has something to hide from the civilized world." But Bush was still unprepared to single out Iraq from his trio of evildoers, speaking of "states like these, and their terrorist allies" as "arming to threaten the peace of the world" and posing "a grave and growing danger." The argument that he would later focus on Iraq was there, but still hypothetical; Bush's people had not yet assembled credible evidence to support it: "They could provide these arms to terrorists, giving them the means to match their hatred. They could attack our allies or attempt to blackmail the United States. In any of these cases, the price of indifference would be catastrophic."

In mid-March 2002, David Manning, a foreign-policy adviser to the British prime minister, Tony Blair, met with Condoleezza Rice to prepare the way for a Blair visit to Bush's Texas ranch where Iraq would be discussed. "Condi's enthusiasm for regime change is undimmed," Manning reported back to London. "But there were some signs since we last spoke of greater awareness of the practical difficulties and political risks." Manning continued:

> From what she said, Bush has yet to find the answers to the big questions:
> - how to persuade international opinion that military action against Iraq is justified;
> - what value to put on the exiled Iraqi opposition;
> - how to coordinate a US/allied military campaign with internal [Iraqi] opposition (assuming there is any);
> - what happens on the morning after?

A few days later the British ambassador to the United States, Christopher Meyer, welcomed Paul Wolfowitz to Sunday lunch and reported their conversation to Blair. Wolfowitz indicated that Bush was leaning toward using threat inflation—fear of Iraqi WMD—to justify war, Meyer wrote:

> [Wolfowitz] took a slightly different position from others in the Administration, who were focused on Saddam's capacity to develop weapons of mass destruction. The WMD danger was of course crucial to the public case against Saddam, particularly the potential linkage to terrorism. But Wolfowitz thought it indispensable to spell out in detail Saddam's barbarism. This was well documented. . . .

Wolfowitz said that it was absurd to deny the link between terrorism and Saddam. There might be doubt about the alleged meeting in Prague between Mohammed Atta, the lead hijacker on 9/11, and Iraqi intelligence (did we, he asked, know anything more about this meeting?). But there were other substantiated cases of Saddam giving comfort to terrorists, including someone involved in the first [1993] attack on the World Trade Center (the latest *New Yorker* apparently has a story about links between Saddam and Al Qaeda operating in Kurdistan).

There is something plaintive in Wolfowitz's appeal to the British for information about the supposed meeting between Atta and Iraqi intelligence in Prague five months before September 11. *The New York Times* had first reported the supposed contact in late October 2001, attributing the story to the Czech minister of the interior. Then, early in 2002, the Czech president, Václav Havel, had called the White House personally to caution Bush that there was actually no evidence for the contact, which Bush would nevertheless continue to use in promoting his war. But Wolfowitz's cautions and concerns about focusing the argument for war on WMD indicate that the argument was taking shape within the Bush administration.

Jack Straw, Blair's foreign secretary, wrote the prime minister on 25 March outlining an argument Blair might use to test Bush's assumptions about Iraq during their forthcoming meeting in Crawford, including:

3. The Iraqi regime plainly poses a most serious threat to its neighbours, and therefore to international security. However, in the documents so far presented it has been hard to glean whether the threat from Iraq is so significantly different from that of Iran and North Korea as to justify military action (see below).

What is worse now?

4. If September 11 had not happened, it is doubtful that the US would now be considering military action against Iraq. In

addition, there has been no credible evidence to link Iraq with [Osama bin Laden] and Al Qaeda. Objectively, the threat from Iraq has not worsened as a result of 11 September. What has however changed is the tolerance of the international community (especially that of the US), the world having witnessed on September 11 just what determined evil people can these days perpetuate.

The difference between Iraq, Iran and North Korea

5. By linking these countries together in his "axis of evil" speech, President Bush implied an identity between them not only in terms of their threat, but also in terms of the action necessary to deal with the threat. A lot of work will now need to be [done] to delink the three, and to show why military action against Iraq is so much more justified than against Iran and North Korea. The heart of this case—that Iraq poses a unique and present danger—rests on the facts that it:

- invaded a neighbour;
- has used WMD and would use them again;
- is in breach of nine [United Nations Security Council] resolutions.

By summer the argument was in place and the work of delinking Iraq from North Korea and Iran under way. Though Bush's ambitions were global, he had always been more interested in challenging Iraq than in taking on the other two states, something he avoided doing throughout his two terms as president. The war he increasingly wanted was his father's war, left unfinished, and his primary motivation for wanting it was the same as his father's: to make an example of Iraq to scare away potential competitors to American hegemony. Not surprisingly, then, he and his advisers—many of them, Dick Cheney in particular, alumni of his father's administration—decided to make the same case for attacking Iraq that Bush senior had made: that Saddam Hussein was secretly developing weapons of mass destruction, nuclear weapons in particular, and must be prevented from doing so lest he pass them to terrorists to use against the United States.

Paul Wolfowitz confirmed that decision in an interview the following year with the journalist Sam Tanenhaus. "The truth is," Wolfowitz told Tanenhaus, "that for reasons that have a lot to do with the U.S. government bureaucracy, we settled on the one issue that everyone could agree on, which was weapons of mass destruction as the core reason." Wolfowitz went on to assert, "But . . . there have always been three fundamental concerns. One is weapons of mass destruction, the second is support for terrorism, the third is the criminal treatment of the Iraqi people. . . . The third one by itself . . . is a reason to help the Iraqis but it's not a reason to put American kids' lives at risk, certainly not on the scale we did it. That second issue about links to terrorism is the one about which there's the most disagreement within the bureaucracy."

Sir Richard Dearlove, the director of MI6, the British equivalent of the CIA, traveled to Washington for war talks in July 2002 and reported to Blair on 23 July that he found "a perceptible shift in attitude" among members of the Bush administration. "Military action was now seen as inevitable. Bush wanted to remove Saddam through military action justified by the conjunction of terrorism and WMD. But the intelligence and facts were being fixed around the policy." There would be debate later, when this secret Downing Street memorandum saw the light of day, about what "fixed around the policy" meant. The context seems clear enough: The Bush administration intended to make a case for war like the case Bush's father had made in 1990, by picking out intelligence "facts" that lent themselves prima facie to the WMD/terrorism interpretation or that could be so interpreted—"fixed" in the sense of "attached to."

If Iraq, for example, proved to be attempting to import sixty thousand high-strength aluminum tubes from China, as it did, those tubes would be identified as potential centrifuge rotors for uranium enrichment even if their specifications were wrong for such rotors but right for artillery-rocket casings. Iraq experts, and even the U.S.'s own Department of Energy, might argue against the more malevolent interpretation, but why should their opinion count? The judges to be convinced were the members of Congress who would be asked to authorize the war and the American people, and neither population was expert in centrifuge rotors and rocket casings or immune to threat inflation. As Dearlove explained to Blair, "It seemed clear that Bush had made up his mind to take military action, even if the timing was not yet decided. But the case was thin. Saddam was not threatening his neighbours, and his WMD capability was less than that of Libya, North Korea or Iran." Threat inflation would bolster the case, as it had bolstered the case against the Soviet Union throughout the Cold War, when it had been the primary political strategy of the U.S. military-industrial complex and its conservative allies in both political parties. If it had worked through all the ups and downs of America's relationship with the Soviet Union, it ought to work at least as well against Iraq.

For the nuclear part of its argument, the Bush administration settled on two related "facts" to make its case for waging preventive war against Iraq. One was the aluminum tubes, which Iraq had attempted to buy from China in 2001. The other was an alleged attempt by Iraq to buy and import 500 metric tons of uranium yellowcake from the impoverished but uranium-rich western African country of Niger. Together, these incidents were supposed to demonstrate a renewed Iraqi effort to develop nuclear weapons.

Such supposition might have foundered on the awkward fact that years of highly visible effort would be necessary to turn aluminum tubes into centrifuge cascades, to operate such centrifuges long enough to enrich natural uranium to weapons grade, and then to construct the weapons themselves—in which case, why rush into war? The Bush administration anticipated this argument with a barrage of assertions about the uncertainty of the intelligence and the pressure of time. That Iraq had expelled

IAEA and UNSCOM inspectors in 1998 played into the administration's hands, allowing it to plausibly claim that Saddam had put his weapons complex back to work on WMD during the four-year interim. Both Richard Butler and Hans Blix had believed at the time that the Iraqi dictator had done so, though they quickly changed their minds as the IAEA turned up evidence to the contrary in the months before the war.

Cheney began the administration barrage. In a major speech to the Veterans of Foreign Wars at their national convention in Nashville on 26 August 2002, the vice president claimed to "now know that Saddam has resumed his efforts to acquire nuclear weapons. Among other sources, we've gotten this from the firsthand testimony of defectors—including Saddam's own son-in-law, who was subsequently murdered at Saddam's direction. Many of us are convinced that Saddam will acquire nuclear weapons fairly soon." Since Hussein Kamel had specifically informed his UNSCOM and IAEA interviewers in August 1995 that "all weapons—biological, chemical, missile, nuclear were destroyed," a fact that Cheney knew, the vice president's invocation of Kamel's testimony as evidence to the contrary is breathtaking in its audacity. Kamel's testimony was still secret in August 2002; when it was finally made public, in late February 2003, the Bush administration with equal audacity would use it selectively to continue making its case for war to the United Nations and the world.

Condoleezza Rice weighed in next, on the Sunday before the one-year anniversary of the September 11 attacks. In an interview with Wolf Blitzer on CNN's *Late Edition*, she pointed to the absence of inspectors to argue for intervention in Iraq. "We know that in the last four years there have been no weapons inspectors in Iraq to monitor what [Saddam] is doing," she told Blitzer, "and we have evidence, increasing evidence, that he continues his march toward weapons of mass destruction." Blitzer asked how much longer the United States could wait. "No one can give you an exact time line as to when he is going to have this or that weapon," Rice said, "but given what we have experienced in history and given what we have experienced on September 11, I don't think anyone wants to wait for the 100 percent surety that he has a weapon of mass destruction that can reach the United States, because the only time we may be 100 percent sure is when something lands on our territory." The national security adviser next mentioned "high-quality aluminum tubes that are really only suited for nuclear weapons programs, centrifuge programs," as evidence of a revived Iraqi effort to develop a bomb, putting the aluminum-tube argument in place in the public discourse. Then, most famously, she linked two familiar Washington tropes into a threatening image of disaster that Bush would soon borrow for his own use: "The problem here is that there will always be some uncertainty about how quickly he can acquire nuclear weapons. But we don't want the smoking gun to be a mushroom cloud."

Bush built on these earlier claims by his vice president and national security adviser in his first nationally televised speech on Iraq, in Cincinnati, Ohio, on 7 October 2002. "Iraq has attempted to purchase high-strength aluminum tubes," he said, repeating the administration mantra, and added for good measure, "and other equipment needed for gas centrifuges, which are used to enrich uranium for nuclear weapons." He repeated Rice's formulation that, "facing clear evidence of peril, we cannot wait for the final proof—the smoking gun—that could come in the form of a mushroom cloud." At the last minute, he had agreed to leave out of his speech the other component of the nuclear argument his administration had settled upon, yellowcake from Niger, because the CIA had warned him off. As a congressional investigation report explained later, "Referring to the sentence [in Bush's speech draft] on uranium from Africa, the CIA said, 'remove the sentence because the amount is in dispute and it is debatable whether it can be acquired from the source. We told Congress that the Brits have exaggerated this issue. Finally, the Iraqis already have 550 metric tons of uranium oxide in their inventory.' "

Despite this warning, Bush's people still included a reference to the supposed purchase in the next draft of the Cincinnati speech, so the CIA faxed another review to the White House that listed three reasons for removing the assertion from Bush's speech: "(1) The evidence is weak. One of the two mines cited by the source as the location of the uranium oxide is flooded. The other mine cited by the source is under the control of the French authorities. (2) The procurement is not particularly significant to Iraq's nuclear ambitions because the Iraqis already have a large stock of uranium oxide in their inventory. And (3) we have shared points one and two with Congress, telling them that the Africa story is overblown and telling them this is one of the two issues where we differed with the British."

Bush left the Niger story out of his Cincinnati speech. It wasn't needed; the House of Representatives on 10 October and the Senate on 11 October passed a joint resolution authorizing him to use force against Iraq "as he determines to be necessary and appropriate."

JOE WILSON, the Foreign Service officer who had worked to free the hostages Iraq had held prior to the first Gulf War, had gone on in the 1990s to serve as U.S. ambassador to Gabon and São Tomé and Príncipe and then as senior director for African affairs on the Clinton National Security Council. He had retired from government service in 1998, the year he married an elegant blonde undercover CIA agent named Valerie Plame, and had taken up international consulting. He knew Africa well, and in February 2002, when the CIA had asked him to attend a meeting about Niger, he had been happy to do so.

He learned at the meeting, he wrote subsequently, that "a report purporting to be a memorandum of sale of uranium from Niger to Iraq had aroused the interest of Vice President Dick Cheney. His office, I was told, had tasked the CIA to determine if there was any truth to the report. I was being asked now to share with the analysts my knowledge of the uranium business and of the Nigerien personalities in power at the time the alleged contract had been executed, supposedly in 1999 or early 2000. The Nigeriens were the same people I had dealt with during and after my time at the National Security Council, people I knew well." Wilson was able to tell the analysts what he had learned on his most recent trip to Niger, two years previously: that four countries—France, Germany, Spain, and Japan—jointly owned the Niger uranium-mining concession, that its ownership and organization hadn't changed in twenty-five years, and that "Niger had not actually sold uranium on its own since the collapse of the uranium market in the mid-1980s."

After further discussions, the CIA sent Wilson to Niger to look into the allegation of uranium sales to Iraq. The first information he collected there came from the U.S. ambassador, a career foreign service officer named Barbro Owens-Kirkpatrick. She told Wilson she had already discussed the allegation with the president of Niger, who denied it and explained why such a deal was impossible. The Marine general in charge of U.S. military relations with African countries had also investigated the charge, she added, and had also concluded it could not possibly be true.

Talking to old contacts and investigating further on his own, Wilson learned that uranium mining in Niger was limited to two mines in the middle of the country in the Sahara Desert that were managed by the French nuclear materials company COGEMA on behalf of the four concessionaires; "but only COGEMA," he wrote, "has actual possession of the ore from the time it is in the ground until it arrives at its destination." Five hundred tons of additional yellowcake production would have represented almost a 40 percent increase in annual production, which "would have been absolutely impossible to hide from the other partners." In short, the sale of a large volume of Nigerien uranium ore to Iraq never happened. Nor did Iraq need to risk flaunting U.N. sanctions to secretly acquire foreign uranium when comparable volumes of indigenous ore were available from its own mines. Nor, of course, could natural uranium be used to make a bomb with-out enrichment of its .0072 percent content of fissile U235 to 90 percent U235, a laborious process requiring the construction and extended operation of large numbers of as-yet-nonexistent centrifuges.

Wilson reported his findings to a CIA officer over Chinese takeout at his home in Washington in March 2002. He had no further official contact with the CIA for a year and a half. He next heard of the Niger claim in George Bush's 28 January 2003 State of the Union speech, when Bush deviously avoided challenging the CIA's repeated assessment that the sale had never occurred by attributing the intelligence to the British. "The British govern-ment," the president notoriously said, "has learned that Saddam Hussein recently sought significant quantities of uranium from Africa." Bush also mentioned the discredited aluminum tubes, claiming they were "suitable for nuclear weapons production." The two claims, both false, together comprised the only physical evidence that Bush adduced to support his claim of a renewed Iraqi bomb program.

SADDAM HUSSEIN was fully aware of the Bush administration's efforts to pick a fight. In the summer of 2002, the intelligence analyst John Prados has written, "Baghdad offered to let UN weapons inspectors return and resume the disarmament process that had lain fallow since 1998." At first the Iraqis debated condi-tions with UNMOVIC and Hans Blix, Prados reported, but "as the drumbeat of Bush rhetoric about regime change continued, Baghdad's reluctance seemed to disappear." Blix negotiated a new inspection resolution with the interested parties at the U.N., the United States in particular, through the end of October, at which time he met with Cheney and then Bush at the White House.

Blix thought Cheney, who did most of the talking during their meeting, "gave the impression of a solid, self-confident—even overconfident—chief executive." The vice president made it clear "that inspections, if they do not give results, cannot go on forever, and said the U.S. was 'ready to discredit inspections in favor of disarmament.' " That, Blix wrote, was "a pretty straight way, I thought, of saying that if we did not soon find the weapons of mass destruction that the U.S. was convinced Iraq possessed (though they did not know where), the U.S. would be ready to say that the inspectors were useless and embark on disarmament by other means." The meeting with the president, whom Blix thought boyish and animated, was less substantial. "He explained to us that the U.S. genuinely wanted peace," Blix recalled. "With some self-deprecation, he said that, contrary to what was being alleged, he was no wild, gung-ho Texan bent on dragging the U.S. into war. He would let the Security Council talk about a resolution—but not for long." Blix read the meetings as affirming, despite the administration's increasing criticism of the inspection process, that "the U.S. was with us for now."

After the U.N. adopted a new resolution on 8 November 2002 demanding of Iraq, as Blix wrote, "immediate, unconditional and active cooperation" and threatening possible armed action for any further material breach in compliance, Blix went to work putting together an inspection program. "We counted on keeping some two hundred people in Baghdad," he wrote, "in addition to a number of biological, chemical, missile and multidisciplinary teams of about ten inspectors each. . . . We had planned for a number of helicopters with a total of about forty people serving them. Computers, communication equipment (including secure lines) and whatnot were all on order. We knew a great many sites we wanted to inspect and a great many questions we wanted to ask." With Iraq's bitter but complete commitment to open inspections, UNMOVIC and the IAEA under Mohamed ElBaradei went in for a first round in late November.

Blix's notes for a presentation to the UNMOVIC commissioners after his November visit to Baghdad pulse with the urgency of the inspection effort:

Should we expand our staff? 100 inspectors in Iraq by Xmas. Can we go much faster? Doubtful. A state military organization is something different. It is ready, trained for deployment [and] supplied with a ready infrastructure. We have to create much of that. If too large, we might easily risk chaos. Already now straining of capacity. More rooms needed in Baghdad. More space needed in New York. Will take a little time. We have a number of potential chief inspectors with special training. 80 on the roster have responded positively for engagement by now. This is a good result. One month before Xmas! But sending out 8 missions simultaneously a day. The planning part will not be easy: 100 people. How many jeeps? How many helicopters? How many cameras? Lucky we have had time to train 300. What would have happened [if we had tried to inspect] in 2000? Risky to overreach. New training course in January. Slow growth. More Arabs [needed]. More women.

Blix told me about one strategy he used to push back against the American pressure to declare Iraq in material breach: He asked the CIA to give him a list of its most suspicious sites first. It did; he sent in his inspectors; nothing turned up. "What we came to discover," he wrote later, "was that no sites given to us by intelligence were ever found to harbor weapons of mass destruction."

While Blix was finding nothing at exactly the places where the CIA believed he should have found hidden WMD, CIA director George Tenet and his deputy John McLaughlin presented what they called "The Case"—against Iraq—to Bush, Cheney, Rice, and White House Chief of Staff Andrew Card on 21 December. Bush was underwhelmed by the presentation, a thin gruel of chemical-weapons precursor agents, test stands for medium-range rockets, drones capable of reaching Azerbaijan, meetings between Saddam and his nuclear scientists. As Bob Woodward reconstructed the CIA presentation, "Bush turned to Tenet. 'I've been told all this intelligence about having WMD and this is the best we've got?' " Tenet responded, famously, "It's a slam dunk case!" According to Woodward, Bush judged Tenet's basketball-slang reassurance "very important" and sent the CIA's leadership off to find some lawyers to juice up the presentation. "Needs a lot more work," Woodward quoted Bush. "Let's get some people who've actually put together a case for a jury."

Much of what followed is well known. Condoleezza Rice published an op-ed in *The New York Times* on 23 January 2003 titled "Why We Know Iraq Is Lying." It claimed that Iraq's December weapons declaration, twelve thousand pages long, "fails to account for or explain Iraq's efforts to get uranium from abroad," a guarded reference to the discredited report of the yellowcake deal. Bush himself, in his 28 January State of the Union Address, repeated the familiar litany, none of it supported by credible evidence: ties to Al Qaeda, an "advanced nuclear-weapons development program," mobile biological weapons labs, aluminum tubes "suitable for nuclear-weapons production," and the sixteen words attributing the Niger deal report to "the British government." Bush built his disastrous war on Nigerien yellowcake never mined or shipped and Chinese aluminum tubes with the exact specifications of an Italian artillery-rocket casing that Iraq was trying to reverse-engineer.

On the last day of January 2003, in the Oval Office, the president of the United States told the prime minister of Great Britain and his advisers that war was inevitable and had already been "penciled in for 10 March." According to a British eyewitness, Bush then calmly discussed ways of provoking war if the U.N. failed to authorize military action, including flying a U.S. U-2 spy plane over Iraq painted in U.N. colors to provoke antiaircraft fire, turning up an Iraqi defector prepared to brief the press about hidden WMD, or assassinating Saddam Hussein.

The double bind in which Iraq found itself and of which the Bush administration took advantage was the decision, after 1991, to destroy its WMD without keeping records of having done so. "How much, if any, is left of Iraq's weapons of mass destruction and related proscribed items and programs?" Blix asked the U.N.

Security Council rhetorically in a briefing on 14 February, continuing,

> So far, UNMOVIC has not found any such weapons, only a small number of empty chemical munitions, which should have been declared and destroyed. Another matter—and one of great significance—is that many proscribed weapons and items are not accounted for. To take an example, a document which Iraq provided suggested to us that some 1,000 tonnes of chemical agent were "unaccounted for." One must not jump to the conclusion that they exist. However, that possibility is also not excluded. If they exist, they should be presented for destruction. If they do not exist, credible evidence to that effect should be presented.

But having secretly destroyed the weapons and items, Iraq had no records to produce, while Blix could not certify Iraq to be in compliance so long as records were lacking. Worse, the U.S. insisted any materiel that Iraq could not prove it had destroyed must be assumed to still exist, hidden somewhere in a warehouse or perhaps underground.

And so it came again to war between Iraq and the United States, a war driven this time by deep fear of further terrorist attacks on the American homeland, "the first case of a war," as Blix would say later, "the primary aim of which is to secure verified disarmament." (But Blix would add, "It is hard to resist the reflection that in terms of lives and suffering, property and money, the war was a very costly way of concluding that there were no WMD.") As the international community moves seriously toward nuclear disarmament in the decades to come, such a war might well be a last resort against a resistant proliferator. It was not a last resort in 2003. It was a war of convenience for the frightened leadership of a nation that Blix would describe that year as "evidently the superior military power in the world: Mars on the Earth," a war engaged prematurely, before the U.N.

inspection process was complete. It did not, of course, end when and as its instigators expected.

SADDAM HUSSEIN WAS captured on 13 December 2003. Across the next six months, as he waited in prison for trial, he was interviewed at length by an Arabic-speaking FBI agent, George L. Piro. Piro wrote that he won the former Iraqi dictator's confidence by "spend[ing] several sessions discussing non-threatening topics [which] allowed Hussein the opportunity to talk freely and boast of past accomplishments." The FBI agent then gradually introduced more challenging subjects into the interviews. By the twenty-fourth interviewing session, the former Iraqi dictator was willing to explain why he had expelled the U.N. inspectors from Iraq in 1998, the decision that had set him up for charges that he was hiding clandestine stocks of WMD. Not at all, he said in Piro's paraphrase:

> Even though Hussein claimed Iraq did not have WMD, the threat from Iran was a major factor as to why he did not allow the return of the UN inspectors. Hussein stated he was more concerned about Iran discovering Iraq's weaknesses and vulnerabilities than the repercussions of the United States for his refusal to allow UN inspectors back into Iraq. In his opinion, the UN inspectors would have directly identified to the Iranians where to inflict maximum damage to Iraq. . . . Hussein indicated he was angered when the United States struck Iraq in 1998. Hussein stated Iraq could have absorbed another United States strike for he viewed this as less of a threat than exposing themselves to Iran.

Hussein also acknowledged to Piro "that when it was clear that a war with the United States was imminent [i.e., in the summer of 2002], he allowed the inspectors back into Iraq in hopes of averting war. Yet it became clear to him four months before the war that the war was inevitable." He told Piro ruefully that he had wanted to have a relationship with the United States "but was not given the chance, as the United States was not listening to anything Iraq had to say."

Nor was the United States listening to the United Nations in its rush to war. Mohamed ElBaradei told the U.N. Security Council on 27 January 2003, four days before George W. Bush informed Tony Blair that the war was "penciled in for 10 March," that the casus belli for such a war would be removed in a matter of months. "To conclude," he said, "we have to date found no evidence that Iraq has revived its nuclear weapons program since the elimination of the program in the 1990s. . . . Provided there is sustained proactive cooperation by Iraq, we should be able within the next few months to provide credible assurance that Iraq has no nuclear weapons program." Those few months, the reserved Egyptian lawyer added, "would be a valuable investment in peace, because they could help us avoid a war."

The primary reason the Bush administration chose not to delay its war with Iraq was not, as the administration claimed, to end combat before the brutal heat of Middle Eastern summer made conditions difficult for U.S. troops. Two or three months' delay—from March to May or June—with the prospect of forestalling a war that could be expected to produce hundreds of thousands of Iraqi military and civilian casualties should have been an easy humanitarian call for an administration that professed to believe it would be welcomed by the Iraqi people with open arms. A more self-serving reason that Bush and Cheney decided to cut short the U.N. inspection process was the one reported by Christian Alfonsi in his book *Circle in the Sand*: to avoid allowing the war to run into 2004, a U.S. presidential election year:

> Cheney had absorbed two bitter lessons from the first Bush administration's failed confrontation with Iraq in 1992. The first was that Saddam invariably grew more aggressive when the

United States was distracted by other security concerns. The second was that it was impossible to muster the domestic and international support for major U.S. military action during a presidential election year. . . .

In Cheney's mind there were two necessary predicates to these lessons: a final showdown with Iraq would have to take place in 2002 or 2003, not during the election year of 2004; and because Saddam's entire strategy for survival would be based on delaying U.S. action until 2004, no accommodation by Iraq, not even acceptance of robust UN weapons inspections, could be allowed to forestall American military action.

The United States and its thin "coalition of the willing" began bombing Iraq on 19 March 2003. The brief war that followed forced regime change, but by most other measures it was a profound disaster. No weapons of mass destruction were found, nor any active program to produce them. About five thousand American and coalition combatants were killed and an equal number of Iraqi combatants. Civilians fared far worse; reliable estimates of war-related civilian violent deaths (such as the Iraq Family Health Survey and the Associated Press) put the number at around 100,000—150,000 through June 2006. More than 4.7 million Iraqis were uprooted. Much of the country's infrastructure was destroyed and has had to be rebuilt at American expense. The Nobel Prize–winning economist Joseph Stiglitz and his associate Linda Bilmes estimate the cost to the United States of the wars in Afghanistan and Iraq, including projected costs for lifetime medical treatment of U.S. casualties, as $3 trillion. Only the Second World War cost more—$5 trillion in 2007 dollars.

The tragedy, Hans Blix told me ruefully one day, was the waste of lives and treasure. "After the war," Blix said, "Kofi Annan and I sat down and estimated the cost of disarming Iraq by inspection versus disarming by war. We estimated that inspection would have cost eighty million dollars—and would have worked as well."

SIXTEEN THE TWILIGHT
OF THE BOMBS

THE DEBACLE OF THE George W. Bush years extended beyond a poorly planned, profligate war justified with inflated threats. The Bush administration also officially withdrew the United States from the Anti-Ballistic Missile Treaty to pursue ground-based missile defenses, continuing the Republican strategy of championing dubious defensive systems over negotiated arms controls. It left the Comprehensive Nuclear Test-Ban Treaty unratified, collecting dust on the Senate floor. It abandoned the Clinton administration's imminent grand bargain with North Korea in favor of belligerent confrontation, to which the beleaguered Communist state responded by withdrawing from the Nuclear Nonproliferation Treaty and crafting and testing its first nuclear weapons. It lifted sanctions on Pakistan imposed to penalize that South Asian country for going nuclear. It sought to develop nuclear "bunker-buster" bombs as well as so-called mini-nukes and to prepare the way for renewed nuclear-weapons testing. It agreed to help India develop its nuclear infrastructure outside the NPT, to supply it with five hundred metric tons of uranium per year, and to allow it to extract plutonium from its spent fuel.

Yet despite the Bush administration's demonstrated distaste for arms negotiations, it pursued major reductions in the number of weapons in the U.S. nuclear arsenal, aligning its efforts with Russia and even embodying them in a treaty when its former Cold War foe insisted. From about 10,000 warheads on U.S. delivery vehicles at the end of the Cold War, the Bush administration had reduced the numbers by January 2009 to about 2,600, while Russian warheads had been reduced from 15,000 to about 4,800. The two countries maintained extensive reserves, however, so that their actual combined nuclear arsenals were estimated as of January 2009 to comprise not 7,400 but 22,400 warheads, 96 percent of world inventory. (Seven other nuclear-weapons states accounted for the remaining 4 percent: France, about 300 nuclear weapons; China, about 240; Britain, about 185; Israel, about 80; India, about 60; Pakistan, about 60; North Korea, fewer than 10.)

In the absence of major conflict, current or foreseeable, between the U.S. and any other nuclear-weapons state, these reduced but still excessive numbers of weapons are a burden and a danger, disconnected from the promising realities of the post–Cold War world. They are expensive, costing the United States alone more than $50 billion a year to maintain—although such a large allocation to U.S. defense contractors may partly explain why the nuclear arsenal continues to be held at such a high level long after the end of the Cold War. "By way of comparison," wrote the nuclear-stockpile expert Stephen Schwartz, "the 2008 nuclear weapons–related 'budget' exceeds all anticipated government expenditures on international diplomacy and foreign assistance ($39.5 billion) and natural resources and the environment ($33 billion). It is nearly double the budget for general science, space and technology ($27.4 billion), and it is almost fourteen times what the U.S. Department of Energy (DOE) has allocated for all energy-related research and development."

Besides maintaining large nuclear arsenals, the two leading nuclear powers have kept considerable numbers of their loaded nuclear weapons on high alert, "waiting," wrote the analyst Michael Mazarr, "to retaliate instantly against attacks that no one anymore expects to come," risking accidental or inadvertent use.

Much of this inertia on the U.S. side has represented politics as usual, the continuing standoff between Republicans and

Democrats over national security policy. During the George W. Bush years in particular, menacing largely replaced diplomacy as the American strategy of choice, and not only Iraq was threatened with war but also Iran and North Korea, the three nodes of Bush's "axis of evil." In its final months, however, the Bush administration rejected Israel's proposal to bomb Iran's developing nuclear facilities on its own and America's behalf, acquiescing instead to an Israeli attack on the Gaza Strip during the U.S. presidential interregnum intended to stop persistent Hamas mortar and rocket attacks launched from Gaza into Israel.

The Bush administration's showy belligerence had concealed a surprising lack of interest in nuclear policy. The ambassador and arms negotiator Linton Brooks was appointed head of the National Nuclear Security Administration (NNSA) in May 2003. In 2007, shortly after he left office, he told me that with the exception of the president himself, "the administration's leadership has not paid very much attention to nuclear issues." That was particularly true at the Pentagon, Brooks said. "So nuclear things were left to lower levels. I think part of it is simply that Rumsfeld's agenda was transformation, and he never thought nuclear weapons were very important. Then 9/11 happened and with the intensity of that, none of his senior people spent any time on nuclear weapons. So the issue devolved down into the bureaucracy, which led on the one hand to a sort of Cold War attitude of 'We can't give up anything,' and on the other hand to the present status"—in 2007—"where the principal deputy under secretary for policy, Ryan Henry, really thinks nuclear weapons are the Coast Guard Auxiliary, they're the horse cavalry, they were important once but they're ancient history now."

Brooks attributed the large reductions the U.S. agreed to make beginning in 2004 to Bush himself. "It's not something the bureaucracy generated and the president approved," he told me. "The bureaucracy generated something much bigger and the president sent it back, saying, 'I said "lowest level" and that's what I meant.' So his instincts were good." Not only a Cold War mentality drove the administration's opposition to arms negotiations, Brooks added. "It's also the ideology. It sometimes looks like the answer to any economic problem for this administration is tax cuts for upper-income brackets. The defense analogue is national missile defense. If the North Koreans are making threats, the solution is national missile defense. If bin Laden wants to kill us, the solution is national missile defense. This administration is very skeptical of arms control. They have a good argument that arms control is for adversaries and we don't want the Russians to be adversaries, so it's inappropriate. But they're also just generally skeptical of its benefits. Paul Wolfowitz told me once that when it would help you can't get it, and when you can get it you don't need it. So I think the combination of, one, the threat isn't there; two, nuclear weapons are yesterday's news; and three, the distraction of 9/11—well, except for the problem of nuclear terrorism, the administration hasn't thought much."

THE PROBLEM OF nuclear terrorism is more obscure and more complicated than it has been seen to be within the U.S. government and in the media. Rumors of a large number of missing Soviet-era "suitcase" bombs, rumors given credence in the late 1990s in public statements by the retired Russian Army general and presidential candidate Alexander Lebed, have faded with Lebed's death in a helicopter crash in 2002. Since the thirty-kilogram backpack weapons probably depended on tritium gas injection to boost their otherwise minimal yield, and tritium has a short half-life, any such weapons stolen in the last days of the Soviet Union would be defunct by now, good at best for a nasty radioactive fizzle. Russia has officially denied any loss of backpack nuclear weapons. Had such weapons made their way to Chechnya, as the Russian press speculated, they would certainly have been used by now.

No nuclear weapons are known to have been stolen in any country since their first development by the United States in 1945.

Whether this fact is testimony to the quality of the security that nuclear weapons are rightly accorded in every country that has them, or whether thieves judge attempting to acquire such complicated, dangerous, and well-guarded explosives not to be worth the risk remains to be seen. U.S. and Russian nuclear weapons are outfitted with complicated physical and electronic locking mechanisms with defensive features that may be deadly; weapons in countries such as Pakistan are protected the way South Africa's were, by being stored partly disassembled, with their fissile components divided among several locations in guarded bunkers or vaults. The theft of a nuclear weapon anywhere would activate every resource the international community could muster, with shooting on sight the minimum rule of engagement.

Because nuclear weapons are well protected, national-security bureaucracies have postulated that a terrorist group that wants to acquire a nuclear capability will be forced to build its own bomb or bombs. Enriching uranium or breeding plutonium and separating it from its intensely radioactive matrix of spent fuel are both well beyond the capacity of subnational entities. The notion that a government would risk its own security by giving up control of a nuclear weapon to terrorists is nonsensical despite the Bush administration's use of the argument to justify invading Saddam Hussein's Iraq. A nuclear attack on United States interests by a terrorist group using a donated bomb would certainly lead to a devastating nuclear counterattack on the country that supplied the weapon, provided the supplier could be determined—a near certainty with nuclear forensics and other means of investigation.

A terrorist group in possession of a homemade or stolen nuclear device is assumed to be undeterrable, however, and probably would be. "The more than 10,000 warheads in the U.S. nuclear stockpile on Sept. 11, 2001," Stephen Schwartz wrote to the point, "had no impact on al Qaeda's calculations that day or in all the days that followed." More than any other single threat, more even than fear of a large-scale anthrax attack, the fear after September 11 that the next such assault might be nuclear changed the views of government leaders everywhere. The theory and practice of nuclear deterrence, whatever its real merits, had made the long nuclear standoff between the United States and the Soviet Union nerve-wracking but tolerable. Suicidal terrorists armed with homemade nuclear weapons are a fresh nightmare.

But could a terrorist group build a deliverable atomic bomb? The United States has quietly explored the question for years. The earliest and perhaps best-known investigation was conducted in the mid-1960s at what was then the Lawrence Radiation Laboratory in Livermore, California (Lawrence Livermore today). The project was called the Nth Country Experiment; its purpose was to explore the "technical problems facing a nation wishing to acquire a small stockpile of nuclear weapons"—in other words, to see if a nonnuclear state without access to secret technical information could successfully design and build a nuclear weapon. A state has more resources than a terrorist group, to be sure, but the experiment was set up to test whether a minimal team—in this case, two young American physicists, recent Ph.D.'s without nuclear-weapons-design knowledge—could invent, on paper, a workable atomic bomb. "The goal of the participants," their instructions read, "should be to design an explosive with a militarily significant yield."

The two novices succeeded, after three man-years of work. Significantly, they decided at the outset of their project, after a little preliminary consideration, that designing a gun bomb would be too *easy*—would not adequately show off their abilities—and moved on to the successful design they presented to their superiors, which was an implosion device.

In the late 1980s, several experienced Los Alamos weapons designers, including Carson Mark, Ted Taylor, and Jay Wechsler, published a report which attempted to answer the question, "Can terrorists build nuclear weapons?" Experienced professionals can find it difficult to forget what they know, and it would seem the Los Alamos designers were not able to return themselves to a state of technical naïveté. What they called a "crude design" turned out to be an implosion device.

For a "crude design," they wrote, "terrorists would need something like 5 or 6 kg of plutonium or 25 kg of very highly enriched uranium (and more for a gun-type device)." The Los Alamos designers thought it "exceedingly unlikely" that any single individual could acquire all the necessary knowledge and skills to make an atomic bomb by himself, so they assumed "that a team would have to be involved. . . . Their number could scarcely be fewer than three or four and might well have to be more." They would need months; they would need a secure location; they might very well irradiate themselves fatally by accident or blow themselves up. But if a team of terrorists weathered all these challenges, the Los Alamos designers concluded, it should be able to produce a weapon with a minimum yield of several tons of TNT equivalent, and very possibly of one hundred tons or more. Indeed, they wrote, "devices employing metal in a crude design could certainly be constructed so as to have nominal yields in the 10 kiloton range—witness the devices used in 1945." The Hiroshima bomb—a gun-type weapon—exploded with a yield estimated to have been equivalent to 13,500 tons of TNT, 13.5 kilotons.

An Ohio State University political scientist named John Mueller has argued that a terrorist attack with a nuclear weapon is extremely unlikely. Mueller has made a career of healthy skepticism about nuclear strategy, countering the persistent American politics of nuclear threat inflation with sensible arguments and solid facts. In a 2009 research paper for the International Commission on Nuclear Non-proliferation and Disarmament, he examined in detail the question of what he called "the atomic terrorist."

Mueller minimizes—in my opinion, correctly—the risk of terrorists' stealing a nuclear weapon or acquiring one by donation, for the reasons I've already reviewed. He correctly eliminates plutonium as a likely terrorist explosive, although he does so for the wrong reasons. Plutonium is not, as Mueller and many others seem to think, more dangerous to work with than uranium—not significantly more radioactive or toxic—but it is far more suscep-tible to predetonation during assembly. In plain English, firing one piece of plutonium into another would result in a meltdown, not a substantial explosion. That was why Los Alamos under Rob-ert Oppenheimer scrambled to invent the implosion method of assembly in the final year of the Pacific War: A sphere crushed to critical density by high explosives doesn't have time to predetonate.

Acquiring enough HEU would be difficult, Mueller argues. No market for it exists; it's carefully guarded; inside collabora-tors would have to fear being killed upon delivery rather than paid off; governments would deploy extensive security forces and offer huge rewards when the theft or diversion was discovered; crossing international borders with stolen HEU would be chal-lenging. All these arguments ring true.

Less certain is Mueller's bomb-construction scenario. He thinks the terrorist team would need engineers and specialists, a machine shop, and at least months "or even a year" to fash-ion its bomb, and perhaps it would, but none of those require-ments seems extravagant. He quotes Stephen Younger, the Los Alamos physicist and weapons designer who served as direc-tor of the Defense Threat Reduction Agency during George W. Bush's first term, emphasizing the "daunting problems associ-ated with material purity, machining, and a host of other issues." Younger concluded, "to think that a terrorist group, working in isolation with an unreliable supply of electricity and little access to tools and supplies, could fabricate a bomb or IND [impro-vised nuclear device] is far-fetched at best." Younger seems to be describing Al Qaeda trying to build a bomb in the caves of Tora Bora—where else would the supply of electricity be unreliable and tools and supplies scarce?—and his condescension toward the bomb-making capabilities of terrorists may be complacent.

I would certainly prefer to believe that a terrorist bomb is beyond the technical and organizational skills of terrorists. Two personal experiences with physicists deeply knowledgeable about nuclear-weapons design leave me skeptical of such a conclusion.

In 1986, when I helped the Nobel Laureate physicist Luis W. Alvarez write his memoirs, Alvarez commented one day on the importance of keeping track of highly enriched uranium. Speaking of a quantity sufficient to form a supercritical mass, he told me, "You can make a fairly high-level nuclear explosion just by dropping one piece onto another *by hand*." Alvarez had been intimately involved in the development of the first atomic bombs, and knew whereof he spoke. Some years later I gave a talk at the National Atomic Museum in Albuquerque during which I quoted Alvarez's comment. An audience member from one of the nearby weapons labs, Los Alamos or Sandia, told me afterward with some enthusiasm, probably speaking out of turn, "Yes, and if you can accelerate it even a little you can get a *much bigger* explosion."

Equally unsettling was my encounter with Ted Taylor, the former Los Alamos weapons designer whom John McPhee credits in his book *The Curve of Binding Energy* with having pioneered the miniaturization of U.S. nuclear weapons. I interviewed Taylor after the 1993 truck-bomb attack on the World Trade Center, the precursor to 9/11. Speculating about nuclear terrorism, Taylor told me he'd wondered how many people it would take "to start World War III." To build a nuclear weapon, he meant, and detonate it under conditions that would lead the nation that was targeted to believe some other nuclear power was behind the attack and to retaliate with a nuclear strike, beginning a catastrophic nuclear exchange. He said he'd concluded it would only take one person. I thought then and think now that one person would suffice only if that person were Ted Taylor. But even if Taylor, who died in 2004, was one of a kind, his informed speculation that a minimum number of conspirators with the right training and skills might succeed in building a homemade nuclear weapon is chilling.

As long ago as 1977, the U.S. Office of Technology Assessment confirmed a small-group scenario:

> A small group of people, none of whom have ever had access to the classified literature, could possibly design and build a crude

nuclear explosive device. They would not necessarily require a great deal of technological equipment or have to undertake any experiments. Only modest machine-shop facilities that could be contracted for without arousing suspicion would be required. The financial resources for the acquisition of necessary equipment on open markets need not exceed a fraction of a million dollars. The group would have to include, at a minimum, a person capable of researching and understanding the literature in several fields and a jack-of-all trades technician.

Which is, of course, an approximate description of the subsequent South African program that led to the successful design and construction of a small arsenal of uranium gun bombs.

All these expert conclusions assume the availability of sufficient HEU to make at least one bomb. Where would Taylor's lone gunman find one hundred pounds of uranium metal? I discovered one answer to that question, and confirmation of Alvarez's suicidal hand-assembly scheme, in a report on nuclear security by Matthew Bunn and Anthony Wier of the Project on Managing the Atom at Harvard's Belfer Center. The two Harvard experts wrote:

Setting off a nuclear explosion with HEU can be done rapidly enough that [U.S. Department of Energy] internal security regulations require that security for U.S. nuclear sites where enough material for a bomb is present be based on keeping terrorists out entirely, rather than catching them as they leave the site, to avoid "an unauthorized opportunity . . . to use available nuclear materials for onsite assembly of an improvised nuclear device"—that is, to prevent terrorists from being able to set off a nuclear explosion while they were still inside the facility where they stole the HEU.

Since terrorists who broke into a U.S. (or some other) nuclear site where HEU was available in critical quantities would hardly have the time or tools needed to build a bomb on-site, the DOE requirement for perimeter defense confirms the Alvarez scenario. Bunn and Wier wrote further that the Senate Foreign Relations Committee at one point "asked the three U.S. nuclear weapons laboratories whether terrorists, if they had the nuclear material, could make a crude but workable nuclear bomb. The answer given was 'yes.' " Within a few months "the laboratories had actually built a gun-type device, using only components that, except for the nuclear material itself, were off the shelf and commercially available without breaking any laws. The device was actually brought into a secure Senate hearing room to demonstrate the gravity of the threat."

If an improvised nuclear device is relatively easy to make once the fissile explosive has been obtained, then the fundamental requirement for security from nuclear terrorism must be rigorous control of plutonium and (especially) highly enriched uranium. As two security specialists, Ivo Daalder and Jan Lodal, concluded in 2008:

> U.S. nuclear policies remain stuck in the Cold War, even as the threats the United States faces have changed dramatically. Today, the gravest threat comes from the possibility of terrorists bent on delivering a devastating blow against the United States acquiring the capacity to do so with nuclear weapons. This threat is compounded by the dangers of nuclear proliferation, as more and more countries hedge against potentially negative developments in their regions by acquiring the wherewithal to build the bomb. Then there is the increasing global demand for nuclear energy, which will spread the infrastructure necessary to produce fissile nuclear materials still wider. The world, in short, is on the verge of entering an age of more nuclear weapon states, more nuclear materials, and more nuclear facilities that are poorly secured— making the job of the terrorists seeking the bomb easier and the odds that a nuclear weapon will be used greater.

Some of this argument is threat inflation, to be sure, but enough of it is realistic to be disturbing. At the opening of the second decade of the twenty-first century, with both nations and subnational entities becoming capable of fielding nuclear arsenals, the world faces a stark choice: eliminate nuclear weapons and secure their fissile explosives or expect them to be used.

RICHARD BUTLER has a name for that choice: he calls it the axiom of proliferation. "It was identified by the Canberra Commission," he told a group of students in Monterey, California, one spring day in 2008, "and in some ways I think it was its highest achievement: *As long as any state has nuclear weapons, others will seek to acquire them.*"

Australia had taken the lead among states in examining nuclear abolition. In 1995, between Butler's work on the indefinite extension of the NPT and the CTBT, he had heard from Canberra about an additional but complementary assignment. The Australian prime minister, Paul Keating, had encountered a journal article that had stirred him to action. "The article was about how ridiculous and threatening nuclear weapons are," Butler told me. "Keating read it and said, 'This is an appalling situation. We should find some way to get rid of nuclear weapons.' " After discussing the question with his foreign minister, Gareth Evans, Keating decided to empower a wide-ranging commission. Evans asked Butler to undertake the work, and from that fortuity the Canberra Commission on the Elimination of Nuclear Weapons was created in November 1995 with Butler as its chairman and a charter "to propose practical steps toward a nuclear weapon free world including the related problem of maintaining stability and security during the transitional period and after this goal is achieved."

Butler invited seventeen knowledgeable and experienced experts and former government officials to join the commission, including Lee Butler, the retired chief of the U.S. Strategic Air Command; Michael Carver, a British lord who had been chief of general staff and chief of defense staff as well as commander in chief of the Far East in the British Army; the Sri Lankan diplomat

Jayantha Dhanapala; Rolf Ekéus; the Japanese nuclear engineer and former ambassador Ryukichi Imai; the former U.S. secretary of defense Robert McNamara; the Chinese ambassador for disarmament affairs Qian Jiadong; the former French prime minister Michel Rocard; Joseph Rotblat, the Manhattan Project physicist and Pugwash Conference president who won the 1995 Nobel Peace Prize; the Russian astrophysicist Roald Sagdeev, who had been Mikhail Gorbachev's science adviser; and the only woman, Maj Britt Theorin, a former Swedish ambassador for disarmament and a member of the European parliament.

They debated across three continents between November 1995 and August 1996, when their report was presented to the Australian prime minister and subsequently to the United Nations and the Conference on Disarmament. "They were an extremely interesting and colorful group," Butler told me:

> Maj Britt Theorin was a classic abolitionist, literally wearing beads and sandals; she would pull out her magic wand and ask why couldn't we just declare nuclear weapons illegal and bring the world together? She was a handful. At the other end of the spectrum, Michel Rocard came on board by arranging to issue a statement of reservations—France might want to retain a few nuclear weapons, you know. In the middle of the spectrum, Rolf Ekéus and Joe Rotblat, among others, were immensely helpful. Lord Carver, like most military men, took the view that nuclear weapons were useless and stupid and that we ought to get rid of them—anyone who has had the button in his hand will tell you that it's a horror. Bob McNamara was terrific. There were times when he was rivetingly bright. He left his ego off the table; there was none of that "I was American secretary of defense" nonsense. All were agreed that the elimination of nuclear weapons was a sound purpose, but it wasn't a group that found ready agreement.

In that, I suggested, they seemed to be representative of their countries and the agendas they brought to the table—a practice run, as it were, of what a negotiation to eliminate nuclear weapons might look like had they carried their governments' portfolios in that regard. Butler agreed. They came to consensus in the end.

The Canberra Commission report opened with a statement of plain truths about nuclear weapons that decades of nuclearist sophistry have obscured:

> The destructiveness of nuclear weapons is immense. Any use would be catastrophic.
>
> Nuclear weapons pose an intolerable threat to all humanity and its habitat, yet tens of thousands remain in arsenals built up at an extraordinary time of deep antagonism. That time has passed, yet assertions of their utility continue.
>
> These facts are obvious but their implications have been blurred. There is no doubt that, if the peoples of the world were more fully aware of the inherent danger of nuclear weapons and the consequences of their use, they would reject them, and not permit their continued possession or acquisition on their behalf by their governments, even for an alleged need for self-defense.
>
> Nuclear weapons are held by a handful of states which insist that these weapons provide unique security benefits, and yet reserve uniquely to themselves the right to own them. This situation is highly discriminatory and thus unstable; it cannot be sustained. The possession of nuclear weapons by any state is a constant stimulus to other states to acquire them.

(The last sentence quoted, of course, is a consensus version of the axiom of proliferation that Butler stated more succinctly in Monterey.)

The U.S. secretary of defense, Robert Gates, in the last months of George W. Bush's second term as president, rephrased the Canberra Commission's axiom from a nuclearist point of view. In doing so, he inadvertently confirmed it. In an October 2008 speech to the Carnegie Endowment for International Peace, Gates said, "As long as others have nuclear weapons, we must maintain some level of these weapons ourselves." The reasons Gates gave for maintaining a nuclear arsenal were "to deter potential adversaries and to reassure over two dozen allies and partners who rely on our nuclear umbrella for their security, making it unnecessary for them to develop their own." Gates may have noticed the obvious weakness in his argument—that eliminating nuclear weapons would eliminate any nuclear threat from "potential adversaries"—because he added the secondary condition that our allies and partners (implicitly, those who have not acquired nuclear weapons) need our protection—or else, Gates speculated, they would proliferate themselves. But such extended deterrence was revealed long ago to be a deceit, as Henry Kissinger notoriously cautioned a NATO conference in Brussels all the way back in 1979:

> We must face the fact that it is absurd to base the strategy of the West on the credibility of the threat of mutual suicide. . . . The European allies should not keep asking us to multiply strategic assurances that we cannot possibly mean, or, if we do mean, we should not want to execute, because if we execute we risk the destruction of civilization.

In fact, states have sought nuclear arsenals when they perceived their existence to be threatened, a perception that any program of nuclear elimination must address. (States have gone nuclear secondarily for "prestige," a wasting asset in a world that increasingly stigmatizes nuclear possession and is likely in the course of time to make such possession a crime against humanity.) Extended deterrence would survive in a world without nuclear weapons, bilaterally or through regional security alliances such as NATO, but it would be conventional. No nuclear power in any case has used nuclear weapons against an opposing belligerent, either conventionally or nuclear-armed, in more than sixty years. Nations, including the United States and the former Soviet

Union, have preferred to accept stalemate and even defeat, as in Vietnam and Afghanistan, rather than escalate to nuclear war. Is there better evidence of the military uselessness of nuclear weapons than six decades of futility?

"How do you prevent states from seeking nuclear weapons?" Butler asked rhetorically. "No state should have them," he told me. "Then, by definition, no one will seek to get them."

Expressed so abstractly, the Canberra Commission's fundamental argument for nuclear elimination sounds naïve. What about cheating? Wouldn't there always be an advantage to be gained in a world without nuclear weapons by cheating—by clandestinely building or reconstituting a nuclear arsenal, or simply by holding back a few nuclear weapons when other states reduce and then eliminate their own? Such in fact has been one major argument that nuclearists have offered against nuclear elimination: that it will be impossible to guarantee that all nuclear weapons have been eliminated and no new ones devised.

The Canberra Commission's answer to that fundamental fear was verification, but it understood that verification could never be conclusive. A world without nuclear weapons would be a world living with a degree of risk of cheating. How much risk the parties to nuclear zero would be willing to accept is a political question. But that is nothing new, the commission's report pointed out:

> Effective verification is critical to the achievement and maintenance of a nuclear weapon free world. Before states agree to eliminate nuclear weapons they will require a high level of confidence that verification arrangements would detect promptly any attempt to cheat the disarmament process. . . . A political judgment will be needed on whether the levels of assurance possible from the verification regime are sufficient. All existing arms control and disarmament agreements have required political judgments of this nature because no verification system provides absolute certainty.

Butler expressed this argument to me more colorfully in a telephone conversation. "What about rogues and criminals? The answer is, they couldn't bust the system because we would use conventional means to prevent them. The world would rise up against such people."

Monitoring for the Comprehensive Nuclear Test-Ban Treaty had already reached such a sophisticated level by 2006, when the monitoring network was only 60 percent complete, that more than twenty CTBT seismic stations detected the first North Korean nuclear test of 9 October as far away as South America, even though its explosive yield was less than one kiloton. Besides 170 seismic stations arrayed across the world, the CTBT's monitoring system includes eleven hydroacoustic stations capable of hearing the explosion of a fifty-pound TNT test charge ten thousand miles away; sixty infrasound stations listening for low-frequency sound waves from above-ground nuclear tests; and eighty radionuclide stations sniffing for bomb-derived radioactive particles and radioactive noble gases. Once the CTBT is fully in force, wrote the *Science* magazine reporter Daniel Clery, "its executive council, if faced with a suspected test . . . can call for the CTBT's ultimate verification measure: an on-site inspection. Within days of a suspected test, a team of up to 40 people can be on the scene and scouring an area up to 1000 square kilometers using overflights, mobile radionuclide detectors, microseismic arrays to detect aftershocks, gamma-ray detectors, ground-penetrating radar, magnetic and gravitational field mapping, and electrical conductivity measurements."

What if a suspected violator refuses to cooperate? That would be a material violation of the CTBT, potentially invoking a full range of responses from the international community, up to and including invasion. Richard Butler's world that would "rise up against such people" is no peacemaker fantasy. It's the world of this narrative, the world you've been reading about, acting imperfectly but with steady determination and increasing confidence on behalf of nuclear limitation and foreclosure: from

Mikhail Gorbachev's and Ronald Reagan's initiatives to end the Cold War, to the voluntary disarming of the former Soviet republics and the securing of nuclear materials, to the U.S. and Russia's deepening mutual arms reductions, to the long effort to roll up Saddam Hussein's nuclear-weapons program, to the up-and-down negotiations with North Korea that have nevertheless prevented another Korean war, to international diplomatic pressure brought to bear effectively on India and Pakistan, to the persistent march forward of negotiations toward treaties to limit nuclear testing and proliferation. Revolutions are not imposed by fiat; they move from conception to reality in the practical experience of accomplishing them and living them through. Working through the day-to-day challenges of a world finally freed from the burden of a long, polarizing ideological conflict, hardly aware of where we were going, we find ourselves in the second decade of the twenty-first century well along the way to eliminating nuclear weapons once and for all.

IT SHOULD COME AS no surprise that resistance increases as we approach closer to that goal. In the years since the Canberra Commission issued its report, other commissions have offered proposals for the elimination of nuclear weapons. Hans Blix chaired a Swedish-sponsored international commission in 2006, Australia's Gareth Evans an international commission cochaired by Japan and Australia in 2008. Inspired by the Reagan-Gorbachev summit at Reykjavik in 1986, the U.S. statesmen George Shultz, Sam Nunn, Bill Perry, and Henry Kissinger came together twenty years later at the invitation of Shultz and the physicist Sid Drell to organize an ongoing program for advancing the elimination of nuclear weapons. They have sustained it with public statements, extensive analysis, and private discussions with national leaders in the United States and abroad. Barack Obama endorsed their call to eliminate nuclear weapons when he became president. All these various groups and individuals, and many others besides, have agreed fundamentally on both the need for nuclear elimination and the political and technical steps necessary to achieve such a transforming goal.

"For fifteen or twenty years now," Butler told me in frustration in 2009, "we have not lacked clear knowledge of the nature of the problem, of its urgency, and of the steps that can be taken to solve it. What we're confronted with, however, is political cowardice—politicians kicking the ball down the road. 'We agree with you,' they say, 'but we have a few rednecks among our constituents. Can we do it after the next election?' However one skins the cat, it comes down to this: As long as nuclear weapons exist, they will proliferate, they will be used, and any use will be catastrophic. We know exactly what needs to be done. We could do it in a morning. All the nuts-and-bolts stuff might take another five or ten years."

Whether it will be done depends on the political courage of national leaders, in the United States first of all. Barack Obama pledged to make reducing and eliminating the world's lethal stockpiles of nuclear weapons a central goal of his administration. In the spring of 2009, the new young president of the United States told the world from a public square in Prague:

> The existence of thousands of nuclear weapons is the most dangerous legacy of the Cold War. No nuclear war was fought between the United States and the Soviet Union, but generations lived with the knowledge that their world could be erased in a single flash of light. Cities like Prague that existed for centuries, that embodied the beauty and the talent of so much of humanity, would have ceased to exist.
>
> Today, the Cold War has disappeared but thousands of those weapons have not. In a strange turn of history, the threat of global nuclear war has gone down, but the risk of a nuclear attack has gone up. More nations have acquired these weapons. Testing has continued. Black market trade in nuclear secrets and nuclear materials abound. The technology to build a bomb

has spread. Terrorists are determined to buy, build or steal one. Our efforts to contain these dangers are centered on a global non-proliferation regime, but as more people and nations break the rules, we could reach the point where the center cannot hold.

Obama then reformulated Richard Butler's axiom of proliferation as an assertion of personal and American responsibility:

Some argue that the spread of these weapons cannot be stopped, cannot be checked—that we are destined to live in a world where more nations and more people possess the ultimate tools of destruction. Such fatalism is a deadly adversary, for *if we believe that the spread of nuclear weapons is inevitable, then in some way we are admitting to ourselves that the use of nuclear weapons is inevitable.*

Just as we stood for freedom in the 20th century, we must stand together for the right of people everywhere to live free from fear in the 21st century. And as the only nuclear power to have used a nuclear weapon, the United States has a moral responsibility to act. We cannot succeed in this endeavor alone, but we can lead it, we can start it.

So today, I state clearly and with conviction America's commitment to seek the peace and security of a world without nuclear weapons.

We won't do it in a morning, and the nuts-and-bolts stuff, given mutual suspicions, will probably take more than five or ten years. Obama's first secretary of defense, Robert Gates, outspokenly opposed it, as did a host of political and military-industrial leaders who feared cheating or a decline in government largess or who balked at giving away the long-standing political advantages of threat inflation.

India, Pakistan, Israel, and North Korea are the hard cases, though each has security needs that the world community must sooner or later organize to meet. India and Pakistan began pursuing confidence-building measures, with some success, after a near-nuclear war over Kargil in 1999. Israel is willing to discuss joining a Middle Eastern nuclear-free zone, though its terms for doing so are demanding. North Korea continues to pursue an alliance with the United States that might provide it with light-water reactors to boost its electrical supply.

Will eliminating nuclear weapons make the world safe for conventional war? If by conventional war one means massed tanks and foot soldiers, such war is already obsolete. Bill Perry's high-tech battlefield sensors and precision weapons, demonstrated with increasing effectiveness in two wars between the United States and Iraq, made it so. The onrushing trend in military armaments is toward what one analyst calls "weapons of precise destruction." Even ICBMs can now be fitted (if they must be) with conventional warheads; when a missile warhead can be delivered via GPS within a three-foot circle across five thousand miles, a small charge of high explosives will do. Nuclear weapons, never weapons of warfare except in the grandiose imaginations of air-power fantasists, have reverted to their original function: They are terror weapons. Are we terrorists?

So-called collateral damage—killing civilians in the course of military attacks—is increasingly condemned in a world in which it has become increasingly visible to television, cell-phone cameras, and the Web. More fundamentally, every large population in the world has passed through at least the first stage of the demographic transition; with declining birth and death rates, families produce fewer children; as numbers of children per family decline, parents are progressively less willing to see their children pressed into military service to be slaughtered in war. The demographic transition signals increased global economic well-being, itself a stimulus to negotiated rather than belligerent relationships between groups and nations. That technological and economic interconnection fosters nonviolent relations has been a questionable argument in favor of technological advance, but it appears today finally to have reached a takeoff point.

Such a change on a world scale finds precedent in the progressive decline in *private* violence in the West across six hundred years as governments centralized, established professional armies, and restrained the Hobbesian violence of the commons. The middle class emerged demanding protection in exchange for the taxes it paid; ordinary citizens gained access to courts of law for the nonviolent settlement of disputes. Homicide rates were on the order of 50 per 100,000 people in medieval Europe; social control over private violence limits those rates to about 1.5 per 100,000 in Europe today. (They are higher in the United States, partly because of the ubiquity of guns, but not much higher—5.6 per 100,000 in 2007. They are highest in states where governments are weak and social controls inadequate—50 per 100,000 in Sierra Leone, 49.1 in El Salvador, 20 in Kazakhstan, 16.5 in Russia.)

The tightening web of social controls over *public* violence is just the interconnected net of national and international efforts I have described in this book. If it seems stumbling and ad hoc, it is no more so than were social controls over private violence as they began to emerge in early modern Europe. This time around, with that history behind us and with modern resources and communications (and a far greater threat to the human world looming over it than private violence ever was), the transition will not require six hundred years. If not in my lifetime, probably in the lifetime of my children, and certainly in my grandchildren's lifetimes, weapons of mass destruction will be outlawed, as Blix's commission, among other entities, has already notably proposed. In time, possession of a nuclear weapon will be judged a crime against humanity. Such a judgment would only codify what is already an evident fact.

I BEGAN THIS WORK of writing the history of the nuclear age in 1979, when I was forty-two. It appeared to me then—it appeared to many people then—that the future would burn out in nuclear holocaust if the nuclear powers continued on their reckless course of waging bitter ideological conflict behind incendiary palisades of missiles and bombs. I had been a novelist before and a magazine journalist; I brought no special knowledge to the work, only a commitment as a citizen to understand and to witness to my convictions.

Early in my research, long before the Internet, I happened to be scanning the shelves of a Midwestern library for books that might inform me about the numbers of deaths from twentieth-century wars. One title caught my attention, a slim volume with the curious name *Twentieth Century Book of the Dead*. I pulled it down from the shelf, opened it, and was immediately drawn in. Its author was a Scotsman, Gil Elliot. A few pages along, with quiet ferocity, he redefined the whole ugly twentieth-century business of war and mass killing:

> It is absurd to look upon the hundred million or so man-made deaths of the twentieth century as the "cost" of the conflict, as though they were the casualty returns of a field commander. They are more directly comparable with the scale of death from disease and plague which was the accepted norm before this century. Indeed, man-made death has largely replaced these as a source of untimely death. This is the kind of change that Hegel meant when he said that a quantitative change, if large enough, could bring about a qualitative change. The quality of this particular change becomes clear if we connect the present total of deaths with the scale of death inherent in the weapons now possessed by the large powers. Nuclear strategists talk in terms of hundreds of millions of deaths, of the destruction of whole nations and even of the entire human race. The moral significance is inescapable. If morality refers to relations between individuals, or between the individual and society, then there can be no more fundamental moral issue than the continuing survival of individuals and societies. The scale of man-made death is the central moral as well as material fact of our time.

I took this paradigm-shifting book home, read it, and then reread it, hardly stopping to sleep, sought and eventually found a copy of my own (it had been published in a small U.S. edition in 1972, had gone mostly unnoticed, and was correspondingly rare). It has been my handbook and guide for understanding nuclear man-made death now for more than thirty years.

I tracked Elliot down through his publisher—he lived in London—and wrote him a letter of unqualified praise. Somewhat surprised, he responded. We began a correspondence. When my research for *The Making of the Atomic Bomb* took me to Europe, I stopped off in London to meet him. We've stayed in touch through all these years of work. Inevitably, I find myself turning again to *Twentieth Century Book of the Dead* as this last volume of my nuclear history draws to a close.

Elliot devised a method for numbering the man-made dead of the twentieth century—you can read his book, if you can find a copy, to see how he does so—but even more profoundly, he identified for the first time the right way to think about the problem of man-made death. It's the right way because it points to a solution, one that our species has already devised and tested and made to work against an older agent of slaughter, epidemic disease. But let him explain:

> Our societies are dedicated to the preservation and care of life. Official concern ceases at death, the rest is private. Public death was first recognized as a matter of civilized concern in the nineteenth century, when some health workers decided that untimely death was a question between men and society, not between men and God. Infant mortality and epidemic disease became matters of social responsibility. Since then, and for that reason, millions of lives have been saved. They are not saved by accident or goodwill. Human life is daily deliberately protected from nature by accepted practices of hygiene and medical care, by the control of living conditions and the guidance of human relationships. Mortality statistics are constantly examined to see if the causes of death

reveal any areas needing special attention. Because of the success of these practices, the area of public death has, in advanced societies, been taken over by man-made death—once an insignificant or "merged" part of the spectrum, now almost the whole.

When politicians, in tones of grave wonder, characterize our age as one of vast effort in saving human life, and enormous vigor in destroying it, they seem to feel they are indicating some mysterious paradox of the human spirit. There is no paradox and no mystery. The difference is that one area of public death has been tackled and secured by the forces of reason; the other has not. The pioneers of public health did not change nature, or men, but adjusted the active relationship of men to certain aspects of nature so that the relationship became one of watchful and healthy respect. In doing so they had to contend with and struggle against the suspicious opposition of those who believed that to interfere with nature was sinful, and even that disease and plague were the result of something sinful in the nature of man himself.

Elliot went on to compare what he called "public death," meaning biologic death, and man-made death:

[I do not wish] to claim mystical authority for the comparison I have made between two kinds of public death—that which results from disease and that which we call man-made. The irreducible virtue of the analogy is that the problem of man-made death, like that of disease, can be tackled only by reason. It contains the same elements as the problem of disease—the need to locate the sources of the pest, to devise preventive measures and to maintain systematic vigilance in their execution. But it is a much wider problem and for obvious reasons cannot be dealt with by scientific methods to the same extent as can disease.

And, a little later, he concluded this first attempt at synthesis: "In fact, the manner in which people die reflects more than any other fact the value of a society."

Hermann Biggs, an American public-health pioneer, made a similar observation at the beginning of the twentieth century. "The reduction of the death rate," Biggs wrote in 1911, "is the principal statistical expression and index of human and social progress."

To advance the cause of public health it was necessary to depoliticize disease, to remove it from the realm of value and install it in the realm of fact. Today we have advanced to the point where international cooperation toward the prevention, control, and even elimination of disease is possible among nations that hardly cooperate with each other in any other way. No one any longer considers disease a political issue, except to the extent that its control measures a nation's quality of life, and only modern primitives consider it a judgment of God.

In 1999, for the first time in human history, infectious diseases no longer ranked first among causes of death worldwide. Public health, a discipline that organizes science-based systems of surveillance and prevention, was primarily responsible for that millennial change in human mortality. Half of all the increases in life expectancy in recorded history occurred within the twentieth century. Most of the worldwide increase was accomplished in the first half of the century, and it was almost entirely the result not of medical intervention but of public-health measures directed to primary prevention. Not surgeons cutting or doctors dispensing pills but better nutrition, sewage treatment, water purification, the pasteurization of milk, and the immunization of children extended human life. Half of all Americans alive today are alive because of public-health improvements. Without such improvements, 69 million of us would have died before reproducing; a further 69 million would never have been born. The number alive because of public-health improvements in the United States alone—138 million—is larger than the total number of man-made deaths worldwide in the twentieth century directly or indirectly caused by war. Public health is medicine's greatest success story and a powerful model for a parallel discipline, which I propose to call *public safety*.

Where the largest-scale instruments of man-made death are concerned, the elements of that discipline of public safety have already begun to assemble themselves: materials control and accounting, cooperative threat reduction, security guarantees, agreements and treaties, surveillance and inspection, sanctions, forceful disarming if all else fails.

Reducing and finally eliminating the world's increasingly vestigial nuclear arsenals may be delayed by extremists of the right or the left, as progress was stalled during the George W. Bush administration by rigid Manichaean ideologues who imagined that there might be good nuclear powers and evil nuclear powers and sought to disarm only those they considered evil. Nuclear weapons operate beyond good and evil. They destroy without discrimination or mercy: whether one lives or dies in their operation is entirely a question of distance from ground zero. In Elliot's eloquent words, they create nations of the dead, and collectively have the capacity to create a world of the dead. But as Niels Bohr, the great Danish physicist and philosopher, was the first to realize, the complement of that utter destructiveness must then be unity in common security, a fundamental transformation in relationships between nations, nondiscrimination in unity not on the dark side but by the light of day.

Violence originates in vulnerability brutalized: It is vulnerability's corruption, but also its revenge. "Perhaps everything terrible," Rainer Maria Rilke once wrote, "is in its deepest being something helpless that wants help from us." As we extend our commitment to common security, as we work to master man-made death, we will need to recognize that terrible helplessness and relieve it—in others, but also in ourselves.

Half Moon Bay
2005–2010

NOTES

For full references, see Bibliography (p. 417).

PROLOGUE

4   *"The principle of common security . . ."*: Palme (1982), p. 176.

5   *"The task of ensuring security . . ."*: Quoted in Sigal (2000), p. 19.

5   *the United States had forced Taiwan:* Hersman and Peters (2006), pp. 546–48.

6   *"If one country keeps . . ."*: Quoted in Chernyaev (2000), p. 77.

7   *allowed its ally to test . . . Lop Nur:* Reed and Stillman (2009), p. 252.

9   *"Despite certain promising developments . . ."*: Spector (1990), pp. 303–4.

10 *A regional nuclear war . . . entire world:* Toon et al. (2007).

11 *"As long as any state has . . ."*: Cited by Richard Butler, class presentation, Monterey Institute of International Studies, Monterey, CA, 2008.

ONE "PRESIDENT BUSH'S FRANKENSTEIN"

16 *"In June 1982 . . . President Reagan . . ."*: Howard Teicher affidavit, Document 61, *National Security Archive Electronic Briefing Book No. 82*, "Shaking Hands with Saddam Hussein: The U.S. Tilts toward Iraq, 1980–1984," edited by Joyce Battle, pp. 2–4.

16 *Saddam "was pleased . . ."*: Department of State telegram, "Subject: Rumsfeld Mission: December 20 meeting with Iraqi President Saddam Hussein," Document 31, *National Security Archive Electronic Briefing Book No. 82*, p. 1.

16 *("I do not remember even one discussion . . ."*: Quoted in Bergman (2007), p. 43. Bergman documents the Israeli program at length at p. 40ff.

17 *"Aziz refused even to accept:"* Howard Teicher affidavit, p. 4.

17 *In 1981, striking from the air:* Yengst et al. (1996), p. 331.

18 *"the deciding factor in this decision . . ."*: Kay (1995), p. 111.

18 *Iraq rebuilt and extended Tuwaitha:* See Albright et al. (1999).

19 *"Al Tuwaitha was visited . . ."*: Kay (1995), p. 119.

19 *Iraq began buying uranium abroad:* Table 1, Iraq Survey Group Report, https://www.cia.gov/library/reports/general-reports-1/iraq_wm, accessed 20 Nov. 2008.

20 *Just as, after . . . underestimate Iraq:* See Kay (1995), pp. 116–17.

20 *"In this connection . . ."*: Quoted in Rhodes (1987), p. 511.

21 *"The fact is that during . . ."*: UNMOVIC working document, 6 Mar. 2003, p. 6 (online).

21 *"The maximum level of radiation . . ."*: Gary Milhollin, "Comments on the 'Al-q'aq'a Bomb," p. 2, Iraq Watch (online).

22 *In 1988 it decided formally:* Albright (2002), p. 1.

23 Precursor materials for WMD: See the Center for Grassroots Oversight, www.historycommons.org.

23 *"In September 1988 . . .":* Scott (1996), p. 1652.

23 *"I came immediately . . .":* Ibid., p. 1655.

24 *an incriminating Socratic dialogue:* "Middle East: The Big Sting," *Time,* 9 Apr. 1990 (online).

24 *"A purchase order . . .":* Robert Reinhold, "Artful Hunt for Smuggler Suspects," *New York Times,* 29 Mar. 1990.

24 *Daghir dithered for months:* Ibid.

24 *"On arrival at Heathrow . . .":* Scott (1996), p. 1652.

25 *"At this stage . . .":* Ibid.

25 *Iraqi agent Ali Daghir:* Ali Daghir has steadfastly maintained that he was entrapped and that the capacitors he was shipping to Iraq were commonplace, a fact disputed by the officials who investigated his case. Daghir did succeed in having his conviction overturned on appeal on the grounds that the trial judge made a technical mistake in his jury instructions. Daghir then tried to win compensation for his conviction-related business losses but never succeeded in doing so. He also continued to be restrained by the U.S. government from doing business in Iraq.

25 *"Iraq may be close . . .":* David Fairhall, "Trigger Parts Point to Impending Test," *The Guardian* (London), 29 Mar. 1990.

26 *enrichment by gaseous diffusion:* For details see Albright (2002), pp. 14–15.

26 *"The Soviets have strong cards . . .":* Quoted in Waas and Unger (1992) (online).

26 *"had advised the president-elect . . .":* Friedman (1993), p. 133. The rest of the quotation follows on the referenced page.

27 *"Normal relations between . . .":* Ibid., Appendix B, p. 322.

27 *Baker endorsed:* See a partial facsimile of this memorandum at Ibid., Appendix B, p. 323.

28 *"one of the largest banks in Italy . . .":* Henry B. Gonzalez, *Congressional Record, House of Representatives,* 28 Apr. 1992, p. H2694.

28 *An intense Bush administration . . . cover-up:* See Friedman (1993), p. 215, passim.

28 *Bush himself participated:* Ibid., p. 215; Gonzalez, *Congressional Record, House of Representatives,* 25 July 1992, p. H9502.

29 *"Despite all this, the United States . . .":* Gonzalez, *Congressional Record, House of Representatives,* 21 Sept. 1992, p. H8820.

30 *"The memo states . . .":* Ibid., p. H8821.

30 *"the current Middle East crisis":* Friedman (1993), Appendix B, p. 339ff.

30 *"In short, these are the facts . . .":* Gonzalez, *Congressional Record,* 21 Sept. 1992, p. H8824.

31 *"President Bush's Frankenstein":* Quoted in Friedman (1993), p. 224.

31 *"Let the Gulf regimes know . . .":* Quoted in Wilson (2005), p. 97.

31 *"Brothers, . . . the weakness of a big body . . .":* Quoted in "Vietnam: Setting the Stage," presentation by Peter W. Rodman to the Conference on the Real "Lessons" of the Vietnam War, Center for National Security Law, University of Virginia School of Law, Charlottesville, VA, Friday, 28 Apr. 2000 (online).

32 *"By Allah, we will make . . .":* Quoted in Alfonsi (2006), p. 11.

32 *"Iraq came out of the war . . .":* "Excerpts from Iraqi Document on Meeting with U.S. Envoy," *New York Times International,* 23 Sept. 1990 (online), p. 2.

33 *"So what can it mean . . .":* Ibid., p. 4.

33 *Glaspie responded:* This and following statements quoted from ibid., p. 5ff.

34 Glaspie-Saddam transcript: Glaspie subsequently testified before Congress that the transcript from which I have quoted, which was made public by Iraq on 11 Sept. 1990, had been "maliciously" edited by the Iraqis "to the point of inaccuracy." She claimed she told Saddam in no uncertain terms that the United States would act if Iraq invaded Kuwait. The California Democrat Tom Lantos responded, "Let me tell you, very few people were sure [at that time] that we would move militarily. . . . For you to say in retrospect that Saddam Hussein absolutely knew that we would move in a military way is simply absurd."

34 *"The United States and Iraq both . . .":* Quoted in Wilson (2005), pp. 102–3.

35 *electronic funds transfers:* These and subsequent details from Hart (n.d.).

35 *"Their reports were very pointed . . .":* Ibid., pp. 6–7.

TWO CUTTING SADDAM'S SINEWS

36 *"This will not stand . . .":* Quoted in Baker (1995), p. 276.

36 *"I know you're aware . . .":* Ibid., p. 277.

37 *Wilson met with Saddam:* Wilson (2005), p. 118ff.

37 *"Convey to President Bush . . .":* Alfonsi (2006), p. 113.

37 *"Saddam was worried . . .":* Wilson (2005), p. 123.

38 *The king . . . was easily persuaded:* Gordon and Trainor (1995), p. 52.

38 *"After the danger is over . . .":* History Commons (online), citing multiple sources.

38 *"Dick Cheney called me . . .":* Powell (1995), p. 467.

38 *"Within a couple of weeks . . .":* Ibid., p. 469.

38 *"but a variety of military . . .":* Arkin and Fieldhouse (n.d.), Week Nine.

39 *that would not be enough for one bomb:* Thomas C. Reed, personal communication, 15 Dec. 2008.

39   *twenty kilograms:* Lyman (1995), p. 2.
39   *missile capable of reaching Tel Aviv:* Hamza (2000), p. 237.
39   *"These tests were credited . . .":* Yengst et al. (1996), p. 338.
39   *delivered by . . . longer-range missiles:* Ibid., p. 335.
39   *the bomb would be notably unstable:* Ibid., p. 334.
39   *"It was a stupid idea . . .":* Thomas C. Reed, personal communication, 15 Dec. 2008.
40   *"We had learned that they . . .":* Wilson (2005), p. 141.
40   *"A half-century ago . . .":* Quoted in Alfonsi (2006), p. 99.
40   *"sharp divisions within George . . .":* Ibid., p. 101.
41   *"was convinced that military . . .":* Ibid., p. 86.
41   *The solution, devised by . . . Pickering:* See ibid., p. 102ff.
41   *"The Bush administration . . .":* Ibid., p. 107.
42   *"the consensus opinion . . .":* David Kay interview, 2007.
42   *Pakistani derivative of the Chinese design:* Reed and Stillman (2009), p. 252.
43   *"gaining profits . . .":* Iraqi intelligence document 1/165, reproduced in Albright and Hinderstein (2004).
43   *"November 28 [1990] . . .":* Bush and Scowcroft (1998), p. 418.
44   *"what began as a strategic . . .":* Ronald Reagan (4 Mar. 1987), "Address to the Nation on the Iran Arms and Contra Aid Controversy," Ronald Reagan Presidential Foundation.
44   *"somewhat to the right . . .":* Quoted in Rhodes (2007), p. 119.
44   *"I think you have to preserve . . .":* "Cheney in His Own Words," *Frontline*, "The Dark Side," PBS (online).
45   *"*SENATOR KENNEDY:* . . .":* Ibid.
45   *"It's such a vital problem . . .":* Quoted in Alfonsi (2006), pp. 151–52.
46   *"I also warned him . . .":* Baker (2006), p. 298.
46   *"holding on to the hostages . . .":* Wilson (2005), p. 164.
47   *"That meeting with the king . . .":* Ibid., p. 165.
47   *"They ran the analysis . . .":* David Kay interview, 2007.
47   *"showed that there was uranium-238 . . .":* Nichols (2001).
47   *"Some of us believed . . .":* Ibid.
48   *"The reactor that did it . . .":* David Kay interview, 2007.
48   *"Those who would measure . . .":* Andrew Rosenthal, "Mideast Tensions; Visiting U.S. Troops in the Desert, President Talks Tough About Iraq," *New York Times,* 23 Nov. 1990.
48   *"which concluded . . .":* Arkin and Fieldhouse (n.d.), Week Seventeen.
49   *"In the [government of Israel's] view . . .":* Alfonsi (2006), p. 141. I follow Alfonsi's argument here.
49   *"capability to produce . . .":* Quoted in Arkin and Fieldhouse (n.d.), Week Seventeen.
49   *"Thus, . . . two weeks before . . .":* Ibid., Week Eighteen.
49   *eighteen nuclear-production sites:* Yengst et al. (1996), p. 333.
50   *"This was indeed a new era . . .":* Arkin and Fieldhouse (n.d.), Week Twenty-five.

51 *"During the second week . . ."*: David Kay interview, 2007.
51 *at least 50 wells:* This and other details of the Kuwaiti oil-well fires from Hirschmann (2005).
51 *"use oil for self-defense"*: Quoted in ibid., p. 13.
52 *"The Gulf War was . . ."*: Quoted in Chollet and Goldgeier (2008), p. 12.
52 *"Yes, and do what?"*: Quoted in Alfonsi (2006), p. 257.
52 *"I think that the proposition . . ."*: Richard Cheney, "The Gulf War: A First Assessment," Soref Symposium, 29 Apr. 1991 (online).
53 *"used to generate data . . ."*: Perry (1991), p. 69.
54 *"Operating together . . ."*: Ibid., p. 77.
54 *"tanks destroyed . . ."*: Ibid., p. 67.
54 *"While it is certainly not . . ."*: Ibid., p. 66.
54 *"Our wisest defense experts . . ."*: Bundy (1991), pp. 86–87.
55 *"no feeling of euphoria . . ."*: Bush and Scowcroft (1998), pp. 486–7.
55 *"when the [Iraqi] troops straggle home . . ."*: Ibid., p. 487.

THREE TRUE COURAGE

56 *"had forfeited any capacity . . ."*: Quoted in Krasno and Sutterlin (2003), p. 4.
56 *"There were those who . . ."*: Gallucci (2001), p. 2.
57 *"For the international community . . ."*: Perricos (2001), p. 1.
57 *"that the [IAEA] . . ."*: Gallucci (2001), p. 2.
57 *"the responsibility to designate . . ."*: Ibid.
57 *"nuclear weapons or nuclear-weapons-useable material . . ."*: United Nations S/RES/687 (1991) (online), C-12.
58 *"twisting middle-aged minds . . ."*: Gallucci (2001), p. 2.
58 *"sort of first . . ."*: Robert Gallucci interview (2002), "Conversations with History," UC Berkeley (online), p. 2.
59 *"the magnitude of the destruction . . ."*: Ibid.
59 *"but I was told . . ."*: Gallucci (2001), p. 3.
59 *"there are lots of commissions . . ."*: Ibid.
60 *"I had never met David . . ."*: Ibid.
60 *"the U.S. military was anxious . . ."*: David Kay interview, 2007.
61 *"Many of the IAEA staff . . ."*: "Iraq's Nuclear Weapons Capability and Inspections in Iraq," Joint Hearing before the Subcommittees on Europe and the Middle East, and International Security, International Organization and Human Rights of the Committee on Foreign Affairs, House of Representatives, 103rd Congress, First Session, 29 June 1993, Jay Davis testimony, p. 63.
61 *"We had a different view . . ."*: Gallucci Interview "Conversations with History," p. 4.
61 *"The first thing we needed . . ."*: Gallucci (2001), p. 3.
62 *"Not only did they not show up . . ."*: Ibid.
62 *"We had no secure telephones . . ."*: David Kay interview, 2007.

63 *"no frictions with the U.S. . . ."*: Hans Blix interview, 2004.

63 *"We were all scared . . ."*: Nichols (2001), p. 4.

64 *"I had to go out and lease . . ."*: David Kay interview, 2004.

64 *"The first few trips required true courage . . ."*: Gallucci (2001), pp. 7–8.

64 *"the city was still struggling . . ."*: "David A. Kay" (interview), *Chemical & Engineering News*, Vol. 82, No. 31 (2 Aug. 2004), pp. 28–33 (online).

65 *"The inspectors came from all over . . ."*: Gallucci (2001), p. 8.

65 *"as a dog on a leash"*: Blix (2004), p. 22.

65 *"An even more serious . . ."*: Ibid., p. 23.

65 *In secret high-level meetings in Iraq:* See Iraq Survey Group Final Report at www.globalsecurity.org.

66 *Tariq Aziz, among others, speculated:* Ibid.

66 *"This first declaration . . ."*: Perricos (2001), p. 2.

66 *"had a little bit more content . . ."*: Ibid.

66 *"The first inspection . . ."*: Ibid.

66 *"To our surprise, Tuwaitha was . . ."* Ibid., p. 3

67 *"Inspectors had to walk . . ."*: Ibid.

67 *"they would be difficult . . ."*: "Consolidated Report on the First Two IAEA Inspections Under Security Council Resolution 687 (1991) of Iraqi Nuclear Capabilities." International Atomic Energy Agency, 11 July 1991.

67 *"The surprise that we had . . ."*: Perricos (2001), p. 4.

68 *"We had not only to measure . . ."*: Ibid.

68 *A later report:* IAEA (1991).

68 *"but in some significant cases . . ."*: Ibid., p. 5.

68 *"The overall impression . . ."*: Ibid.

69 *"Dimitri talked to . . ."*: David Kay interview, 2007.

69 *"a photo analyst . . ."*: Ibid.

69 *"At that point he called . . ."*: Ibid.

70 *"The team found that . . ."*: Perricos (2001), p. 2.

70 *"didn't find what . . ."*: Nichols (2001), p. 2.

71 *"unusual . . . with unusually large . . ."*: IAEA (1991), p. 1.

71 *"took hundreds of pictures . . ."*: Perricos (2001), p. 9.

71 *"John's first assignment . . ."*: "John M. Googin," Memorial Tributes, National Academy of Engineering 8 (1996), 120–24.

72 *"I can still see him . . ."*: Perricos (2001), p. 9.

72 *"may have had a dim . . ."*: David Kay interview, 2007.

72 *"We analyzed all the available . . ."*: Nichols (2001), p. 2.

72 *"One of the intelligence . . ."*: Ibid.

FOUR **FOLLOWING THE CALUTRON TRAIL**

74 *"We got on our bus . . ."*: Nichols (2001), p. 2.

74 *photographing boxed material through a fence:* Davis and Kay (1992), p. 24.

74 *"running around Tuwaitha . . .":* Gallucci (2001) (online).

74 *"that it might be a good idea . . .":* Ibid.

75 *"I had brought . . .":* Nichols (2001), p. 3.

76 *"just a dusty area . . .":* Ibid.

76 *"We quite literally wrote the script . . .":* U.S. Committee on Foreign Affairs (1993), p. 31.

76 *"took a walk beforehand . . .":* David Kay interview, 2007. Unless otherwise specified, all David Kay statements in this chapter come from this source.

78 *"The David Kay cowboys . . .":* Gallucci (2001), pp. 9–10.

79 *"Rolf Ekéus felt that . . .":* Trevan (1999), p. 98.

79 *Central Command details:* Ibid., p. 76.

80 *"all concealment task forces . . .":* Quoted in Ritter (1999), p. 109.

80 *"The inspectors arrived . . .":* Perricos (2001), p. 10.

80 *"At one time or another . . .":* "Report on the Third IAEA On-Site Inspection in Iraq Under Security Council Resolution 687" (1991), p. 6.

81 *"where the inspectors asked . . .":* Perricos (2001), p. 10.

82 *one of his colleagues:* Khidhir Hamza.

82 *the entire CERN library of computerized-magnet-design programs:* Albright and O'Neill (1999).

82 *an alternative design with a solid iron core:* "In fact, Jafar ultimately settled on another design . . . which in one respect has some similarity with the original [CERN] proposal, i.e., the use of magnetized cylinders of steel," Gsponer and Hurni (1995), p. 24.

82 *"If that was the model . . .":* Sidney Drell, personal communication, 2 Feb. 2009.

82 *"it was quite possible . . .":* Gsponer and Hurni (1995), p. 20.

82 *"There was no sense . . .":* BBC News interview with Gordon Corera, 12 August 2004 (online).

83 *The strategic aim of these programs:* See Barzam (2001).

83 *"Jaffar tried to explain . . .":* Perricos (2001), p. 10.

83 *"Near the end of our stay . . .":* Nichols (2001), p. 3.

84 *"When Blix suddenly realized . . .":* Reported by Paul White, Los Alamos group interview, 2007.

84 *"The revelation that Iraq . . .":* Blix (2004), p. 24.

84 *"the Soviet ambassador . . .":* Ibid., p. 23.

84 *"We traveled all around Iraq . . .":* Frank Pabian, Los Alamos group interview, 2007.

85 *"a sand-covered Los Alamos report . . .": Los Alamos NewsBulletin,* Summer 1991.

85 *"most of the material . . ."* Davis and Kay (1992), p. 24.

86 *enough HEU for one or two bombs:* Phillips, in the *Los Alamos News-Bulletin,* Summer 1991, says 12 kilograms, but Davis and Kay (1992), p. 25, write that "At design levels, Tarmiya could have produced 15–30

kg per year of highly enriched uranium . . . enough to make one or two bombs per year."

86   *"The facility at Tarmiya . . .":* Statement of IAEA Director General to IAEA Board of Governors, Vienna, Austria, 17 July 1991 (online).

86   *"It is now being asked . . .":* Ibid.

87   *"What we didn't have . . .":* Gallucci (2001).

87   *"Sometime during that August . . .":* Ibid. All Gallucci quotations in this section come from this source unless otherwise specified.

88   *"It just went against his Swedish . . .":* David Kay interview, 2007. All Kay quotations in this section come from this source unless otherwise specified.

90   Inspection time schedule: "First Report on the Sixth IAEA On-Site Inspection in Iraq Under Security Council Resolution 687" (1991), 22–30 September 1991, Appendix, Chronology of Team Activities, p. 5ff.

91   *"Al-Atheer Plant Progress Report":* Included as an appendix to the IAEA report on its sixth Iraq inspection, translated at http://www.iraqwatch .org/un/IAEA/s-23122.htm.

92   *"within time variations . . .":* Al-Atheer progress report, Appendix, p. 18.

92   *"20 detonation tests":* Ibid., p. 16.

92   *"our scientists requested to refer . . .":* Imad Khadduri, "Iraq's Nuclear Non-Capability," www.dissidentvoice.org, 21 Nov. 2002 (online).

95   *6:20 a.m. on 24 September:* "First Report Sixth IAEA Inspection," Appendix, Chronology of Team Activities, p. 6.

97   *"We are currently in nighttime . . .":* "U.N. Inspector's Words: 'We're Prepared to Stay,' " *New York Times,* 25 Sept. 1991.

98   *a football game using a water bottle:* Kay actually said a roll of toilet paper, but several of his fellow parking-lot attendees corrected him.

98   *Gallucci would hint:* Gallucci (2001). See especially this talk's Q. & A.

100   *"There was always the plausible . . .":* Ibid., p. 14.

101   *"did a lot to energize . . .":* Ibid., p. 12.

101   *"Project 6000, also known as Al Atheer . . .":* CIA 65819 6581901, online at www.globalsecurity.org.

101   *"The proud calutrons . . .":* Perricos (2001), p. 12.

101   *"Finding this smoking gun . . .":* Ibid., p. 11.

102   *"Saddam had witnessed firsthand . . .":* Alfonsi (2006), p. 343.

FIVE   **THE LITTLE SUITCASE**

105   *"I'm tired as hell . . .":* Quoted in Chernyaev (2000), p. 369.

105   *Eduard Shevardnadze . . . presaged:* "The reformers have gone into hiding. A dictatorship is approaching. No one knows what this dictatorship will be like . . ." Quoted in Pryce-Jones (1995), p. 375.

105 *"For those in the know . . .":* Remnick (1994), p. 447.

106 *Vladimir Kryuchkov . . . learned of their discussions:* Andrew and Mitrokhin (1999), p. 513; Albats (1994), pp. 282–83.

106 Cheget: My primary source of information on the *Cheget* system is Tsypkin (2004).

106 *"responsible for directing the activities . . .":* United States (1992a), pp. 71–72.

107 *a lavish presidential dacha:* For a satellite view, see Google Earth N 44º 23′ 30.84″, E 33º 45′ 27″.

107 *Thirty-two-man KGB personal bodyguard:* Gorbachev (1991), p. 23.

108 *"Let him . . . a 'state of emergency' ":* Gorbachev (1996), p. 600.

108 *"a quiet old man . . .":* Yeltsin (1994), p. 72.

109 *"The situation is catastrophic . . .":* Quoted in Remnick (1994), p. 450.

109 *"the state would fall apart":* Quoted in ibid., p. 452.

109 *Pugo . . . had sneaked off:* Gorbachev (1996), p. 634.

109 *Lukyanov . . . a friend of Gorbachev:* Pryce-Jones (1995), p. 419, believes historians have confused Anatoly with another Lukyanov, Andrei, who was close to Gorbachev as an undergraduate at Moscow State University; but see Gorbachev (1991), p. 45: "For forty years, from our student days, we [i.e., Anatoly] had enjoyed comradely relations."

109 *"Yanayev . . . was already . . . drunk":* Quoted in Remnick (1994), p. 452.

110 Cheget *terminal . . . disconnected:* 4:32 p.m. Tsypkin (2004), p. 2. Gorbachev gives the time he learned of the arrival as 4:50 p.m. Bonnell et al. (1994), p. 161.

110 *"[He] asked me about the condition . . .":* Tsypkin (2004), p. 2.

110 *"Many cars were piling up . . .":* Chernyaev (2000), p. 405.

110 *"Evidently they are going to try . . .":* Bonnell et al. (1994), p. 162.

110 *"a conversation with deaf-mutes":* Ibid., p. 164.

111 *"I was told that the cause . . .":* Tsypkin (2004), p. 3.

111 *The general staff . . . could launch:* Ibid., p. 5.

111 *Gorbachev was "no longer capable . . .":* Quoted in Bonnell et al. (1994), p. 339.

112 *"the race to Foros":* Remnick (1994), p. 486.

113 *The* Cheget *team had been removed:* As recorded in Raisa's diary: "At five p.m. the senior security guard reported that the signaling unit had been withdrawn." Gorbachev (1996), p. 635. This action is confirmed in the testimony of the *Cheget* team leader quoted in Tsypkin (2004), p. 4.

113 *"left for Moscow . . .":* Ibid.

114 *"We consider this a sign . . .":* Gorbachev (1996), p. 639.

114 *"I talked on the telephone . . .":* Ibid., p. 641. N.B. *"I said to them . . . 'garrison' "* interpolated from MG's original statement at Bonnell et al. (1994), p. 166.

114 *"judging by their reaction . . .":* Chernyaev (2000), p. 421.

114 *"It was then . . .":* Gorbachev (1996), p. 641.

115 *"she threw herself on the seat . . .":* Chernyaev (2000), p. 423.

115 *"We lived through . . .":* Gorbachev (1996), p. 640.

115 *"I have come back from Foros . . .":* Ibid., p. 642.

115 *"The conference was probably . . .":* Sam Nunn interview, July 2008. All Nunn quotations in this chapter not otherwise attributed come from this source.

116 *"You have to assume . . .":* "Coup Chiefs Likely Controlled Nuclear Bombs," *Toronto Star,* 24 Aug. 1991, p. A11.

118 *"are more stringent . . .":* United States (1992c), p. 7.

118 *"We do not invest . . .":* Ibid., p. 4.

119 *"Under the conditions present . . .":* Ibid., p. 7.

119 *Indeed, once Gorbachev's* Cheget *was deactivated:* Tsypkin (2004), p. 5.

119 *"that the situation that occurred . . .":* United States (1992c), p. 6.

120 *"was a significant source . . .":* Barton Gellman, *Washington Post,* 28 Aug. 1991, p. A18.

120 *"in virtually real time . . .":* Bruce Blair, personal communications, 1 Sept. 2008.

120 *"Let me describe . . .":* United States (1992c), p. 5.

121 *"special processing . . .":* Ibid.

121 *"actually devised . . . to streamline . . .":* Ibid., p. 17.

122 *"There is an important lesson . . .":* Ibid., p. 9.

122 *"sufficient to eradicate Europe . . .":* Stanislav Shushkevich interview, Apr. 2003.

122 *In Kazakhstan 104 . . . work to do:* Podvig (2001), p. 24.

SIX MANY LITTLE MONSTERS

123 *Sam Nunn's family background:* Sam Nunn interview, Washington, 9 July 2008. All Nunn quotations in this chapter not otherwise attributed come from this source.

125 *"I remember very well . . .":* Shields and Potter (1997), p. xiii.

126 *"He and three or four . . .":* Ibid.

126 *Nunn, NATO, and forward basing:* Nunn (2008), p. 1.

126 *"withdrawal of significant numbers . . .":* Goodby (2006), p. 107.

126 *"we had a major problem . . .":* Shields and Potter (1997), p. xiii.

127 *"In particular, I believed . . .":* Ibid., p. xvi.

127 *"Civil war in a country . . .":* United States (1992a), p. 2.

127 *"another form of defense . . .":* Ibid.

127 *"foolish":* Quoted in John Lancaster et al., "Citing Soviet Strife, Cheney Resists Cuts; Possible Civil War, Famine Noted by Pentagon Chief," *Washington Post,* 30 Aug. 1991, p. A1.

127 *"premature":* Quoted in Ann Devroy, *Washington Post,* 30 Aug. 1991, p. A1.

127   *"cut into the muscle of defense . . .":* "The President's news conference in Kennebunkport, Maine," 2 Sept. 1991, George H. W. Bush Public Papers.

128   *"to assist the Soviet Union . . .":* Sam Nunn, "A Helping Hand, Not a Blank Check," *Washington Post,* 15 Sept. 1991, reproduced in United States (1992a), p. 82.

128   *the earliest statement . . . belived to be:* "The Cold War has ended and we are entering a new era, one in which many of the old prescriptions lack curative powers. We face a new kind of nuclear threat and we need a new strategy to meet it. Deterrence is a necessary but no longer sufficient element of that strategy. We should begin now to work through together how to deal with nuclear dangers that cannot be reached by the threat of retaliation.

"The threat of accidental or unauthorized nuclear attack is of this character. The chance of such an attack may be small, but the consequences would be incalculable. Unless we are willing to conclude that the recently failed coup is the last serious crisis for the Soviet Union, and unless we disregard the growing Third World threat, we must deal with this possibility," United States (1992a), p. 76.

128   *"both the House and the Senate . . .":* Shields and Potter (1997), p. xvi.

128   *"the broadest and most . . .":* Bush and Scowcroft (1998), p. 546.

129   *"Cheney's distaste for . . .":* Ibid., p. 545.

129   *"concerned that the North . . .":* Bush and Scowcroft (1998), p. 545.

129   *"largely a gesture . . .":* Quoted in Cumings (2004), p. 55.

129   *"directing that the United States . . .":* Bush's speech is reproduced in full in United States (1992a), pp. 83–87, with a Fact Sheet following.

130   *"There were some differences . . .":* Bush and Scowcroft (1998), p. 547.

131   *"Prior to shipment to Russia . . .":* Blair (1993), pp. 102–3.

131   *"involved removing tritium . . .":* Blair (1993), p. 313, n. 134.

131   *"We ran into a buzz saw":* United States (1992a), p. 256.

132   *"The results of that election . . .":* Ibid.

133   *Senator Richard Lugar . . . had arranged:* According to Richard Combs in Shields and Potter (1997), p. 43.

133   *"none of the other three . . .":* Campbell et al. (1991), p. 33.

134   *"Like the German rocket scientists . . .":* Ibid., p. 42.

134   *"such as the Middle East":* Ibid., p. 64.

134   *"There was a remarkable consensus . . .":* United States (1992a), p. 154.

135   *"a start":* Ibid., p. 257.

136   *"was as unfocused . . .":* Baker (1995), p. 559.

136   *"We will maintain . . .":* "Chicken Kiev Speech," Wikisource, accessed 25 Sept. 2008.

136   *"I think Bush was realizing . . .":* Stanislav Shushkevich interview, Apr. 2003.

137   *"Dick wanted to see . . .":* Baker (1995), p. 560. Emphasis in original.

137   *"Yugoslavia with nukes":* e.g., ibid., p. 562.

137   *"though we all agreed . . .":* Ibid., p. 561.
138   *"Shevardnadze would leave his apartment . . .":* Ibid., p. 569.
138   *Baker's Princeton speech:* United States (1992a), pp. 223–37.
139   *"The President is a little late . . .":* United States (1992a), p. 258.
139   *"We received the equipment . . .":* Stanislav Shushkevich interview, Apr. 2003.
140   *"We do not envision any . . .":* Quoted in Paine and Cochran (1992), p. 14.
140   *"The administration was suggesting . . .":* Ibid., p. 15.
142   *"Throughout its first three years . . .":* NRDC (1992), p. iv.
143   *"a private venture . . .":* Ibid., p. i.
145   *"one senior official . . .":* Ibid., p. ii.
145   *"not to accept . . .":* Quoted in Reiss (1995), p. 92.
145   *a date the Russian military determined:* Ibid., p. 93.
146   *"It was immediately apparent . . .":* Neff (1998), n.p.
147   *an op-ed essay:* Thomas L. Neff, "A Grand Uranium Bargain," *New York Times*, 24 Oct. 1991, p. A25.
147   *"If the material in each . . .":* Neff (1998), n.p.
147   *"We have spent too much . . .":* NRDC (1992), p. 15.
147   *"Mikhailov said that the weapons . . .":* Ibid., p. 14.
148   *"Jim, can you clean . . .":* Quoted in Lambright (2002), p. 55.
148   *"Watkins finalized decisions . . .":* Ibid., p. 74.
148   *"When I became head of state . . .":* A full transcript of Gorbachev's televised resignation speech appears at Gorbachev (1996), pp. xxvi-xxix.
149   *"A second call confirmed . . .":* Reed (2004), p. 2.

SEVEN WAITING FOR FORTY YEARS

150   *"Yasser Arafat, leader of the Palestine . . .":* Ustiugov (1993), p. 34.
151   *"With the support of the nation . . .":* Nazarbayev (2001), p. 47.
152   *"If the international community . . .":* Baker (1995), p. 581.
152   *"Shushkevich was at pains . . .":* Ibid., p. 582.
152   *"Kravchuk was similarly cooperative":* Ibid.
152   *"Prior preparation prevents . . .":* Baker (2006), p. 5.
152   *"Our mission . . . was to tell . . .":* Thomas Graham interview, 2004.
153   *"There was not much disagreement . . .":* Graham (2002), p. 134.
153   *"Early on they indicated . . .":* Ibid.
154   *"deep snow everywhere . . .":* Thomas Graham interview, 2004.
154   *"They were very desperate . . .":* Ibid.; Graham (2002), p. 134.
154   *"Kazakhstan, of course . . .":* Graham (2002), p. 135.
154   *At a traditional banquet . . . hers:* Ibid.
155   *"new and very expensive . . .":* United States (1992a), p. 11.
155   *"Let me describe some . . .":* Ibid., pp. 11–12.
156   *"The brain drain problem . . .":* Quoted in *Arms Control Today*, January/February 1992, p. 40.

157 *"The United States judged . . .":* Graham and LaVera (2003), p. 372.

157 *a thorough 1988 U.S. Office of Technology Assessment study:* U.S. Congress (1988), p. 126.

157 *"I propose that we find . . .":* Ronald Reagan, "Address to the 39th Session of the United Nations General Assembly," New York, N.Y., 24 Sept. 1984.

158 *joint verification experiments:* See "Joint Statement Following the Soviet–United States Summit Meeting in Moscow," 1 June 1988, Reagan Papers, University of Texas.

158 *"a rip-roaring snowstorm":* Los Alamos Science 24 (1996), p. 7, p. 10.

158 *Miz and Contactor:* Sandra Blakeslee, "Soviets Prepare for Verification at Nevada Test Site," *New York Times,* 15 Aug. 1988.

159 *"He was then the director . . .":* Ibid., p. 7.

159 *"Then he said, 'Don . . .' ":* Ibid., p. 10.

159 *"They were absolutely . . .":* Los Alamos Laboratory group interview, 2007.

159 *"When we walked around . . .":* Mikhailov (1996), p. 70.

159 *"In contrast to our test site . . .":* Ibid., p. 71.

160 *someone from the . . . Russian royal family:* Quoted in Blakeslee, "Soviets Prepare."

160 *"the side product was . . .":* Sig Hecker interview, 2001.

161 *he and his allies . . . funding:* Los Alamos Science 24 (1996), p. 16.

161 *"Our guys came back from Geneva . . .":* Sig Hecker interview, 2001.

161 *"It was too radical . . .":* Ibid.

162 *"He said Bush is concerned . . .":* Ibid.

162 *"an astonishing suggestion . . .":* Younger (2009), p. 30.

163 *"I've been waiting for this moment . . .":* Sig Hecker lecture, Stanford University New Century Seminar, 18 Oct. 2005.

163 *"Then it was just born instantly . . .":* Sig Hecker interview, 2001.

163 *"From the moment we stepped . . .":* Los Alamos Science 24 (1996), p. 20.

164 *"Academician Khariton told us . . .":* Sig Hecker, "An American Tribute to Academician Yuli Borisovich Khariton," lecture for presentation at the Khariton Scientific Conference, Arzamas-16, Russia, 27 Feb. 1999.

164 *"He said it was very simple . . .":* Hecker, Arzamas-16 lecture, 1999.

164 *"The cost of failure . . .":* Los Alamos group interview, 2007.

164 *"those who in case of failure . . .":* Hecker, Arzamas-16 lecture, 1999.

165 *"an oasis in a third-world country . . .":* Sig Hecker, "Today's Nuclear Challenges," unpublished notes, Director's Colloquium, Lawrence Livermore Laboratory, 7 Jan. 1998.

165 *"The problem wasn't 'loose nukes' . . .":* Ibid.; Sig Hecker interview, 2001.

165 *"the system of grave consequences":* Hecker, "Today's Nuclear Challenges," 1998.

166 *"I started talking to the Russians . . .":* Sig Hecker interview, 2004.

166 *"The list of topics . . .":* Los Alamos Science 24 (1996), p. 22.

166 *"Just about instantly he gave us . . .":* Ibid., pp. 23–24.

166 *National Security Council balked:* Ibid., p. 24.

167 *"from Secretary Cheney . . .":* United States (1992c), p. 40.

168 *"I was not the head . . .": Los Alamos Science* 24 (1996), pp. 24–25.

168 *"During that trip . . .":* Ibid., p. 25.

168 *"I'm tired of Americans . . .":* Ibid.

168 *"we were on extremely thin ice":* Ibid., p. 26.

169 *"There were many people . . .":* Ibid.

169 *"Prior to my first trip . . .":* Younger (2009), p. 31.

169 *"intended to prevent . . .":* Stephen Younger, "Why Are Nuclear Weapons Important?" Videotaped lecture, Los Alamos Study Group, 21 June 1999.

169 *Sam Nunn led a Senate delegation:* see United States (1992b).

170 *"The success of these countries . . .":* United States (1992b), p. 2.

170 *"to generate funds . . .":* Ibid., p. 5.

170 *"will be very difficult at best":* Ibid.

170 *no Nunn-Lugar funds had yet been expended:* Ibid., p. 11.

170 *"strong hints that Ukraine . . .":* Ibid., p. 12.

171 *"assailed by nationalists . . .":* Sigal (2000), p. 254.

171 *"an almost exclusive [Bush] administration focus . . .":* Goodman (1995), p. 148.

171 *"a potent memo":* Ibid.

171 *"a pathetically inadequate response":* Kalb (1994), p. 220.

171 *"hot-button issue . . .":* Ibid., p. 222.

172 *"The place in history . . .":* Quoted in ibid., p. 107.

172 *"Baker indicated that he . . .":* Goodman (1995), pp. 148–49.

172 *"The president opened the meeting . . .":* Ibid., p. 149.

173 *"And no one is sure . . .":* Quoted in Kalb (1994), p. 106.

173 *"was rather cagey . . .":* Baker (1995), p. 661.

173 *"haggled over the protocol . . .":* Ibid., p. 662.

173 *"Finally Zlenko got the message":* Ibid., p. 663.

173 *"The START protocol was done . . .":* Ibid., p. 664.

174 *"In Lisbon I made the rounds . . .":* Graham (2002), p. 136.

174 *"Early the next morning . . .":* Ibid.

174 *"infuriated" . . . "There's nothing worse . . .":* Baker (1995), p. 664.

174 *"explained how each was to enter . . .":* Graham (2002), p. 136.

175 *"Finally . . . at 8:10 p.m. . . .":* Baker (1995), p. 665.

175 *Dick Cheney balked:* Graham (2002), p. 137.

EIGHT   **PREVENTIVE DEFENSE**

179 *"Our deputies don't care . . .":* Skootsky (1995), entry for 7 Jan. 1992.

181 *"all nuclear strategic offensive arms . . .":* Quoted in ibid., entry for 20 May 1992.

181 *At the United Nations' Earth Summit . . . budget:* Reported in Marples (1996), p. 131.

181 *Belarus signed a Nunn-Lugar agreement:* Skootsky (1995), entry for 22 Oct. 1992.

181 *"We want to get rid . . .":* Quoted in ibid., entry for 6 Jan. 1993.

183 *preventive defense:* See Carter and Perry (1999).

183 *"When we took office . . .":* Ibid., p. 77.

184 *"With Bill Perry leading . . .":* Talbott (2002), pp. 108–9.

184 *"Through the fall . . .":* Talbott (2002), p. 108.

184 *"because we started out . . .":* Linton Brooks interview, 2007.

185 *"It required a reduction . . .":* Elizabeth Sherwood-Randall, personal communication, 18 Oct. 2005.

185 *"You listen to those folks . . .":* Quoted in Talbott (2002), p. 104.

185 *"It was all called nonproliferation . . .":* Linton Brooks interview, 2007.

186 *"bypassing his own government's . . .":* Talbott (2002), p. 118.

186 *"Progress on the storage facility . . .": Los Alamos Science* 24 (1996) p. 33.

187 *"a 'concentration camp' state . . .":* Potter et al. (1994), p. 47.

187 *"Nobody even considered . . .":* Quoted in Jessica Eve Stern, "Cooperative Activities to Improve Fissile Material Protection, Control, and Accounting," in Shields and Potter (1997), p. 312.

187 *"As [our] contacts grew . . .": Los Alamos Science* 24 (1996), pp. 33–34.

187 *"I do not know who . . .":* Neff (1998) (online). All Neff quotations in this section come from this (unpaginated) source unless otherwise specified.

188 *"This process . . . would ensure . . .":* Timbie (2004), p. 166.

188 *each problem in turn was . . . resolved:* For a detailed account, see Timbie (2004).

189 *"The Kazakh government had no idea . . .":* Graham Allison Senate testimony, Subcommittee on European Affairs (1995), p. 79.

189 *"By mid-1993 . . .":* William C. Potter, "Project Sapphire," in Shields and Potter, eds. (1997), p. 348.

190 *"He found himself in a vault . . .":* Cockburn and Cockburn (1997), p. 142.

191 *Twenty-seven . . . signed on . . . technicians:* Riedy (1995), p. 7.

191 *"was to assay . . .":* Background briefing, Kazakhstan's nuclear fuel, Office of the Assistant Secretary of Defense (Public Affairs), 23 Nov. 1994 (online), p. 7.

192 *"emergency drills . . .":* Ibid.

192 *"I was running the meetings . . .":* Jessica Stern interview, 2004.

192 *"By fall, . . . who was going to pay . . .":* Ibid.

192 *"It was a very big endeavor . . .":* Background briefing, Kazakhstan's nuclear fuel, op. cit., p. 7.

192 *2.37 metric tons of material stock:* Shields and Potter (1997), p. 355, n. 18; Defense Nuclear Facilities Safety Board memorandum for G. W. Cunningham, technical director, "Staff observations of Department of

Energy (DOE) and Lockheed Martin Energy Systems' (LMES) support of Project Sapphire," 21 Dec. 1995, p. 2 (online).

193   *"But it came back not . . .":* Cockburn and Cockburn (1997), p. 157.

193   *Bill Perry was working . . . Nurmagambetov:* Togzhan Kassenova, personal communication, 2007.

193   *the Ukrainian parliament voted:* Jentleson (2000), p. 125.

193   *"when it pledged . . .":* William Martel in Schneider and Dowdy (1998), p. 93.

193   *"The team, I want to tell you . . .":* Hazel O'Leary, DOD News Briefing: Secretary of Defense William J. Perry, et al., 23 Nov. 1994 (online), p. 3.

194   *"Many of the new Republicans . . .":* Alfonsi (2006), pp. 347–48.

195   *"putting together an orientation . . .":* Ibid., p. 348.

195   *Acquiring it cost . . . supplies:* "Kazakhstan: Project Sapphire," Nuclear Threat Initiative Research Library, www.NTI.org.

196   *"The joke was on . . .":* Cockburn and Cockburn (1997), p. 159.

196   *"were sitting there in the cockpit . . .":* Quoted in Tirpak (1995), p. 7.

196   *Memorandum on Security Guarantees:* Togzhan Kassenova, personal communication, 2007.

197   *The United States . . . exchanged instruments:* Jentleson (2000), p. 110.

197   *China also weighed in:* Togzhan Kassenova, personal communication, 2007.

197   *"Under the Cooperative Threat . . .":* Perry (1996), online.

197   *"I joined my Russian . . .":* Perry (1996) (online).

197   *"the single most important accomplishment . . .":* Sig Hecker, New Century Seminar, Stanford University, 18 Oct. 2005.

NINE   LEAVING THE *LAAGER*

199   *forty thousand tons of . . . concentrate:* Horton (1999), p. 4.

199   *"The secret income flows . . .":* David Fig, "Apartheid's Nuclear Arsenal: Deviation from Development," in Cock and Mckenzie (1998) (online).

199   *four kilograms of highly enriched uranium:* U.S. State Dept. to American Embassy, Vienna, 31 Dec. 1964 (National Security Archive, online).

200   *"South Africa has imported . . .":* Bill Brubeck (of NSC) to McGeorge Bundy, 17 Aug. 1964 (National Security Archive, online).

200   *South Africa began . . . early 1960s:* Albright, Berkhout, and Walker (1997), p. 379.

200   *demonstrated an indigenous . . . in 1967:* Purkitt and Burgess (2005), p. 39.

200   *Construction . . . began in 1969:* Ibid., p. 38.

201   *"proselytizing the PNE . . .":* Mark Hibbs, "South Africa's Secret Nuclear Program: From a PNE to a Deterrent," *Nuclear Fuel* 18(10), p. 3.

201   *South Africa began secretly . . . in 1961:* U.S. Central Intelligence Agency, partly declassified top-secret report cited at Digital National Secu-

rity Archive, South Africa chronology; *South African agreements with Israel:* Hersh (1991), p. 264.

201 *"During the 1970s . . .":* Stumpf (1995), p. 3.
202 *Stumpf cites:* Ibid.
202 *"This pressure by the USA . . .":* Ibid.
202 *Stumpf complains further:* Ibid.
202 *"South African scientists . . .":* Ibid., pp. 27–28.
202 *"Senior South African politicians . . .":* Ibid., p. 15.
204 *"In comparing a gun device . . .":* Hibbs (1993), pp. 1–2.
205 *three deep boreholes:* Cochran (1994), p. 163.
206 *"an unmarked light aircraft . . .":* Richelson (2006), p. 279.
206 *In the days ahead . . . over Vastrap:* Ibid.
206 *"romantic notion about . . .":* Quoted in ibid., p. 281.
206 *"the necessary channels . . .":* Leonid Brezhnev to James Callaghan, 10 Aug. 1977, quoted in Tweedie (2008), p. 1.
206 *"that although he knew . . .":* Quoted in ibid., pp. 1–2.
206 *"The United States and other . . .":* Richelson (2006), p. 281.
207 *"long-standing [South African] program . . .":* quoted in ibid.
207 *"continue to monitor . . .":* Quoted in ibid.
207 *"as the onset of . . .":* Purkitt and Burgess (2005), p. 43.
207 *(The share of its weapons budget . . . 1982.):* Ibid., p. 254.
208 *"assassinations, torture, and smuggling . . .":* Ibid., p. 60.
208 *"studies of implosion . . .":* Ibid., p. 62.
210 *An all-sky . . . double flash:* Hones et al. (1981), pp. 7–8.
210 *"the Intelligence Community has high . . .":* National Security Council memorandum for the Secretary of State et al., "South African Nuclear Event," 22 Oct. 1979, p. 1. (National Security Archive, online.)
211 *"might then support nuclear weapons . . .":* Ibid., p. 2.
211 *"the South Africans have the capability . . .":* Ibid., p. 8.
211 *"not clear that there . . .":* Quoted in Richelson (2006), p. 291.
212 *" 'If there was anything . . .' ":* Quoted in CIA Interagency Intelligence memorandum, "The 22 September 1979 Event," stamped Jan 25, 1980, p. 9. (National Security Archive, online.)
212 *"might find out . . .":* Ibid., p. 8.
212 *Stanford Research Institute study gave odds:* Oetzel and Johnson (1980).
212 Alvarez: The Adventures of a Physicist: Luis W. Alvarez (New York: Basic Books, 1987). For Alvarez's discussion of the ad-hoc Vela committee's investigation, see p. 248ff.
213 *"My mandate was . . .":* Quoted in Hersh (1991), p. 277.
213 *"The Israelis might have conceivably . . .":* CIA, "The 22 September 1979 Event," p. 9.
214 *"If the South Africans had considered . . .":* Ibid., p. 10.
215 *"former Israeli government officials . . .":* Hersh (1991), pp. 271–72.
215 *"We created the South . . .":* Chris McGreal, "Brothers in Arms: Israel's Secret Pact with Pretoria," *The Guardian* (U.K.), 7 Feb. 2006 (online).

216 *"When we came to the crossroads . . .":* Ibid.
216 *The number of South Africans drafted . . . doubled:* Purkitt and Burgess (2005), p. 55.
216 *"would have been akin . . .":* Albright (1994) (online).
217 *thirty grams of Israeli tritium:* Albright (1993), p. 6.
217 *"replace the seven . . .":* Quoted in ibid., p. 5.
217 *"Phase 1 called for . . .":* De Villiers et al. (1993), pp. 100–101.
218 *"the questions that must be answered . . .":* Pabian (1995), p. 18.
218 *"was due in large part . . .":* Ibid., p. 10.
219 *"questioned about the reasons . . .":* Quoted in ibid., p. 19, n. 80.
219 *"The Y Plant was closed . . .":* De Villiers et al. (1993), p. 104.

TEN A MILLION AND A TRILLION

220 *"could dramatically adjust . . .":* Gallucci (2001), p. 14.
221 *"The air war . . . leveled North Korea . . .":* Cumings (2004), p. 27.
222 *"Destroying the last major . . .":* Crane (2000), p. 160.
222 *"skeptical of the feasibility . . .":* Quoted in ibid., p. 162.
222 *"North Korea decried . . .":* Crane (2000), p. 162.
223 *"in accordance with Far East . . .":* Ibid.
223 *"were dominated by discussion . . .":* Ibid., p. 163.
223 *"eighteen of twenty-two . . .":* Ibid., p. 168.
223 *"They are prepared for war . . .":* Memorandum, Hungarian Foreign Ministry, 16 Feb. 1976, "History of North Korean Attitudes Toward Nuclear Weapons and Efforts to Acquire Nuclear Capability," Cold War International History Project e-dossier, 17 May 2005 (hereafter "North Korean e-dossier").
224 *"Our specialists reported . . .":* Document 7, "Conversation between Soviet Ambassador in North Korea Vasily Moskovsky and Soviet specialists in North Korea," 27 Sept. 1963, North Korean e-dossier.
224 *Kim Il Sung, visited the U.S.S.R.:* Document 11, Report, Embassy of Hungary in North Korea to the Hungarian Foreign Ministry, 13 Mar. 1967, North Korean e-dossier.
224 *"The Soviet side asked . . .":* Document 17, Report, Embassy of Hungary in the Soviet Union to the Hungarian Foreign Ministry, 12 Nov. 1969, North Korean e-dossier.
225 *"conspiracy concocted by the USSR . . .":* Quoted on Nuclear Threat Initiative website, China Profiles, Nuclear Nonproliferation Treaty.
225 *"The DPRK side . . . made a request . . .":* Document 22, Report, Embassy of Hungary in North Korea to the Hungarian Foreign Ministry, 15 April 1976, North Korean e-dossier.
226 *"Until the 1960s . . .":* Savada (1993), Chapter 1, subsection on economic development (online).
226 *"that the DPRK was in . . .":* Document 26, Report, Embassy of Hun-

gary in North Korea to the Hungarian Foreign Ministry, 8 Dec. 1976, North Korean e-dossier.

227 *"If we compare the output . . ."*: Document 29, Report, Embassy of Hungary in North Korea to the Hungarian Foreign Ministry, 23 Feb. 1979, North Korean e-dossier.

228 *"Kim Il Sung is believed . . ."*: Mansourov (1995), p. 26.

228 *"a mill for concentrating . . ."*: Ibid.

228 *"In the 1980s and with the coming . . ."*: Reed and Stillman (2009), p. 261.

229 *"affirmed that the DPRK . . ."*: Document 35, Report on the Visit by Erich Honecker to the DPRK, 18–21 Oct. 1986, North Korean e-dossier.

230 *"The long-term goal . . ."*: John Lewis, Center for International Security and Cooperation seminar at Stanford University, 17 Nov. 2006.

230 *(The Soviet Union . . . demise:* Wit et al. (2004), p. 54.

231 *"What's the use of a few . . ."*: Quoted in Sigal (1998), p. 34.

231 *"It became increasingly clear . . ."*: Harrison (2002), p. 32.

232 *"So I was there and it . . ."*: Hans Blix interview, 2005.

234 *"senior Defense Department official . . ."*: David E. Sanger, "North Korea Plan on Fueling A-Bomb May Be Confirmed," *New York Times,* 15 June 1992.

235 *"So I began to press . . ."*: Hans Blix interview, 2005.

235 *One scenario . . . implosion bomb:* Albright (1994a), p. 67.

236 *Lee Butler . . . James Woolsey:* Cited in Cumings (2004), p. 65.

236 *Able Archer:* See my *Arsenals of Folly,* p. 163ff.

236 *"I'm running out of demons . . ."*: Quoted in Nichols (2004), p. 108.

237 *"the first North Korean nuclear crisis":* Wit et al. (2004), p. 26.

237 *"The recent example of Iraq . . ."*: Ibid., p. 35.

237 *"it was clear to all . . ."*: Ibid., p. xv.

238 *9.5 kilograms of plutonium:* Albright and O'Neill (2000), p. 116.

238 *"In a telex to Pyongyang . . ."*: Wit et al. (2004), p. 43.

238 *"a short, stocky man . . ."*: Ibid., p. 52.

238 *"I knew that the North . . ."*: Robert Gallucci interview, 2002.

239 *"Not surprisingly . . ."*: Wit et al. (2004), p. 53.

240 *"Now, according to the chief. . . ."*: Ibid.

240 *the two sides issued a joint statement:* Ibid., Appendix B, p. 419ff.

241 *"bold new instructions":* Quoted in ibid., p. 71.

241 *"remove the fuel rods . . ."*: Quoted in ibid., p. 74.

241 *"Model One, the happy model . . ."*: Unless otherwise specified, this and following Gallucci statements come from my Robert Gallucci interview, 2002.

242 *"in making the proposal . . ."*: Wit et al. (2004), pp. 75–76.

242 *"suggested that the United States . . ."*: Ibid., p. 77.

243 *"was a full hour-long . . ."*: Graham (2002), p. 232.

243 *"Clearly, . . . the consequences . . ."*: Wit et al. (2004), p 83.

243 *"North Korea cannot be . . ."*: Quoted in Reiss (1995), p. 260.

244　*"more likely than not":* Quoted in ibid., p. 287.

244　*"If we pull an Osirak . . .":* Quoted in Wit et al. (2004), p. 104.

244　*a recent war game:* Cited in ibid., p. 102.

245　*"We can't find nuclear . . .":* Quoted in ibid., p. 104.

245　*"bellicosity . . . more of a negotiating . . .":* John Lancaster and Ann Devroy, "U.S. Weighs Deployment of Patriots to S. Korea," *Washington Post,* 27 Jan. 1994.

245　*(By one careful contemporary estimate:* Hayes (1994), p. 5.

245　*Clinton was said to be "likely" to approve:* Michael R. Gordon, "U.S. Said to Plan Patriot Missiles for South Korea," *New York Times,* 26 Jan. 1994, p. A1.

246　*"all the activities in the DPRK's . . .":* Statement by a spokesman for the General Department of Atomic Energy of the Democratic People's Republic of Korea, 18 Mar. 1994, Pyongyang. IAEA publications, INFCIRC/437, Attachment 1, www.iaea.org (online).

246　*"thanked us for our . . .":* Ibid.

246　*"that the Agency . . .":* Quoted in D.P.R.K. General Department of Atomic Energy Statement of 18 March 1994.

246　*"We are ready to respond . . . Seoul is not far . . .":* quoted in Sigal (1998), p. 107, and (a variant version) Oberdorfer (2001), p. 304.

247　*"We don't know anything . . .":* Mark Thompson, "Well, Maybe a Nuke or Two," *Time,* 11 Apr. 1994 (online).

247　*"out of place . . .":* Josette Shiner and Michael Breen, "Another Sharp 'No' from Kim Il-sung," *Washington Times,* 19 Apr. 1994, p. A1.

247　*"The only way that . . .":* Steve Komarov, "N. Korea Sounds a Conciliatory Note," *USA Today,* 19 Apr. 1994, p. 4A.

247　*"Except for . . . one senior-level . . .":* Creekmore (2006), p. 19.

248　*"a bombshell":* Wit et al. (2004), p. 169.

248　*"four or five nuclear bombs":* "US Security Policy in Korea." Address by Secretary of Defense William Perry to the Asia Society, Washington, 3 May 1994 (online).

248　*"If North Korea were to break . . .":* Ibid.

249　*The North's pointed . . . reactor:* Albright and O'Neill (2000), p. 126, n. 10, gives this date, citing "an IAEA official," which I take to be the most credible source. Oberdorfer (2001), p. 309, gives 8 May without attribution. Wit et al. (2004), p. 172, presumably drawing on Gallucci's notes, write, "Kang told Gallucci that unloading would begin on May 4." An outside limit is the North's communication with the IAEA on 12 May that it had already started unloading, cited in Sigal (1998), p. 115.

249　*He sent off his inspectors . . . 15 May:* Wit et al. (2004), p. 175.

249　*with Dimitri Perricos in charge:* Oberdorfer (2001), p. 309.

249　*fourteen hundred fuel rods . . . more inspectors:* Wit et al. (2004), p. 184.

249　*"They just dumped the fuel . . .":* Sig Hecker interview, 2004.

249　*"a big mess . . .":* Quoted in Oberdorfer (2001), p. 309.

250 *"You think of the United Nations . . ."*: Robert Gallucci interview, 2002.

250 *"the United States could not fight . . ."*: Wit et al. (2004), p. 176.

250 *"the possibility of North Korean . . ."*: Ibid., p. 178.

250 *"When asked by the president . . ."*: Ibid., p. 181.

250 *"at that time they still . . ."*: Sig Hecker interview, 2004.

251 *"must not be allowed . . ."*: William J. Perry and Ashton B. Carter, "The Crisis Last Time" (op-ed), *New York Times,* 19 Jan. 2003.

251 *"sanctions mean war . . ."*: Peter Grier, "China May Be Wild Card in N. Korea Drama," *Christian Science Monitor,* 7 June 1994.

ELEVEN GREAT LEADERS

252 *North Korea had been trying . . . invitation:* Creekmore (2006), p. 61.

252 *"I spent over three hours . . ."*: Robert Gallucci interview, 2002. Unless otherwise specified, all further Gallucci statements in this chapter derive from this source.

253 *"that North Korea wanted . . ."*: Creekmore (2006), p. 62.

253 *"that the United States . . ."*: Wit et al. (2004), p. 63.

254 *"We are not going to let you . . ."* Quoted in Oberdorfer (2001), p. 326.

254 *"with access to all . . ."*: Oberdorfer (2001), p. 325.

254 *"Carter emphasized his strong view . . ."*: Creekmore (2006), pp. 65–66.

254 *Carter flew . . . similarly rebuffed:* Sigal (1998), p. 152.

255 *"too close an identification . . ."*: Creekmore (2006), pp. 339–40, n. 38.

255 *"With rumors of shortages . . ."*: Ibid., p. 108.

256 *Other foreign embassies in Seoul:* Wit et al. (2004), p. 217.

256 *"The crossing at Panmunjom . . ."*: Jimmy Carter, "Report on Our Trip to Korea, June 1994," Appendix F in Creekmore (2006), p. 320. (Hereafter "Carter Report.")

256 *"over an almost-empty . . ."*: Ibid.

257 *"that spelled out . . ."*: Creekmore (2006), p. 135.

257 *"We strongly affirm . . ."*: Quoted in ibid., p. 140.

258 *confidential message from Carter to Clinton:* For Carter's summary, see Carter Report, p. 321.

258 *"We are heading toward . . ."*: Quoted in Creekmore (2006), p. 151.

258 *"over which President Clinton . . ."*: Creekmore (2006), pp. 151–52.

259 *"We must have a way . . ."*: Quoted in Wit et al. (2004), p. 224.

259 *"The central problem is . . ."*: Quoted in Creekmore (2006), p. 160.

259 *"If the U.S. had helped us . . ."*: Quoted in ibid., pp. 160–161.

260 *"He accepted all my proposals . . ."*: Carter Report, p. 322.

260 *"asked him each time . . ."*: Carter Report, p. 322.

262 *Gallucci . . . making himself inconspicuous:* see photo at Wit et al. (2004), between p. 204 and p. 205.

262 *Creekmore said the former president . . . commitments:* Creekmore (2006), p. 180.

263   *"That killed the . . . sanctions . . .":* Quoted in ibid., p. 179.

263   *"a very important . . .":* Quoted in ibid., p. 331.

264   *"occasioned the largest municipal-bond . . .":* Wit et al. (2004), p. 266.

265   *"They hated the idea . . .":* Stossel (2005), p. 14.

265   *"From the standpoint . . .":* Wit et al. (2004), p. 332 (original italics).

266   *"The missiles cannot reach . . .":* New York Times Magazine, 19 Oct. 2003, p. 41.

TWELVE THE CORNERSTONE OF PEACE AND STABILITY

267   *"Look around you . . .":* Thomas Graham, Jr., interview, 2004.

267   *"There was nothing there . . .":* Ibid.

268   *"the centerpiece of international . . .":* Graham (2002), p. 257.

268   *"Although few agreed . . .":* Ibid., p. 260.

268   *"I traveled all over . . .":* Thomas Graham, Jr., interview, 2004.

269   *"an impossibility . . .":* Graham (2002), p. 262.

269   *"the cornerstone of international . . .":* Ibid.

269   *"many countries stressed . . .":* Ibid., pp. 262–63.

271   *"and the Russians . . .":* Ibid., p. 137.

271   *"the greatest disarmament . . .":* Jentleson (2000), p. 111.

271   *"laid out very clearly . . .":* Chollet and Goldgeier (2008), p. 44.

271   *"wanted the United States to remain . . .":* Ibid., p. 51.

271   *"That was just nutty . . .":* Ibid., p. 45.

272   *"The September decision was . . .":* Lambright (2002), pp. 75–76.

273   *"It was a whole different world . . .":* Sig Hecker interview, 2004. All the following Hecker statements in this chapter derive from this source unless otherwise specified.

274   *"Reliability testing is not . . .":* Graham (2002), pp. 240–41.

275   *"I had not been able . . .":* Ibid., pp. 241–42.

275   *"Who will speak for the moratorium . . .":* Ibid., p. 242.

275   *"Hazel, however . . .":* Ibid.

276   *"It was an inspirational . . .":* Ibid., pp. 242–43.

276   *"Hazel brought with her . . .":* Ibid., p. 243.

278   *"Stockpile Stewardship . . . consists of two . . .":* Statement of Dr. Victor H. Reis, 1999 Congressional Hearings Supporting the National Security Strategy, House Armed Services Committee, 2 Feb. 1999 (online).

278   *"For three years running . . .":* Ibid.

279   *"A very large part . . .":* Odom (1998), p. 215.

282   *"Israeli officials . . . writes":* Graham (2002), p. 270.

282   *"None of that material . . .":* Ibid., p. 286.

283   *"could not live forever . . .":* Ibid., p. 269.

283   *"Mexico was determined . . .":* Ibid., p. 275.

283   *"had kept open the nuclear option . . .":* Ibid., p. 276.

283   *"Countries began to join . . .":* Ibid., p. 279.

284 *"Several important NAM ambassadors . . .":* Ibid., p. 291.

284 *"The treaty did not create . . .":* Quoted in ibid., p. 287.

285 *"the principal elements . . .":* Butler (2001), p. 53.

285 *"The treaty had served . . .":* Ibid., pp. 45–47.

285 *"a series of documents . . .":* Ibid., p. 47.

285 *"to seek its cooperation . . .":* Ibid., p. 48.

286 *"It was during the long flight . . .":* Ibid.

286 *"the possible final form . . .":* Ibid.

286 *"At the request of others . . .":* Ibid., p. 49.

287 *"a CTBT by 1996 . . .":* Graham and LaVera (2003), p. 106.

288 *"Though [political commitments] do not . . .":* Bedjaoui (1991), p. 268.

288 *"the nuclear issue . . .":* Untitled UNSCOM document, "UNSCOM/ IAEA SENSITIVE, *NOTE FOR THE FILE,"* undated, available at http:// www.globalsecurity.org/wmd/library/news/iraq/un/unscom-iaea _kamal-brief.htm, p. 1.

289 *"12 ton, then 9 ton . . .":* Ibid., p. 4.

289 *"All chemical weapons . . .":* Ibid., p. 13 (emphasis added).

290 *"In retrospect, . . . the French tests . . .":* Graham (2002), p. 248.

290 *"Several of them . . .":* Thomas Graham, Jr., interview, 2004.

291 *"that they would break . . .":* Graham and LaVera (2003), p. 1379.

291 *"countries favoring the treaty . . .":* Hansen (2006), p. 44.

292 *"I stood just feet away . . .":* Butler (2001), p. 65.

THIRTEEN THE DOG ATE MY HOMEWORK

293 *"nuclear apartheid":* Quoted in Perkovich (1999), p. 373.

294 *"reevaluate the country's . . .":* Quoted in ibid.

294 *At least one test device:* Perkovich (1999), p. 374.

294 *"The situation was more urgent . . .":* Ibid., p. 375.

295 *"profoundly shocked the Iraqi . . .":* Rolf Ekéus (rapporteur's summary), From UNSCOM to UNMOVIC: The Future of Weapons Inspections in Iraq. Washington Institute Special Policy Forum, 18 July 2000 (Poli- cyWatch #477), p. 1 (online).

295 *"had been responsible . . .":* Quoted in Cockburn and Cockburn (1999), p. 199.

296 *"In a locked chicken shed . . .":* Ibid., p. 200.

296 *"Do you think I could harm . . .":* Quoted in ibid., p. 207.

296 *"He would return to Baghdad . . .":* Quoted in ibid., p. 197.

296 *"UNSCOM would be spying . . .":* Duelfer (2009), p. 117.

297 *"Since the U-2 could loiter . . .":* Ibid., p. 32.

297 *"no indication of Iraq . . .":* IAEA 4th Consolidated Report (S/197/779), 6 Oct. 1997, p. 4.

297 *"There were no documents . . .":* Duelfer (2009), p. 112.

298 *"The Iraqis had provided . . .":* Ibid., pp. 154–55.

298 *"verify the unverifiable . . .":* Ibid., p. 154.

298 *"Head of UNSCOM . . .":* Butler (2000), p. 61.

303 *"I've spent a lifetime . . .":* Butler (2000), p. 63. Italics in original.

303 *"Butler came in at an extremely . . .":* Duelfer (2009), p. 137.

303 *"would quickly take advantage . . .":* Ibid., p. 138.

304 *"to flood Iraq . . .":* Ibid.

304 *"Iraqi propaganda began . . .":* Butler (2000), p. 110.

304 *"Saddam had every reason . . .":* Ibid., p. 124.

305 *"stood transfixed, watching . . .":* Ibid., p. 126.

305 *"Many Republicans were . . . demoralized . . .":* Alfonsi (2006), p. 363.

306 *"Saddam Hussein is a convicted . . .":* Quoted in ibid., p. 359.

307 *"the only sure way . . .":* Quoted in ibid., p. 364.

307 *"The Kristol/Kagan analysis . . .":* Brent Scowcroft, "Taking Exception: The Power of Containment," *Washington Post,* 1 Mar. 1998, Op-ed Section, p. C7.

307 *"We would have been forced . . .":* George H. W. Bush and Brent Scowcroft, "Why We Didn't Remove Saddam," *Time,* 2 Mar. 1998, p. 31.

308 *"We may soon face a threat . . .":* Elliott Abrams, et al., letter to William J. Clinton, 26 January 1998, online at http://www. newamerican century.org/iraqclintonletter.htm.

310 *"efforts to remove . . .":* Iraq Liberation Act of 1998, Section 3 (online).

310 *"The government believed . . .":* Perkovich (1999), p. 384.

311 *a cost . . . $2.5 billion:* Ibid., p. 437.

311 *Vajpayee made the final decision to test:* According to a reliable intelligence source who prefers anonymity.

311 *"George, there aren't going to be . . .":* Quoted in Talbott (2004), p. 47.

312 *"We needed to make sure . . .":* Transcript, 17 May 1998 Indian Department of Atomic Energy press conference, online at www.fas.org.

312 *The AEC announced:* Quoted in Zhimin and Feizhi (1998) (online).

312 *"I can now believe stories . . .":* Quoted in Talbott (2004), p. 49.

313 *"Dr. Khan reminded . . .":* Rai Muhammad Saleh Azam, "When Mountains Move—the Story of Chagai," online at www.defencejournal. com/2000/june/chagai.htm.

314 *"About equal . . .":* Jeremiah News Conference, 2 June 1998, p. 4., at www.fas.org/irp/cia/product/jeremiah.html.

314 *"In retrospect, the U.S. . . . .":* Jamie McIntyre, "Explaining Why U.S. Intelligence Failed to Anticipate Indian Nuclear Tests," CNN Worldview, 2 June 1998.

315 *"was basically a Democratic . . .":* Keith Hansen interview, 2007.

315 *"By the end of September . . .":* Deibel (2002), p. 147.

316 *"with no guarantee . . .":* Ibid., p. 148.

316 *"Clinton had not mounted . . .":* Ibid., p. 151.

316 *"wrote on the day . . .":* Ibid., p. 157.

317 *"It would be a mistake . . .":* Ibid., p. 160.

317 *"the problem of nuclear weapons . . .":* Butler (2001), p. 11.

FOURTEEN REGIME CHANGE

321 *"One of the keys . . .":* Quoted in Kim Cobb, "Writer Says Bush Talked About War in 1999," *Houston Chronicle,* 1 Nov. 2004, p. A10 (online at http://downingstreetmemo.com).

322 *"The only way we can hope . . .":* Al Gore, "Defeating Hussein, Once and for All," *New York Times* Op-ed, 26 Sept. 1991 (online).

322 *"In general . . . the formula . . .":* Ibid.

322 *"From 1993 to early 1998 . . .":* Burgos (2008), pp. 241–242.

323 *"In the rhetorical contestation . . .":* Ibid., p. 223.

323 *"This unilateral destruction . . .":* "Amb. Richard Butler's Presentation to the UN Security Council," June 3, 1998, p. 2 (online at www.fas .org).

324 *"only 13 targets on the list . . .":* William Arkin, "The Difference Was in the Details," *Washington Post,* 17 Jan. 1999, p. B1 (online).

324 *"insisted that the United States . . .":* Ibid.

324 *"Iraq's nuclear and chemical materials . . .":* Fred Kaplan, "Strikes Didn't Finish Job US Set Out to Do," *Boston Globe,* 21 Dec. 1998 (online).

325 *After the 1998 bombing:* Duelfer (2009), pp. 159–60.

325 *"It would have been normal . . .":* Duelfer (2009), pp. 163–64.

325 *"There was never any answer . . .":* Duelfer (2009), p. 160.

325 *"on the grounds that this new . . .":* Scott Ritter, "The Case for Iraq's Qualitative Disarmament," *Arms Control Today,* June 2000 (online at www.armscontrol.org).

326 *"From 1994 to 1998 . . .":* Ibid.

326 *"Responsibility for overseeing . . .":* Ibid.

327 *"By December 1998 . . .":* Mohamed ElBaradei, "The Status of Nuclear Inspections in Iraq," statement to the United Nations Security Council, New York, 27 Jan. 2003 (online at www.IAEA.org).

327 *"From an Iraqi perspective . . .":* Duelfer (2009), p. 165.

328 *"Our continued insistence . . .":* Ibid., p. 167.

329 *"How close is the peril . . .":* Quoted in Pollack (2004).

330 *"The opening premise . . .":* Suskind (2004), pp. 73–74.

330 *"should examine our military options . . .":* Ibid., p. 75.

330 *"The risk to US and Alliance . . .":* Quoted in ibid., pp. 77–78.

330 *"From the start . . .":* Quoted in ibid., p. 86.

331 *"impacted the World Trade Center":* Associated Press, 26 Nov. 2001, quoted in Allan Wood and Paul Thompson, "An Interesting Day: President Bush's Movements and Actions on 9/11," www.historycommons .org.

331 *"I was sitting outside the classroom . . .":* White House, 4 Dec. 2001, quoted in ibid.

332 *"Today, we've had a national tragedy . . .":* "Remarks by President Bush at Emma Booker Elementary School." Federal News Service transcript, 11 Sept. 2001 (online).

332 *"And for the record . . ."*: Full transcript of bin Laden's speech, Al Jazeera English archive, 1 Nov. 2004 (online).

333 *2,954 victims:* The number was initially given as 2,974 but revised downward two years later.

333 *"a great opportunity"*: Quoted in Dan Balz and Bob Woodward, "America's Chaotic Road to War; Bush's Global Strategy Began to Take Shape in First Frantic Hours After Attack," *Washington Post,* 27 Jan. 2002 (online).

333 *"The Pearl Harbor of the twenty-first . . ."*: Quoted in ibid.

FIFTEEN **THE HARD STARE INTO THE ABYSS**

334 *"At 2:40 p.m. that day . . ."*: Woodward (2004), pp. 24–25.

334 *"opportunity"*: Quoted in ibid., p. 25.

334 *"If we go after Saddam . . ."*: Quoted in ibid.

334 *on* Meet the Press *. . . "No"*: Quoted in Frank Rich time line: "What the White House Knew, and When It Knew It," www.frankrich.com.

335 *"Bush told Rice . . ."*: Woodward (2004), p. 26.

335 *"Get Tommy Franks looking . . ."*: Quoted in ibid., p. 2.

336 *no U.S. cases since 1992: U.S. Morbidity and Mortality Weekly Report* 51(53) 37, 2004.

336 *"reasonable . . . but I must say . . ."*: "Cheney: 'Reasonable' to Assume Anthrax Cases Linked to Terrorists," CNN.com, 12 Oct. 2001 (online).

337 *"In a sense, September 11 . . ."*: Matthew Engel and Anthony Sampson, "Attack on Afghanistan: US War Aims: Sabre-rattling at Saddam: Threat to Baghdad Is Way of Keeping Options Open," *The Guardian* (London), 10 Oct. 2001, p. 4 (online).

338 *"Everyone who had entered . . ."*: Mayer (2009), Chapter 1 (Kindle edition).

338 *"when the White House sensor . . ."*: Ibid.

338 *"had convinced the President . . ."*: Ibid.

338 *On 29 October Cheney literally:* Ibid.

338 *"Officials who worked . . ."*: Ibid.

339 *A story about Lundgren . . . next day:* Rick Weiss and David Brown, "Inhalational Anthrax Is Suspected in Conn. Woman," *Washington Post,* 21 Nov. 2001, p. A01.

339 *He probably discussed it with Cheney:* Woodward (2004), p. 4.

339 *"I think the seminal event . . ."*: Weisberg (2008), p. 191.

340 *"cut and run early"*: Quoted in Weisberg (2008), p. xvii.

340 *"The key thought about this . . ."*: Quoted in Woodward (2004), p. 34.

341 *"Since the end of the Gulf War . . ."*: Alfonsi (2006), pp. 385–86.

342 *"Saddam Hussein agreed . . ."*: Quoted in Jim Lobe, "Baghdad Veers Back into Washington's Crosshairs," *Taiwan Economic News,* 4 Dec. 2001 (online).

342 *"axis of evil"*: "The President's State of the Union Address," 29 Jan. 2002 (online).

343 *"From what she said . . .":* Memorandum, David Manning to Tony Blair, 14 Mar. 2002 (online).

344 The New York Times . . . *interior:* Patrick E. Tyler with John Tagliabue, "Czechs Confirm Iraqi Agent Met with Terror Ringleader," *New York Times,* 27 Oct. 2001 (online).

344 *Václav Havel, had called White House:* Frank Rich time line (online).

344 *"3. The Iraq regime . . .":* Jack Straw to Tony Blair, 25 Mar. 2002 (online).

346 *"The truth is . . . that for reasons . . .":* U.S. Department of Defense news transcript, "Deputy Secretary Wolfowitz Interview with Sam Tanenhaus, *Vanity Fair*" (online).

346 *"a perceptible shift in attitude . . .":* "The Secret Downing Street Memo," *Sunday Times* (London), 1 May 2005 (www.timesonline.co.uk).

347 *"It seemed clear that Bush . . .":* Ibid.

348 *"We know that in the last four years . . .":* CNN *Late Edition* with Wolf Blitzer: Interview with Condoleezza Rice, aired 8 Sept. 2002, CNN .com transcript (online).

349 *Bush built . . . Cincinnati, Ohio:* Remarks by the president on Iraq, Cincinnati, Ohio, 7 Oct. 2002 (online).

349 *"Referring to the sentence . . .":* U.S. Select Committee on Intelligence (2004), pp. 56–57.

350 *"a report purporting to be . . .":* Wilson (2005), p. 14.

351 *"Niger had not actually . . .":* Ibid., p. 15.

351 *The first information . . . true:* Ibid., p. 21.

351 *"but only COGEMA . . .":* Ibid., p. 23.

351 *"would have been absolutely . . .":* Ibid., p. 24.

352 *"The British government . . .":* "Transcript of the State of the Union, Part 8: Iraq," CNN.com, 29 Jan. 2003.

352 *"Baghdad offered to let . . .":* Prados (2004), p. 27.

352 *"gave the impression of a solid . . .":* Blix (2004), p. 86.

353 *"He explained to us that the U.S. . . .":* Ibid.

353 *"immediate, unconditional and active . . .":* Ibid., p. 89.

353 *"We counted on keeping . . .":* Ibid., p. 90.

354 *"Should we expand . . .":* Hans Blix, "Introduction to the 11th Session of the College of Commissioners/Notes for the Executive Chairman of UNMOVIC, Dr. Hans Blix/ New York, 26 November 2002." Hans Blix, personal communication.

354 *"What we came to discover . . .":* Blix (2004), p. 93.

354 *George Tenet . . . "The Case":* Woodward (2004), pp. 247–49.

354 *"Bush turned to Tenet . . .":* Ibid., p. 249.

355 *"Why We Know Iraq Is Lying":* Condoleezza Rice, *New York Times* op-ed, 23 Jan. 2003.

355 *Bush then calmly . . . Saddam Hussein:* Reported by David Manning, chief foreign policy adviser, in a memo to Tony Blair. Frank Rich time line, pp. 26–27.

355 *"How much, if any, is left . . .":* Hans Blix, "Briefing of the Security Council, 14 February 2003" (online at IAEA.org).

356 *"the first case of a war..."*: Hans Blix, "Notes for introduction to a seminar in Stockholm, 5 April 2003," p. 6. Hans Blix, personal communication.

356 *"It is hard to resist the reflection..."*: Hans Blix, "The UN, Iraq, Weapons of Mass Destruction and the Use of Force—The View of a Nordic Lawyer," Riga Graduate School of Law, 20 May 2005, p. 11. Hans Blix, personal communication.

357 *"spend[ing] several sessions..."*: FBI Interview Session 00, Saddam Hussein, 21 March 2004, p. 5 (online at National Security Archive).

357 *"Even though Hussein claimed..."*: FBI Interview Session 24, Saddam Hussein, 11 June 2004, p. 2 (online at National Security Archive).

357 *"that when it was clear that..."*: Ibid., pp. 3–4.

358 *"To conclude, ... we have to date..."*: Mohamed ElBaradei, "The Status of Nuclear Inspections in Iraq," statement to the United Nations Security Council, New York, 27 Jan. 2003, p. 6 (online at www.IAEA.org).

358 *"Cheney had absorbed two..."*: Alfonsi (2006), pp. 394–95.

359 *Joseph Stiglitz... 2007 dollars:* Joseph Stiglitz and Linda Bilmes, "The three trillion dollar war," Timesonline, 23 Feb. 2008.

359 *"After the war..."*: Hans Blix interview, 2004.

SIXTEEN THE TWILIGHT OF THE BOMBS

360 *Yet despite... fewer than 10.):* Federation of American Scientists (online).

361 *"By way of comparison..."*: Schwartz and Choubey (2009), pp. 6–7.

361 *"waiting... to retaliate..."*: Mazarr (1999), p. 1.

362 *"the administration's leadership..."*: Linton Brooks interview, 2007. All Linton Brooks quotations in this chapter come from this source unless otherwise attributed.

364 *"The more than 10,000 warheads..."*: Stephen Schwartz, "Letter to the Editor: Nuclear deterrence," *Washington Times,* 12 Feb. 2009.

365 *"technical problems facing a nation..."*: Frank (1967), p. v.

365 *"The goal of the participants..."*: quoted in Oliver Burkeman, "How Two Students Built an A-bomb," www.Guardian.co.uk, 24 June 2003, p. 4.

365 *"Can terrorists build nuclear weapons?"*: Mark et al. (1987) (online).

366 *John Mueller... extremely unlikely:* See Mueller (2009).

366 *"the atomic terrorist"*: Ibid.

366 *as Mueller... seem to think:* Ibid., p. 6: "Because of the dangers and difficulties of transporting and working with plutonium, a dedicated terrorist group, it is generally further agreed, would choose to try to use highly enriched uranium."

367 *"or even a year"*: Ibid., p. 9.

367 *"daunting problems associated..."*: Quoted in ibid.

368 *John McPhee . . .* The Curve of Binding Energy: McPhee (1974).

368 *"A small group of people . . .":* Quoted in Bunn and Wier (2004), p. 20.

369 *"Setting off a nuclear explosion . . .":* Ibid.

370 *"asked the three U.S. nuclear . . .":* Ibid., pp. 20–21.

370 *"U.S. nuclear policies remain . . .":* Daalder and Lodal (2008), pp. 80–81.

371 *"It was identified by . . .":* Richard Butler, Monterey Institute of International Studies, Monterey, California, 2008.

371 *"The article was about . . .":* Richard Butler, telephone interview, 2009.

371 *"to propose practical steps . . .": Report of the Canberra Commission on the Elimination of Nuclear Weapons,* Aug. 1996 (online), p. 3. Hereafter Canberra Commission report.

372 *"They were an extremely interesting . . .":* Richard Butler interview, 2009.

374 *"As long as others have . . .":* Robert Gates, "Nuclear Weapons and Deterrence in the 21st Century," Carnegie Endowment for International Peace, 28 Oct. 2008 (online).

374 *"We must face the fact . . .":* Quoted in Sloan (1983), p. 57.

375 *"Effective verification is critical . . .":* Canberra Commission report, p. 13.

376 *"What about rogues . . .":* Richard Butler, telephone interview, 2009.

376 *Monitoring for the Comprehensive Nuclear Test-Ban Treaty:* See Clery (2009).

376 *"its executive council . . .":* Ibid., p. 385.

380 *"weapons of precise destruction":* See David Blair, "How to Defeat the United States: The Operational Military Effects of the Proliferation of Weapons of Precise Destruction," in Sokolski (1996), Chapter 4.

382 *"It is absurd to look upon . . .":* Elliot (1972), pp. 5–6.

383 *"Our societies are dedicated . . .":* Ibid., p. 8.

384 *"[I do not wish] to claim . . .":* Ibid., pp. 8–9.

384 *"In fact, the manner . . .":* Ibid., p. 10.

385 *"The reduction of the death . . .":* Quoted in Rosen (1958), p. 440.

386 *"Perhaps everything terrible . . .":* Rilke (1984), Letter Eight.

BIBLIOGRAPHY

Abella, Alex (2008). *Soldiers of Reason: The RAND Corporation and the Rise of the American Empire.* New York: Harcourt.

Adams, James (1984). *The Unnatural Alliance.* New York: Quartet Books.

Albats, Yevgenia (1994). *The State Within a State: The KGB and Its Hold on Russia—Past, Present, and Future.* New York: Farrar, Straus & Giroux.

Albright, David (1993). "Slow but Steady." *Bulletin of the Atomic Scientists* 49, 5–6.

———(1994a). "North Korean Plutonium Production." *Science and Global Security* 5, 63–87.

———(1994b). "South Africa and the Affordable Bomb." *Bulletin of the Atomic Scientists* 50, 37–47.

———(2002). "Iraq's Programs to Make Highly Enriched Uranium and Plutonium for Nuclear Weapons Prior to the Gulf War." (Online at www.isis-online.org.)

Albright, David, and Corey Hinderstein (2004). "Documents Indicate A. Q. Khan Offered Nuclear Weapons Designs to Iraq in 1990; Did He Approach Other Countries?" (Online at www.isis-online.org.)

Albright, David, and Kevin O'Neill (1999). "Iraq's Efforts to Acquire Information About Nuclear Weapons and Nuclear-Related Technologies from the United States." (Online at www.isis-online.org.)

———eds. (2000). *Solving the North Korean Nuclear Puzzle.* Washington: ISIS Press.

Albright, David, Corey Gay, and Khidhir Hamza (1999). "Development of the Al Tuwaitha Site: What If the Public or the IAEA Had Overhead Imagery?" (Online at www.isis-online.org.)

Albright, David, Frans Berkhout, and William Walker (1997). *Plutonium and Highly Enriched Uranium 1996: World Inventories, Capabilities and Policies.* Oxford, U.K.: Oxford University Press.

Alexander, George L. (1992). *Forceful Persuasion: Coercive Diplomacy as an Alternative to War.* Washington: United States Institute of Peace Press.

Alfonsi, Christian (2006). *Circle in the Sand: Why We Went Back to Iraq.* New York: Doubleday.

Allin, Dana H. (1995). *Cold War Illusions: America, Europe and Soviet Power, 1969–1989.* London: Palgrave Macmillan.

Allison, Graham (2005). *Nuclear Terrorism: The Ultimate Preventable Catastrophe.* New York: Henry Holt.

Allison, Graham, et al., eds. (1993). *Cooperative Denuclearization: From Pledges to Deeds.* Cambridge, MA: Center for Science and International Affairs.

———(1996). *Avoiding Nuclear Anarchy: Containing the Threat of Loose Russian Nuclear Weapons and Fissile Material.* Cambridge, MA: MIT Press.

Andrew, Christopher, and Vasili Mitrokhin (1999). *The Mitrokhin Archive: The KGB in Europe and the West.* New York: Penguin.

Arbatov, Alexei, and Vladimir Dvorkin (2006). *Beyond Nuclear Deterrence: Transforming the U.S.-Russian Equation.* Washington: Carnegie Endowment for International Peace.

Arkin, William M., and Richard W. Fieldhouse (1985). *Nuclear Battlefields: Global Links in the Arms Race.* Pensacola, FL: Ballinger.

———(n.d.). *The Gulf War: Secret History.* Stars and Stripes (www.stripes .com).

Arkin, William M., Robert S. Norris, M. Hoenig, and Thomas Cochran (1987). *Nuclear Weapons Databook, Volume III: U.S. Nuclear Warhead Facility Profiles.* Pensacola, FL: Ballinger Publishing.

Armitage, M. J., and R. A. Mason (1983). *Air Power in the Nuclear Age.* London: Palgrave Macmillan.

Arnold, Lorna (1995). *Windscale, 1957: Anatomy of a Nuclear Accident.* London: Palgrave Macmillan.

Asculai, Ephraim (2002). *Verification Revisited: The Nuclear Case.* Washington: ISIS Press.

Astore, William J. (2008). "Leaving Cheyenne Mountain." *Nation* 286, 22–24.

Atkinson, Rick (1993). *Crusade: The Untold Story of the Persian Gulf War.* Boston: Houghton Mifflin.

Baker, James A., III (1995). *The Politics of Diplomacy.* New York: Putnam.

———(2006). *Work Hard, Study, and Keep Out of Politics! Adventures and Lessons from an Unexpected Public Life.* New York: G. P. Putnam's Sons.

Ball, Desmond (1988). *Strategic Nuclear Targeting.* Ithaca, NY: Cornell University Press.

Barnet, Richard J. (1960). *Who Wants Disarmament?* Boston: Beacon Press.

Barry, John (2003). "Exclusive: The Defector's Secrets." *Newsweek,* 3 March, 6.

Barzam, Amatzia (2001). "An Analysis of Iraqi WMD Strategy." *Nonproliferation Review,* Summer, 25–39.

Bedjaoui, M., ed. (1991). *International Law: Achievements and Prospects.* Boston: Martinus Nijhoff.

Behrens, J. W., and Allen D. Carlson, eds. (1989). *50 Years With Nuclear Fission.* Washington: American Nuclear Society.

Bennett, Andrew (1999). *Condemned to Repetition? The Rise, Fall, and Reprise of Soviet Russian Military Interventionism, 1973–1996.* Cambridge, MA: The MIT Press.

Bergman, Ronen (2007). *The Secret War With Iran: The 30-Year Clandestine Struggle Against the World's Most Dangerous Terrorist Power.* New York: Free Press.

Beschloss, Michael R., and Strobe Talbott (1993). *At the Highest Levels: The Inside Story of the End of the Cold War.* Boston: Little, Brown.

Betts, Richard K. (1987). *Nuclear Blackmail and Nuclear Balance.* Washington: Brookings Institution Press.

Bhatia, Shyam, and Daniel McGrory (2000). *Brighter Than the Baghdad Sun: Saddam Hussein's Nuclear Threat to the United States.* Washington: Regnery.

Blacker, Coit D. (1993). *Hostage to Revolution: Gorbachev and Soviet Security Policy, 1985–1991.* New York: Council on Foreign Relations.

Blackett, P. M. S. (1948). *Fear, War, and the Bomb: Military and Political Consequences of Atomic Energy.* New York: McGraw-Hill.

Blair, B. G., Jonathan Dean, Steve Fetter, et al., eds. (1999). *The Nuclear Turning Point: A Blueprint for Deep Cuts and De-Alerting of Nuclear Weapons.* Washington: Brookings Institution Press.

Blair, Bruce G. (1993). *The Logic of Accidental Nuclear War.* Washington: Brookings Institution Press.

Blair, Bruce G., Thomas B. Cochran, et al. (2008). *Towards True Security: Ten Steps the Next President Should Take to Transform U.S. Nuclear Weapons Policy.* Cambridge, MA: UCS Publications.

Blair, David (1996). "How to Defeat the United States: The Operational Military Effects of the Proliferation of Weapons of Precise Destruction." In Henry Sokolski, ed., *Fighting Proliferation: New Concerns for the Nineties.* Maxwell AFB, Alabama: Air University Press (online).

Blechman, Barry M., ed. (2009). *Russia and the United States.* Washington: Henry L. Stimson Center.

Blix, Hans (2004). *Disarming Iraq.* New York: Pantheon.

———ed. (2006). *Weapons of Terror: Freeing the World of Nuclear, Biological and Chemical Arms.* New York: United Nations.

Blumenthal, Sidney (1988). *Rise of the Counter Establishment: From Conservative Ideology to Political Power.* New York: HarperCollins.

Bobbitt, Philip, Lawrence Freedman, and Gregory F. Treverton, eds. (1989). *US Nuclear Strategy: A Reader.* New York: New York University Press.

Boldin, Valery (1994). *Ten Years That Shook the World: The Gorbachev Era as Witnessed by His Chief of Staff.* New York: Basic Books.

Bonnell, V. C., Ann Cooper, and Gregory Freidin, eds. (1994). *Russia at the Barricades: Eyewitness Accounts of the August 1991 Coup.* Armonk, NY: M. E. Sharpe.

Bracken, Paul (1983). *The Command and Control of Nuclear Forces.* New Haven, CT: Yale University Press.

———(1999). *Fire in the East: The Rise of Asian Military Power and the Second Nuclear Age.* New York: Harper Perennial.

———(2003). "The Structure of the Second Nuclear Age." *Orbis* 47, 399–413.

Brinkley, Joel, and Stephen Engelberg, eds. (1988). *Report of the Congressional Committees Investigating the Iran-Contra Affair, with the Minority Views.* New York: Times Books.

Brzezinski, Zbigniew (2007). *Second Chance: Three Presidents and the Crisis of American Superpower.* New York: Basic Books.

Builder, Carl H. (1994). *The Icarus Syndrome: The Role of Air Power Theory in the Evolution and Fate of the U.S. Air Force.* Piscataway, NJ: Transaction Publishers.

————(1995). *Rethinking National Security and the Role of the Military.* Santa Monica: RAND.

Bukharin, Oleg (1997). "The Future of Russia's Plutonium Cities." *International Security* 21, 126–58.

————(1998). "Securing Russia's HEU Stocks." *Science and Global Security* 7, 311–31.

Bundy, McGeorge (1988). *Danger and Survival: Choices About the Bomb in the First Fifty Years.* New York: Random House.

————(1991). "Nuclear Weapons and the Gulf." *Foreign Affairs,* Fall.

Bundy, McGeorge, William Crowe, and Sidney Drell (1993). *Reducing Nuclear Danger: The Road Away from the Brink.* Washington: Brookings Institution Press.

Bunn, George, and Christopher Chyba, eds. (2006). *U.S. Nuclear Weapons Policy: Confronting Today's Threats.* Washington: Brookings Institution Press.

Bunn, Matthew (2007). *Securing the Bomb 2007.* Washington: Nuclear Threat Initiative.

Bunn, Matthew, and Anthony Wier (2004). *Securing the Bomb: An Agenda for Action.* Washington: Nuclear Threat Initiative.

Bunn, Matthew, Anthony Wier, and John P. Holdren (2003). *Controlling Nuclear Warheads and Materials: A Report Card and Action Plan.* Washington: Nuclear Threat Initiative.

Burghart, D. L., and Theresa Sabonis-Helf, eds. (2004). *In the Tracks of Tamerlane: Central Asia's Path to the 21st Century.* Washington: National Defense University Press.

Burgos, Russell A. (2008). "Origins of Regime Change: 'Ideapolitik' on the Long Road to Baghdad, 1993–2000." *Security Studies* 17:2, 221–256.

Burroughs, John (1997). *The (Il)legality of Threat or Use of Nuclear Weapons: A Guide to the Historic Opinion of the International Court of Justice.* Munich: Lit Verlag.

Bush, George H. W., and Brent Scowcroft (1998). *A World Transformed.* New York: Vintage.

Butler, Richard (2000). *The Greatest Threat: Iraq, Weapons of Mass Destruction and the Crisis of Global Security.* New York: Public Affairs.

————(2001). *Fatal Choice: Nuclear Weapons and the Illusion of Missile Defense.* Boulder, CO: Westview Press.

Campbell, K. M., et al., eds. (2004). *The Nuclear Tipping Point: Why States Reconsider Their Nuclear Choices.* Washington: Brookings Institution Press.

Campbell, Kurt M., Ashton B. Carter, Steven E. Miller, and Charles A. Zraket (1991). *Nuclear Fission: Control of the Nuclear Arsenal in a Disintegrating Soviet Union.* Cambridge, MA: Center for Science and International Affairs.

Canberra Commission on the Elimination of Nuclear Weapons (1996). *Report of the Canberra Commission on the Elimination of Nuclear Weapons.* Canberra, Australia: Commonwealth of Australia.

Carlson, John (2009). "Introduction to the Concept of Proliferation Resistance." International Commission on Nuclear Non-proliferation and Disarmament (online).

Carter, Ashton B. (1992). "Reducing the Nuclear Dangers from the Former Soviet Union." *Arms Control Today,* Jan.–Feb., 10–14.

Carter, Ashton B., and William J. Perry (1999). *Preventive Defense: A New Security Strategy for America.* Washington: Brookings Institution Press.

Chari, P. R., Pervaiz Iqbal Cheema, and Stephen P. Cohen (2007). *Four Crises and a Peace Process: American Engagement in South Asia.* Washington: Brookings Institution Press.

Chernyaev, Anatoly (2000). *My Six Years with Gorbachev.* University Park, PA: Pennsylvania State University Press.

Chinoy, Mike (2008). *Meltdown: The Inside Story of the North Korean Nuclear Crisis.* New York: St. Martin's Press.

Chollet, Derek, and James Goldgeier (2008). *America Between the Wars.* New York: Public Affairs.

Christopher, Warren (1998). *In the Stream of History: Shaping Foreign Policy for a New Era.* Palo Alto, CA: Stanford University Press.

Cirincione, Joseph, Jessica T. Mathews, and George Perkovich (2004). *WMD in Iraq: Evidence and Implications.* Washington: Carnegie Endowment for International Peace.

Claire, Rodger (2004). *Raid on the Sun: Inside Israel's Secret Campaign That Denied Saddam the Bomb.* New York: Broadway Books.

Clarke, Richard A. (2004). *Against All Enemies: Inside America's War on Terror.* New York: Free Press.

Clery, Daniel (2009). "Test Ban Monitoring: No Place to Hide." *Science* 325, 382–85.

Clinton, Bill (1994). *National Security Strategy of the United States 1994–1995: Engagement and Enlargement.* Washington: Potomac Books.

———(1995). *National Security Strategy of Engagement and Enlargement: 1995–1996.* Washington: Brassey's.

Cochran, Thomas B. (1994). "Highly Enriched Uranium Production for South African Nuclear Weapons." *Science and Global Security* 4, 161–76.

Cochran, Thomas B., and Robert Standish Norris (1992). "Russian/Soviet Nuclear Warhead Production." *Nuclear Weapons Databook NWD 92–1.* Washington: Natural Resources Defense Council.

Cochran, Thomas B., Robert S. Norris, and Oleg A. Bukharin (1995). *Making the Russian Bomb: From Stalin to Yeltsin.* Boulder, CO: Westview Press.

Cock, Jacklyn, and Penny Mckenzie, eds. (1998). *From Defence to Development: Redirecting Military Resources in South Africa.* Capetown: David Philip.

Cockburn, Alexander (2003). "Meet the Prime WMD Fabricator." *Nation,* Aug. 18/25, 12.

Cockburn, Andrew, and Leslie Cockburn (1997). *One Point Safe.* New York: Doubleday.

Cockburn, Andrew, and Patrick Cockburn (1999). *Out of the Ashes: The Resurrection of Saddam Hussein.* New York: HarperCollins.

Cohen, Avner (1998). *Israel and the Bomb.* New York: Columbia University Press.

Cohen, Avner, and Steven Lee, eds. (1986). *Nuclear Weapons and the Future of Humanity: The Fundamental Questions.* Lanham, MD: Rowman & Littlefield.

Cohen, Stephen F. (2000). *Failed Crusade: America and the Tragedy of Post-Communist Russia.* New York: W. W. Norton.

Committee on International Security (1994). *Management and Disposition of Excess Weapons Plutonium.* Washington: National Academies Press.

———(1997). *The Future of U.S. Nuclear Weapons Policy.* Washington: National Academies Press.

Committee on International Security and Arms Control (2005). *Monitoring Nuclear Weapons and Nuclear-Explosive Materials.* Washington: National Academies Press.

Corera, Gordon (2006). *Shopping for Bombs: Nuclear Proliferation, Global Insecurity, and the Rise and Fall of the A. Q. Khan Network.* New York: Oxford University Press.

Corey, Robin (2006). *Fear: The History of a Political Idea.* New York: Oxford University Press.

Cox, Arthur M. (1975). *The Myths of National Security: The Peril of Secret Government.* Boston: Beacon Press.

Crane, Conrad C. (2000). *American Airpower Strategy in Korea 1950–1953.* Lawrence: University Press of Kansas.

Creekmore, Marion, Jr. (2006). *A Moment of Crisis: Jimmy Carter, the Power of a Peacemaker, and North Korea's Nuclear Ambitions.* New York: Public Affairs.

Crocker, Chester A. (1992). *High Noon in Southern Africa: Making Peace in a Rough Neighborhood.* New York: W. W. Norton.

Cumings, Bruce (2002). *Parallax Visions: Making Sense of American–East Asian Relations.* Durham, NC: Duke University Press.

———(2004). *North Korea: Another Country.* New York: New Press.

Daalder, Ivo, and Jan Lodal (2008). "The Logic of Zero: Toward a World Without Nuclear Weapons." *Foreign Affairs,* Nov.–Dec., 80–95.

Dahl, Robert Alan (1985). *Controlling Nuclear Weapons: Democracy Versus Guardianship.* Syracuse, NY: Syracuse University Press.

Danner, Mark (2007). "Words in a Time of War: On Rhetoric, Truth and Power." In Andras Szanto, ed., *What Orwell Didn't Know: Propaganda and the New Face of American Politics.* New York: Public Affairs Press (online).

Davis, Jay C., and David A. Kay (1992). "Iraq's Secret Nuclear Weapons Program." *Physics Today,* July, 21–27.

Deibel, Terry L. (2002). "The Death of a Treaty." *Foreign Affairs* 81, 142–61.

Deudney, Daniel (1983). *Whole Earth Security: A Geopolitics of Peace.* Worldwatch Institute (online).

Deutsch, Morton (1986). "Folie à Deux: A Psychological Perspective on Soviet-American Relations." In Karns, Margaret P., ed., *Persistent Patterns and Emergent Structures in a Waning Century.* New York: Praeger.

De Villiers, J. W., Roger Jardine, and Mitchell Reiss (1993). "Why South Africa Gave Up the Bomb." *Foreign Affairs* 72, 98–109.

DeVolpi, Alexander, Vladimir E. Minkov, Vadim A. Simonenko, and George S. Stanford (2004). *Nuclear Shadowboxing: Contemporary Threats from Cold War Weaponry.* Kalamazoo, MI: Fidlar Doubleday.

Dhanapala, Jayantha, with Randy Rydell (2005). *Multilateral Diplomacy and the NPT: An Insider's Account.* Geneva: UNIDIR.

Drell, Sidney D. (1993). *In the Shadow of the Bomb: Physics and Arms Control.* College Park, MD: AIP Press.

———(2007). *Nuclear Weapons, Scientists and the Post–Cold War Challenge: Selected Papers on Arms Control.* Hackensack, NJ: World Scientific.

Drell, Sidney D., and George P. Shultz, eds. (2007). *Implications of the Reykjavik Summit on Its Twentieth Anniversary: Conference Report.* (Conference held October 11–12, 2006, at the Hoover Institution, Stanford University.) Stanford, CA: Hoover Institution Press.

Drell, Sidney D., and James E. Goodby (2003). *The Gravest Danger: Nuclear Weapons.* Stanford, CA: Hoover Institution Press.

———(2009). *A World Without Nuclear Weapons: End-State Issues.* Stanford, CA: Hoover Institution Press.

Duelfer, Charles (2009). *Hide and Seek: The Search for Truth in Iraq.* New York: Public Affairs Press.

Dumas, L. J., and Marek Thee, eds. (1989). *Making Peace Possible: The Promise of Economic Conversion.* Oxford: Pergamon.

Eden, Lynn (2004). *Whole World on Fire: Organizations, Knowledge & Nuclear Weapons Devastation.* Ithaca, NY: Cornell University Press.

Ehrman, John (1996). *The Rise of Neoconservatism: Intellectuals and Foreign Affairs, 1945–1994.* New Haven, CT: Yale University Press.

Elliot, Gil (1972). *Twentieth Century Book of the Dead.* New York: Charles Scribner's Sons.

Embassy of the Republic of Kazakhstan and Nuclear Threat Initiative (2006). *Kazakhstan's Nuclear Disarmament: A Global Model for a Safer World.* Washington: Embassy of Kazakhstan.

Farr, Warner D. (1999). *The Third Temple's Holy of Holies: Israel's Nuclear Weapons (Counterproliferation Paper No. 2).* Maxwell Air Force Base, AL: USAF Counterproliferation Center, Air War College (online).

Foster, K. R., David E. Bernstein, and Peter W. Huber, eds. (1999). *Phantom Risk: Scientific Inference and the Law.* Cambridge, MA: MIT Press.

Frank, W. J., ed. (1967). Summary Report of the *N*th Country Experiment. UCRL-50249. Livermore, CA: Lawrence Radiation Laboratory (online).

Franke, V. C., ed. (2002). *Security in a Changing World: Case Studies in U.S. National Security Management.* Westport, CT: Praeger.

Freedman, Lawrence (1981). *The Evolution of Nuclear Strategy.* London: Macmillan.

Friedman, Alan (1993). *Spider's Web: The Secret History of How the White House Illegally Armed Iraq.* New York: Bantam.

Gallucci, Robert (2001). "Reflections on Establishing and Implementing the Post–Gulf War Inspections of Iraq's Weapons of Mass Destruction Programs." Address delivered at ISIS conference on "Understanding the Lessons of Nuclear Inspections and Monitoring in Iraq: A Ten-Year Review." (Online at www.isis-online.org.)

Ganguly, Sumit, and Devin T. Hagerty (2005). *Fearful Symmetry: India-Pakistan Crises in the Shadow of Nuclear Weapons.* Seattle: University of Washington Press.

Garthoff, Raymond L. (1994). *The Great Transition: American-Soviet Relations and the End of the Cold War.* Washington: Brookings Institution Press.

Gat, Azar (1998). *Fascist and Liberal Visions of War: Fuller, Liddel Hart, Douhet, and Other Modernists.* Oxford: Clarendon Press.

Gates, Robert M. (1997). *From the Shadows.* New York: Simon & Schuster.

Gerson, Joseph (2007). *Empire and the Bomb: How the U.S. Uses Nuclear Weapons to Dominate the World.* London: Pluto Press.

Glasstone, Samuel, ed. (1977). *The Effects of Nuclear Weapons,* 3rd Edition. Washington: United States Atomic Energy Commission.

Goldblat, Josef, ed. (2000). *Nuclear Disarmament: Obstacles to Banishing the Bomb.* London: I. B. Tauris.

Goldgeier, James M., and Michael McFaul (2003). *Power and Purpose: U.S. Policy Toward Russia After the Cold War.* Washington: Brookings Institution Press.

Goldstein, Avery (2007). *Deterrence and Security in the 21st Century: China, Britain, France, and the Enduring Legacy of the Nuclear Revolution.* Stanford, CA: Stanford University Press.

Goldwin, Robert A., and Robert A. Licht, eds. (1990). *Foreign Policy and the Constitution.* Washington: AEI Press.

Goodby, James E. (2006). *At the Borderline of Armageddon: How American Presidents Managed the Atom Bomb.* Lanham, MD: Rowman & Littlefield.

Goodman, A. E., ed. (1995). *The Diplomatic Record 1992–1993.* Boulder, CO: Westview Press.

Goodpaster, Andrew J. (1995). *An Evolving US Nuclear Posture: Second Report of the Steering Committee Project on Eliminating Weapons of Mass Destruction; Report No. 19.* Washington: Henry L. Stimson Center.

Gorbachev, Mikhail (1991). *The August Coup: The Truth and the Lessons.* New York: HarperCollins.

———(1996). *Memoirs.* New York: Doubleday.

———(1999). *Gorbachev: On My Country and the World.* New York: Columbia University Press.

Gordon, Michael, and Bernard E. Trainor (1995). *The Generals' War: The Inside Story of the Conflict in the Gulf.* Boston: Back Bay Books.

Graham, Thomas, Jr. (2002). *Disarmament Sketches: Three Decades of Arms Control and International Law.* Seattle: University of Washington Press.

Graham, Thomas, Jr., and Damien J. LaVera (2003). *Cornerstones of Security: Arms Control Treaties in the Nuclear Era.* Seattle: University of Washington Press.

Grinspoon, Lester, ed. (1986). *The Long Darkness: Psychological and Moral Perspectives on Nuclear Winter.* New Haven, CT: Yale University Press.

Grosscup, Beau (2006). *Strategic Terror: The Politics and Ethics of Aerial Bombardment.* London: Zed Books.

Gsponer, André, and Jean-Pierre Hurni (1995). *Iraq's Calutrons: Electromagnetic Isotope Separation Beam Technology and Nuclear Weapon Proliferation.* Geneva: ISRI.

Hafemeister, David W. (1997). "Reflections on the GAO Report on the Nuclear Triad: How Much Was Enough to Win the Cold War; Was It Freud or Newton?" *Science and Global Security* 6, 383–93.

———(2005). "Presidential Report to the Congress: Net Benefit Analysis of US/Soviet Arms Control." *Science and Global Security* 13, 209–17.

———(2007). *Physics of Societal Issues: Calculations on National Security, Environment, and Energy.* New York: Springer.

———ed. (1991). *Physics and Nuclear Arms Today.* College Park, MD: American Institute of Physics.

Halperin, Morton H. (1987). *Nuclear Fallacy: Dispelling the Myth of Nuclear Strategy.* Cambridge, MA: Ballinger.

Halperin, Morton H., and Jeanne M. Woods (1990). "Ending the Cold War at Home." *Foreign Policy* 81, 128–43.

Hamza, Khidhir (2000). *Saddam's Bombmaker.* New York: Scribner.

Hansell, Cristina (2009). "Internationalizing Nunn-Lugar: Lessons for Future Multilateral Cooperative Threat Reduction Projects." International Commission on Nuclear Non-proliferation and Disarmament (online).

Hansen, Chuck (1988). *U.S. Nuclear Weapons: The Secret History.* New York: Orion Books.

Hansen, Keith A. (2006). *The Comprehensive Nuclear Test Ban Treaty: An Insider's Perspective.* Stanford, CA: Stanford University Press.

Harney, Robert, Gerald Brown, and Matthew Carlyle (2006). "Anatomy of a Project to Produce a First Nuclear Weapon." *Science and Global Security* 14, 163–82.

Harrison, Selig S. (1992). *Korean Endgame: A Strategy for Reunification and U.S. Disengagement.* New York: Century Foundation.

Hart, Fred L., Jr. (n.d.). *The Iraqi Invasion of Kuwait: An Eyewitness Account.* Carlisle Barracks, PA: U.S. Army War College (online).

Harwell, M. A. (1984). *Nuclear Winter: The Human and Environmental Consequences of Nuclear War.* New York: Springer.

Hayes, Peter (1994). "Defiance Versus Compliance: The DPRK's Calculus Faced with Multilateral Sanctions." Report to Northeast Asia Peace and Security Network. (Online at www.nautilus.org.)

Hayes, Stephen F. (2007). *Cheney: The Untold Story of America's Most Powerful and Controversial Vice President.* New York: HarperCollins.

Hecker, Sig, Steve Younger, Nerses Krikorian, et al. (1996). " 'Side-by-Side as Equals'—An Unprecedented Collaboration Between the Russian and American Nuclear Weapons Laboratories to Reduce the Nuclear Danger." *Los Alamos Science* 24, 1–43.

Hersh, Seymour (1991). *The Samson Option: Israel's Nuclear Arsenal and American Foreign Policy.* New York: Random House.

Hersman, Rebecca K. C., and Robert Peters (2006). "Nuclear U-turns: Learning from South Korean and Taiwanese Rollback." *Nonproliferation Review* 13(3), 539–53.

Hibbs, Mark (1993). "South Africa's Secret Nuclear Program: From a PNE to a Deterrent." *Nuclear Fuel* 18, 3.

Hirschmann, Kris (2005). *The Kuwaiti Oil Fires.* New York: Facts on File.

Hogan, Michael J. (1992). *The End of the Cold War: Its Meaning and Implications.* Cambridge, U.K.: Cambridge University Press.

Holloway, David, William Perry, James Goodby, et al. (2000). *The Anatomy of Russian Defense Conversion.* Walnut Creek, CA: Vega Press.

Hones, E. W., Jr., D. N. Baker, and W. C. Feldman (1981). "Evaluation of Some Geophysical Events on 22 September 1979." *Los Alamos Series,* LA-8672 (online).

Hyland, William G. (1999). *Clinton's World: Remaking American Foreign Policy.* New York: Praeger.

IISS (2008). *Nuclear Programmes in the Middle East: In the Shadow of Iran.* London: International Institute for Strategic Studies.

Ikle, Fred Charles (2005). *Every War Must End.* New York: Columbia University Press.

Independent Commission on Disarmament and Security Issues (1982). *Common Security: A Blueprint for Survival.* New York: Simon & Schuster.

Horton, Roy E., III (1999). "Out of (South) Africa: Pretoria's Nuclear Weapons Experience." USAF Institute for National Security Studies Occasional Paper #27.

Isikoff, Michael, and David Corn (1995). *The Politics of Nuclear Renunciation: The Cases of Belarus, Kazakhstan and Ukraine.* Washington: Henry L. Stimson Center.

Jentleson, B. W., ed., (2000). *Opportunities Missed, Opportunities Seized: Preventive Diplomacy in the Post–Cold War World.* Lanham, MD: Rowman & Littlefield.

Jervis, Robert (1989). *The Meaning of the Nuclear Revolution: Statecraft and the Prospect of Armageddon.* New York: Cornell University Press.

Kalb, Marvin (1994). *The Nixon Memo.* Chicago: University of Chicago Press.

Kampelman, Max M. (1991). *Entering New Worlds: The Memoirs of a Private Man in Public Life.* New York: HarperCollins.

Kassenova, Togzhan (2007). *From Antagonism to Partnership: The Uneasy Path of the U.S.–Russian Cooperative Threat Reduction.* Stuttgart: Ibidem-Verlag.

Kaufmann, Chaim (2004). "Threat Inflation and the Failure of the Market-place of Ideas: The Selling of the Iraq War." *International Security* 29(1), 5–48.

Kaufmann, William W., and John D. Steinbruner (1991). *Decisions for Defense: Prospects for a New Order.* Washington: Brookings Institution Press.

Kaun, David E. (1988). *Where Have All the Profits Gone? An Analysis of the Major U.S. Defense Contractors: 1950–1985.* San Diego, CA: University of California Institute on Global Conflict and Cooperation.

Kay, David (1995). "Denial and Deception: The Lessons of Iraq." In Roy Godson, Ernest R. May, and Gary Schmitt, eds., *U.S. Intelligence at the Crossroads.* Washington: Brassey's, 109–27.

Kazakhstan, Embassy of (2006). *Kazakhstan's Nuclear Disarmament: A Global Model for a Safer World.* Washington: Embassy of Kazakhstan.

Kegley, Charles W. (1990). *The Long Postwar Peace: Contending Explanations and Projections.* New York: HarperCollins.

———(1991). *After the Cold War: Questioning the Morality of Nuclear Deterrence.* Boulder, CO: Westview Press.

Kegley, Charles W., and Eugene R. Wittkopf (1985). *The Nuclear Reader: Strategy, Weapons, War.* New York: St. Martin's Press.

Kelley, Kitty (2004). *The Family: The Real Story of the Bush Dynasty.* New York: Doubleday.

Khalilzad, Zalmay M. (1995). *From Containment to Global Leadership? America and the World After the Cold War.* Santa Monica, CA: RAND.

King, John Kerry (2002). *International Political Effects of the Spread of Nuclear Weapons.* Honolulu: University Press of the Pacific.

Kissinger, Henry (1982). *Years of Upheaval.* Boston: Little, Brown.

Klotz, E. G. (1980). "The U.S. President and the Control of Strategic Nuclear Weapons." Ph.D. thesis, Oxford University.

Krasno, Jean E., and James S. Sutterlin (2003). *The United Nations and Iraq: Defanging the Viper.* Westport, CT: Praeger.

Kreisler, Harry (2002). *Robert Gallucci Interview.* Berkeley, CA: Institute of International Studies, UC Berkeley (online).

Krepon, Michael (2005). *Cooperative Threat Reduction, Missile Defense, and the Nuclear Future.* Basingstoke, U.K.: Palgrave Macmillan.

———(2009). *Better Safe Than Sorry: The Ironies of Living with the Bomb.* Stanford: Stanford University Press.

Krosney, Herbert (1993). *Deadly Business: Legal Deals and Outlaw Weapons; The Arming of Iran and Iraq, 1975 to the Present.* New York: Thunder's Mouth Press.

Lambright, W. H. (2002). "Changing Course: Admiral James Watkins and the DOE Nuclear Weapons Complex." In V. C. Franke, ed., *Security in a Changing World: Case Studies in U.S. National Security Management.* Westport, CT: Praeger, pp. 55–80.

Larkin, Bruce (2008). *Designing Denuclearization: An Interpretive Encyclopedia.* Piscataway, NJ: Transaction Publishers.

Lee, Ergene (2000). "The 1993 North Korean Nuclear Crisis: A Foreign Policy Analysis." Ph.D. thesis, Virginia Polytechnic Institute.

Leebaert, Derek (2002). *The Fifty Year Wound: The True Price of America's Cold War Victory.* Boston: Little, Brown.

Lettow, Paul (2005). *Ronald Reagan and His Quest to Abolish Nuclear Weapons.* New York: Random House.

Levy, Adrian, and Catherine Scott-Clark (2007). *Deception: Pakistan, the United States, and the Secret Trade in Nuclear Weapons.* New York: Walker.

Lewis, Jeffrey G. (2007). *The Minimum Means of Reprisal: China's Search for Security in the Nuclear Age.* Cambridge, MA: MIT Press.

Lewis, John Wilson, and Xue Litai (1988). *China Builds the Bomb.* Stanford: Stanford University Press.

Loeber, Charles R. (2004). *Building the Bombs: A History of the Nuclear Weapons Complex.* Philadelphia: Diane Publishing.

Lyman, Edwin S. (1995). "Iraq: How Close to a Nuclear Weapon?" Nuclear Control Institute (online).

Mann, Edward C., III (1995). *Thunder and Lightning: Desert Storm and the Airpower Debates.* Maxwell Air Force Base, AL: Air University Press.

Mann, James (2004). *Rise of the Vulcans: The History of Bush's War Cabinet.* New York: Viking.

Mansourov, Alexandre Y. (1995). "The Origins, Evolution, and Current Politics of the North Korean Nuclear Program." *Nonproliferation Review,* Spring–Summer, 25–38.

Mark, J. Carson, et al. (1987). "Can Terrorists Build Nuclear Weapons?" In Paul Leventhal and Yonah Alexander, eds., *Preventing Nuclear Terrorism.* Lexington, MA: Lexington Books (online).

Markusen, Ann, and Joel Yudken (1992). *Dismantling the Cold War Economy.* New York: Basic Books.

Marples, David R. (1996). *Belarus: From Soviet Rule to Nuclear Catastrophe.* London: Palgrave Macmillan.

Mayer, Jane (2009). *The Dark Side: The Inside Story of How the War on Terror Turned into a War on American Ideals.* New York: Simon & Schuster.

Mazarr, Michael J. (1999). "Virtual Nuclear Arsenals: A Second Look." *CSIS Web Report.* Washington: CSIS Press (online).

McCormack, Gavan (2004). *Target North Korea: Pushing North Korea to the Brink of Nuclear Catastrophe.* New York: Nation Books.

McNamara, Robert S. (1968). *The Essence of Security: Reflections in Office.* New York: Harper & Row.

———(1986). *Blundering into Disaster: Surviving the First Century of the Nuclear Age.* New York: Pantheon.

McPhee, John (1974). *The Curve of Binding Energy.* New York: Farrar, Straus and Giroux.

Mikhailov, Viktor N. (1996). *I Am a Hawk: Memoirs of Atomic Energy Minister Mikhailov.* Edinburgh: Pentland Press.

Milhollin, Gary (1993). "The Iraqi Bomb." *The New Yorker,* 1 Feb., 47–56.

Mitchell, William (2006). *Winged Defense: The Development and Possibilities of Modern Air Power—Economic and Military.* Mineola, NY: Dover.

Morrison, Philip, and Kosta Tsipis (1998). *Reason Enough to Hope: America and the World of the Twenty-first Century.* Cambridge, MA: MIT Press.

Mosher, David E. (2003). *Beyond the Nuclear Shadow: A Phased Approach for Improving Nuclear Safety and U.S.-Russian Relations.* Santa Monica, CA: RAND.

Moxley, Charles J., Jr. (2000). *Nuclear Weapons and International Law in the Post Cold War World.* Lanham, MD: Austin & Winfield.

Moynihan, Daniel Patrick (1990). *On the Law of Nations.* Cambridge, MA: Harvard University Press.

Mueller, John (2009). "The Atomic Terrorist?" Research Paper, International Commission on Nuclear Non-proliferation and Disarmament (online).

Musharraf, Pervez (2006). *In the Line of Fire: A Memoir.* New York: Free Press.

Nazarbayev, Nursultan (2001). *Epicenter of Peace.* Hollis, NH: Puritan Press.

Neff, Thomas L. (1998). "Liquidating the Cold War." *Physics and Society Newsletter* 27: 1 (online).

Neuneck, Götz, and Otfried Ischebeck, eds. (1993). *Missile Proliferation, Missile Defense and Arms Control: Proceedings of a Symposium Held in Hamburg.* Baden-Baden: Nomos Verlagsgesellschaft.

Nichols, Jere (2001). "Uncovering the Secret Program—Initial Inspections." Panel discussion at ISIS conference on "Understanding the Lessons of Nuclear Inspections and Monitoring in Iraq: A Ten-Year Review." ISIS (online).

Nichols, John (2004). *The Rise and Rise of Richard B. Cheney.* New York: New Press.

Nolan, Janne E. (1999). *An Elusive Consensus: Nuclear Weapons and American Security After the Cold War.* Washington: Brookings Institution Press.

Norris, Robert S., Andrew S. Burrows, and Richard W. Fieldhouse (1994). *Nuclear Weapons Databook: British, French, and Chinese Nuclear Weapons.* Boulder, CO: Westview Press.

NRDC (1992). *Report on the Third International Workshop on Verified Storage and Destruction of Nuclear Warheads, Held in Moscow and Kiev, 16–20 December 1991.* Washington: Natural Resources Defense Council.

Nunn, Sam, with Daryl G. Kimball and Miles A. Pomper (2008). "A World Free of Nuclear Weapons: An Interview with Nuclear Threat Initiative Co-Chairman Sam Nunn" (online).

Obeidi, Mahdi (2004). *The Bomb in My Garden: The Secrets of Saddam's Nuclear Mastermind.* Hoboken, NJ: Wiley.

Oberdorfer, Don (2001). *The Two Koreas: A Contemporary History.* New York: Basic Books.

Odom, William E. (1998). *The Collapse of the Soviet Military.* New Haven, CT: Yale University Press.

Oelrich, Ivan (2004). *Missions for Nuclear Weapons After the Cold War.* Washington: Federation of American Scientists.

Oetzel, George N., and Steven C. Johnson (1980). "Vela Meteoroid Evaluation." SRI International (online).

Olsen, Edward A. (2002). *US National Defense for the Twenty-First Century: The Grand Exit Strategy.* London: Frank Cass.

Ouchi, William G., and Alan L. Wilkins (1985). "Organizational Culture." *Annual Review of Sociology II,* 457–83.

Paine, Christopher, and Thomas B. Cochran (1992). "So Little Time, So Many Weapons, So Much to Do." *Bulletin of the Atomic Scientists* 48, 13–16.

Palme, Olof (Independent Commission on Disarmament and Security Issues) (1982). *Common Security: A Blueprint for Survival.* New York: Simon & Schuster.

Pape, Robert A. (1996). *Bombing to Win: Air Power and Coercion in War.* Ithaca, NY: Cornell University Press.

Park, Robert L. (2001). *Voodoo Science: The Road from Foolishness to Fraud.* New York: Oxford University Press.

Parsi, Trita (2007). *Treacherous Alliance: The Secret Dealings of Israel, Iran, and the United States.* New Haven, CT: Yale University Press.

Paul, T. V. (2000). *Power Versus Prudence: Why Nations Forgo Nuclear Weapons.* Montreal: McGill-Queen's University Press.

Perkovich, George (1999). *India's Nuclear Bomb: The Impact on Global Proliferation.* Berkeley: University of California Press.

———(2009). "Extended Deterrence on the Way to a Nuclear-Free World." International Commission on Nuclear Non-proliferation and Disarmament (online).

Perlmutter, Amos, Michael Handel, and Uri Bar-Joseph (1982). *Two Minutes Over Baghdad.* London: Frank Casso.

Perricos, Dimitri (2001). "Uncovering the Secret Program—Initial Inspections." *Understanding the Lessons of Nuclear Inspections and Monitoring in Iraq: A Ten-Year Review.* ISIS (online).

Perry, William (1996). "Defense in an Age of Hope." *Foreign Affairs,* Nov.–Dec. (online).

———(1991). "Desert Storm and Deterrence." *Foreign Affairs,* Fall (online).

Pfaltzgraff, Robert L. (1990). *National Security Decisions: The Participants Speak.* New York: Lexington Books.

Pillar, Paul R. (2006). "Intelligence, Policy, and the War in Iraq." *Foreign Affairs,* Mar.–Apr. (online).

Podvig, Pavel, ed. (2001). *Russian Strategic Nuclear Forces.* Cambridge, MA: MIT Press.

Pollack, Kenneth M. (2004). "Spies, Lies and Weapons: What Went Wrong?" *Atlantic Monthly,* Jan.–Feb. 2004 (online).

Polmar, Norman, and Robert S. Norris (2008). *The U.S. Nuclear Arsenal: A History of Weapons and Delivery Systems Since 1945.* Annapolis: Naval Institute Press.

Popadiuk, Roman (1996). *American-Ukrainian Nuclear Relations.* Washington: Institute for National Strategic Studies, National Defense University.

Potter, William C., Emily Ewell, and Elizabeth Skinner (1994). "Nuclear Security in Kazakhstan and Ukraine: An Interview with Vladimir Shkolnik and Nicolai Steinberg." *Nonproliferation Review* 2, 45–54.

Powell, Colin (1995). *My American Journey: An Autobiography.* New York: Random House.

Prados, John (2004). *Hoodwinked: The Documents That Reveal How Bush Sold Us a War.* New York: New Press.

Pritchard, Charles L. (2007). *Failed Diplomacy: The Tragic Story of How North Korea Got the Bomb.* Washington: Brookings Institution Press.

Pryce-Jones, David (1995). *The War that Never Was: The Fall of the Soviet Empire 1985–1991.* Troy, MI: Phoenix Press.

Purkitt, Helen E., and Stephen F. Burgess (2005). *South Africa's Weapons of Mass Destruction.* Bloomington: Indiana University Press.

Quester, George H. (1966). *Deterrence Before Hiroshima: The Airpower Background of Modern Strategy.* New York: John Wiley & Sons.

———(1995). *The Nuclear Challenge in Russia and the New States of Eurasia.* Armonk, NY: M. E. Sharpe.

———(2005). *Nuclear First Strike: Consequences of a Broken Taboo.* Baltimore, MD: Johns Hopkins University Press.

Raman, J. Sri (2004). *Flashpoint: How the U.S., India and Pakistan Brought Us to the Brink of Nuclear War.* Monroe, ME: Common Courage Press.

Ramberg, Bennett (1980). *Destruction of Nuclear Energy Facilities in War: The Problem and the Implications.* Lanham, MD: Lexington Books.

Ravenal, Earl C. (1979). *Strategic Disengagement and World Peace: Toward a Noninterventionist American Foreign Policy.* Washington: Cato Institute.

Reed, Thomas C. (2004). *At the Abyss: An Insider's History of the Cold War.* New York: Presidio Press.

———(2008). "The Chinese Nuclear Tests, 1964–1996." *Physics Today* 61, 47–53.

Reed, Thomas C., and Danny B. Stillman (2009). *The Nuclear Express: A Political History of the Bomb and Its Proliferation.* Minneapolis, MN: Zenith Press.

Reiss, Mitchell (1995). *Bridled Ambition: Why Countries Constrain Their Nuclear Capabilities.* Washington: Woodrow Wilson Center Press.

Reiss, Mitchell, and Robert S. Litwak, eds. (1994). *Nuclear Proliferation After the Cold War.* Washington: Woodrow Wilson Center Press.

Remnick, David (1994). *Lenin's Tomb: The Last Days of the Soviet Empire.* New York: Vintage.

Reynolds, Wayne (2000). *Australia's Bid for the Atomic Bomb.* Victoria, Australia: Melbourne University Publishing.

Rhodes, Richard (1987). *The Making of the Atomic Bomb.* New York: Simon & Schuster.

———(1995). *Dark Sun: The Making of the Hydrogen Bomb.* New York: Simon & Schuster.

———(2007). *Arsenals of Folly: The Making of the Nuclear Arms Race.* New York: Knopf.

Richelson, Jeffrey (2006). *Spying on the Bomb: American Nuclear Intelligence from Nazi Germany to Iran and North Korea.* New York: W. W. Norton.

Riedy, Alexander W. (1995). "Project Sapphire Briefing. Meeting of the U.S.-German Study Group on Nonproliferation, Bonn, Germany, 12–13 June" (online).

Rilke, Ranier Maria (1984). *Letters to a Young Poet.* New York: Random House.

Riordan, Michael (1982). *The Day After Midnight: The Effects of Nuclear War.* Fort Bragg, CA: Cheshire Books.

Ritter, Scott (1999). *Endgame: Solving the Iraq Crisis.* New York: Simon & Schuster.

Rosen, George (1958). *A History of Public Health.* Baltimore: Johns Hopkins University Press.

Russell, James A., ed. (2006). *Proliferation of Weapons of Mass Destruction in the Middle East.* London: Palgrave Macmillan.

Sagan, Carl, and Richard Turco (1990). *A Path Where No Man Thought: Nuclear Winter and the End of the Arms Race.* New York: Random House.

Sagan, Scott, and Kenneth N. Waltz (2002). *The Spread of Nuclear Weapons: A Debate Renewed.* Second Edition. New York: W. W. Norton.

Sanger, David E. (2009). *The Inheritance: The World Obama Confronts and the Challenges to American Power.* New York: Harmony Books.

Savada, Andrea Matles, ed. (1993). *North Korea: A Country Study.* Washington: Library of Congress.

Schell, Jonathan (1998). *The Gift of Time: The Case for Abolishing Nuclear Weapons.* New York: Holt.

———(2003). *The Unconquerable World.* New York: Metropolitan Books.

———(2007). *The Seventh Decade: The New Shape of Nuclear Danger.* New York: Metropolitan Books.

Schneider, Barry R., and William Dowdy, eds. (1998). *Pulling Back from the Nuclear Brink.* New York: Routledge.

Schwartz, Stephen I. (1998). *Atomic Audit: The Costs and Consequences of U.S. Nuclear Weapons Since 1940.* Washington: Brookings Institution Press.

Schwartz, Stephen I., with Deepti Choubey (2009). *Nuclear Security Spending: Assessing Costs, Examining Priorities.* Washington: Carnegie Endowment for International Peace.

Schweitzer, Glenn E. (1997). *Experiments in Cooperation: Assessing U.S.-Russian Programs in Science and Technology.* New York: Twentieth Century Foundation.

Scoblic, J. Peter (2008). *U.S. Versus Them: How a Half-Century of Conservatism Has Undermined America's Security.* New York: Viking.

Scott, Richard (1996). *Return to an Address of the Honourable the House of Commons Dated 27 July 1996 for the Export of Defence Equipment & Dual-Use Goods to Iraq and Related Prosecutions.* London: Her Majesty's Stationery Office.

Shahram, Chubin (2006). *Iran's Nuclear Ambitions.* Washington: Carnegie Endowment for International Peace.

Shields, J. M., and William C. Potter, eds. (1997). *Dismantling the Cold War: U.S. and NIS Perspectives on the Nunn-Lugar Cooperative Threat Reduction Program.* Cambridge, MA: MIT Press.

Shulman, Seth (1992). *The Threat at Home: Confronting the Toxic Legacy of the U.S. Military.* Boston: Beacon Press.

Shultz, George P. (1993). *Turmoil and Triumph: My Years as Secretary of State.* New York: Scribner.

Shultz, George P., Sidney D. Drell, and James E. Goodby, eds. (2008). *Reykjavik Revisited: Steps Toward a World Free of Nuclear Weapons.* Stanford, CA: Hoover Institution Press.

Sigal, Leon V. (1998). *Disarming Strangers: Nuclear Diplomacy with North Korea.* Princeton: Princeton University Press.

———(2000). *Hang Separately: Cooperative Security Between the United States and Russia, 1985–1994.* New York: Century Foundation Press.

Simpson, Fiona (2009). "The U.S. Stockpile Stewardship Program: Domestic Perspectives and International Implications." International Commission on Nuclear Non-proliferation and Disarmament (online).

Skootsky, Mark D. (1995). "An Annotated Chronology of Post-Soviet Nuclear Disarmament 1991–1994." *Nonproliferation Review,* Spring–Summer, 64–105.

Sloan, Stanley R. (2005). *NATO, the European Union, and the Atlantic Community: The Transatlantic Bargain Challenged.* Lanham, MD: Rowman & Littlefield.

Sokolski, Henry, ed. (1996). *Fighting Proliferation: New Concerns for the Nineties.* Maxwell Air Force Base, AL.: Air University Press.

Sokov, Nikolai (2000). *Russian Strategic Modernization.* Lanham, MD: Rowman & Littlefield.

Spector, Leonard S., with Jacqueline R. Smith (1990). *Nuclear Ambitions: The Spread of Nuclear Weapons 1989–1990.* Boulder, CO: Westview Press.

Spies, M., and John Burroughs, eds. (2007). *Nuclear Disorder or Cooperative Security: U.S. Weapons of Terror, the Global Proliferation Crisis, and Paths to Peace; An Assessment of the Final Report of the Weapons of Mass Destruction Commission and Its Implications for U.S. Policy.* New York: Lawyers' Committee on Nuclear Policy.

Stengel, Richard, Strobe Talbott, and Nancy Traver (1986). "Does Gorbachev Want a Deal?" *Time,* 13 Oct. (online).

Stumpf, Waldo (1995). "Birth and Death of the South African Nuclear Weapons Programme." In *50 Years after Hiroshima* (Conference Proceedings). Castiglioncello, Italy: USPID (online).

Suskind, Ron (2004). *The Price of Loyalty: George W. Bush, the White House, and the Education of Paul O'Neill.* New York: Simon & Schuster.

Stossel, Scott (2005). "North Korea: the War Game." *Atlantic,* July–August (online).

Szporluk, Roman (2000). *Russia, Ukraine, and the Breakup of the Soviet Union.* Stanford, CA: Hoover Institution Press.

Talbott, Strobe (2002). *The Russia Hand: A Memoir of Presidential Diplomacy.* New York: Random House.

———(2004). *Engaging India: Diplomacy, Democracy, and the Bomb.* Washington: Brookings Institution Press.

———(2008). *The Great Experiment: The Story of Ancient Empires, Modern States, and the Quest for a Global Nation.* Washington: Simon & Schuster.

Tellis, Ashley J. (2001). *India's Emerging Nuclear Posture: Between Recessed Deterrent and Ready Arsenal.* Santa Monica: RAND.

Tellis, Ashley J., C. Christine Fair, and Jamison Jo Medby (2001). *Limited Conflicts Under the Nuclear Umbrella: Indian and Pakistani Lessons from the Kargil Crisis.* Santa Monica: RAND.

Thamm, Gerhardt (1993). "Challenging Paradigms, Finding New Truths, 1969–79" (Declassified 2007). *Studies in Intelligence* 37 (3) (online at www.cia.gov).

———(1993). "Unraveling a Cold War Mystery: The ALFA SSN; Challenging Paradigms, Finding New Truths." Central Intelligence Agency (online).

Thompson, Reginald (1951). *Cry Korea.* London: MacDonald & Co.

Timbie, James (2004). "Energy from Bombs: Problems and Solutions in the Implementation of a High-Priority Nonproliferation Project." *Science and Global Security* 12, 165–89.

Tirpak, John A. (1995). "Project Sapphire." *Air Force* 78 (online).

Toon, Owen B., Alan Robock, Richard P. Turco, et al. (2007). "Consequences of Regional-Scale Nuclear Conflicts." *Science* 315 (5816), 1224–1225.

Trevan, Tim (1999). *Saddam's Secrets: The Hunt for Iraq's Hidden Weapons.* London: HarperCollins UK.

Tsypkin, Mikhail (2004). "Adventures of the 'Nuclear Briefcase': A Russian Document Analysis." *Strategic Insights* 3 (9).

Tweedie, Neil (2008). "Britain Learned of South African Nuclear Programme from USSR." *Daily Telegraph* (London), 13 December.

Underhill-Cady, Joseph B. (2001). *Death and the Statesman: The Culture and Psychology of U.S. Leaders During War.* New York: Palgrave.

United States. Committee on Armed Services, House of Representatives, 102nd Congress, Second Session (1992a). *Preventing Chaos in the Former Soviet Union: The Debate on Providing Aid.* Washington: U.S. Government Printing Office.

United States. Committee on Armed Services, United States Senate, 102nd Congress, Second Session (1992b). *Assisting the Build-Down of the Former Soviet Military Establishment.* Washington: U.S. Government Printing Office.

United States. Committee on Armed Services, United States Senate, 102nd Congress, Second Session (1992c). *Trip Report: A Visit to the Commonwealth of Independent States by Senator Sam Nunn, Senator Richard Lugar, Senator John Warner, and Senator Jeff Bingaman, March 6–10, 1992.* Washington: U.S. Government Printing Office.

United States. Committee on Foreign Affairs, House of Representatives, 103rd

Congress, First Session (1993). *Iraq's Nuclear Weapons Capability and IAEA Inspections in Iraq: Joint Hearing before the Subcommittee on Europe and the Middle East and International Security, International Organizations and Human Rights.* Washington: U.S. Government Printing Office.

United States. Committee on Foreign Relations, United States Senate, 107th Congress, Second Session (2002). *Increasing Our Nonproliferation Efforts in the Former Soviet Union.* Washington: U.S. Government Printing Office.

United States. Select Committee on Intelligence, United States Senate, 108th Congress (2004). *Report on the U.S. Intelligence Community's Prewar Intelligence Assessments on Iraq.* Washington: U.S. Government Printing Office.

United States. Subcommittee on European Affairs of the Committee on Foreign Relations, United States Senate, 102nd Congress, First Session (1992). *Command and Control of Soviet Nuclear Weapons: Dangers and Opportunities Arising from the August Revolution.* Washington: U.S. Government Printing Office.

United States. Subcommittee on European Affairs of the Committee on Foreign Relations, United States Senate, 104th Congress, First Session, 22–23 Aug. 1995 (1995). *Loose Nukes, Nuclear Smuggling, and the Fissile-Material Problem in Russia and the NIS.* Washington: U.S. Government Printing Office.

United States Congress, Office of Technology Assessment (1988). *Seismic Verification of Nuclear Testing Treaties, OTA-ISC-361.* Washington: U.S. Government Printing Office.

United States Department of Defense (1992). *Conduct of the Persian Gulf War, Final Report to Congress, April 1992.* Washington: Department of Defense.

United States Department of Energy (1997). *Linking Legacies: Connecting the Cold War Nuclear Weapons Production Processes to Their Environmental Consequences.* Washington: U.S. Department of Energy.

Ustiugov, Mikhail (1993). "A 'Temporarily Nuclear State.' " *Bulletin of the Atomic Scientists,* Oct. (online).

Utgoff, V. A., ed. (2000). *The Coming Crisis: Nuclear Proliferation, U.S. Interests, and World Order.* Cambridge, MA: MIT Press.

Venter, Al J. (2007). *Allah's Bomb: The Islamic Quest for Nuclear Weapons.* Guilford, CT: Lyons Press.

Waas, Murray S., and Craig Unger (1992). "Annals of Government: In the Loop: Bush's Secret Mission." *New Yorker,* 2 Nov.

Walker, William (1992). "Nuclear Weapons and the Former Soviet Republics." *International Affairs* 68, 255–77.

Weisberg, Jacob (2008). *The Bush Tragedy.* New York: Random House.

Weisman, Alan (2007). *Prince of Darkness: Richard Perle; The Kingdom, the Power, and the End of Empire in America.* New York: Union Square Press.

Wilson, Joseph (2005). *The Politics of Truth: A Diplomat's Memoir.* New York: Public Affairs.

Wilson, Valerie Plame (2007). *Fair Game: My Life as a Spy, my Betrayal by the White House.* New York: Simon & Schuster.

Winik, Jay (1996). *On the Brink.* New York: Simon & Schuster.

Wit, Joel S., Daniel B. Poneman, and Robert L. Gallucci (2004). *Going Critical: The First North Korean Nuclear Crisis.* Washington: Brookings Institution Press.

Wohlforth, William C. (1996). *Witnesses to the End of the Cold War.* Baltimore: Johns Hopkins University Press.

Wood, Houston G., Alexander Glaser, and R. Scott Kemp (2008). "The Gas Centrifuge and Nuclear Weapons Proliferation." *Physics Today* 61, 40–45.

Woodward, Bob (1991). *The Commanders.* New York: Simon & Schuster.

———(2004). *Plan of Attack.* New York: Simon & Schuster.

Woolf, Amy (2008). *U.S. Strategic Nuclear Forces: Background, Developments, and Issues.* CRS Report for Congress RL33630, updated 5 Aug. 2008.

Worden, Mike (2002). *Rise of the Fighter Generals: The Problem of Air Force Leadership, 1945–1982.* Honolulu: University Press of the Pacific.

Wurmser, David. (1999). *Tyranny's Ally: America's Failure to Defeat Saddam Hussein.* Foreword by Richard Perle. Washington: AEI Press.

Yeltsin, Boris (1994). *The View from the Kremlin.* London: HarperCollins.

Yengst, William C., Stephen J. Lukasik, and Mark A. Jensen (1996). *Nuclear Weapons That Went to War (Draft Final Report).* Alexandria, VA: Defense Special Weapons Agency.

Younger, Stephen M. (2008). *Endangered Species: How We Can Avoid Mass Destruction and Build a Lasting Peace.* New York: Harper Perennial.

———(2009). *The Bomb: A New History.* New York: Ecco.

Zarimpas, N., ed. (2003). *Transparency in Nuclear Warheads and Materials: The Political and Technical Dimensions.* Stockholm: SIPRI.

Zhimin, Li, and Li Feizhi (1998). "Impact of South Asia's Nuclear Tests upon the CTBT." Sixth ISODARCO Beijing Seminar on Arms Control, Shanghai, China, 1 November (online).

ACKNOWLEDGMENTS

At one time I intended the material in this book to be part of its immediate predecessor, *Arsenals of Folly*. When that previous work reached more than five hundred manuscript pages and the end of the Cold War, I decided to close it there and take up the post–Cold War years separately. *The Twilight of the Bombs* is that separate and final narrative in what began as a single volume and has now concluded as a four-volume series.

It seems appropriate, then, to acknowledge here collectively the many people who helped me with this multivolume work. I can't begin to list them all, but their names recur in this and previous volumes, none of which I could have written without them.

With this book in particular, Anne Sibbald has been more than an agent; she has been a trusted adviser as well. Mort Janklow's experience and wisdom sustained the enterprise. Jon Segal, my editor at Knopf, encouraged me to explore further when I thought I was finished. He was right, and his good judgment made this a far better book. Richard Butler offered not only his clear memories but also his friendship, which I cherish. Tom Graham has been both a friend and an inspiration. My friends Eduard and Eugenia Wolfson, who lived through the last days of the U.S.S.R., enlivened my research into those difficult years.

I benefited as well from interviews with David Albright, Hans Blix, Linton Brooks, Sid Drell, Bob Gallucci, Jim Goodby, Keith Hansen, Sig Hecker, David Kay, Jack Mulligan, Sam Nunn, Frank Pabian, Stanislav Shushkevich, Jessica Stern, Paul White, and Stephen Younger. My affiliation with Stanford's Center for International Security and Cooperation and its codirectors, Sig Hecker and (in Scott Sagan's absence) Lynn Eden, has been sustaining.

Thanking my wife, Dr. Ginger Rhodes, is far more than a formality. Ginger has worked with me on almost all my books. She's the first to read every chapter, always with enthusiasm. For this final volume, as for many of my earlier books, she tracked down copyright holders and negotiated all the permissions. I respect, admire, and adore her. She, not thermonuclear fusion, makes the sun shine.

PERMISSIONS ACKNOWLEDGMENTS

Excerpts from James A. Baker III, *The Politics of Diplomacy,* copyright © 1995 by James A. Baker III. Used by permission of G. P. Putnam's Sons, a division of Penguin Group (USA) Inc.

Excerpts from Christian Alfonsi, *Circle in the Sand: Why We Went Back to Iraq,* copyright © 2006, 2007 by Christian J. Alfonsi. Used by permission of Doubleday, a division of Random House, Inc.

Excerpts from Richard Butler, *Fatal Choice: Nuclear Weapons and the Illusion of Missile Defense.* Boulder, CO: Westview Press. Copyright © 2003 by Richard Butler. Reprinted by permission of Basic Books, a member of the Perseus Books Group.

Excerpts from Richard Butler, *The Greatest Threat: Iraq, Weapons of Mass Destruction and the Crisis of Global Security.* New York: Public Affairs. Copyright © 2001 by Richard Butler. Reprinted by permission of PublicAffairs, a member of the Perseus Books Group.

Excerpts from Terry L. Deibel, "The Death of a Treaty," *Foreign Affairs* 81, September/October 2002, 142–161. Reprinted by permission of *Foreign Affairs.* Copyright © 2002 by the Council on Foreign Relations, Inc. www.ForeignAffairs.com.

Excerpts from Charles Duelfer, *Hide & Seek: The Search for Truth in Iraq.* New York: Public Affairs Press. Copyright © 2009 by Charles Duelfer. Reprinted by permission of PublicAffairs, a member of the Perseus Books Group.

Excerpts from Thomas Graham, Jr., *Disarmament Sketches: Three Decades of Arms Control and International Law.* Seattle: Institute for Global and Regional Security Studies, copyright © 2002 by University of Washington Press. Reprinted by permission of the University of Washington Press.

Excerpts from Joseph Wilson, *The Politics of Truth: A Diplomat's Memoir.* New York: Public Affairs. Copyright © 2005 by Joseph Wilson. Reprinted by permission of PublicAffairs, a member of the Perseus Books Group.

Excerpts from Joel S. Wit, Daniel B. Poneman, and Robert L. Gallucci, *Going Critical: The First North Korean Nuclear Crisis.* Copyright © 2004 by The Brookings Institution. Reprinted by permission.

Excerpts from Marion Creekmore, Jr., *A Moment of Crisis: Jimmy Carter, the Power of a Peacemaker, and North Korea's Nuclear Ambitions.* New York: PublicAffairs. Copyright © 2006 by Marion Creekmore, Jr. Reprinted by permission.

Excerpts from Gil Elliot, *Twentieth Century Book of the Dead.* New York: Charles Scribner's Sons. Copyright © 1972 by Gil Elliot. Reprinted by permission of Gil Elliot.

Excerpts from Mark Hibbs, "South Africa's Secret Nuclear Program: From a PNE to a Deterrent," *Nuclear Fuel* 18, 3, copyright © 1993 by the McGraw-Hill Companies. Reprinted by permission.

Excerpt from "South Africa's Secret Nuclear Program: From a PNE to a Deterrent" by Mark Hibbs (*Nuclear Fuel,* May 10, 1993). Reprinted by permission of The YGS Group.

ILLUSTRATION CREDITS

PHOTOGRAPHS

U.S. F-117A Stealth Fighter-Bomber: Photo courtesy of U.S. Army
Kuwaiti oil wells: U.N. photo by John Isaac
Coalition Soldiers: Photo courtesy of U.S. Air Force
Electromagnet: IAEA
Iraqi uranium enrichment facility: IAEA
Facility at Al Atheer: Action Team 1991–1998/IAEA
Bush, Yeltsin & Graham: Courtesy of Thomas Graham, Jr.
Khariton & Hecker: Los Alamos National Laboratory
FSU missile silos: U.S. State Department
South African bank vaults: Courtesy of Mungo Poore
South African bombs: Courtesy of Mungo Poore
Yongbyon nuclear reactor: Los Alamos National Laboratory
Carter & Kim Il Sung: Voice of America
Blix & ElBaradei: Government of Australia
Evans & Butler: IAEA photo by Dean Calma
U.N. meeting: U.N. photo
Shakti-1 weapon: Government of India
Pakistan: Television screen image
Bush in schoolroom: Official White House photo by Eric Draper
World Trade Center: Courtesy of U.S. Coast Guard
Situation Room: Official White House photo
Bush at World Trade Center site: Official White House photo by Eric Draper
Anthrax spores: Sandia National Laboratories
Powell: AP photo by Elise Amendola
Aluminum tubes: U.S. State Department
Bush on carrier: Official White House photo by Susan Sterner
Obama: Official White House photo

DIAGRAMS

Pg 60: Bridge crane: Tim James Rhodes, RA. AIA.
Pg 73: Implosion bomb cutaway: Tim James Rhodes, RA. AIA.
Pg 160: Little Boy cross section: John Coster-Mullen
Pg 164: Double flash graph: Tim James Rhodes, RA. AIA.

INDEX

Printed in the United States
by Baker & Taylor Publisher Services